ENCYCLOPÆDIA OF THE THEATRE

Another Book of the Theatre

Art of the Night

The Autobiography of an Attitude

Bottoms Up, An Application of the Slapstick to Satire

Comedians All

The Critic and the Drama

Encyclopedia of the Theatre

The Entertainment of a Nation

Europe After 8:15

Materia Critica

Mr. George Jean Nathan Presents

Passing Judgments

The Popular Theatre

Since Ibsen

Testament of a Critic

The Theatre Book of the Year 1942–43

The Theatre Book of the Year 1943–44

The Theatre Book of the Year 1944–45

The Theatre Book of the Year 1945–46

The Theatre Book of the Year 1946–47

The Theatre Book of the Year 1947–48

The Theatre Book of the Year 1948–49

The Theatre Book of the Year 1949–50

The Theatre in the Fifties

The Theatre of the Moment

The Theatre, The Drama, The Girls

The World in Falseface

ENCYCLOPÆDIA
OF THE
THEATRE
GEORGE JEAN
NATHAN

Fairleigh Dickinson

RUTHERFORD • MADISON • TEANECK

FAIRLEIGH DICKINSON UNIVERSITY PRESS

THE ENCYCLOPEDIA OF THE THEATRE. © 1940 by George
Jean Nathan, © renewed 1968 by Mrs. George Jean Nathan. New
material in this edition © 1970 by Associated University Presses, Inc.

Library of Congress Catalogue Card Number: 75-120099

Reprinted 1970

Associated University Presses, Inc.
Cranbury, New Jersey 08512

ISBN 0-8386-7721-5
Printed in the United States of America

To

Eugene O'Neill

After Many Years

Contents

Contents

D

E

F

G

H

Contents

I

J

K

L

M

N

Contents

O

P

Q

R

S

T

Contents

U

Ugliness versus Beauty . . . Unsympathetic Rôles

V

Vaudeville . . . Victims . . . Victorian Charm . . . Vox et Praeterea Nihil . . . Vue Anglaise . . . Vulgarity

W

Warnings . . . Weakness . . . "Well-son"; "Now-daughter" . . . Why the Guild Foundered . . . Wilder . . . Women and Actresses . . . Women Playwrights . . . Workers' Stage

X

X (Sex-Appeal)

Y

Yen for Thespis . . . Youth and the Verse Drama

Z

Zapfenstreich

Introduction

By CHARLES ANGOFF

Tempus Fugit. On April 8, 1958, George Jean Nathan died, at the age of 76. During his long reign as America's most celebrated, most learned, most perceptive dramatic critic it used to be said that having a play reviewed by him was a fate worse than death. He made plays and he killed them, he made playwrights and he sneered them off into oblivion. Yet the tenth anniversary of his death went almost totally unnoticed in New York City, which he, a world traveler par excellence, loved above all cities in the world.

He deserves better of his city, of his profession, of Broadway, of his nation, and—yes—of the world theatre.

There can be no doubt that he will get his due in the not-too-distant future. It is a commonplace of literary history for the reputation of a man of the first magnitude to slump almost immediately after his death. Often it takes another ten, fifteen, or even twenty years for him to resume his rightful place in the cultural annals of his country and time. Recall what happened to the reputation of Theodore Dreiser. He died in 1947 and only now is the academic world—and the nonacademic world as well—realizing what a massive figure he was. Recall what happened to F. Scott Fitzgerald, who waited for more than ten years after his death in 1940 to begin to achieve the recognition that rightfully was his. There is, further, the case of Sherwood Anderson. The classic case, of course, in American literary history is Herman Melville, who died in 1891, and did not assume his position as a literary giant till more than thirty years later.

Nathan was a dramatic critic who subscribed to the ancient and honorable philosophy that before a man can claim the right to evaluate plays and acting he ought to know something about both, and the more he knows the better. And by knowing Nathan meant what may, with more than a modicum of truth in his case, be characterized as universal knowing. The man's knowledge was truly tremendous. He knew the American theatre, of course, as probably no other critic knew it before him or since. He knew the German theatre and the Austrian theatre and the English theatre and the Spanish theatre and the Portuguese theatre and the Scandinavian theatre. He had read the plays and he had seen many of them. Needless to say, he was also familiar with the classical Greek theatre. But a good critic must not only know; he must perceive deeply into innermost meanings and he must hear silent melodies of the mind. He must be the theatregoing-public's conscience and way-shower. Finally, he must express his knowledge and perceptions in lively language laced with literary allusion and humor. Nathan possessed all these attributes in abundance.

This is revealed amply in the present volume, *Encyclopedia of the Theatre,* first published in 1940. It is the initial volume in a projected series of reprints of Nathan's entire canon of dramatic criticism. Knowledge? When Clare Boothe's *The Women* was produced many acclaimed it as "highly original" because of its all-female cast. Nathan disproved that claim thus:

"Previous plays containing only women: Rodney Ackland's stage adaptation of Hugh Walpole's novel *The Old Ladies* and called *Night in the House,* Cyril Campion's *Ladies in Waiting,* Alice Gerstenberg's *Glee Plays the Game* (it was this same Miss Gerstenberg who wrote the short play, *Overtones,* which anticipated Eugene O'Neill's dual personality drama device in *Days without End*), Christa Winslowe's *Girls in Uniform,* Aimee and Philip

Stuart's *Nine Till Six*, Harold Brighouse's *Smoke Screens,*
Zona Gale's *The Clouds*, several short plays by Gertrude
Jennings, among them *The Bride, I'm Sorry—It's Out!,*
and *Pearly Gates*, Walter Prichard Eaton's *Romance and
Rummage*, Ellis Parker Butler's little comedy *The Revolt,*
Elizabeth Brace's *Quite a Remarkable Person*, Vera Cas-
pary's and Winifred Lenihan's *Blind Mice*, etc., etc."

What about the art of acting? What about "the
Method?" Nathan said the following:

"With no preparation for the stage other than some
minor coaching in voice and reading of Shakespeare,
Fanny Kemble at nineteen and upon a few weeks' notice
was rushed to Covent Garden by her father, threatened
with bankruptcy, to make her debut as Juliet. London
acclaimed her and she became the toast of the town. For
two years afterwards she and her performance were the
topic of rapt conversation wherever people interested in
the theatre gathered. Mary Anderson at sixteen played
the same role in America and caused something of a public and critical sensation. The following year she appeared at the head of her own company and a year later,
at eighteen, took New York with not only her Juliet,
but her Parthenia, Meg Merrilies, Evadne and Bianca as
well. Neither of these grand kids was a heaven-sent
prodigy or genius. Actors and scholars given to learned
gabble on the value of long training, experience, technical education, etc., please meditate.

"The whole matter of acting is enveloped with written
and oral bosh. . . . All the technique in the world
couldn't have aided little eight-year-old Peter Holden in
giving a more telling and beautiful performance in *On
Borrowed Time* than he did give. All the technique from
here to Moscow wouldn't have prevented Eva Le Gallienne's *L'Aiglon* from being as bad as it was. Without
technical equipment of any kind, Joan Bennett, on her
first appearance on the stage, gave a performance in

Jarnegan some years ago more definitely appealing than any twenty girls bursting with technique could conceivably have managed. But, on the other hand, no actor without infinite technical competence could have come within miles of giving such a performance as Lucien Guitry gave in almost every play he appeared in, or as our own George M. Cohan gave in the play *Ah, Wilderness!* The only point I have to add is that such actors as Guitry and Cohan have never for a moment forgotten that the most valuable quality in technique is the genius for rehearsing it painstakingly and then, once the curtain is up, acting as if they never had heard the word.

"Let us, further, proceed to the case of Ethel Waters. The Mlle. Waters, as you know, is the colored lady who for years has entertained musical show customers with ditties concerned with a variety of heat waves, mainly such as affect the feet, the seat, and the Afro-American heart. Last year, the desire for a somewhat more complex species of histrionism overcame her and she abandoned the realm of the musical show to play the leading dramatic role in the Du Bois tragedy, *Mamba's Daughters*. Without previous dramatic acting experience of any kind whatsoever, she became overnight one of the acting toasts of the town, winning such notices from the critics as had not greeted the New York breakfast or dinner eye in a long spell."

Some have said condescendingly, "You can't reckon an artist by a single fine performance." Nathan dug into his ocean of information and said:

"Can't you? When Brahms composed his first symphony, he was initially established, and properly, as the third B in the proud company of Bach and Beethoven. Following the minor experimental scribble, *Galatea, An Eclogue,* Cervantes became immortal with *Don Quixote,* his first novel. And though he never wrote anything afterward even remotely to approach it, his genius remains unquestioned. This is flying pretty high and wide and a bit absurdly in any contemplation of mummers? Maybe so. But, descending precipitately in the scale of values and merely for the sake of the argument, what acting performances in the history of the stage have showed greater histrionic genius, if we are to believe the critical authorities of their time, than the very earliest performances of Tomasso Salvini, the first performances of the brothers Coquelin, Benoit Constant and Ernest Alexandre, at the Theatre Français and the Odeon respectively, or—to come down in the scale somewhat further than we have come down—the first performance ever given on a dramatic stage by the musical comedy girl, Marie Tempest?"

Do you look for humorous, epigrammatic writing in dramatic criticisms? Here is what Nathan had to say about the theatre of 1940:

"It is the weakness of so much of present-day drama that its emotions are fundamentally little more than moving-picture emotions in dinner jackets. Its passions are the puny tremors of puny hearts and spirits to which puny playwrights seek to give size by funneling them through a ceremonious polysyllabic dramaturgy. It lives like a worm; it thinks like a Hollywood movie director; it loves either like a eunuch or a rabbit; it feels like a gigolo; and it dies like a ham Cyrano."

Nathan was never pompous. He did not think it beneath his dignity as a critic to have his say about Hollywood's sex symbols. He said of one of them:

"Not long ago Hollywood, in scholastic conclave assembled, picked out one of its young movie women, Mlle. Ann Sheridan, and formally announced to the American public that she had more sex appeal than any other houri in the whole community. Thus was added still another imbecility to the already rich roster of the California Corinth. That the young lady in question may enjoy a share of sex appeal is quite possible, although, judging from the many photographs of her which I have seen in the public prints, I feel that I personally might be able to resist her devastating puissance with considerable ease and equanimity. But that is not the point. The point is that it is no more possible arbitrarily and specifically to nominate sex appeal for the generality of men than it is possible accurately to predict their unanimous reaction to broccoli and the political philosophy of Walter Lippmann, or even to cures for colds, sleeveless pajamas, and Western sandwiches. What is sex appeal to one man is often a dose of salts to another. If proof were needed, the commonly heard query, 'What does he see in her?' would supply it. And if, further, feminine sex appeal were the positive and firmly fixed attribute that Hollywood apparently thinks it is, there would be hardly a man in America today who wouldn't be going around with a black eye. . . .

"Sex Appeal—and here surely your professor discloses no startling news—is as undefinable as the taste of celery. You can no more tell me or any other man that this or that woman has sex appeal and hope invariably to convince than I can tell you or any other man, even when under the influence of alcoholic liquor. Asked to define sex appeal, the current Hollywood bombshell saucily tossed a theoretically tempting hip and sagely observed: 'Sex appeal is mixed up with charm and personality, the main ingredients of which are a healthy, natural curiosity and an active sense of humor.' Curiosity and an active sense of humor, the young lady should be sadly informed, have driven more originally impressed and palpitating men away from potential sirens than you can shake a stick at.

" 'Next important thing,' continued the irresistible pigeon, 'is to avoid being too shy. Then nobody has any fun.' It is quite possible that maybe nobody has any fun, but it has long been my observation that the shy girl, however much a party killjoy she may be, still oddly enough seems to stir the boys' fancy a heap more than the girl who climbs on the mantel and imitates Beatrice Lillie or the one who sneaks up behind you and whimsically pours a bottle of creme de cacao down your collar. Shyness, though very probably not in Hollywood, is often to sex appeal what onions are to a hamburger."

Was Nathan the best dramatic critic America has yet produced? I incline to think so, but that is immaterial. Was he always "right" in his judgments? Of course not. Only second-rate critics, like second-rate writers in general, are always at their best. He had his blind spots and he had his bizarre enthusiasms. He said of William Saroyan that his talent was "the loveliest and most bouncing that has come the way of the local stage in some equinoxes." I doubt that Nathan's ghost, as it wanders about the boulevards of the hereafter, is very comfortable with the memory of this judgment. On the other hand, Nathan dismissed all of Wilder, including *Our Town*, as "pishposh . . . flapdoodle . . . pepperless, saltless, sexless." This comment will puzzle Nathan's future biographer.

But such aberrations will not diminish his stature in the cultural history of the Twenties, Thirties, Forties, and Fifties. He made enormous contributions. It was he more than any other individual who helped to educate, not only the American public, but also the Broadway producers, to the greatness of Eugene O'Neill. In season and out of season he beat the drums for the author of *Beyond the Horizon, Desire Under the Elms, Strange Interlude, Long Day's Journey* and *The Iceman Cometh.* I believe he was the only major critic who saw the last play for what it was—a mountain of dramatic achievement.

And it was Nathan who was one of the first and certainly the most persistent champion of Sean O'Casey. I was with him on the opening nights of *Juno and the Paycock* and *Within the Gates* in New York City. As we walked back to his hotel, the Royalton, he said of each, "Remember tonight. You've seen a great play. The *Feinschmeckers* tomorrow morning will hem and haw about this or that defect. There are plenty of defects. So are there in the Grand Canyon."

The mystery about Nathan is how this boulevardier—this man who bathed in lilac water, who had some twenty canes, who felt undressed if his shirts didn't have French cuffs, who had some two score topcoats and a score of overcoats and about a hundred neckties, who felt ill at ease in the company of everyday workingmen and workingwomen—how this *flaneur*, this dandy, was at once drawn to the plays of those who found song and glory, as well as misery, in the lives of these very same everyday workingmen and workingwomen. There is still another mystery. He sensed when such plays by other hands were false. He sensed—as time has largely borne him out—that Odets was not writing about real people in the Bronx, but only about his Hollywoodish mind's version of these people. I once asked him how he knew all this. He said, "Easy. I know the same way you know that *Anna Karenina* is a genuine novel about genuine people, even though —I hope you will forgive me for blurting this out—you are not a member of the Romanoff dynasty and have little other royal blood flowing in your veins."

Nathan was drawn to the magic lanterns of life, to the night, to the fleeting joys and sorrows, to the loveliness in impossible aspirations. He often quoted O'Neill's remark, "The only dreams worth having are those which cannot be fully realized." Once—it was during Prohibition days—I heard him debate with Robert Benchley the relative merits of night and evening in the history of civilization. Nathan championed night, because "the essence of woman is night." To Nathan the world of fantasy and of dreams and of yearnings was the only real world. Which is why he loved to go to the theatre and why he enjoyed seeing even poor plays (he would often leave after the first fifteen minutes) : the world of the theatre had a special reality to him. He loved every aspect of it—burlesque and vaudeville included. I have seen him laugh uncontrollably when witnessing a stage clergyman or statesman kicked in the "prat" by a wayward bum. He had little interest in politics, and, in fact, knew little about it. But he once did make one suggestion that may be relevant to our times. He proposed Jimmy Durante for President of the United States on both major tickets, and he gave him a platform: "Free Love and Free Beer." I pointed out to Nathan that there is no such thing as free love. He said, "I know, but you need illusion in politics, as in everything else."

Fairleigh Dickinson University
Rutherford, New Jersey

ENCYCLOPÆDIA OF THE THEATRE

ABACUS BRITANNICUS. Much of the contemporary English polite comedy writing suggests a highly polished and very smooth billiard table with all the necessary brightly poised cues, but without balls.

ABBOTT. During the early rehearsals of *To Quito and Back*, Theatre Guild Director Philip Moeller gathered the principals around him and explained to them his conception of their characters. "You," he said to Leslie Banks, "are a clarinet." "You," he suggested to Joseph Buloff, "are a bassoon." "And you," he observed to Sylvia Sidney, "are an oboe." "Nuts," replied Miss Sidney. "I'm just a girl in love with that man!"

Miss Sidney would admire George Abbott as a director and Mr. Abbott would unquestionably admire Miss Sidney as a critic. There is no arty buncombe about Director Abbott. He doesn't think of his actors as clarinets, bassoons and oboes, or in his most temperamental and crusty moments even as combs musicalized with confidential tissue-paper. He thinks of them simply as more or less competent performers who, if they will do him the honor of keeping sufficiently sober and paying some attention to him, may eventually contrive to give a show that will attract enough customers to permit him, in turn, eventually to build the recherché house at Port Washington which he has been figuring on ever since the money first began to roll in with *Three Men on a Horse*.

Just as every actor's ambition, including even John Gielgud's, is one day to be able to play Hamlet, so it has been Abbott's one day to produce more important plays than the trivial comedies and farces with which he has achieved big box-office success. But every time he has sought to capture his ambition by the tail, the bird has not only eluded his grasp but has derisively given him its generic noise. On each occasion when he has tried to establish himself as a producer and director of more exalted status, he has come a cropper. His métier seems to be rather the stage fabrication of rough-and-tumble popular entertainment, and in that field he has few rivals. The fair share of his shows meet the palate of the proletariat for drama in the form of Mexican jumping beans and by way of merchanting it to the full he converts his players from Moeller's clarinets, bassoons and oboes into kangaroos, chamois and grasshoppers, all constantly on the leap. As a director, he is Yankee Doodle plus, and a lineal descendant — a fact overlooked by his critical appraisers — of that directorial super-George of an earlier day, Mr. Cohan.

The more usual theatre of this later George is the theatre of snappy curtain lines, wisecracking dialogue, allusions to Broadway hotels, mentions of favorite brands of champagne, periodic humorous excursions to the lavatory, sentimental relief in the shape of tender young lovers, and various analogous condiments, all staged as if the author had used a pepper-shaker in lieu of an inkwell. It provides generally amusing if critically negligible stuff, and it also generally provides Abbott, his authors, and his actors with a nice honorarium for their exertions. If Abbott can't be the directorial Hamlet of his dreams, he may at least content himself in being a pretty satisfactory couple of other fellows from Ephesus and Syracuse.

ABOUT SOMETHING. In the continued controversy over whether plays should be About Something or should be simply content to be good entertainment I can't detect much sense. I have seen many thousands of plays, good and bad, since first I hit upon dramatic criticism as a way to live luxuriously without too much brain exercise, and I can't recall more than maybe one or two in all the lot that were not about something. To write a play about nothing at all is probably the most difficult feat on earth, and reserved only to heaven-sent geniuses. And even when such genuises have on rare occasions attempted it, they have found themselves flabbergasted and have discovered, sweat as they might, that their plays refractorily turned out to be about something after all. Shakespeare suffered the humiliation in the instance of both *As You Like It* and *Much Ado about Nothing,* and to a considerable degree also in *Twelfth Night.* Strindberg tried to turn the trick in *The Dream Play* and similarly found himself stumped. And though he then applied his full virtuosity to the business in the case of *The Spook Sonata,* he fell short by some distance, although here considerable progress was noted. Nevertheless, he couldn't entirely make the grade and there were periodic holes in the play when it at least seemed to mean something.

Infinitely lesser but gifted playwrights of modern times — Lady Gregory, for one example — have similarly set themselves the herculean task and have also failed at it. In the entire history of the drama of these times, in point of fact, I can think of one and only one play that from first to last is about absolutely nothing. That play is George M. Cohan's *The Tavern.* There may be one or two others that, to the superficial eye, seem to be about nothing, but it isn't difficult for the trained critical eye to discern that actually they are a disappointment and that they really, however faintly, have something to say about something or other.

To differentiate between plays that are About Something and plays that are merely good entertainment is accordingly a paradox, and a very silly one. It isn't a matter of merely good entertainment; it is merely a matter of good plays. The world for centuries has been helplessly finding good entertainment in good plays about something and finding no entertainment in bad plays equally about something.

Of course, what the controversialists mean by About Something is something closely related to modern times, modern problems and affairs, and modern philosophies, preferably written by someone who doesn't know any too much about what he is writing but who is pretty nobly indignant about it just the same. Melodrama and mentality are twins to such fowl, and profound thought something identical with violent prejudice in swing time. In short, if a play is not about Communism, Fascism, Democracy, Capital or Labor, it is considered to be about nothing. And it is thus that the best play imaginable about some such deep human concern as the love of man for woman or the search for stars in a drear, bleak sky is loftily waved aside, and cheers reserved alone for the worst play imaginable which gravely contends that a capitalist who makes a million dollars a month really ought to pay his employees more than eight dollars a week or that Democracy as visualized by Abe Lincoln is a rather more comfortable form of government than that once practiced by Torquemada.

The attitude has gone to such an extreme that we find even many of the professional critics striking it. As a result, many a play of some merit is contemptuously dismissed and dispatched to an early storehouse grave. Last season, for example, there was produced a play by a young man named Bowers, called *Where Do We Go from Here?* It dealt, with first-rate observation and very fair humor, with the students of a small mid-western college and showed not only the emptiness of their lives in college but the emptiness that spectre-like lay ahead of them in after years. But this wasn't enough for the About Something gourmands. The play, they asserted, lacked sufficient plot, ideas, purpose and weight. They asserted it so loudly, indeed, that the little play soon died. It was, true, a minor play and not particularly important, but it deserved a better critical treatment, I think, and a better fate. There have been numerous other such cases in recent years. Several that come to mind at the moment were Elmer Rice's *The Left Bank,* Teresa Deevy's *Katie Roche,* Robert Ardrey's *Star-Spangled,* Alfred Savoir's *He,* Vincent Lawrence's *A Distant Drum,* George Birmingham's *General John Regan,* George Cohan's *Pigeons and People,* and Lennox Robinson's *Is Life Worth Living?*

ACTING. One thing is always safely predictable and that is that in every theatrical season there will be more nonsense talked and written about the business of acting than any other subject, save perhaps only the orchestration of musical show scores, the youthful beauty of our older and more decayed actresses, and the great good accomplished by the late Federal Theatre Project in augmenting theatrical audiences through the instrumentality of bad plays and worse productions. Acting, however, will unquestionably always get the heaviest play, because the dumber anyone is the more he feels himself privileged and qualified to discuss it, and not entirely without reason. For few people, including actors, know much about the matter and even what the few know is open to question.

When I say that few actors know much about acting I intend neither facile paradox nor specious insult. What I mean is that, while actors may here and there know a great deal about the subject, their knowledge is often confined largely to the other side of the stage's fourth wall, that is, to acting as a craft of and within itself and with small relation to its audience effect. It is for this reason that actors themselves frequently admire performances of their fellows that audiences and critics have small respect for. And it is for this reason also that you will rarely encounter an actor who believes that that performance of his which audiences and critics consider his best is his best. Thus, for example, having seen Sir Cedric Hardwicke in at least a dozen performances both here and abroad and having believed and written that his Canon in *Shadow and Substance,* which was greeted with unanimous acclaim by audiences and critics, was equally to my mind the best of them all, I was not in the least surprised when he subsequently informed me that he considered it his very poorest.

As I look at it, any acting that affects and moves an audience is good acting and any that doesn't, whatever its imposing content of technical dexterity, isn't. Some of the theoretically worst actors in Christendom have now and then made an impression upon audiences that some of the theoretically best now and then have failed to. Nor is it entirely a matter of rôles. That is too easy a way out. Richard Mansfield's Jekyll and Hyde didn't thrill his customers one iota more than the ham Thomas Shea's. Lou Tellegen, one of the sourest actors it was ever my amusement to watch, got his audiences as Armand very much more handily than a half-dozen better actors who have played the rôle. Elisabeth Bergner, who probably knows more about the art of acting than any three Jane Cowls, could never move her audiences one-third as much with her Juliet as Jane Cowl could.

The actor, accordingly, is generally the worst possible critic of acting, save in its academic sense. And the place for acting in its academic sense is less the theatre than it is an actors' club, a player's autobiography, or a greenroom.

Although I fully appreciate that motion picture acting and stage acting are things far apart, there is a point involving the former that may not be completely out of key with and fairly relevant to the question here considered. Some months ago I attended a picture called *Mayerling*. In it Danielle Darrieux gave a performance of positive and lovely effect, as was agreed by everyone who saw it. That is, everyone but a handful of stage actors. These proclaimed uppishly that her performance may have been charming and effective, but that it certainly wasn't acting. All that the rest of us can say in turn is that if it wasn't acting it was a pretty doggone good substitute for it, whatever it was, and that it seemed to us a deal better in its especial circumstance than a carload of expert Stanislavskism would have been. The same with the stage, and avaunt those actors who in one breath argue that type casting is the enemy of all true acting and in the next explain away a grantedly excellent performance on the ground that the player happened to be exactly the right type.

With no preparation for the stage other than some minor coaching in voice and reading of Shakespeare, Fanny Kemble at nineteen and upon a few weeks' notice was rushed to Covent Garden by her father, threatened with bankruptcy, to make her début as Juliet. London acclaimed her and she became the toast of the town. For two years afterward she and her performance were the topic of rapt conversation wherever people interested in the theatre gathered. Mary Anderson at sixteen played the same rôle in America and caused something of a public and critical sensation. The following year she appeared at the head of her own company and a year later, at eighteen, took New York with not only her Juliet, but her Parthenia, Meg Merrilies, Evadne and Bianca as well. Neither of these grand kids was a heaven-sent prodigy or genius. Actors and scholars given to learned gabble on the value of long training, experience, technical education, etc., please meditate.

The whole matter of acting is enveloped with written and oral bosh. Many of our critics, in making out their lists of the best acting performances of a recent season, for example, placed Frank Craven in *Our Town* close up toward the top. There is no denying that Craven was admirable in his rôle of descriptive narrator, but to contend that the performance represented acting save in its most elementary sense is to ridicule the craft of acting. Mr. Craven, in point of fact, didn't act at all, as he himself would unquestionably be the first to allow. He had no character to interpret and he interpreted no character. He simply walked out onto a stage in his own simple and agreeable person and served as compère to the play with his simple and agreeable voice. He didn't even play himself; he was himself. No character name was listed opposite his own in the program. He was, in the playwright's own purpose, of the drama but not in it. He was, as I have said, perfect for the author's and producer's purpose, but if what he did was acting in the true meaning of the term a lot of acting actors are being swindled and the Actors' Equity Association should promptly see to it that they get paid handsomely and to boot for their nocturnal disquisitions at the bars of the Lambs' and Players' clubs and for the impressive extenuating explanations they next morning give their wives.

This confusion as to acting values has become increasingly common. A possible reason therefor was given by the aforementioned Hardwicke several years ago in a lecture at Cambridge. Said Sir Cedric: "The actor's voice has dropped from the declamatory to the almost confiding coo of the crooner, and his gestures are restricted to lighting a cigarette or putting an offending corner of a handkerchief discreetly into its correct place in his jacket pocket. So that now the strain of comprehending a play is thrown entirely on the ear which, because of the absence of adequate gesture, is put to an increasingly severe test. Acting has given way to behavior and tends to become inarticulate. Scenery is so factual that we scarcely notice it. I should say that there is more acting nowadays in a motor-car showroom when a potential customer enters, and certainly more at the average business interview, than there is in the modern theatre. Perhaps we have arrived at a time when only the worst actors aspire to the stage." He then continued: "The cleavage between the theatre of yesterday and that of today is wide and deep. In the drama of yesterday the audience found relief from the repressions of life outside. Today free expression is to be found in life, while the drama is suffering from acute repression."

The confusion I have referred to is confined not alone to the public and to actors themselves but is shared, and lavishly as I have hinted, by those very agents who are paid to exercise their presumably professional analytical knowledge, to wit, the critics. It is true not only now; it has been true for years. The old Bernhardt-Duse critical argument that in some of its aspects resembled a dog fight is too familiar to need recalling. The critical monkeyshines suffered by John Drew on the score of his deportmental naturalness, the critical wooziness over Mimi Aguglia out of which doubtless neither the poor woman herself nor certainly many of the rest of us could make histrionic head or tail, the critical stage-door admiration of Richard Mansfield and the lofty condescension toward Arnold Daly, the galvanic buncombe over a lot of Henry Irving's art (both pro and con), the lush Leslie Carter nonsense, the Mrs. Pat Campbell critical claptrap, the Bergner gooeyhooey — these, similarly, need no recalling. If the public knows utterly nothing about the craft of acting (and why should it, as it doesn't give a hoot so long as it knows what it likes?), and if actors themselves know only that phase of it which is flattering to their own idiosyncratic greasepaint philosophies, it would seem that the critics' analytical education in the subject is also nothing for them to get on a high horse about. (Lest the reader forget, I, too, am a critic.)

Glancing back over what I have written, I observe that even this particular treatise on the acting business is not without its slight trace of confusion. That is what generally happens whenever acting comes up for discussion. Acting should be seen, not written about. Very often, indeed, God knows, it shouldn't even be seen. It is, at its best, like good liquor: it affects one agreeably for the time being and instils in one a pleasant illusion. It can, like the liquor, move one to laughter and to tears, and enter one into a new emotional world. At its worst, like bad liquor, it gives one only a bellyache and a desire to lick the hell out of the bartender, both followed by an acute nausea.

If I seem in the foregoing paragraphs to have disparaged what is known to the acting trade as technique, that surely is not my intention. Technical resource is obviously most valuable to an actor and any critic who argued otherwise would be something of an idiot and fit only for association with actors who believe that technique is the beginning and end of all acting. The trouble is that the great majority of actors do believe that very thing, to the considerable distress of their paying customers. They present themselves to their audiences in the light of pianists who have mastered the technical aspects of their art but who, in the mastering, have lost sight of such important requisites as vitality, warmth and imagination. They have all the perfection of modern re-frigerating plants and a proportionate percentage of chill. They devote themselves to impressing other actors who share their admiration of pure technique at the expense of impress-ing audiences who have paid to be warmed and moved. They lecture their rôles instead of playing them. They are superb hams hanging futilely in a Ghetto delicatessen.

All the technique in the world couldn't have aided little eight-year-old Peter Holden in giving a more telling and beautiful performance in *On Borrowed Time* than he did give. All the technique from here to Moscow wouldn't have prevented Eva Le Gallienne's *L'Aiglon* from being as bad as it was. Without technical equipment of any kind, Joan Ben-nett, on her first appearance on the stage, gave a perform-ance in *Jarnegan* some years ago more definitely appealing than any twenty girls bursting with technique could con-ceivably have managed. But, on the other hand, no actor without infinite technical competence could have come within miles of giving such a performance as Lucien Guitry gave in almost every play he appeared in, or as our own George M. Cohan gave in the play *Ah, Wilderness!* The only point I have to add is that such actors as Guitry and Cohan have never for a moment forgotten that the most valuable quality in technique is the genius for rehearsing it pains-takingly and then, once the curtain is up, acting as if they never had heard the word.

Let us, further, proceed to the case of Ethel Waters. The Mlle. Waters, as you know, is the colored lady who for years has entertained musical show customers with ditties concerned with a variety of heat waves, mainly such as affect the feet, the seat, and the Afro-American heart. Last year, the desire for a somewhat more complex species of histrionism overcame her and she abandoned the realm of the musical show to play the leading dramatic rôle in the Du Bois' tragedy, *Mamba's Daughters.* Without previous dramatic acting experience of any kind whatsoever, she became overnight one of the acting toasts of the town, winning such notices from the critics as had not greeted the New York breakfast or dinner eye in a long spell. Nor were the critics, including myself, the only ones who saw in her performance something uncommonly expert and impressive. The opening night audience, along with subsequent audiences, paid her a like tribute. Actors and actresses, too, flocked to the Empire to view her and came away agog over her virtuosity. And old theatrical hands of all sorts similarly found themselves moved and cheering.

In all this we have, I think, still yet another dose of convincing evidence that when people talk about the art of acting they often talk humbug. There are, of course, actors of age and experience who are masters of their craft and who may deserve, from the æsthetically miscellaneous and the more sentimentally inclined commentators — together with the less deliberative share of the public — the honor of being dubbed artists. But when I, for one, think of Miss Waters and various others like her in past years who, without what may be called preparation of any sound species, have jumped casually onto a stage and covered themselves with acting glory, I am more disposed than ever to nominate most of the so-called acting art a load of lovely moonshine. To argue in Miss Waters' case that she had the benefit of the skillful Mr. McClintic's direction is, it seems to me, arguing around the corner. For if acting is an art, it is a pretty peculiar one to be able to be imparted to a novice, with such immensely telling effect, in only a few weeks' rehearsal time. And to argue, in turn, that the Mlle. Waters may be a rare genius and hence an exception is to argue with no acquaintance with theatrical facts. For there have, as I have pointed out, been similar cases; not a few, but many.

So impressed with Miss Waters' art was the acting profession itself that, upon reading the New York *Times* review of her performance (the only one that didn't go overboard on her behalf), a representative group of players waxed so indignant that they paid for a large advertisement in that journal proclaiming their wholesale admiration of her great talent, duly appending to the proclamation their illustrious monikers. And so impressed with the advertisement was the *Times* critic that he galloped back to the Empire and the following Sunday generously indited two columns of retraction, allowing that he had been a victim of the grippe when he first appraised Miss Waters and that, now he was fully recovered and himself again, he thought her pretty hot stuff when it came to the sock and buskin business.

But Miss Waters was not the only toast of *Mamba's Daughters*. Others in it to confound staunch supporters of the doctrine of the art of acting were a young Negro named Bryant, whose previous experience had been confined largely to serving as a master of ceremonies in a Harlem vaudeville house, and a young Negress named Fredi Washington who had previously appeared in a single straight play, several colored song and dance chowders, and in minor rôles in a jitney movie or two. Both were hailed by critics, actors and public as sumpin'. And both fully deserved it. No better performances in relatively analogous rôles had any of us seen by twenty times more experienced white players.

I can hear your protest to the effect that Negroes are naturally gifted for acting and that this may account for the phenomena of the fine performances of Waters and the others. That Negroes are congenitally expert actors is one of the most foolish articles in the American Credo; most of them that we see on the dramatic stage are either downright bad or pretty indifferent. They may be congenitally adept hoofers and in some cases singers, but comparatively few of them elect seriously to tackle acting. They appear to consider it either as below them or as an invasion of their leisure. With minor exception, they don't seem to like it and are bored with it.

But to return to the motif. If acting is an art and generally not rather an accident of suitable rôle and personality, reflect upon the true and convincing performance of the small youngster, Helen Renée, in the late unlamented *Dear Octopus*. Or, God forgive me, take a look at the little boy in the film, *Kentucky*, and see his profoundly affecting emotional performance in the long scene wherein, crying his heart out over his father's shooting, he runs protestingly alongside the departing Federal cavalry troop. Consider, also, the understudy in the Chicago company of *Kiss the Boys Goodbye* — a young and inexperienced girl named Fairleigh — who jumped into the difficult leading rôle on the second night and gave a performance which almost everyone connected with the enterprise maintained was not only better than that previously given by the regularly assigned actress but as good as that given by the practised actress in the New York company. (It was, it should further be noted, not an entirely imitative performance.) Reflect, too, on a variety of such exceptional performances as have been given by young Sylvia Sidney the first time she stepped on a stage in *Crime* and stole the show from all the older actors in it, by young Stephen Courtleigh as Lincoln in *Prologue to Glory*, by a number of Federal Theatre amateurs in various productions, and by two of the children in *Seen But Not Heard*.

Last season no less than four or five young men practically without any antecedent training proved themselves uncommonly adept actors in the ill-starred *Where Do We Go*

from Here? The same thing was true the season before in
the cases of *So Proudly We Hail* and *Bright Honor.* William
Haade, who had never been on a stage before, took all the
acting honors in *Iron Men;* the amateur company that played
200 Were Chosen won high praise for the expertness of their
performances; and Eddie Dowling, who hitherto had been
known only as a song and dance man, laid hold of his first
dramatic rôle last season in *Here Come the Clowns* and gave
what was generally agreed to be one of the finest performances of the year. The acting of any number of Abbey Theatre novices stands high in the Irish histrionic records; and so
it goes. One might extend the list indefinitely.

Think then, in turn, of the wretched performances often
given by actors and actresses of wide experience, players
who regard themselves as artists and who are also so regarded by the public. You will have no difficulty reeling
them off in dozens, from Ethel Barrymore's Juliet to Lionel
Barrymore's Macbeth and from Walter Hampden in *Achilles
Had a Heel* and half a dozen other plays to Philip Merivale
in *Lorelei* and several others and Blanche Yurka in a comprehensive repertoire.

But, condescendingly smile the objectors, you can't
reckon an artist by a single fine performance. Can't you?
When Brahms composed his first symphony, he was initially
established, and properly, as the third B in the proud company of Bach and Beethoven. Following the minor experimental scribble, *Galatea, An Eclogue,* Cervantes became
immortal with *Don Quixote,* his first novel. And though he
never wrote anything afterward even remotely to approach
it, his genius remains unquestioned. This is flying pretty
high and wide and a bit absurdly in any contemplation of
mummers? Maybe so. But, descending precipitately in the
scale of values and merely for the sake of the argument,
what acting performances in the history of the stage have
showed greater histrionic genius, if we are to believe the
critical authorities of their time, than the very earliest per-

formances of Tomasso Salvini, the first performances of the brothers Coquelin, Benoît Constant and Ernest Alexandre, at the Théâtre Français and the Odéon respectively, or — to come down in the scale somewhat further than we have come down — the first performance ever given on a dramatic stage by the musical comedy girl, Marie Tempest?

ACTORS (ENGLISH). That English actors are greatly superior to our own when it comes to the performance of polite comedy is still freely to be accepted as fact. But, however successful they are in impressing their English audiences in the case of modern drama involving the deeper amorous passions, it is gradually becoming evident that they are unimpressive — at times, indeed, even slightly ridiculous — to American audiences. Their clipped speech, over-precision of diction and congenital and apparently unconquerable chill of comportment combine in American eyes and ears to make their dramatic protestations of heat and passion often indistinguishable from so many self-conscious cucumbers. Just as the individual American can seldom persuade himself not to smile at the average Frenchman's characteristic abundant air of indignation, whatever its justification, or at the average Chinaman's express-train volubility, whatever its intelligence in turn, so Americans in theatrical audience assembled can't keep from grinning just a little at Englishmen's amorous incalescence, however meritorious the histrionism that merchants it.

AMATEUR GROUPS. It would have profited the countless amateur theatrical groups currently spread throughout the nation to have made a quick excursion to New York and to have learned from the late Experimental Theatre, Inc., exactly what they shouldn't do about things. I can, in this connection, think of no better guide and mentor. For this latest amateur organization to brave the breastworks of professional Broadway achieved a virtuosity in muddleheadedness that amounted to sheer genius. Gathering together a number of ambitious novices calling themselves the New York Players, it selected for their initial divertissement Strindberg's *The Bridal Crown*, which would provide pretty difficult histrionic going for a Comédie Française company and which, even if the latter were good in it, which is doubtful, would provide even more difficult theatregoing for any audience other than one composed of Scandinavian dramatic critics, and then only if they were hogs for rococo symbolical folklore.

Having in the name of art picked Strindberg at his worst, the Experimental group thereupon persuaded a Russian named Jilinsky to direct and stage it. What Russians do in such circumstances is doubtless sufficiently familiar to you. If you have forgotten, I remind you. First, they form a union of two with the man at the electrical switchboard and peremptorily see to it that the evening is devoted almost exclusively to shooting fancy colored lights up, down and around the stage, evidently in the belief that all plays should have been written by Loie Fuller. Secondly, when they are at a loss what to tell the stageful of actors to do, they invariably have them stand around in static groups and thrust out their hands with palms upturned. And, thirdly, they so slow down and gloomify the tempo of the play that you can't distinguish whether you are sitting in a theatre or a hearse. But in order to profit by the lesson, the country's amateur organizations would have had to make that excursion in a hurry. The Experimental Theatre's exhibit lasted just one night.

AMERICAN LYRIC THEATRE.   There can be no question that the design of the recently founded American Lyric Theatre is heartily commendable. Financed by a phalanx of tony and well-heeled art lovers, it announces as its purpose " the enrichment of American culture through the encouragement and support of the musical, dramatic, and choreographic arts, the creation of opportunities for singing opera in English, the cultivation of the taste of the American people by producing works in the form of lyric drama, and the stimulation of compositions for the lyric stage by American authors and composers." That, however, American culture was perceptibly enriched by its first two productions is a poor bet even in Chinese money.

The productions in point were "an American folk opera" called *The Devil and Daniel Webster,* by Douglas Moore and Stephen Vincent Benét, and "a musical romance based on the melodies of Stephen Foster" called *Susanna, Don't You Cry,* by Clarence Loomis and Sarah Newmeyer. The former was a hitch-hiker gesture in the right direction but without the slightest indication of a lift. The latter was a woefully amateurish cuckooing of the formula of *Blossom Time,* etc., which could not have got by the youngest office-boy outside the Messrs. Shubert's office. The former may generously be put down as a mistake by the Lyric Theatre group, but in the case of the latter the group condemned itself as without taste, judgment, and theatrical intelligence of any kind.

Mr. Benét's book, derived from a story of his published in *The Saturday Evening Post,* was a paraphrase of the Faust legend visited upon a New England community in the 1840's and involved the trial and rout of Mephistopheles, who would claim the soul of a New Hampshire son of the soil, by Orator Webster. It was almost completely dramaless and never more so than when Mr. Moore periodically embroidered it with his genteel and wholly respectable, if generally impotent, score. The lyrics, with their allusions to pies, farmyard esoterica, and the like, might have passed critically in print but they warred against any musical accompaniment and, in the singing, impressed the sensitive ear with much of the discomfort that would be attendant upon simultaneously listening to a violin concerto and reading *On a Slow Train through Arkansas.*

The second exhibit, which consisted in an effort to string

together Foster's familiar songs with a story that was a mixture of adulterated *Showboat* and most of the outworn stencils of long bygone musical comedy, was — as noted — entirely disastrous. Worse, it was so strained and silly that it, in turn, could not have got by the youngest office-boy outside the Messrs. Krimsky's gate and if conceivably it could have would have proved too foolish even for their beer-hall burlesque stage. Foster's melodies taken singly may woo the proper sentimental reaction but when, as in this instance, they were piled on top of one another without surcease for a couple of hours they gagged the ear with the copiousness of their sweet molasses and suggested that even *Yes, We Have No Bananas*, to say nothing of *The Music Goes 'Round and 'Round*, would have been a rich and welcome palliative.

The intention of the American Lyric Theatre — like the intention of so many other individuals and groups in our theatre — to emphasize and encourage America for America's sake in the arts is a proud and happy one, and one that has my full endorsement. But it sometimes leads to regrettable consequences. It has already, in the dramatic theatre, led to some pretty awful jingo rubbish and to some almost as bad juvenile philosophy and thematic whoopdedoodle. And it has now, in the instance of the Lyric group, led to two exhibits that should boost business enormously for such alien and un-American products as *Der Rosenkavalier* or even a revival of, God help us, *Olivette*. It would be a good idea if this theatrical chauvinism were quietly, wisely and soon to take stock of itself and ponder the danger of its present excesses. To believe that you can convert claptrap into something that isn't claptrap simply by smearing its surface with red, white and blue paint is to court not only the ribald snickers of criticism but any reputable American audience's resentment of the capitalization of cheap American appeal.

AMERICAN PLAYWRITING. American playwriting by and large enjoys all the attributes of a violin, save only its melodiousness. The necessary guts are there, but the bow lacks the gift of evoking poetic song from them.

ANNEXATION OF ENGLAND. A Broadway wit, recently asked what he thought of the European nations' determination to annex large slices of one another's territory, replied that he didn't know much about that but was nevertheless certain of one other thing, and that was that the United States was gradually annexing England — actor by actor. There seems to be some truth in the remark. The American stage has been so crowded with English actors in late seasons that if things keep up it will probably in the near future be impossible to find an American actor left, save perhaps in some Boston stock company — and then doubtless only in the minor rôle of a policeman or a messenger boy, or on one of the Indian reservations — and then, in turn, only as a super in one of the lesser war dances. As for the movies, Hollywood is presently so chock-a-block with English players that when a director has need of a short *a* in an actor he has to send scouts as far north as Seattle to find someone to come down and supply it.

Where all this is eventually going to lead is difficult to foretell. Despite the heroic attempts of the Actors' Equity Association to make the American stage safe for American actors, the Association doesn't seem to be able to do much but hold meetings at the Hotel Astor and work itself into a futile lather. While these meetings, that last for days, are going on and while the American actors are making long speeches protesting that it is all a terrible shame and an awful catastrophe and that three-quarters of them haven't soles on their shoes and are gradually starving to death, the ships down around Fourteenth street are quietly unloading English actors by the ton. Perhaps there is only one way out for the American actors. While all the English actors are over here, let them sneak quietly over to London, change their names to Basil, Nigel, Napier and Cosmo, or in the case of the girls to Esme, Daphne, Pamela and Vi, and annex the English actors' old London jobs.

APPRENTICE SCHOOLS.   It is my judgment, based upon personal investigation over the period of the last three years, that the majority of the apprentice schools connected with the rural summer theatres constitute little more than easy graft and a racket and are, further, of scarcely any worth to the students who hopefully enroll in them. In addition, the atmosphere surrounding some of them might profitably be looked into by parents solicitous of the moral welfare of their progeny.

There is a considerable difference between the prospectuses sent out by many of the schools and what the students actually and realistically get once they have paid the demanded tuition fees. Some of the apprentice workshops offer as advance bait the name or names of well-known, passé actors and actresses who are to head the coaching staffs. These quondam celebrities are, true enough, subsequently and duly to be found in the schools, but in many of them the matriculant is lucky if they show up in classroom for more than a few minutes a day, as it seems to be the practice — once the money is in — to have most of the instruction conducted by persons of obscure and dubious theatrical connection, if indeed any, and whose major contributions to the tutelage of the aspiring fledglings seem to consist in the recommendations (1) to buy and read Stanislavski's book on acting, (2) to stand daily in the pasture back of the converted cow-stable and yell for an hour at the top of the voice by way of achieving enough volume to be heard some day in the back rows of a theatre, and (3) to walk up and down stairs for another hour a day in order to attain graceful movement and carriage.

The nick for this extraordinary stage education usually varies from two hundred and fifty to five hundred or more dollars, depending largely upon the eminence of the theatrical and dramatic lights whose names adorn the prospectuses and who spend most of the time the kids are getting the above instruction in Ye Olde Beargrease Inn opposite the workshop, heatedly assuring themselves, over the beers, that nothing has been any good in the legitimate theatre since they last appeared in it.

At certain of the cheaper apprentice schools, men and women whose sole practical connection with the stage has been the teaching of poetry in high-schools or the coaching of high-school and secondary college dramatic clubs serve as the only instructors, and it is such that the young hopefuls trust to acquaint them with the inside secrets of the art of Salvini and Sorel. These secrets are guaranteed, once they are mastered, to make a genuine, first-rate, Grade A actor or actress, avidly sought after by the Shuberts, out of even the least promising student, provided only the latter has paid up in full. (Incidentally, so far as the few free scholarships go, only the prettier girls with a lot of convivial sex appeal peculiarly ever seem to get them.) The aforesaid rich secrets, I have discovered after extensive sleuthing, consist in learning how to repeat the letters A, B and C with three different shades of expression, how to recite some well-known jingle first tragically, then humorously, and then the way an old character actor or actress would speak it, how to stoop or kneel in such a manner that the knees won't give off a loud cracking sound, and how to walk off a stage without bumping into the side of a door.

Add here and there to this wonderful histrionic guidance a bit of fencing (invaluable to girl students in fighting off the amatory advances of the school coaches and directors) and maybe an explanation of the difference between pink and purple makeup, and you have a pretty accurate synopsis of the average apprentice school swindle.

ART. Not long ago, one of our most celebrated captains of industry said to me that, when it came to the greater part of modern art, he preferred the comic strips. He added that not only, however, was he afraid to say so to others, for fear they would deride him as a Babbitt, but that I, as well, would doubtless put him down in the same category. When I assured him that I would do nothing of the kind and that to a very considerable degree I heartily agreed with him, he was so surprised and overcome that he ordered up another bottle of champagne.

The notion that a man — and particularly a business man — who fails to appreciate most of modern art is an ignoramus and fit only for association with street-cleaners and fashionable society enjoys an exuberant life. Yet more often than not it is the enthusiastic admirer of modern art in the aggregate who should properly bear the stigma. Let us, by way of clinical investigation, take a look at the things in this modern art which excite the latter's respect and devotion.

First, we have surrealist painting. Its high priest is one Dali and its avowed purpose, so far as any one who hasn't had more than ten drinks can make out, is to interpret objects and even emotions in terms of the subconscious. But what it looks like is the window of a junk shop seen through the eyes of a somewhat inebriated monkey who imagines he is gazing at a Harlem wedding. Its impression upon any slightly more advanced and more sober member of civilization has best been described by a sound artist who observed that it was akin to looking at an egg in the morning to see what time it was and then boiling the clock for three minutes.

Secondly, there is the modern literary art as exemplified by Gertrude Stein. I offer an example of the Stein genius: "Might have as would be as would be as within nearly as out. It is very close and closed. Closed closed to let letting closed close close close in justice in join in joining. This is where to be at water at snow snow show show one one sun and sun snow show and no water no water unless unless why unless. Why unless why unless they were loaning it here loaning it intentionally. Believe two three. What could be

sad beside beside very attentively intentionally and bright."
Comment unnecessary.

Thirdly, we have such modern opera as Marc Blitzstein's *The Cradle Will Rock*. The curtain goes up and we
behold the performers in their street clothes seated in several rows of kitchen chairs. There is no scenery and there is
no orchestra. The score is entrusted to a single piano. One
by one and then two by two the performers come down stage
and sing something to the effect that it is awful when you
are broke and mistake a bit of spit on the sidewalk for a
dime or that if the laboring man doesn't get his due pretty
damned quick there is going to be hell to pay. When each
number is finished the participants go back and sit in the
kitchen chairs, the man at the piano thereupon announcing
that the next scene — if there were any scenery — will represent a night club or a steel mill or — if there were any costumes — a big costume party on the Waldorf-Astoria roof.
At the conclusion, the actors come down close to the audience and yell that union labor is determined to fight for its
rights. The curtain falls and the audience goes up to El
Morocco or the Stork Club *en masse*.

Fourthly, we engage the modern art of pantomime and
the dance, one of whose foremost exponents is Angna Enters.
I describe briefly a few of the latest revelations of this widely
endorsed artiste. First, *A Modern Totalitarian Hero*. In this
number Miss Enters puts on an elaborate and gaudy Fascist
uniform, with a gas mask serving as a helmet. After cavorting around the stage with the goose-step and Heil-Hitler
salute, she suddenly stoops and picks up a rose. She fondles
the bloom until she is pricked by a thorn. This makes her
very angry and she throws the rose to the floor and steps on
it, thereupon exiting imperiously. Next, *Danse Macabre*. In
this, the great artiste trots out the ancient vaudeville and
musical comedy number in which a man dances with a dress-
maker's dummy, the sole difference in the case of our great
modern artiste being that she does it all with a straight face

and doesn't wind up with the old comedian's gag: " Well, anyway, I don't have to buy *her* a beer! " Then, *End of a World, Paris, August, 1914,* in which our great artiste impersonates a woman attending a concert and goes through various bored motions and facemakings while, from outside, come the sounds of martial music. There is also the item — a paraphrase of the idea in Noël Coward's *Dance, Little Lady* — in which a bored young woman drinking, smoking cigarettes and hoofing it in a night club finally passes out.

Fifthly, the modern art of interior decoration. The chief feature of this art is to take all the old soft, comfortable stuffing out of the seats of the chairs, remove the old comfortable arm rests, and so construct the chairs that if you lean back in them more than six inches they will topple over and land you on your heinie. Another big feature is to take all the pictures off the wall and paint on it instead either the March of the Wooden Soldiers or two fourteen-foot-long calla lilies. Still another piquant and very popular feature is the substitution of minature pin-trays for ash-trays, necessitating the depositing of one's cigar or cigarette ashes either in one's pocket or under the settee. And a still further feature is the placing of a tall screen embellished with doughnuts made of cellophane in such a position that it falls over and hits one on the head every time one tries to move out of the drawing-room into the dining-room.

Sixthly, there is the modern art of music. This is too long a subject to go into here, but I offer a sufficiently revelatory example in Ravel's piano concerto for the left hand alone. This was written to order for Paul Wittgenstein, a left one-armed piano performer, and it was rumored at the time of Ravel's death not long ago that he was working on a piano concerto for one Henri Mouchoir, who lost both his arms in a train wreck in 1932.

In the seventh place, we have the modern art of architecture which has resulted in, among other things, a wealth of buildings resembling Brown Derbies and other such

Michel Los Angelo headaches. In the eighth place, there is the modern art of stage décor, which has resulted, among other things, in ten dollars' worth of cardboard representing the Palace of Schönbrunn. In the ninth place, we have the modern art of Picasso which here and there substitutes pieces of leather, thumb nails, tacks and pieces of string for the paints of Rubens and Raphael. And in the tenth place, we have the modern art of poetry which substitutes such blank verse as

> Tell me, sweet, do not
> tell me, oh,
> for why do they
> oh, why,
> do tell me if
> at end of day
> is why
> or why
> or when

for the music of Shelley and Keats and Swinburne.

Let the business men who are maligned and ridiculed for not going into swooning raptures over all this modern art at last get up on their hind legs and give the Bronx cheer to their critics. And if they need a professional critic to lend additional volume to that cheer, they are at liberty to call up the present writer and tell him where they are holding the meeting.

AUTOBIOGRAPHIES. With very few exceptions, actors who confect autobiographical volumes put a dunce's cap on themselves coincidentally with the word *Finis*. The competent actor usually comes out of his book as one whose competence seems either excessively dubious or at best predicated on reasons quite different from those he offers. The charming actor, whether competent or not, usually emerges as something of a dissuading ass. The only species, in point of fact, that comes off with even faint honors seems to be the actor who hasn't anything much to recommend him critically and professionally (someone like Billy Bryant, the showboat mime, for example), who doesn't make any bones about it, and who just goes ahead and rattles off a lot of good-natured and amusing stories about his life and lack of art.

Speaking of the biographies of artists, Shaw once said that they all contain at least two anecdotes, one to illustrate the miraculous powers of the hero's brain, and another to exhibit his courage and dexterity in personal combat. The autobiographies of actors frequently adhere to much the same formula, particularly if the actors happen to be English. In that case, we are pretty sure to get the author's high tribute to his cerebral copings with Shakespeare and other classics, along with the implication that his interpretations are in all likelihood the only sound ones and that nobody else, especially the critics, knows what is really what in the matter, along with a due share of stories about his service and activities in the World War. These latter customarily present him, through the mist of a heavily manufactured modesty, as a stoic and realistic soldier or aviator for all his antecedent occupation with the world of make-believe, and are accompanied by details which reveal him to his admiring readers as one gifted in the simultaneous bayoneting of a Hun and the cynical quotation of Macbeth's first speech in Act 1, Scene VII, to say nothing of one who nonchalantly took the mud of Flanders in his stride quite as if it were the dance floor of the Embassy Club.

If the English actor happens to be of the non-classical species, of relatively younger years, and one whose art lies in the composition and acting of fashionable drawing-room comedy, what we get is several hundred pages of fluent chit-chat punctuated with photographs displaying him from the lovable age of six to his proud epiphany as a full-fledged leading man in the rôle of young Lord Sacheverell Pincus in his first great success, *Riviera Rigadoon.* The aforesaid chit-chat is purveyed in ferociously ingratiating terms, is so strainedly meek and modest that at times the reader fears the author will fall backward in a faint, and consists mainly of six recitations of what the witty Mrs. Pat Campbell once remarked to the author, two passages indicating his polite generosity upon encountering dramatic critics who had panned him, ten equally charming tributes to the ten actresses who have played in his various plays, several instances of advice which he received from famous older actors and playwrights, all of which he attests he was grateful for but which he resolutely rejected, a five hundred word paragraph telling of his enormous pride at the King and Queen's attendance of the five hundredth performance of one of his plays, and a chapter in which he describes, in humorously apologetic fashion, his early attempts at acting (Gerald Du Maurier brusquely informed him he should take up insurance salesmanship instead), his unsuccessful hawking of his early plays (Charles Cochran brusquely informed him he should devote himself to writing tupenny fiction instead), and the dinner dear old Gerald and dear old Charlie tendered him some years later at the Garrick Club on the occasion of his first overwhelming success.

The autobiographies of American actors vary principally only in detail. The same early hardships and the same belated recognitions are trotted through the routine paces. So are the anecdotes recounting the time when the scenery in Ashtabula, Ohio, fell on the author, who was acting Banquo's ghost, hit him a stunner on the head and caused him when he came to embarrassingly to recite his old lines from *The Ticket-of-Leave Man;* the time the manager vamoosed with the money and he stole down the fire-escape of a hotel in Des Moines, Iowa, in order to evade his room bill and was caught in the jam of the rest of the company doing the same thing; and the time Bill Brady, by way of desperately economizing on expenses, persuaded him not only to double as Uncle Tom and Simon Legree but to play Little Eva and both the bloodhounds, to say nothing of tooting a cornet in front of the theatre before the performance, serving as an usher, and selling gumdrops between the acts.

If the American actor is of vintage years his book will inevitably contain a diatribe against the old theatrical syndicate headed by Klaw and Erlanger. He will demonstrate at length how the Syndicate throttled theatrical art, of which he was so august and important a part, and how only his own great resource in getting them to put up a tent for him in El Paso, Texas, and installing chairs for him in an old barn in Waco saved the day for the American theatre. Having duly exhausted his indignation over Klaw and Erlanger by page 253, he then proceeds to get all boiled up again over the machinations of the Shuberts and it is only some hundred or so pages later that he recovers his equanimity sufficiently, after sharply telling off all the dramatic critics, to convey to the reader a final intimation of his own enduring eminence.

The books of lady actors are in general fabric and essence not greatly dissimilar to those of their gentlemen friends, and enjoy few variations. The same encounters with world celebrities are sprinkled through the pages; if the actress is English, there will be examples of the witty manner in which she put them to embarrassed rout; if she happens to be American, there will be traces of feigned schoolgirl humility and awe at the kind things they said to her when they forced their way through the crowd of admirers in her dressing-room or showed up unexpectedly and surprisingly one day for tea in her cozy apartment overlooking some river or other, or in slightly less affluent circumstances maybe only a garden. (" Lawdy, lawdy, Miss Jo," flutters Sally, her colored maid, " Ah bets it'll be President Roosevelt, d' King o' England and Mistah Einstein comin' in here to see you-all next! ") Also in evidence are the sympathetic humors of beginning days, with parents skeptical of their daughter's ambition, with the red velour curtain pulled off the parlor window to serve as a costume for our heroine's appearance as Portia in a neighborhood kids' attic exhibit, with the first word of encouragement spoken by the local stock company leading woman sought out after a Wednesday matinée, with the unrewarding and endless visits to producers' offices, and with the matchless thrill of the day when at long last our little sweetheart got the chance to walk on as a Nubian slave in the second road-company of *Quo Vadis*.

The autobiographies of English and American actresses appear to differ chiefly in one important detail. Whereas English actresses all seem to have had fathers, American actresses seem for the most part to have had only mothers. In most of the books written by the American girls if papa is mentioned at all, which is rarely, he seems either to have died (often from over-indulgence in alcohol) the day our heroine was born or to have deserted mama when our heroine was one year old. English fathers, on the other hand, seem to have stuck around for years. But in America it is dear old patient mother who has had to do all the chores to help our baby keep life in her body and to assist and guide her on her career. It is thus that whereas the English autobiographer divides her gratitude between her father and mother (with an overlapping fraction reserved, if she be past fifty-five, for a note of encouragement from Ellen Terry or, if she be under forty-five, for one from Sybil Thorndike), the American actress bestows hers mainly upon her mother, reserving what share is left over for her pet dog.

It is an uncommon actress who doesn't seem to devote almost as much affection to her pet dog as to her histrionic art. Fewer dogs and more acting would benefit the stage no end.

Aside from this, the autobiographies of both the English and American girls are, as noted, for the major part as generally alike as the usual remark about two peas. Both are at great pains to assure the reader how much they love the theatre — " it is the breath of life to me; it is my whole existence; without it, I could not live "; both are obsessed by one or more little superstitions upon which they dwell at considerable length and in relation to which they offer several droll personal experiences; both go in for lavish praise of their various leading men (most of whom they in all probability disliked intensely and fought with); and both invariably have at least one story to tell about how they and the company they were in triumphed over an earthquake, flood or some other catastrophe of nature which threatened to keep them from getting to their destination in time for a performance.

The greatest difficulty experienced in these memoirs, whether male or female, is the author's clearly obvious struggle at least in part to suppress the actor's natural conceit and vanity and to give the book a winning veneer of modesty. As I have said before, this is a trying compromise for any actor and it isn't long before his book betrays his disrelish of it and automatically again reverts to first principles. The one thing a mime seems never able to learn is that while one may offer a mental and intellectual superiority with grace and profit, it is the mark of bounderism to offer a personal and emotional superiority. The complete absence of any trace of the former and the crude and transparent effort and failure to conceal the latter are what make nine out of every ten actors' autobiographies the pickledust they are.

But the leading deficiency of the autobiographers is their uniform evasion and prevarication. To read many of them is to believe that actors and actresses invariably lead a life as sexless as a dead rabbit's; that they are — even often when they marry — coldly indifferent to the anatomical divertissements of the rest of the human family; that they are, in short, so many male and female virgins who would be shocked to death if, in the first instance, a pretty ingénue gave them the naughty eye or, in the second, if a handsome leading man pinched them on the cheek. Forgive at least one reader for laughing. Also forgive the laughter of at least one reader when he finds in none of the books such piquant episodes as those related to the authors' regular squabbles over money matters, fights with minor actors and actresses who threatened to steal certain moments of a play, scraps with playwrights over lines and scenes, and all the other customarily and scrupulously deleted anchovies.

It is a characteristic and peculiarity of most such autobiographies that their authors reserve their most copious admiration for fellow players who have died and who thus are no longer in a position to offer their vanity any active and serious competition. Here and there, of course, you will encounter some fairly sweet words about an associate who is still alive — about an actor if the littérateur is an actress, about an actress if the littérateur is an actor, though seldom the other way 'round — but the real Grade A goosegrease goes in the main to one or more of the dear departed.

There is, too, invariably one producer or manager who is nominated not only an uncommon genius but who is further affectionately endorsed as a wonderful friend, ever thoughtful, ever gently understanding and considerate, and ever intuitive as to the author's various difficult and trying problems. All the other managers and producers for whom the author has worked are indirectly implied to be lice. The actor rarely any longer comes right out and says so — that sort of thing went out of fashion, as I have indicated, when the older hams exhausted animosity toward the Syndicate and, later, the Shuberts — but it isn't hard to read between the lines.

With so many actors these days going in for writing and so many writers these days going in for acting, it is small wonder that both arts are suffering some pretty cruel wallops. The only hope, so far as the particular art of histrionic literature goes, seems to rest in the kind of actor who not only can't write but who can't act either. Such a one, for example, as the Billy Bryant I have earlier mentioned. I append a sample of Billy's belletristic charm and intelligence.

After telling how he has been polling his Ohio River show-boat audiences as to who is the World's Worst Actor, Billy continues:

"I'm safe as long as I can buy long underwear to play Hamlet in, but people keep ringing radio actors in on me and I'm worried. I get a good, solid vote like 'Bryant is the worst. After five years I know' — and then somebody cuts into my lead by writing 'I think Ben Bernie is worse. He smokes cigars while he acts. Until you can smell up your acting the same way you'll have to be content to be second worse.' I may have to go out there in *Agnes, The Switchman's Daughter* and really show 'em some bad acting to hold my lead."

AUTOGRAPH MANIA. That the autograph mania has swept the country like a locust plague, with its bugs performing to the distress and often agony of the public sidewalks in every sizable American city, isn't particularly exclusive news. But that it is the entirely new manifestation that many believe it to be is hardly in keeping with the facts. It has been in operation for years and, where once it functioned indoors, has now simply moved out-of-doors.

Its news is thus not in its presence, but in the increased magnitude of that presence. We have had autograph fiends with us for more than fifty years, and they have often been just as crazy as members of the bigger swarm that currently makes any public function a discommodious, if not life-risking, thing to attend. The idea that all autograph fiends are dirty little boys and girls with soiled pads in their hands — an idea promulgated by almost everyone who so much as even mentions the topic — is a fanciful one. Any number of the so-called fiends whom I enjoy the dubious privilege of knowing personally are in other respects fully adult, and many of them occupy positions in the more exalted strata of human affairs. But, as I have said, they are every bit as persistent and just as idiotic as any small boy or girl who crowds into theatre lobbies, railway stations, airports, restaurants and night clubs in search of the signatures of the somewhat more celebratedly idiotic.

From the latest price quotations on autographs, culled from various catalogues of professional merchants of autographs, we may determine the comparative taste, prejudice, intelligence and collector-acumen of the two classes of fiends, based upon the quoted values of all kinds of signatures. These catalogues, it must be remembered, are designed not for the autograph hunting riffraff but for the theoretically more elect and presumably more intelligent collectors. What do we find? We find that, among this more intellectually snooty and cultured class, the autograph of the late John Gilbert, the movie actor, is quoted for sale at two dollars, while that of Richard Mansfield, one of the most famous dramatic actors of the American theatre, is listed at exactly half that price. The urchins seem to have a considerably more astute conception of relative artistic values. In the capacity of private investigator, I discover from them that whereas the signature of Fredric March, the movie actor, is sold by them for fifteen cents, that of Alfred Lunt, the stage actor, brings fifty cents.

The catalogued sale price of Helena Modjeska's and Annie Pixley's autographs are respectively a dollar and a half and five dollars, a sweet indication of the preferences and critical values of the elect in the way of actresses. And while the quotation on the signature of Ellen Terry is only two dollars, the price asked for that of Mrs. Pat Campbell is three and a quarter, which is analogously like asking more for a share of stock in a defunct gold mine than for one in American Tel. and Tel. The kid collectors, on the other hand, value Katharine Cornell's autograph at fifty cents and Eva Le Gallienne's at ten, and they demand three times more for Helen Hayes' than for Eugenie Leontovich's, which implies, whether they know it or not, that they are rather better critics than their purportedly sharper minded elders.

Consider the latter's taste and judgment in other directions. According to the catalogued price lists, they regard Palmer Cox, creator of the *Brownies,* worth a dollar more as an artist than Millais (the prices are five and four dollars respectively); Frances Hodgson Burnett, author of *Little Lord Fauntleroy,* worth a dollar and a half more as a literary genius than William Dean Howells (three and a half versus two); Victor Hugo worth ten dollars less than James Whitcomb Riley (seven-fifty versus seventeen-fifty); and Leonard Merrick fifty cents more precious than John Ruskin (three fifty versus three). The autograph-collecting youngsters exchange autographs among themselves, they tell me, at the rate of a dollar for Sinclair Lewis as against two bits for Edna Ferber, seventy-five cents for Ellen Glasgow against a dime for Faith Baldwin, and six William Lyon Phelpses for one Theodore Dreiser. The superior taste and judgment of the maligned sidewalk-infesting brats is obvious.

The preferences of the older and more sedate collectors are generally, as a matter of pure statistical record, a lot more comical than those of the kids. Upton Sinclair seems to the collecting elect to be worth six dollars and Mark Twain only four — and two of Mark's autographs, at that, for the one price! General Phil Sheridan, one of the heroes of the Civil War, is appraised at a mere couple of dollars, while Drake De Kay, a Union general about whom few persons have ever heard, is considered a hot bargain at four simoleons and a half. In the way of college presidents, Eliphalet Nott, quondam head of Union College, is worth a dollar more than Theodore D. Woolsey, once president of Yale, a dollar and a half more than James Mather, once president of Harvard, twice as much more than H. T. Durant, founder of Wellesley, and more than merely twice as much more than Mark Hopkins, erstwhile president of Williams. Mary Garden brings a dollar, which is the same value placed upon J. H. Rainey, a former colored member of Congress. Grover Cleveland is estimated at being less than one-third as precious as Calvin

Coolidge, and Chester A. Arthur is worth seven dollars and a half, only a little less than Thomas Jefferson. Martin Van Buren is considered a big bargain at five dollars and Warren Gamaliel Harding an even bigger one at fifteen, whereas James Madison goes begging at four dollars and Ulysses S. Grant at six.

But the humor doesn't stop here. G. M. Dallas, vice-president under Polk, is esteemed at seventeen dollars and a half, whereas you can get James Monroe, Franklin Pierce, Andrew Johnson, James A. Garfield, James Buchanan, John Quincy Adams, Millard Fillmore, and several other American Presidents for less than one-fourth that amount. Charles VI, Emperor of the Holy Roman Empire, is worth four dollars, which puts him on an equal price level with Joseph Hergesheimer. John Hancock, signer of the Declaration of Independence, is quoted at the same figure as Al Smith. Alexander Dumas is worth a couple of dollars less than Ezra Pound (four versus six). Swinburne is rated at the same figure as Sara Teasdale, and Abraham Lincoln seems to be worth only as much as W. H. Taft.

After talking with at least two dozen of the youngsters who hang around the New York theatres, moving picture palazzos and other such centers where celebrities of one sort or another are wont to gather, I have gleaned the following autograph market quotations that obtain among them. Among the playwrights, Eugene O'Neill rates a dollar, Elmer Rice a quarter, George S. Kaufman a quarter, Robert Sherwood a quarter, and Owen Davis a dime. Among the actors, Maurice Evans brings fifty cents, Jimmie Durante forty cents, William Gaxton fifteen cents. Among the actresses, aside from those already mentioned, Judith Anderson is rated at thirty-five cents, Helen Menken at fifteen, Nazimova at thirty, Lynn Fontanne at twenty-five, and Gypsy Rose Lee at twenty. Among the movie actors, Clark Gable is quoted at fifty cents, Ronald Colman and Herbert Marshall at forty-five, Charlie Chaplin at fifty, Gary Cooper at thirty, and Francis Lederer, Cesar Romero, Robert Young, Gilbert Roland, Eric Linden and John Boles at six cents each. Among the movie girls, Grace Moore is worth half a dollar, Kay Francis twenty cents, Mary Pickford fifteen cents, Janet Gaynor fifteen cents, Constance Bennett fifteen cents, Katharine Hepburn a quarter, Myrna Loy a quarter, Ginger Rogers fifty-five cents and Joan Crawford sixteen. And in the world of sports, one Jack Dempsey is worth three Max Schmelings, one Joe Louis is worth twelve Braddocks, and you can, the kids tell me, get all the Gene Tunneys and Maxie Baers you want for a dime.

It doesn't look as if those little pests are such terribly dumb critical clucks after all.

B

BAITERS OF CRITICS. In every theatrical season some producer, playwright or actor makes a fool of himself by getting
into a fight with one or more of the critics. Whether the fight
is with fists or with print doesn't matter. In either case the
fellow is eventually bound to find himself with his bloomers
down. Nor does it matter if he is in the right and the critic
in the wrong. The cards are stacked against him from the
outset. They are not stacked by the critics; they are stacked
by himself. And why are they thus stacked? Because in
every instance recorded in the local theatrical history of the
last thirty years the critic-baiter has been recognized by the
public as smarting under the sting of his own failure, because
in all that time no consistently sound, reputable and important producer, playwright or actor, whether in success or periodic failure, has bothered about critics the one way or the
other, and because the American public abides by the national tradition that any man, even a critic, should have the
right to speak his mind freely and without restriction, even
if he hasn't a mind and is by way of being a consummate ass.

The two most recent theatrical armigerents to overlook
this and to emerge with their shirt-tails hanging out were
Mr. Jack Kirkland and Mr. Jed Harris. Not so very long ago,
the former offered to the public his idea of a dramatization
of John Steinbeck's series of character studies of the California paisano, *Tortilla Flat*. His idea took the form of sedulously filtering out of Steinbeck's work every trace of its humorous understanding, gentleness and pity and of leaving
in his dramatization only the dregs of its vulgarity. This vulgarity, in turn, which in Steinbeck was forthright, honest,

healthy and clean, Kirkland converted into Minsky innuendo, smut and outright dirt. The critics to a man naturally took him severely to task and the public, agreeing with the critics, remained away from his play to such a degree that it was yanked off the stage after only a few days' showing.

What, then, did Kirkland do? Did he properly hide himself in shame, even in disgrace? Did he go out and get quietly and consolingly drunk? Did he take private stock of himself and, like any intelligent man under the same circumstances, conclude that he had made a miserable botch of his job and vow to himself that, by God and by Jupiter and by the beards of Mohammed and Emanuel Swedenborg, he would do better the next time or, by God and by Zeus and by the navels of Buddha and Frank Buchman, he'd know the reason why? He didn't. Believing that the critics and not he were responsible for his ignominious downfall, he picked out Richard Watts, of the *Herald-Tribune,* as the symbol of the critical cabal against him, trailed Watts to his favorite bar, and took a swing at him. Five minutes later what was left of Kirkland was gathered together, placed in an empty beer case, and delivered at his hotel by several good, officiating Christians, who accidentally and very unfortunately dropped the beer case twelve times on the way.

Mr. Harris put on a revival of Ibsen's *A Doll's House* which indicated to the majority of the critics that he had apparently mistaken for it J. Hartley Manners' *Peg o' My Heart* and had produced the latter instead. Although anyone who knew the least thing about Ibsen and his play fully concurred in the critics' estimate, Harris, as is his wont every time he personally makes a mess of a job, became good and indignant at those who had found him out. On such occasions, unlike Kirkland, however, he refrains from making an idiot of himself by taking pokes at the critics' jaws and landing in a beer case. He prefers to make an idiot of himself by giving out interviews and thus safeguarding and preserving his health, if not his intelligence.

Harris' extenuation of himself for his Ibsen inexperience took this form: "There is no man in New York writing dramatic criticism today who has any creative force; they're critics only because they have jobs. When their papers fold they're no longer critics. I've never seen so many men so ill-equipped for their jobs as the boys now reviewing for the New York dailies. They're a nice lot of fellows, intelligent and certainly honest. But do they know anything about the theatre? Why, except for Mr. Atkinson, there's not one who would be missed if he dropped out. . . . Critics don't have to pay for their mistakes and there's no denying that what they write has an immediate effect on the seat-buying public. . . . And now take Woollcott, Woollcott's now an actor. One of my regrets is that I did not appreciate Woollcott more when he was writing reviews."

Let us analyze.

1. If there is no newspaper critic with any creative ability and if there is none who knows anything about the theatre why did Harris engage John Anderson, of the *Journal-American,* to adapt plays for him, why has he often consulted with at least three of them on his productions, why (until the *American* folded) did he exercise so much interest in a play that Gilbert Gabriel, that paper's critic, was writing, and why have so few critics in New York — up to the Ibsen production — been safe from his solicitous telephone inquiries as to the merits of play manuscripts he was considering?

2. The critics, says Harris, are intelligent and certainly honest, but, he asks, do they know anything about the theatre? If the critics are intelligent and honest (as to the intelligence, though certainly not the honesty, of maybe one or two of them, I am not so entirely optimistic as Harris), what is there so complex and inscrutable about the theatre in most of its manifestations that it should elude their comprehension and their ability accurately to report on it? Surely, any half-way intelligent truck-driver or even theatri-

cal producer shouldn't have difficulty in knowing everything there is to be known about the theatre as it has been represented by such of Mr. Harris' own more recent productions as *The Lake, Life's Too Short, The Fatal Alibi, Wonder Boy* and *Spring Dance.* If it is not too impolite, may one further ask how much any man who produces such plays as these, all worthless and all prompt failures, himself knows about the theatre?

3. " Except for Mr. Atkinson (of the *Times*) there's not one who would be missed if he dropped out." By a strange coincidence, Mr. Atkinson was the only critic who gave Harris' production of *A Doll's House* a completely laudatory notice.

4. " Critics don't have to pay for their mistakes." But don't they? If they make enough of them, they have to pay with their reputations, their careers, and their very jobs. There is no more lasting place for the dolts among critics than for the dolts among theatrical producers.* In the last two decades at least a half-dozen critics have been dismissed from their jobs on New York newspapers because of critical incapacity.

5. " One of my regrets," says Harris, " is that I did not appreciate Woollcott more when he was writing reviews." By another strange coincidence, Woollcott ballyhooed Harris' production of *A Doll's House* over the radio.

I can quite understand that such men as Kirkland and Harris get sore when criticism drives to the dump something upon which they have expended their time and best efforts and which, though it isn't worth the powder to blow it up, they nevertheless persuade themselves is pretty fine. That is human nature, not only with the Kirklands and Harrises, but with the majority of men. But what I can't understand is why they don't slyly convert that soreness into a skillful and convincing, if completely incompetent, irrelevant, immaterial and bogus, proof that the critics, though obviously

---

* *Mr. Harris has retired to Hollywood.*

wholly right, are not only wrong in their specific cases but beautifully dumb in a lot of other more or less related directions. The trouble, of course, is that men like Kirkland and Harris have no talent for such intellectual pranks. But any man who has could have a heap of fun and could win not only a share of the public to his side but also those critics who admire a good show, even when it is at their own expense. I therefore suggest that the next time some playwright, producer or actor becomes indignant at something I have written of him, however much he may appreciate its fact and truth, he ask me to compose an attack upon myself for him to sign and to give out under his own name. I have been of such magnanimous service to several disgruntled jackasses on at least four occasions in the past and never once have I failed to convince a great many other jackasses that I didn't, in my critical capacity, know what I was talking about and should promptly be committed to the doghouse. The trick isn't at all difficult. But I shall not give it away here. I'd dislike so soon to lose the amusement of seeing the Kirklands being carted off in beer cases and the Harrises making themselves indistinguishable from the Morris Gests of twenty years ago.

Ballyhooey.   Three and more decades ago, those sons of Munchausen who are known to the world as theatrical press-agents were at the top of their own especial and peculiar pole of glory. It was a great period for the boys. Assuming — not without a considerable degree of intelligence — that the theatregoers of the time were for the most part a lot of impressionable children, they addressed their circus efforts to an I.Q. of about six percent, and found their acumen duly and richly rewarded.

They found, for instance, that by spreading fables to the effect that an actress substituted milk for water in her bath, the public would flock to behold the exotic creature. They discovered that by informing the boobs that another actress had such a delicate nervous constitution that it was impossible for her to play unless the street in front of the theatre was covered with tan-bark to deaden the traffic noises, the aforesaid boobs would gallop to the box-office to gape at her. They found that by broadcasting the news that a not half bad-looking girl named Polaire was the homeliest woman extant, crowds would pour their money into the till to have a look at her.

Anything went in those days, provided only it lacked any element of truth and was completely nonsensical. As one who lived through the era and followed its publicity voodoo with a close and amused eye, I can recall three and only three theatrical press-agent yarns out of thousands that betrayed even a modicum of relatively intelligent persuasion. And the three in question, for all that, were almost as big frauds as all the others.

The first of the three was a story sent out by the press-agent for Charles and Rose Coghlan in a play called *The Royal Box*. Playing in it with her father and aunt was Gertrude Coghlan, then a young girl. Her rôle was a small one and called for her to do a bit of the balcony scene from *Romeo and Juliet*. All that the audience could see of her was her body from the waist up, the flowered rail of the balcony hiding the rest of her. It was necessary for her to make a quick change of costume to go into the scene and the press-agent allowed that Papa Charles and Aunt Rose, who were the stars of the occasion, suggested to her that, inasmuch as the audience couldn't see her skirt, it would be a good idea for her to simplify and hasten matters merely by putting on a fancy bodice.

The press-agent then went on to record at length how Gertrude tried it a few times and found that she simply couldn't play the romantic scene with her old woolen skirt clashing with the beautiful bodice and jarring her extremely sensitive mood. Unless she was in the full costume of Juliet, the scene, as far as her acting went, went to pieces. So, agreeing with her, her papa and aunt inserted a short time-killing scene which would give her the necessary minutes to make the complete change. Foolish stuff, true enough, but at least with a relieving small dose of conviction.

The second instance was to the credit of the publicity mouthpiece for David Belasco. Dave, according to his Munchausen, had long pondered the three Aristotelian unities of time, place and action and, pondering, had arrived at the conclusion that Aristotle, the dummkopf, had overlooked a most important fourth. This fourth, it appeared, was — in the press-agent's phraseology — the unity of blood. That is to say, Dave argued that the trouble with the acted drama was that the various members of a family, as cast by the average producer, never showed the faintest resemblance to one another and might as well be members of entirely different families. Dave, announced his publicity ambassador, was going to change all that. In his productions, an audience would be able, through his careful casting of the rôles, quickly to detect the suggestion of related family looks.

More bosh, to be sure, and even a little extra-boshful to anyone who stopped for a moment to reflect that members of the same family often look no more alike than as many drugstore candies, but relatively sensible, at that, when compared with the period's stories of vaudeville acrobats studying for grand opera and a whole company of actors planning to scale Mount Everest during the summer vacation.

The third yarn concerned the celebrated farce writer, Charles H. Hoyt. When Hoyt produced *A Contented Woman* with the beautiful Caroline Miskel, whom he married, in the leading rôle, his hired ballyhooer published the tale that he wrote the play for the especial purpose of slyly and obliquely persuading Miss Miskel that a woman's place was not in public life but at home with her loving spouse. Which, generally, was the play's theme and plot. Sure enough, Miss Miskel presently deserted the stage and retired to domesticity. The story made a wide impression.

People thought Hoyt an uncommonly shrewd and wily old bird. But one thing spoiled the proper effect of his press-agent's fable. The reason Miss Miskel went back to the fireside was that the play was so poor it quickly failed. Which not only left Miss Miskel but the press-agent out of a job.

Theatrical press-agency has experienced a great change since those days. Seldom any longer are we regaled with the old tales of actresses' stolen jewels, stars who have discovered gold mines in their back yards, producers who plan to produce a play simultaneously in all the countries of the globe, and similar donkey-bait. The public of today has grown up and is no longer a goat for such taradiddle. As a consequence, press-agency has come to smell less of the circus ring and shell game and has gained an increased decorum and sense. Now and again, to be sure, some throwback to the ancient order will pop into print with a gob of the old-time flapdoodle, but it makes an impression on nobody and it isn't long before its confector finds himself minus a pay envelope.

The new press-agency has brought into the field a new type of ballyhooer. The best in the business today are men of wit and humor who are nice hands at literature, men who are students of the more serious side of the theatre, and men who appreciate that facts are infinitely more convincing than fiction. Richard Maney's various stories about the Mad Mahout of Broadway, Billy Rose, are destined to become classics of the publicity craft. They are immensely amusing; they are adroitly composed; far from making their subject a hero, as the old-time press-agency would have done, they truthfully make him a slightly absurd but very interesting and even lovable human being; and they arouse the vital curiosity about him and his ventures. Maney's stories about the mock melodramas at the American Music Hall have been similarly humorous, piquant and able performances. They have created the proper air and atmosphere around the productions and their exaggerations have been in strict accordance with the spirit of the enterprise.

The late Ray Henderson's press-agency of Katharine Cornell was a model of its kind. Dignified and informative, it never stooped to the old honkytonk technique. And it helped not a little in raising Miss Cornell in the popular esteem. Only on one occasion did Henderson bend a bit toward the past tradition and that was in his stories about Miss Cornell's dog, Flush, who appeared with her in *The Barretts of Wimpole Street*. Oliver Sayler's press-agency in connection with the Russian players was often sound enough to be clipped and filed away by aspiring students of the drama and acting. Barrett Clark's appearances in a publicity rôle are invariably accompanied by articles reflecting his well-grounded knowledge of the modern drama. And there are others such. If an actress represented by any one of them were to lose not only her jewels but her clothes, lingerie, husband, lover, cook and pet canary to boot, you'd never get a line about it from them.

BANKHEAD. Among my histrionic skepticisms, Tallulah Bankhead has since her beginning bulked pretty large. I could never see in her much more than a scintillant personality with a decidedly minor acting equipment, and her considerable critical success in London nine years ago seemed to me, after due on-the-spot investigation and research, to be grounded largely on the facts that, with her wild and woolly ways and manner, she was a novelty to a stage whose women generally comport themselves as if they all had been written by Pinero and that, further, in two of her exhibits she had taken her clothes off, which always gets the sedate London critics.

In *The Little Foxes*, however, Tallulah made your Solon eat a slice of humble-pie. Her performance of the vicious, stone-hearted, rapacious female who gets what she goes after, whatever the price, was a capital job, admirably poised and excellently detailed, and in addition devoid of all the hitherto cut-and-dried Bankhead quirks and mannerisms. I appreciate, of course, that critics who have been skeptical of an actress in other rôles often at length fall for her when she shows up in one that presents her as what the he-man school of English playwrights, embracing the Messrs. Coward, Novello, *et al.*, designate as a bitch. But as Tallulah has played that species of rôle before, and has usually played it poorly, no such excuse may be assigned for the respect here paid to her performance in the Hellman exhibit.

BEAUTY AND THE CRITICAL BEAST.　One of the most damaging philosophies that latterly has befallen the theatre is the theory that if an actress knows how to act it isn't at all necessary for her to be beautiful, or even fairly good-looking. This is all very well for the professional critics, three-fourths of whom are hypocrites anyway when it comes to the matter, but it has become increasingly painful for the greater part of the public.

There are occasions, of course, when an actress' looks do not count the one way or the other. If she is an old woman or is playing the rôle of an old woman is one such occasion. If the rôle is that of an unattractive or a repulsive female is another. And if the actress, whatever the rôle, is by way of being something of a genius in the histrionic art is still another. But since we have very few such geniuses and since the great majority of our acting girls are run of the mill, this subject of looks may well be weighed by the playgoing congress.

The theatre's purpose, end and sole reason for being is the projection of the mood of beauty. But in recent years the forces of dramatic art have combined against it. These forces, notably naturalism and realism, have carried themselves to such a length that the real beauty that lies in dramatic poetry has been largely banished from the theatre.

Realistic drama only once in a great while possessed of beauty, stage settings that haplessly vouchsafe either a realistic over-elaboration or a bogus simplicity, rich costumes poverty-stricken in grace and charm, superficial wit, dirty humor as funny as unwashed ears, and commonplace imagination in a dozen and one directions have further tended to nullify the stage's romantic allure. And it is because of all this that loveliness and beauty in its women have become an increased desideratum.

A theatre with beautiful women is, critics or no critics, a theatre that becomes alive and thereafter living and singing in the memory. Duse will linger in the romantic imagination long after Bernhardt is forgotten. Janet Achurch was dead even in the later days of her own theatrical life, but Ellen Terry will not die for a hundred years to come. It isn't always so, true enough, but it is so in most cases. I last year asked Charles Cochran, the well-known British producer, about the particularly beautiful young English actress named Vivien Leigh, whom I had never beheld on the stage. " Can she act? " I inquired. " Not much," replied Charlie. " Then how do you account for the extravagantly good notices the London critics have given her? " I wanted to know. Charlie smiled. " She is," he rejoined, " the only good-looking new actress they've had a chance of seeing on the London stage in the last dozen years."

There is no reason to sneer at the London critics. They simply betrayed that homesickness for beauty in one bearing or another which their theatre had so long denied them and their constituency.

Many plays fail of their complete and proper effect because the actresses cast in their important rôles fail to visualize either the playwrights' or the audiences' concept of the women they play. In the season before last, a play about Lincoln went to pieces in the audience's imagination the moment the actress assigned to play Ann Rutledge popped into view. Last season another play about Lincoln successfully

stroked the audience's imagination and in part contributed to
its own great success by casting in the same rôle a girl with
all the sad and lovely romance in the world in her face. And
please don't tell me it was merely a difference in acting competence. Both rôles were and are so elementary and simple
that almost any actress could play them with her hands tied
behind her back and even if directed by Max Reinhardt with
his elegant white kid gloves on. It was all purely a matter
of looks; the Longmire girl had them and the other girl didn't
have them.

The moving pictures, in their own way, have achieved
success because they have given the public dramatic heroines who look as the public imagines them. They have
achieved doubled success when they have given the public
dramatic heroines who look three times more like what they
should look like than the public has been able to imagine
them. And they have achieved their supreme success when
they have practically got rid of drama and have merely substituted very beautiful women for it. A Hedy Lamarr is
worth more to the movie box-office than a hundred *Hamlets*.

The movies, of course, are a low form of art and the
movie public may be regarded with considerable condescension, but just the same even the snootiest theatrical critic
must allow that the pictures have shown some critical sense
in this particular regard and that the picture public isn't altogether so abhorrently dumb. There is a touch, a wee touch,
of that peculiar public in even the best of us. Katherine
Locke may be a better Ophelia than Celia Johnson, but once
the analytical gabble of the Critics' Circle is over I'll take
Celia and so, you have my word for it, will most of my colleagues, whatever they punditically and professionally try to
tell you. And so will you, you more honest and honorable
layman!

It is the same in countless other instances. If two equally
talented actresses play Candida, it will be the presentation
with the more personable and attractive of the twain that

will project itself deepest into an audience's emotions. The Juliets of Mary Anderson and Julia Marlowe will be remembered long after the Juliets of dozens of competent piefaces have passed from the recollection. Hauptmann's *And Pippa Dances* has failed in every country where it has been shown because they have never been able to find the actress with the required looks, the creature that Hauptmann imagined and wrote, to play it. Max Beerbohm, it is said, would not write for the theatre because he appreciated that the delicately lovely women his pen would create could be cast only once in every twenty or thirty years.

As a professional theatre critic of more than three decades' experience, I have, after reading new plays in manuscript, periodically suggested in print long in advance the names of certain actresses who might bring the necessary beauty and loveliness to the leading rôles. In a number of instances producers have hospitably followed the presumptuous suggestions and in each and every instance the public has responded properly to the choice. Why? Simply because there has always been uppermost in my mind not the actress as actress so much as the actress as girl or woman. Did she look the rôle as I imagined the author sentimentally saw it or at least as I myself thus definitely saw it? Did her previous performances imply the personal, physical and spiritual possession of those qualities that the rôle hinted at? Did my picture of her, rightly or wrongly, seem to me the picture the rôle should visually create and project? To the Marines with acting as acting; that was of secondary importance.

The trouble with many producers is that they think of actresses primarily as actresses, without taking into casting consideration the woman (aside from the actress) that the public and critics subsequently have to look at. In the case of certain plays, it may not matter. But in the case of most plays, it matters a great deal. The producers should remember that we not only have to listen to actresses but we also have to look at them. And for our three dollars and eighty-

five cents they might throw in at least eighty-five cents' worth
of something to look at.

BELASCOISM. When one recalls that Elizabeth B. Ginty
spent a considerable portion of her earlier life as secretary
and general factotum to the late David Belasco, one may
the more readily understand the rachitic quality of her play
about Jesse James, *Missouri Legend*. It isn't that the lady
didn't try sincerely and hard to make a sound job of it. She
undoubtedly, to the best of her ability, did. But that ability, whatever it may have been in the first place, showed so
clearly the effects of long and intimate association with the
late gooroo of greasepaint that her exhibit needed only a
half dozen Tiffany lamps, a five thousand dollar Paisley
shawl thrown over the piano, and a slightly more realistic
rainstorm — and perhaps its title changed to *The Boy of the
Golden West* — to take us all right back to her old boss'
heyday.

So insidious was the Belasco influence upon her that
the lady did not, apparently, herself realize it. In a press
interview she allowed that she cared little for the work of
women playwrights because, she said, they were given to
an excess of sentiment. Yet, though she thus implied that
she herself was free from any such excess, her own play betrayed it to an extent that would have warmed her mentor's
heart. It is true that she followed in some measure the James
biographical record, but she so massaged fact with the soothing syrup of sentimental theatrical hokum that it frequently
became indiscernible to the categorical eye. We were, accordingly, vouchsafed a play in which the notorious bandit's
climactic deed consisted in paraphrasing the well-known
old scene from *Turn to the Right* and stealing from the bank
messenger the two hundred dollars which he (Jesse) gave
the poor widow to pay off the mortgage on her house. And
we thus got a Jesse who could not abide a man who used
cuss words, who was obstreperously religious, who brushed

away a tear whenever he thought of his dear wife and children, who was seven hundred and fifteen times more honorable than Joseph Stalin, who talked wistfully of his dear, departed mother, and who was tenderly dusting off her picture when he met his end.

It wasn't, as has been noted, that some of these sentiments were not to a degree attributable to the hero of our youth. It was rather that Miss Ginty heated the degree up to one hundred and five in the shade. The J.J. that emerged was, consequently, not a bandit with a soft side so much as a softy with a bandit side. If, whatever solemn reference tomes the author nosed, our Jesse was anything like that, Street and Smith certainly swindled us out of a lot of dimes in the early Nineties. Nor were Miss Ginty's literary style and humor sufficiently incandescent to atone for her empirical debunking exercise. Her rustic dramatic belles lettres were of the species which inevitably embraces the line, "What might your name be, stranger?," and her humor was of the variety which unappeasably concerns itself with posteriors, whether of horses or of bustle-amplified females.

BEST SELLERS. Dramatized best sellers, it has long been maintained, make doubtful theatrical properties. In the history of American publishing, twenty-one novels have reached a sale of more than a million copies. These are the best sellers de luxe. Of the twenty-one, ten have thus far been dramatized for the professional stage. Of the ten dramatizations, eight were big successes, to wit, *Ben Hur, The Virginian, The Trail of the Lonesome Pine, David Harum, Trilby, Treasure Island, The Little Shepherd of Kingdom Come,* and *Pollyanna.* The dramatizations of the remaining two, *The Sheik* and *The Girl of the Limberlost,* were made by wretched hacks, were cheaply and wretchedly produced in third-rate theatres, and were listed as failures. Yet even the producers of those two broke better than even on them.

BIOGRAPHICAL DRAMA.   Novices in the field of the biographical play imagine that a more or less faithful and accurate recording of historical personality and event constitutes drama. It does nothing of the kind. What it most often constitutes is merely a phonograph record played over television. Drama is not fact and truth but the seductively deceptive simulacrum of fact and truth.

BIRABEAU.   It is evident that André Birabeau, unlike most of his French colleagues, can at one and the same time read German and not be indignant. What he has done in his little play, *Dame Nature,* is waggishly to Frenchify and boulevardize Wedekind's famous children's tragedy, *The Awakening of Spring.* Laying hold of the Swiss-German's tragic tale of youngsters at the critical age of puberty, he pulls off its crêpe and embellishes its dark contours with gay, and here and there pastel and tender, colors. Wedekind's little Melchior and Wendla are renamed André and Leonie and, like the former, are ignorant of sex. Also like the former, Dame Nature draws them together and a baby results. But unlike Melchior and Wendla, who wind up respectively in a reformatory and a grave, André and Leonie wind up in a comedy that simultaneously smiles sympathetically at their predicament and brings them themselves to smile superiorly at any such gratuitous condescension. The Wedekind play, it is needless to remark, should out of respect for it not be brought into comparison with any such minor divertissement, and it is not. Two treatments of the same basic theme are the sole consideration intended.

Therefore, amiably to pursue. In the German play the elders view the youngsters' problem with solemn faces and ponderous moralizings. In the French play, when confronted by the situation, they humorously comfort themselves with the assuaging reassurance that at least it wasn't the father of André who got Leonie into trouble. In the German exhibit, the mother, spilling tears over her daughter, wails gloomily that at her daughter's age the secrets of sex had also cruelly been withheld from her. In the French, the mother casually touches her nose with her forefinger and lightly observes, when she gets the startling news that the one responsible for Leonie's baby is her own young son, that it is all very peculiar, as she had always thought boys didn't reach manhood until they began to smoke. In the German play, Melchior's little boy friend is so shocked by the ugliness of sex that he shoots himself. In the French, André's little boy friend is so vicariously tickled by its charm that he grabs André's air rifle and forgets himself shooting at paper pigeons. Now let the Nazi Angermacher, who can at one and the same time read French and boil with indignation, even up matters by Germanizing into tragedy one of Birabeau's farce-comedies.

BLUTWURST. Although the public is apparently again so hungry for the theatre that if several actors so much as smear their faces with greasepaint and get up on a stage and say hello the box-office seems to have difficulty in handling the customers, it is a rueful critical fact that most of the dramatic provender isn't nourishing enough to sustain a canary. It is something of a pity, for the producers can't go on feeding a dramatically starved public with doughnut holes and expect it, in turn, to go on paying caviar prices for them. The public may conceivably, as is often alleged, have a hospitable stomach for theatrical pastries but there must nevertheless come a time when it will crave and demand a little blutwurst for a change. Today it may be so arbitrarily eager for the theatre that even when the Barter Players come up from the South for a night and offer a plugged-penny *Macbeth* in exchange for some raspberries or a dubious egg (both of which, though eminently congruous, are by way of being an overcharge), it will actually indicate its irrepressible theatrical ardor — *vide* the newspaper reports — by offering instead such honoraria as a Mallard duck, an Andalusian goat, a bottle of vintage champagne, a basket of broccoli, a ten pound Virginia ham, and a first edition of Huneker, each of which in turn would be an even saucier and more exorbitant overcharge for most of the new plays presented at from three to four dollars, plus tax, in the Broadway theatres. But the situation cannot and will not continue. The shell game is never long good for money in the same place.

BOOKS. The conventional critical objection to such Broadway musical exhibits as *Three Waltzes* and *Between the Devil* is that the books, or librettos, are not only woefully inferior to the scores but that they are at the same time old-fashioned, stale and dull. Although a great deal of the criticism holds water and I fully concur in it, it nevertheless strikes me that there is something to be said for the other side. It would, true enough, be pretty hard to find a book duller than that of *Between the Devil,* and certainly the three-generation love story of *Three Waltzes* has already served enough time to be paroled, but even so I speculate why criticism should be so harsh with exhibits of this kind when it allows itself to be so lenient in other more or less analogous directions.

I allude, obviously enough, to the opera. If the book of *Three Waltzes* is old-fashioned, stale and dull, what of the libretto of *La Sonnambula,* or *Lakmé,* or *La Favorita,* or *Cavalleria Rusticana,* or *L'Africaine,* or *Manru,* or *La Traviata,* or *Der Freischütz,* or some of the others? If any such librettos were to be merchanted on Broadway today, the yell of derision would be audible for miles around, yet no one complains when year after year one is asked to listen to their endless repetition at the opera. Any such comparison is nonsensical? Why? Well, for one thing, you say, it is a matter of music. But the music of *Three Waltzes* is by and after Johann Strauss, Sr., Johann Strauss, Jr., and Oscar Straus and so surely is not to be dismissed as contemptible. Well, for another thing, you say, the opera librettos mentioned were originally deserving and are now agreeably accepted as pleasant mementoes. But the *Three Waltzes* story was also originally and relatively deserving and might now also be agreeably accepted as a pleasant memento. And were the opera librettos mentioned really as originally deserving as you say? One, after a vaudeville by Scribe, was old-fashioned and dull even in 1831; another was derived by a couple of hacks from a play already stale in 1840; still another after a play also already more than stale; and another still by the same worn-out Scribe whose librettos have done so much to depress opera.

Nevertheless, you say, the lyrics of these operas are infinitely superior to those of some such exhibit as *Three Waltzes*. You are, I have the honor of telling you, a snob and a faker. The *My Heart Controls My Head* lyric in the latter is just as good as, if not better than, the *Tutto è gioja* in the Bellini opera, the *To Live Is to Love* every bit as good as the *Fior di giaggolo* in the Mascagni, the *Our Last Waltz Together*, the *Springtime* and the *Do You Recall?* fully as good as, indeed considerably better than, such lyrical exercises as the sailors' chorus in the Meyerbeer opera, the villagers' jingle in *Manru*, and the *Ah, fors è lui* in the *Camille* extraction. Well, well, you say, but nobody listens to the words and lyrics in opera; it is the music alone that matters. Well, well, I reply, why then must anyone listen so arbitrarily and insistently to the words and lyrics of something like *Three Waltzes* when its music has been garnered from the world's masters of three-quarter time? Well, well, well, you say, but the singing voices make a difference. Kitty Carlisle's voice in *Three Waltzes* was of operatic quality and, besides, unlike the majority of female opera singers, she is very good-looking and can act. Michael Bartlett, in the same operetta, had sung in grand opera in Italy and elsewhere.

So many people — and that includes critics — are such bloody hypocrites.

These frequent loud complaints against books and librettos on the part of various professional grousers would seem to indicate that they go to an operetta principally to hear the words, which has always seemed to me to be like going to a barroom principally to talk to the bartender. Such fowl are musical teetotalers or, if not exactly that, at least whip-hands on the musical waterwagon. They would talk to a girl while dancing *Roses from the Southland* or the *Blue Danube* with her. They would discuss ornithology with their brides while listening to the song of the nightingale. They would lament the political changes in Germany during the swan-song of Isolde. They would feel the quality of the paper on which Joseph Conrad sings his beautiful literary melodies. They would argue about diaphonics, the Stuttgart pitch, and the criticisms of Ernest Newman during the Ninth Symphony. To hell with 'em!

BOX-OFFICE BOOZE. It is the maternal dodge of spinster playwright-directors like Rachel Crothers to make the dipsomaniac husbands in their plays sympathetic characters by directing the actors playing the rôles to comport themselves as if they had never drunk anything stronger than sauerkraut juice and not only didn't like it but were stricken with remorse for their intemperance and debauchery.

CAVEAT EMPTOR. In the light of present conditions, the reading public that relies upon critical guidance for its theatregoing should be warned to equip itself with not merely a grain but a sizable bag of salt. I do not refer to the custom of critics in the hot weather period of the year lazily to let down defective summer musical shows. It is, where the critic doesn't openly and engagingly admit his equivocation, an unscrupulous and properly resentable swindle, but since the public is for the most part alive to it, it doesn't any longer much fool anybody. The person who buys a ticket to a summer musical that has been touted by the reviewers knows full well that he is taking a chance, and accordingly has no one but himself to blame.

What I refer to, rather, is the personal sympathy for one or another group or institution which, allowed free rein by the critics, influences them to sidestep the truth as to the demerits of various exhibits and to bamboozle the people who read and follow them. With decidedly minor honorable exception, the theatre reviewers, for one example, permitted their understandable compassion for the so-called Refugee Artists Group to distort the fact about the latter's show, *From Vienna*. To read what they wrote, the theatregoer was persuaded that the show was not only pretty jolly stuff but as such thoroughly worth his cash outlay. It was unhappily, I regret to report, nothing of the kind. It was for the most part a pretty dull and tedious show and, speaking from a strictly theatrical point of view, not worth the money that was charged for it. That was the plain and readily to be determined unvarnished criticism of it.

That the persecuted, homeless and brave little band of writers, actors, singers and dancers who presented the show were deserving of every possible encouragement and assistance is, of course, too obvious to be repeated. Such encouragement and assistance should have been extended to them by critics as well as other folk. But in the case of any critic of any professional integrity whatsoever the encouragement and assistance should have been wholly apart and sharply distinguished from his expressed and published critical opinion. His pity, help and generosity should have been his own private and personal dispensation and should have been firmly kept within that bound. He had no right to cheat his editor, his paper, his public and his own professional probity by letting his heart run away with him, however tender and condign the cause. A bad show, he should have appreciated, is a bad show whether it is put on by liberty-enjoying Americans or exiles from the opprobrious dictatorships.

What is more, such prevarication on the refugees' behalf couldn't be of much real assistance to them. They may have got a little money out of it for a little while, but the public couldn't be victimized for long, and the refugees themselves, with slight exception, soon found to their double distress that the critics had lied to them about admirable competences which they did not possess and about future jobs which did not materialize.

A similar though not so excessive personal sympathy here and there corrupted honest criticism in the case of the Federal Theatre Project's exhibits, especially when rumors first began to be bruited about that the Project was doomed. Many of the critics are so full of commiseration for people out of work and so stout in their relief convictions that they allowed these otherwise unchallengeable and eminently praiseworthy emotions to color their reports not only on certain of the Project's plays and players but on the mass achievement of the Project itself. Poor plays and poor performances were thus prettily glossed over in the name of

faith, hope and charity, and an enterprise that the aforesaid
critics themselves knew perfectly well was far from being
theatrically, dramatically and artistically what it should be
was whooped up by them as something that even a blind
man with an ounce of judgment could quickly have seen
for what it factually was.

CENSORS. The sardonic drollery of censorship has rarely
been better illustrated than in the actions of Mr. John
Spencer, official theatrical blue-penciler to the city of Boston. When Elmer Rice's play, *American Landscape*, was
shown there previous to its New York engagement, it seemed
that Mr. Spencer's moral sense was outraged by the appearance in the script of several ejaculations involving the use of
the name of the Deity in conjunction with swearing. So outraged, indeed, was the gentleman that he demanded they be
deleted instanter; otherwise, he roared, the show would be
forbidden to go on. " I will not have the morals of my city
befouled! " cried he.

Directly preceding the Rice play, there ran for several
immensely prosperous weeks in Boston the Abbott-Rodgers-
Hart musical show, *The Boys from Syracuse*, as bawdy an
exhibit as even morally abandoned New York has seen in
some time. But did Censor Spencer so much as lift a finger
against it? Censor Spencer did not. It all seemed jake to
him; in fact, it may be inferred that he was entertained no
end. Otherwise, why his silence? We thus come to the brace
of points I have in mind.

For some reason I have never been able to deduce, it is
the general conviction of censorship, first, that there is something offensively blasphemous and even grossly immoral in
some such objurgation as " God damn Hitler " or " Christ! Is
Göbbels a louse! " It is apparently censorship's idea that God
and the Saviour are grievously offended by visiting any such
request or addressing any such query to Them and that, to
be wholly proper, to meet with Their wholesale favor and

inordinately to please Them, the phrasing should be " God bless Hitler " or, in the instance of the Saviour, an interrogation as to whether He did not consider Mr. Göbbels one of His own pet creatures. Secondly, it is evidently the theory of censorship that a bawdy line spoken straight is more conducive to immorality than the same line accompanied by such emotional stimulants as low lights, soft music and semi-nude women. It is thus that censorship, as symbolized by the great city of Boston, considers a *God damn* more harmful to the morals and chastity of its citizens than a scene in *The Boys from Syracuse* in which a woman goes to bed with her husband's brother, the articulation of the name of the Saviour more corruptive of the morality of the young than a musical show evening like the above devoted to promiscuous adultery, and a drama like *Strange Interlude* morally objectionable because O'Neill didn't think to add some hot tunes and hot babies to it.

Like Censor Spencer, however, *The Boys from Syracuse* seemed to me to be a pretty good show.

CORNELL.　It is whispered to me by my privately employed Whisperer No. 6 that S. N. Behrman wrote *No Time for Comedy* with the Lunts in mind and that the Lunts, upon reading it, politely rejected it. The Lunts thus join me in a minority report on it. Although most of the newspaper reviewers fondled it in terms which they customarily reserve for the best plays of Somerset Maugham and the worst ones of Maxwell Anderson and although the first-night audience bravoed it with the gusto that it in turn habitually bestows upon any very poor play with one of its favorite actresses in it, it strikes me as being the feeblest comedy job that its gifted author has done in some years. Nor was it materially helped by Katharine Cornell's performance.

Miss Cornell, whatever her virtues in the field of the more serious drama, is no comédienne. (If you argue that her Candida disproves it, I quietly reply, first, that no actress, comédienne or anything else, has so far failed to make a good impression in the rôle and, secondly, that calling *Candida* a comedy in the usual theatrical sense is as far-fetched as calling *The Second Mrs. Tanqueray* a problem play.) Everything about Miss Cornell — her voice, tragic mask, physical comportment, gestures, and general histrionic layout — belies her as a comédienne, and her performance in the brittle Behrman exhibit accordingly and helplessly converted what should have been lightly gliding comedy into something that was destructively dramatic. That Mr. McClintic, her husband, foresaw the inevitable was clearly reflected in his affectionate effort to conceal her comedy shortcomings by craftily, if bogusly, directing the play into a relatively serious mood which was remote from its natural design. I observe that my colleague, Mr. Anderson, wrote flatteringly that Miss Cornell " plays comedy with a sort of wistful and shining gravity which gives Mr. Behrman's play a substance it simply doesn't possess." It seems to me — aside from a mild speculation as to how anyone can give substance to the substanceless simply by treating it gravely — that this was akin to admiring, on the other hand, an actress who might remove substance from a substantial play by playing it with a wistful and shining levity.

CORPSES AND CRITICS. Hearing an owl hoot under my window last night, my thoughts naturally turned to dramatic critics. In their turning they became obsessed by a startling and disconcerting idea. Is it possible that, by and large, the great majority of our theatrical guides and mentors do not much care for a play unless it has a corpse in it?

If the idea strikes anyone as fantastic, a little reflection will offer some convincing proof. Two of the three plays which thus far have won the Critics' Circle's annual prize have pleasured the boys with corpses, Maxwell Anderson's *Winterset* vouchsafing them at least three and John Steinbeck's *Of Mice and Men* forcing them to be content with two. And while the third play, Anderson's *High Tor*, didn't have some of the desiderate stiffs in it, it was only because you can shoot all night and not kill men who are already dead.

Even the lesser contenders for the critics' awards have been funeral parlors. *Idiot's Delight, Daughters of Atreus, Johnny Johnson, On Borrowed Time, The Wingless Victory, Golden Boy, Our Town, Dead End* and *The Little Foxes* have each and all fully met the critical demand that at least one character, or preferably from two to a half dozen or so, be soon or late maneuvered into a state of rigor mortis. With the institution of an honorable citation to the season's best foreign play, *Shadow and Substance,* with its heroine dead at the finish, immediately and duly got the laurel.

Producers and playwrights, sagaciously privy to the critics' prejudice, try to woo them by catering to their whim. The former put on revivals of both the older and newer classics which are particularly luxuriant in mortal remains, and the more luxuriant they are the more the critics admire them. *Hamlet,* their favorite show at all times, at its conclusion resembles a Chinese battlefield. Other such happily accepted revivals of recent seasons as *Richard II, Julius Caesar, Hedda Gabler, The Sea Gull, The Plough and the Stars, Romeo and Juliet, Othello* and the like, while not all quite so fruity with cadavers, have gratified the boys with from one to three or four. And when it came to *Outward Bound,* with almost its entire cast of characters dead before the curtain went up, their delight knew no limit. As for our leading playwrights, O'Neill, the top of them all, is unquestionably the critics' darling because he rarely offers them a play without at least one human carcass in it and sometimes gives their joy no bounds by shuffling off enough mortal coils to flabbergast the late Frank Campbell.

Our other better-known dramatists sapiently follow O'Neill's lead and, like him, get rich from the critics' good notices. Maxwell Anderson, as has been hinted, has recently failed to get the critics' approval only on such occasions as he has carelessly neglected to provide a play with a defunct body, for example, *The Star-Wagon* and *Knickerbocker Holiday*. Robert Sherwood was fully acclaimed by the reviewers only when he stopped writing plays like *The Queen's Husband* and *This Is New York*, which had no one dead in them, and began killing 'em off in *The Petrified Forest* and *Idiot's Delight*. His current *Abe Lincoln in Illinois*, while it contains one death, is doubtless completely acceptable to the critics only because they know that Abe is due to pop off after the final curtain. If Sherwood had shown them Abe actually being shot and gasping his last, they would have been triply tickled.

Clifford Odets got where he is today by giving the reviewers corpses as if they were luscious filets mignons, and with the same critically appetizing result. Elmer Rice began to see the light in *Street Scene* and since then, with but intermittent very negligent and deplorable exception, has provided the desired spectacle of organic remains. Even the humorous George Kaufman has taken a hand in the coffin business and has cashed in with plays like *Stage Door, Merrily We Roll Along* and *Dinner at Eight*. And so with many of the rest. Zoë Akins promptly bought ten gold bathtubs every time she read the good notices that were given a play of hers in which the leading actress turned to lugubrious clay just before the last curtain. Sidney Kingsley purchased himself a country estate when he got wise to the critics' crêpey caprice. And Bayard Veiller, Edward Sheldon, Laurence Stallings and any number of other playwrights of the last twenty years have similarly profited from the dishing out of the craved-for reliquiæ.

Things have got to the point, indeed, where the critics admire, if not always exactly corpses, at least bogus or potential corpses in their comedies and farces. They loved *Room Service* because someone pretended to be dead in it. To them the episode was, by unanimous consent, the tastiest in the whole exhibit. The mere idea that one of the leading characters might be dead from a sock on the head overjoyed them in the case of *Three Men on a Horse.* They cried it up for *Missouri Legend,* in which the Jesse James record was treated waggishly, not only because Jesse became a stiff in the last act but also because the aforesaid stiff was thereupon celebrated with some low, corpsey barroom balladry.

Although when *Tobacco Road,* to turn to the more serious drama, originally opened, some of the critical boys didn't at once entirely cotton to it, after it had been running for a year or two they thought things over, figured out the corpses in it, and promptly began to eat their preliminary criticisms. Now they refer to it very affectionately. *Broadway,* with its mortal artillery, remains their favorite American melodrama. *What Price Glory?,* with its second act curtain descending upon a corpse, is close to their fancy as a great American drama. *Mourning Becomes Electra,* with its death and desolation, is aces in their esteem. *Berkeley Square,* in which almost all the characters are dead before the play begins, like *Outward Bound* got them where they lived. Murder exhibits like *The Trial of Mary Dugan* find them boisterous boosters. And let almost any actor play the rôle of a successful murderer and his notices will sound like those Mussolini gives himself.

Among the more modern French classics, *Cyrano de Bergerac,* which ends with Schnozzle a corpse, is dear to their hearts. Among the more modern German, *The Weavers,* with its curtain similarly descending upon an old fellow's dead body, is equally dear. And among the more modern English, *Saint Joan,* with Joan fried at the stake, is their pet of pets. It is unnecessary for me to mention the Russian drama and its corpses. The critics passionately venerate nine-tenths of it.

When the reviewers, ex and present, themselves try their hands at drama they immediately betray their esteem for stiffs. Alexander Woollcott, turning playwright, thus duly inserted a corpse into his *The Dark Tower*. A. E. Thomas spent a whole play talking about corpses in *Merely Murder*. Carleton Miles, going over to playwriting, contented himself with nothing less than the Lizzie Borden case, making it over into an exhibit called *Nine Pine Street*. His next play, *Portrait of Gilbert*, also dealt with a cadaver. John W. Gassner, tackling the dramatic form, has a play coming along called *Tower beyond Tragedy*, which is ancient Greek in its mortality statistics. Frederic Hatton, quondam drama critic on the Chicago *Evening News*, not only had a corpse but actually a whole cemetery full of them in his *Love, Honor and Betray*. John Anderson's appetite for hearse-food persuaded him to undertake the revision of *The Fatal Alibi*, as Stark Young's doubtless persuaded him in turn to tackle his proficient new version of *The Sea Gull*. Clayton Hamilton and Channing Pollock are among the numerous other former critics who have supplied their brothers still on the aisles with the longed-for mortal remains.

If Abie had killed his Rose, Anne Nichols would unquestionably have got such notices that she'd have made twice as much money as she did.

COWARD. Noël Coward seems to have been undone by the very sophistication for which he was so long and miscellaneously venerated. His recent contributions to the stage consist largely of recollections and chronicles of his world-weariness, fashionable ennui, and general disillusion. His sophistication, in short, has synchronously achieved its apogee, saturation point and bottom-bump, and he apparently has nothing any longer to sell us but his own vast personal boredom. And personal boredom has been a pretty doubtful theatrical commodity since Oscar Wilde's relieving wit was buried in the sod.

CRITICAL CENSORSHIP. The best thing that has lately been accomplished by the New York drama critics is the removal of any further necessity for outside metropolitan censorship of the theatre. Although, of course, it is not beyond the realm of probability that some external and officious sniff-nose, itching for a little factitious importance, may horn in now and again, he will only make a fool of himself if he does, for the critics are doing an all-sufficient job and one that is apparently fully satisfactory to the public. This was made evident once again in the case of *Journeyman*, dramatized from the Erskine Caldwell novel by the Messrs. Hayes and Alexander. Utterly worthless as drama and merchanted solely on its pornography, the exhibit was so unanimously condemned by the reviewers that its box-office began sprouting cobwebs the very next morning. And it was thus invited to limbo along with every other similarly worthless and deliberately dirty play that has recently shown its face on the local stage, to wit, *Tortilla Flat, Wise Tomorrow, Love in My Fashion, The Greatest Show on Earth, If I Were You, I Must Love Someone* and *Clean Beds*.

But if, as is quite possible, you believe that this critical censorship is based upon morals and is therefore at once suspect and artistically deplorable, you are mistaken. Save in the instance of one single reviewer, the Rev. Dr. Mantle, of Joe Patterson's *Daily News*, who is of so high a critical morality content that Joe himself gets religion every time he reads one of his reviews of even a Tony Sarg marionette show, morals have nothing to do with it. And that is the commendable point. The critical attack is directed wholly and entirely against artistic and dramatic trumpery. If it were solely a case of morals, the attack would certainly include such plays as *Amphitryon 38, Of Mice and Men* and *The Shoemakers' Holiday*, all of which drew enthusiastic reviews. It is dirt unredeemed by dramatic integrity that the critics, though their personal souls may be destined for roasting in hell, are determined to exile from the theatre and thus guarantee against outside censorship authentic dramatic integrity which, for all criticism cares, may be as dirty as it pleases.

CRITICAL PRESCRIPTION. The average person regards even his favorite dramatic critic with a measure of the same skepticism and antagonism that he secretly reserves for his doctor. He may be willing to concede that both are satisfactorily grounded in experience, that their judgment is often safely followable, and that their professional understanding is commendable. But just the same he paradoxically rather resents them. Though he pays both of them for their services, it is his as it is every man's nature to gag at being given advice, at being instructed even to his own undeniable benefit, and at being told that he doesn't know how to look out for himself.

The sagacious critic, appreciating this prejudice, accordingly avoids irritating his sensitive patient as the Occidental medico does and pursues instead the practice of the Oriental. He doesn't wait until his patient is ill and irritable; he bends his best efforts to keeping him from being ill. This he accomplishes by indoctrinating him with the highest and most tonic standards of drama, with a gradual improvement of dramatic taste, and with the proper resistance to corrupting theatrical bacilli. And almost before he himself knows it, the patient, who might otherwise be hostile to him, is cordially and acquiescently his. But he must, fully to cajole that patient, have the necessary critical bedside manner. He must deftly conceal too august a wisdom in ingratiating humor; he must lend positiveness some alleviating grace; he must embroider assertion with modesty, or at least an affectation of modesty.

CRITICISM BY COMPARISON. Although my good brothers, the reviewers, may not know it — or if they do, will indignantly deny it — it seems to me that more and more are they falling into the habit of criticism by comparison, that whimsical and often equivocal practice. There have been any number of recent examples, but the most revelatory, I think, is to be had in the instance of the Mercury Theatre's production of *Julius Caesar*. The night preceding its opening, the critics were summoned to pass upon the merits of the Laurence Rivers production of *Antony and Cleopatra*, with Tallulah Bankhead as Cleo. You have been sufficiently informed long ere this of Mlle. Tallulah's Queen of the Nil (no *e*, please, Mr. Printer; don't make something out of nothing), of Prof. Strunk's undergraduate conception of the Shakespearean text, of the elaborate conventionality of the scenic equipment and costuming, and of the disastrous aspect of the whole works. The reviewers came, saw, and duly, properly and appropriately condemned the display in terms extra-theatrically reserved for the description of the more puissant and empyreumatic cheeses and the novels of F. Marion Crawford.

Then, on the heels of this undoubted and incontrovertible mess, came the Mercury Theatre effort noted. It disclosed a mirage of intelligence, a mirage of inventiveness, some fair acting performances, and an investiture that combined a share of superficial impressiveness with a winning financial economy. The shock of contrast bowled the boys over, with a single exception. Dismissing calm, considered and rational criticism, they rebounded from the previous night's débâcle like so many excited rubber balls. Tallulah's show was so rotten that Orson Welles' became a masterwork. And if the criticisms of Tallulah's were demolishing, those of Welles' sounded like Sam Goldwyn describing one of his own movies.

I do not wish too greatly to detract from the Mercury Theatre's achievement; it had, surely, a few commendable points. But its *Julius Caesar* no more deserved the kick-back, hysterical and all-embracing praise visited upon it than Leslie Howard's Hamlet deserved the wholesale denunciation it got simply on the score that John Gielgud's was not quite so deficient. Let us consider the reviewing reaction. The Bankhead *Antony and Cleopatra* was staged in the older tradition; the Welles *Julius Caesar* in the modern-plus. The former's stage was given over to a wealth of shining costumes and lavish settings; the latter's to ordinary modern clothes, bare walls and a simple interplay of lights. The reviewers anathematized the former as being ridiculously outmoded and hailed the latter as the height of originality and imagination. If, to anyone acquainted with the producing art of Russia and pre-Hitler Germany, this was not criticism by contrast and comparison and as criticism therefore suspect, I take the liberty of wondering how the reviewers would have estimated this *Julius Caesar* if it had been preceded the night before not by the elaborately orthodox stage production of Tallulah's defective *Antony and Cleopatra* but by the elaborately orthodox stage production of Maurice Evans' admirable *King Richard II*. If the liberty I take is deemed excessive, may I politely request the reviewers to look into their files and reconcile their high opinions of Evans' physical production with their low opinions of Tallulah's.

The Mercury exhibit, as I have remarked, was rapturously praised for its imagination and originality. The imagination and originality were confined largely to identifying the text with modern times and events and playing it in modern dress. So far as the imagination and originality of identifying a Shakespearean text with modern times and events goes, *Julius Caesar* was presented in that manner in Russia fully a dozen years ago; *Hamlet* was presented in the same manner in Germany four years before the advent of Hitler; and there have been various such re-treatments of other of the Bard's plays in book form. As to the modern dress idea, we have already had it, in New York alone, in the cases of *The Taming of the Shrew* and *Hamlet*. Imagination, accordingly, in the reviewers' minds, is apparently to be defined as anything either hypothetically or factually different, irrespective of sound merit. And originality as anything that one missed seeing because one didn't happen to be abroad that year.

We come critically to the business of playing the historical tragedy of *Julius Caesar* in modern clothes. This strikes me as being akin to playing *The Prisoner of Zenda* in overalls, or *Charley's Aunt* in togas. I may be peculiar, but Brutus dressed like Alfred Knopf, Metellus Cimber in the wardrobe of the dramatic critic for *Variety*, Portia in a Bergdorf-Goodman number, and Trebonius looking for all the world like me in my last year's serge suit seem a lot less to me like Brutus, Metellus Cimber, Portia and Trebonius, however exuberously I exercise my imagination, than so many actors who have boozily wandered into the Shakespearean proceedings from Prezzolotti's spaghetti joint just around the corner. What is more, I am so peculiar that I can't help having something of a time of it trying to reconcile modern dress with characters whose means of conveyance are chariots, who go about with swords, who have to refer to their business lounge suits as cloaks and robes, and who are governed by praetors. And I am not used, whether Shakespeareanly, critically or alcoholically, to a lean and hungry Cassius played by an actor weighing at least one hundred and eighty-five pounds and who looks as if, just before the show began, he had eaten Dinty Moore out of house and home.

The greatest enthusiasm of the critics in the instance of the Mercury exhibit, however, proceeded from their exceptional conviction that the Mercury stage had at last clarified the play, as if Shakespeare's readily intelligible and very simply understood tragedy needed clarification. Far from clarifying the already perfectly clear, the Mercury company actually beclouded and garbled much of the play in its endeavor to give it the flavor of a modern parable. It not only frequently beclouded and garbled it, indeed, but often made it slightly ridiculous, as witness an attribution of the totalitarian philosophy to Shakespeare, the temporary conversion of the hypocritical Antony into a bogus saint and of the intelligent and contemplative Brutus into a debatable foghead, the propaganda against dictatorship with dictatorship at the end magnificently and unassailably triumphant, etc. The next greatest critical enthusiasm was for the additional clarification that modern dress afforded the play. Just how lines read in serge suits become automatically clearer than the same lines read in togas, except perhaps for movie fans, is hard to make out. Since modern clothes never helped the critics appreciably to grasp, let us say, Pirandello, and if it is all merely a matter of costume, why wouldn't it be a good antithetical idea for future producers to help matters by putting Pirandello's characters in ancient Roman dress? In fact, I have a much better idea. To make everything completely clear all around for the boys, why not play all plays stark naked? The third biggest critical enthusiasm was for the staging, only bare walls, platforms of different levels, and lights being used. This, as I have noted, was proclaimed imagination and originality *tout-tout.* As for a similar employment of lights, let the critics be reminded of the productions at least twenty years ago of Linnebach and Pasetti in Munich. As for a similar employment of platforms of different levels, let them be referred to the productions of Jessner and Pirchan in Berlin at about the same time. And as for the bare walls, let them be prompted on the earliest productions of the celebrated Habimah troupe.

CRITICISM OF CRITICISM. Directly before I was cajoled through the combined serpentine wiles of the editor of a certain periodical and several auxiliary gratis flagons of sack to conduct a drama department for the education and enlightenment of his culture-hungry masses, there performed for some months on my future pages an egregious wight named Potter who enthusiastically nominated himself an arch-Archer and proceeded forthwith to attempt to prove to the drama critics that he was the only man in the world who knew what they weren't talking about. Most critics, this bird contended, were blockkopfs of a low and measly cut, far better suited to serve as interior decoration of lunatic asylums than as acceptable commentators on the theatrical arts. Among those thus laid out was your present preceptor who, like all critics something of a pert rooster, contented himself with an airy and very lordly wave of dismissal, accompanied by a sotto voce crack on the high probability that the fellow was merely some disgruntled ex-actor or other such theatrical sorehead, and hence one to be contumeliously sniffed.

Lately, however, I have been munching the matter and, although I still have the honor to consider the M. Potter an ahss and many of his expressed opinions peculiarly imbecile, it strikes me that we ought to have more of this business of criticism of critics, provided only it be pursued by persons of some intelligence and perception. In his thoroughly interesting, recently published attack on the English critics, *The Flying Wasp,* Sean O'Casey, that admirable dramatist, says: " To make things secure for themselves, they have built up a cozy protection by bringing into being a nice little code of laws which say that no one criticized by them should have the indecency or vulgarity to answer them back. A grand little code of honor — for the critics. The critic is to have a mile of space in a year in which to let himself go . . . while those who aren't under the veil of Isis can't have an inch. . . . If this curious and comfortable (for the critics) unwritten law remains unresisted, it will soon come that almost anything that a critic may say must be received with everlasting acceptance and silence."

There is no reason in the world, I wholeheartedly agree with O'Casey, why such a state of affairs, presuming it to exist, should be permitted to exist. If criticism is a healthy thing for the theatre, criticism of criticism should be an even healthier. Let any person who detects any nonsense written by a critic — and a lot is written every season — proclaim it as loudly as he can and throw it back into the critic's face. It would do everyone good, including the critic himself. The only trouble seems to be that the answerers of critics' nonsense in this country are often quite as nonsensical as the critics themselves, which gets us nowhere. And if the business is to be set going, we ought to get somewhere. Otherwise criticism of criticism, perhaps going on to criticism of criticism of criticism, and proceeding then even to criticism of criticism of criticism of criticism, will drive us all crazy, and God knows a lot of us are already crazy enough as it is.

What has brought me to a sympathy with O'Casey's and even Potter's point of view are certain of the critical performances upon an experiment of my own, not long ago offered to the public in book form. This experiment, called *The Avon Flows*, consisted in an effort to show in Shakespeare's own language what would have happened to the Romeo-Juliet marriage had the lovers lived. For the purposes of the demonstration I employed parts of three of the Bard's plays, to wit, *Romeo and Juliet, Othello* and *The Taming of the Shrew*, clearly stating and heavily emphasizing in a conspicuous prefatory note that the Shakespearean line remained throughout absolutely unchanged and intact, that not so much as a single word of my own had been incorporated into the text, and that my sole contribution to the orchestration of the three plays, aside from the job of the orchestration itself, was a few stage directions.

I am not a playwright; I lay no claim to being a playwright; and I haven't the faintest wish or desire to be a playwright. I have enough to do laying claim to being a critic. But as the experiment naturally and inevitably had to take the dramatic form, I suppose it was only to be expected that certain critics, both dramatic and literary, would argue that it was as a playwright I offered myself. And consequently, were I playwright, I can — through the incompetence and befuddlement of some of the reviews — appreciate the impatience with certain critical fish that must be felt by such real playwrights as O'Casey.

Whether the result of the Shakespearean paraphrase which I attempted was good or bad isn't the point. The point is that, good or bad, or even considerably worse than bad, some of the criticisms of it, whether favorable or unfavorable, showed that the critics in question knew utterly nothing of the work of Shakespeare. I offer a sample in evidence. Writing in the New York *American*, my old friend Charles Hanson Towne delivered himself as follows: "His first act consists of several transposed scenes from the play as Shakespeare wrote it, and then your modern Mr. Nathan enters with his own lines, his own remoulding of the chief characters, with the introduction of others we knew not of." The fact, plain enough to anyone who knows even faintly his Shakespeare and his *Romeo and Juliet* in particular, is that, far from Mr. Nathan entering with his own lines, there is not a single line that isn't Shakespeare's very own. Nor is there the introduction of any character who does not figure among the dramatis personæ of the three Shakespearean plays named.

But the real critical humor was yet to come. "Who," asked Charley, "would have suspected Mr. Nathan of being a poet in his own right? He has a few high moments in playing the part, as when he has Juliet say:

> ' Why, this is not a boon;
> 'Tis as I should entreat you wear your gloves,
> Or feed on nourishing dishes, or keep you warm,
> Or sue to you to do a peculiar profit
> To your own person.' "

Doesn't Charley know that it was Shakespeare and not Mr. Nathan, whom he charmingly flattered, who wrote those lines?

"And," flatteringly continued Charley, "he (Mr. Nathan) can end his own scenes on rhymed couplets with no little skill." Every one of the rhymed couplets, I regret to say, is Shakespeare's.

"But," protested Charley after placing this undeserved laurel on my brow, "why does Mr. Nathan permit Romeo to say: 'Yes, you have seen Paris and she together'?" Mr. Nathan didn't permit Romeo to say it, Charley, Shakespeare did, as you will discover by consulting the text.

We come now to the real critical custard-pie. "You may be shocked at a few of the lines," wrote Charley, "and either Shakespeare or Bacon, according to your belief, might turn in his grave could he read such a passage as this:

> ''Tis not a year or two shows us a man:
> They are all but stomachs, and we all but food;
> They eat us hungrily, and when they are full
> They belch us!'"

It is possible that Bacon might turn in his grave could he read the passage, but hardly Shakespeare, for he himself wrote it, as Charley, if he takes the trouble, may find out by referring to Act III, Scene IV, of *Othello*.

Leaving the nutritious critical performance of Mr. Towne, we engage no less a critic than Brooks Atkinson of the New York *Times*, my respected brother in the New York Drama Critics' Circle, observing: "Since she (Juliet) appears to be married all through the second act it is a little astonishing in the first scene of the third act to find that apparently she has to be married all over again." It would truly be a little astonishing, as Brooks says, if she has to be, but there is no slightest suggestion that she has to be. What she has to be, after having left her lord and master, is be *wooed* all over again. Brooks should buy himself a dictionary. Therein he will find that, while *woo* may in certain instances imply a soliciting or seeking in marriage, it just as often means simply "to court", "to ask with importunity", "to seek to influence or persuade", "to invite", "to endeavor to prevail upon to do or to grant something", "to try to obtain or bring about", and "to make love". But as

the good Brooks is personally slightly puritanical, his interpretation of the Shakespearean word may be understandable.

Clifton Fadiman, of *The New Yorker,* whose criticisms
I always read with pleasure, never gave me more robustious
pleasure (in a theatrical if not critical sense) when, in the
midst of a very favorable review of the Shakespearean paraphrase, he pulled this: "He tells us what we have always
wanted to know: to wit, what would have happened *if the
star-crossed lovers had married."*

Dr. William John Tucker, professor of English at the
University of Arizona and guest critic to that luscious journal of the desert, the Tucson, Arizona, *Citizen,* worked himself up into a frightful stew over the audacity of any mere
dramatic critic and one confessedly not a dramatist meddling
with Shakespeare. Hark to his enraged howl: "It isn't true.
It isn't decent. It is literary blasphemy. There may be some
people who will regard it as a demonstration of the author's
wit, but there are also some Philistines who will not hesitate to declare that it proves him to be a barbarian or a
blatherskite. The people, as the people, will, I hope, be
healthy-minded enough to indicate their disgust in the most
effective way. We shall see! At whatever cost of pain to individuals literature must be purified from this taint."

It is evident that the indignant professor's acquaintance with the drama is rather less than negligible. If it
were even infinitesimally more considerable he would have
to list among the tainters, barbarians and blatherskites — all
of them guilty of paraphrasing the classics — various such
low fellows of the past as Plautus and Terence, who similarly paraphrased the Greeks, and Voltaire and Racine, who
were guilty of the same crime, along with such modern
knaves as Gerhart Hauptmann, who has audaciously fashioned a new version of *Hamlet,* and Sir James M. Barrie, who
re-edited *The Taming of the Shrew* by way of proving that
it was Katherine who tamed Petruchio and not Petruchio
who tamed Katherine. Then, too, of course, the good Prof.,

if he were sufficiently educated in the drama, would have to list Shakespeare himself among the aforesaid blatherskites, for if ever a low dog brazenly took hold of ancient dramatic treasures and re-stated them in his own terms it was old Will himself, thank God.

Prof. Tucker, incidentally, had better stay away from the present-day Russian theatre. If he were to see what it has done to *Hamlet*, the poor fellow would swoon.

As a concluding portrait of critical awareness, I give you the performance of Mr. Peter Monro Jack, in the New York *Times*. (Everybody on that paper but the sports writer, it seems, tossed pennies at me, but the sports writer is yet to be heard from.) Thus, seriatim, M. Jack:

1. "Paris, who speaks exactly four lines in the first act and does not seem to know anyone in the cast but Capulet. . . ."

The Shakespearean line clearly and explicitly states that not only Capulet but Lady Capulet and Juliet's nurse (*vide* their eulogies of him) know and are known to Paris. Furthermore, it is obviously Paris who is dancing with Juliet at the opening of the first act's fourth scene.

2. "Without Othello's Moorishness, it is hard to believe Iago-Tybalt's lines that Juliet (Desdemona) will, soon after the marriage, 'begin to heave the gorge, disrelish and abhor this Romeo' etc. Why, no, not at all; this is much too strong language to use against the admirable Romeo of the first act."

It is properly hard for M. Jack or anyone else to believe the lines unless he knows his Shakespeare well enough to recall that Iago was and is here still ever a hypocrite, a self-server and a deliberate liar. Even so, however, it isn't a case of "soon after the marriage," as M. Jack conveniently misquotes, but "some years later" — maybe so many as eight or even ten.

3. "As the scene progresses, a gleam of comprehension pervades his (Romeo's) features — why, with the evidence before us, it is impossible to tell,"

If a man suspects his wife of infidelity and then hears from an unimpeachable source that his suspicion was falsely and basely aroused by a scoundrel, why is it impossible to tell why a gleam of comprehension should pervade his features?

4. " A completely new character, nowhere to be found in the Othello act, though possibly intimated in Shakespeare's *Romeo and Juliet,* appears before us, one who can understand Juliet's nurse and Desdemona's Emilia."

Who this " new " character that our critic had in mind is, I can't, even after having my colored valet (an Oxford graduate and a quondam Shakespearean actor of parts) reread the paraphrase aloud to me fourteen times, quite decipher. But grant that there conceivably might be such a " new " character. What of it? Doesn't Shakespeare himself periodically in his plays introduce " new " characters in just the manner and for just the means our doverwilson laments?

5. " Together with a stage direction that we are still puzzling over, in which Juliet speaks *acidulously.*"

What is puzzling about it? Go over into your paper's dramatic department and borrow that dictionary that Brooks Atkinson has probably by this time bought. In it you will find *acidulously* very simply and quite obviously defined as " slightly sour; figuratively, sour in feeling or expression; sharp; caustic; harsh."

It becomes apparent that what some of our Shakespearean critics need and need badly are copies of Shakespeare and Webster.

CRITICS BETWEEN SEASONS.   If there is anything duller than a dramatic critic who remains on the writing job between seasons, please tell me. A dramatic critic's business is obviously the criticizing of drama and when there is no drama to criticize and he stalls his customers by talking about a lot of other things he is likely to present himself in the light of a public accountant playing ticktacktoe. It isn't so much that what he writes may not be interesting. It is rather that, interesting or not, it isn't what his public expects or wants of him. You don't call in and pay a piano-tuner to discourse on politics, theology, and amiability of the colored upstairs maid.

Yet critics, with no plays at hand to review, persist in doing that very thing, or something like it. English critics in the off-season, for example, are fond of confecting touching little essays on the Sussex downs (preferably when a soft mist settles over them), the morning song of the larks in Surrey, the excellence of the French wines they found on their holiday trips to Paris, and the beauteous barmaid they ran across in Cheltenham. Even Walkley and Shaw in their critical heyday were not above it. When he had no plays to write about, Walkley used to devote himself to pieces on the new armadillo in the Zoo, the new psychometry, the black-birds perched in the Chaumontel pear trees near his country house, Charles I's infirmity, so-called American civilization, the art of letter writing, hotel entertainments, election cir-culars, and lipsticks. (If you doubt it, consult his collection of articles published under the title, *More Prejudice*.) As for Shaw, when the theatre was for the time being denied him, you'd get his ideas on Fabianism, vegetarianism, the dangers of bicycling, and what a devil of a time his sore foot was giving him. There were also little pieces describing the joys of sitting on the grass in the quiet countryside.

Our American critics during the loafing period similarly fill space in divers ways. Just before going off the deep end altogether, you are likely to get end-season papers from them on Chekhov's influence on Aurania Rouverol or some other such topic more or less directly related to the theatre. But then the real subterfuge begins. There will be lyrics to Nature, as contacted somewhere in Connecticut or New York State, arguing that watching a potato grow is ten times more inspiring than watching a dozen performances of *Hamlet*. There will be, from the more migratory and adventurous brethren, communiqués from far points on the piquancy of eating breakfast in a Chungking hotel while a Japanese airplane drops bombs into one's coffee, on the Neon signs in Tokyo that remind the correspondents exactly of Broadway, and on the surprising circumstance that no one in Hollywood seems to talk about anything but moving pictures. There is also sure to be at least one article about a ship's concert and maybe one other on the automobile trip the writer took up Nantucket way.

Critics without plays remain dogs without tails.

DANCING GIRLS. The ridicule of Adolf Hitler because his eye and fancy are fetched by pretty dancing girls is itself retroactively ridiculous. It is doubly ridiculous, indeed, in view of the fact that the dancing girls who have captivated his imagination are Americans. For in such Yankee dancing darlings, past and present, the stages of the world have found a romantic fascination that few of even the greatest dramatic actresses and none of the greatest singers have been able to supply. Unser Adolf's admiration is simply a somewhat belated echo of the tribute paid our hoofing honeys by the kings and princes of Europe. The late King Edward's veneration of Edna May and King Alfonso's taste for the Dolly sisters are as well known as the quondam Prince of Wales' delight in Adele Astaire. Presented to the latter for the first time at a private party, Miss Astaire duly curtseyed and then, in her characteristic free-spoken manner, asked him what she did now. " Now," he replied, placing his arm about her waist, " you dance with me."

The history of the modern American stage is rich in dancing girls who will probably be remembered longer than many of their talented dramatic sisters. Della Fox is still vitally fresh in the memories of those who would be hard put to it to recall the names of more than two or three celebrated American dramatic actresses of her day. Lotta Faust still stands for a whole period in the theatrical life of New York, as does Marilyn Miller. A hundred theatregoers still remember Ann Pennington's knees for every one or two who can remember what rôles Nance O'Neil, say, played during all the years La Belle Pennington was tossing her tootsies.

Irene Castle's name, even after these many years, is as familiar to the present generation as Eleanor Powell's. Dorothy Dickson, deserting the America that had for years applauded her, went to London and became for fifteen years the still-remembered toast of the town.

But maybe I confine my remarks too greatly to American-born pets, though surely when we consider a roster that embraces such a plurality as Bessie McCoy, Helen Hale, Bonnie Maginn, Eva Fallon, Aimée Angeles, Minnie Ashley, Mae Murray, Pauline Chase (the famous Polly), Marie George, Marion Sunshine, Edna Wallace, Anna Laughlin and Violet McMillen, to say nothing of Marie Doro (one of the most thrilling of the lot in her early dancing incarnation), Christie McDonald, Florence Pritchard, Irene Bentley, Sandol Milliken, Ruth Peebles (I fell hard for her in my sophomore year; Hitler would have tried to steal her from me), Julia Sanderson, Phyllis Rankin, May Naudain, Erminie Clark, Mary Eaton and young Grace McDonald — when, recovering my breath, we consider such a list, as I was saying ten minutes back, we may be justified in the confining. Furthermore, Hawaii is American, and there doubtless has never been a more attractive dancing daisy than Pualani Mossman, lately visible on the stage of *Hellzapoppin*. And, furthermore still, let us not overlook the delightful Merissa Flores, half Mexican, half Irish, but born in California and an American, and the equally delightful Cuban-parented Eva Reyes, born in Tampa, both of whom have become favorites here.

Nevertheless, American or non-American, it is always the dancing girl the world over who most satisfactorily massages the fancy of the male of the species. For more years than one can recall, Mistinguett, even now at sixty-odd, has been and remains the darling of masculine Paree. Lilian Harvey for years took hold of the Berlin imagination to a degree than no Elisabeth Bergner or Helene Thimig could hope to equal. Jessie Matthews has had the London boys going for many seasons, and recently a young and lovely dancing lass from Mexico — Carmen Molina her name — has thrown all kinds of warm rainbows across the male audiences of New York. It extends to the screen. What Europe, like America, crowds the movie houses to look at isn't some film artiste who can eat drama alive, but Ginger Rogers.

What is it that thus lifts these terpsichorean maidens into the fanciful clouds? I allow myself the freedom of a few guesses. In the first place, they represent more than anyone else the romance of the theatre, the vague tinsel dream that persists in so many men from the innocent days of boyhood. In the second place, their performances are enveloped with music and lights and colors which in combination become associated with them in the imagination. In the third place, the costume of the dance is usually feminine plus; its twirling skirt and its laces and flounces, its gay ribbons and its soft silks swing themselves rhythmically and irresistibly into the masculine pleasure. And in the fourth and most important place, the average dancing girl is designed with a greater anatomical perfection and is considerably better-looking than four out of five of her dramatic and singing colleagues. Otherwise, she wouldn't be a dancing girl or, if she stubbornly were, she would be a pretty quick failure.

In all this, obviously, I have in mind the dancing girls of musical comedy and revue. The so-called classical dancers are a race apart, half given to the dance and half to something that passes for dramatic interpretation, and which often is neither. Nor do I refer to the ballet dames, for all their occasional other undeniable high virtues. The very idea of a toe dancer (usually with calves as muscular as Joe Louis' biceps) is damaging to the sentimental reaction of most men, of whom I have the honor to be one. No, it isn't these profound females to whom I address today's valentine. The critics may respect them, and correctly, but the man that is the critic wouldn't buy them a supper even if his wife were dying of tuberculosis and if the champagne were free. Proficiency and romance are not always twins; a slender leg is twice as sociologically inspiring as a piano one, however great a virtuoso the latter; a lovely face will launch a thousand more gala ideas than one saggy and wrinkled from the strain of years of pseudo-classical dance practice.

There is an implication of moonlight and palm trees in the natural dancing of a Pualani that two decades of experience in the Russian ballet art couldn't possibly contrive to suggest. There is a bright and appealing physical music in the dancing of such charming youngsters as Grace McDonald and Carmen Molina that occupies a little niche of its own. There is an excitement in the dance of the fair, dark Cuban Estela that you would never find in all the second-act curtain climaxes of all the dramas that Charles Klein and George Broadhurst ever wrote. There was something in the gliding and twirling of Adele Astaire and Marilyn Miller that left a dull, vacant spot on the stage when those girls left it.

This is no way for a serious critic of the theatre and drama to talk? Go chase yourself.

DAVIES. In *Blow Ye Winds*, his most recent dramatic dispensation, Valentine Davies attempted to tell some such story of love and sex as Claude Anet's *Ariane* with the aid of an elaborate stage setting representing a boat. The stage setting of the boat was fine, but things unfortunately stopped there. Why they stopped there does not impose any undue analytical strain upon the critical faculties. In the first place, Mr. Davies, lacking entirely the subtlety and, apparently, much of the woman-experience of even a pleasant second-rater like Anet, succeeded only in contriving the same old boy-meets-girl tale, and with no more variations than a one-finger piano rendition of *My Gal's a Highborn Lady*. Through three long acts and eight long scenes he announced and repeated, like a deaf-mute passionately trying to communicate the A B C's through the sign-language to a blind man, the startling news that when a hitherto aloof woman who prides herself on her great mental gifts finally condescends to surrender her virtue to a man and finds that he is a soothingly apt fellow in the hay, she not only comes to the conclusion that mind maybe isn't everything but also that she likes it. Evidently enraptured by his discovery, Mr. Davies was loath simply to impart it to his audience and let it go at that. So important did it seem to him that he generously confided it to his paying guests at intervals of every five to ten minutes.

In the second place, Mr. Davies elected to make his heroine a Ph.D., and not only a Ph.D. along with the antecedent B.A. and M.A. tacked on, but a practising psychoanalyst to boot. What is more, he made her talk and act like one. Now, unless a playwright has a charming skill and a charming wit, any such female's anatomical affairs are likely to retail all the warm romantic interest and the character herself all the warm romantic appeal of a piece of ice down one's back, and that was precisely the effect registered by Mr. Davies' self-conscious and pseudo-intellectual protagonist. How anyone, including even Mr. Davies' semi-moron hero, might become emotionally excited over such a creature evaded the comprehension.

In the third place, Arthur Hopkins committed the error of staging at least part of this intrinsically fantastic fable in a realistic manner, which only added to its absurdity and impossibility of serious acceptance. What is more, even had a so-called stage realism been proper and suitable, the Hopkins handling of it was still on the humorous side. His set representing the boat was realistic enough, that is, while it was supposed not to be moving. But when, in obedience to the plot and dialogue, it was supposed to be moving and when the characters on it ecstatically described its flight through the waters and when all that the audience saw was the boat remaining solidly stationary in front of a wrinkled blue backcloth, a critic might have been forgiven for rushing right out and sending a prayerful telegram to Langdon McCormick or a cablegram to Gordon Craig, both collect. However, even if the boat had moved, the sailor hero with enough pink makeup on his face to serve an entire *Follies* company wouldn't have much helped the illusion. This sailor hero, in the fourth place, was played by a young actor from the Hollywood art studios who comported himself throughout the evening as if the stage were marked off with camera chalk-lines and as if it were essential that he sedulously confine himself within their bounds, the histrionic impression being of a prisoner pacing a narrow cell. And, in the fifth place, the female Ph.D. and psychoanalyst was a young actress who, doubtless personally and intelligently appreciating that the character which Davies had drawn would not have stimulated the libido of even his miscellaneously inclined sailor, sought to give at least a faint measure of persuasibility to the evening's theme by dressing herself in a series of costume changes infinitely less suggestive of and appropriate to a female Ph.D. and psychoanalyst than to a movie star having the time of her young life at Antibes.

DEATH WATCH. For years you have heard of the so-called Death Watch, that is, the combination of New York dramatic critics and regular first-nighters whose sole purpose is to attend the openings of new plays and mercilessly murder them. You have heard how the first-nighters find their chief pleasure in making audible derisory comments on the plays, how they misbehave so outrageously that the actors on the stage can hardly go on with their lines, and how in the intermissions they congregate in the lobbies and on the sidewalks and arbitrarily roast everything in sight. And you have read how the critics, those malicious and destructive beasts of prey, take the greatest delight in getting into huddles between the acts and agreeing to pan the tar out of any and everything willy-nilly, thus killing off any number of fine plays. Or, if not exactly fine plays, at least plays with enough merit to enjoy a large success if only the critics left them alone.

It is high time that someone dispelled this popularly accepted legend. It is one of the worst frauds ever perpetrated on a gullible public. There is a Death Watch, it is true, but it isn't composed of the critics and the first-nighters. Far from constituting a Death Watch, they constitute in the general run the theatre's staunchest advocates, loyalest friends and biggest and most indiscriminate boosters. If you are reluctant to believe it, read the newspapers and go to the openings and observe the conduct of the first-night audiences. More bad, or at least indifferent plays, are either praised or graciously let down by the majority of the reviewers for the daily press than you can shake a stick at. Take, in the last two seasons alone, such dramatic gimcracks and counterfeits as *The Star-Wagon, French without Tears, Susan and God, Spring Meeting, What a Life, Missouri Legend,* and the like. All of them were given such honeyed notices by many of the critics that the school essays of Pollyanna must have seemed in comparison to have been the work of Strindberg. And so far as the first-nighters are concerned, any play, however odoriferous, that fails to get less than a dozen final curtain calls is a rarity. Unless my powers of observation over a period of three decades have been sadly defective, the first-night audience automatically likes almost everything, and the worse it is the better it seems to like it.

The critics and first-nighters no more constitute a Death Watch than cyanide of potassium constitutes a crêpe Suzette. The Death Watch, strange as it may seem, is made up rather of certain theatrical managers and producers and of most of the actors and actresses who, when out of work, insinuate themselves into the audiences at the opening performances. Although the fact is not known to the public in general, it is and has long been appreciated by the critics and regular first-nighters, who have whimsically shouldered a blame that rightly and properly rests upon these others.

Chief among the real Death Watch is the theatrical producer, Mr. Brock Pemberton. He goes to all the premières, his face the picture of gloom and morbidity, and to so much as look at him sitting in his seat or standing glumly in the lobby is enough to dispirit even the most enthusiastic critic. If ever he likes a play or performance, no one knows it, and if he doesn't like it, which, to put it mildly, is pretty often, a number of the critics will tell you that he is not loath to vouchsafe his opinion between the acts or directly after the show — sometimes, indeed, after seven or eight shows. "Hm," he sourly observed to Critic John Mason Brown on one occasion, "you certainly fell for that Maxwell Anderson guff!" The guff was *High Tor,* which subsequently was awarded the year's prize by the drama critics' own circle.

Mr. William A. Brady is another manager and producer who figures conspicuously in the real Death Watch. And still another is Mr. Arthur Hopkins. Both haven't missed a day in years loudly proclaiming the death of the legitimate theatre. Mr. Brady has given out hundreds of interviews in that time asserting that the theatre hasn't a leg to stand on any longer, and Mr. Hopkins has written an endless series of magazine and Sunday newspaper articles arguing that the theatre has been permanently killed seriatim by everything from the movies to the automobile, from the critics to the radio, and from the first-night audiences to the traffic regulations. And when Mr. Brady and Mr. Hopkins attend the openings, their faces mirror the excessive depression and melancholia of Mr. Pemberton's.

Mr. John Golden, yet another producer, contradicts the belief that the maligned critics and first-nighters are the leading enemies of the theatre and puts the onus on the people directly within the theatre itself. It is the unionization of the industry, he charges, that has done the dirty work. "The actors have their unions, the authors, the managers, the scene designers, the electricians, the stage-hands — yes, even the ushers and the scrub-women! The worst enemy of the theatre today is the people of the theatre," he states. So far, so good. But then Mr. Golden immediately elects himself an honorary member of the Death Watch with the following: "Perhaps the producers are most to blame. The majority of them are amateurs or near-society dilettantes, night-club habitués, angel-backers and shoestring gamblers, with their slipshod, unmoral and — even worse — unprepared productions messing up Broadway."

That Mr. Golden is eminently correct in his animadversions on certain producers, I have already suggested. But that he doesn't present himself in the light of a veritable Death Watch cheer-leader when he issues his blanket destructive criticism of those others whom he refers to above is difficult for anyone closely acquainted with the theatre to believe. Such amateur producers as the Group Theatre, the Mercury, and even the late Theatre Union have in general put on critically sounder plays and done more to inject new life into the drama than Mr. Golden himself. Such producers with a liking for society and the fashionable life as Mr. Gilbert Miller and Mr. Alfred De Liagre, Jr., the former in particular, have certainly not been guilty of "slipshod, unmoral and unprepared productions" and have periodically added considerably to the theatre's more sophisticated pleasures. Mr. George Abbott, Mr. Vinton Freedley and Mr. Sam Harris are just three of a number of producers who like to go to night-clubs, and surely all are producers highly esteemed by critics and audiences. Mr. Eddie Dowling, Mr. Max Gordon and Mr. Guthrie McClintic have angels to back them, and does Mr. Golden really believe that for that reason they are inferior to Mr. Golden, who says that he puts up his own money? Furthermore, the plays put on by shoestring gamblers are not always any more contemptible than some of those put on by the legitimate producing gamblers. I recall, over a period of years, that some of them, indeed, were pretty good.

Assisting the producers in the real Death Watch are

actors and actresses. If ever there have existed destructive
critics, eavesdrop on the comments of the actors and actresses
in an audience when a play is over! Play, players, settings,
lighting and costumes generally get scant mercy from them.
The leading lady's looks (particularly if she happens to be
over thirty-five), the dresses on the women in the company,
the quality of the play compared with that of the one they
themselves last had a run in — everything receives their
strictures. Only at an actors' benefit performance do actors,
when part of an audience, ever find anything to praise.

Mr. Henry Hull, as a member of the Actors' Division of
the Death Watch, takes the following comprehensive fall
out of the members of his profession: " The first-nights savor
somewhat of a combination of Roman arena, a fashion parade, a bull fight and a psychopaths' convention and are just
plain hell for the actors, who are all so damned unbalanced
that they alternately underplay and overstress." Thus, according to Death Watch Hull, there is never an actor who
gives a good performance on an opening night. And thus,
according to Mr. Hull, the critics and first-night audiences
who believe and state that a lot of them often do are plain
fools.

DETEMPERAMENTALIZATION. If things keep going as they
are, the temperamental ham, that bane of the stage, the producer and the audience, will soon be as much a relic of the
past as lidded spittoons, William Jennings Bryan campaign
buttons, and the novels of Beatrice Harraden.

Various things have conspired toward the happy and desired end. Chief among them have been the reinforced look
of hard disapproval which the Actors' Equity Association
itself has bestowed upon any member who permits himself to get out of normal and reasonable hand, the thank-
God attitude of any actor who is lucky enough to get a paying job these days, and the indisposition of audiences any
longer to stand any of the old monkey-business for a mo-

ment. The combined result has been the exile of temperamental jambons to the movies and such a peace backstage in the legitimate theatre as hasn't been approached in the world since Napoleon went into retirement at St. Helena.

Perhaps I exaggerate a bit. Now and again, though at pleasingly protracted intervals, we still hear of some histrio who cuts up a little. But it isn't long before he is quickly put in his place by a prophylactic wallop from a stagehand, a complaint registered with Equity by the producer, a smear of custard from the critics, and some spiritual advice from his pastor. If none of these sedatives, perchance, works, the pork-chop has only two alternatives open to him: either to go to Hollywood, where they will stand for almost anything but good, honest acting or to go back to his old job as a shoe-clerk, insurance salesman, or hinterland stock company mime.

All this, true, is excellent and as it should be, and the theatre has profited enormously from the change. But sometimes I look back just a little wistfully and regretfully at the passing of the old order of things. It certainly, however discommodious it was, provided a lot of extra-dramatic and ribald amusement.

No better show, for example, was ever put on than that proceeding from the temperamental didoes of the late Richard Mansfield. A hambo if ever there was one, Richard had, and exercised, an artistic sensitiveness of such overwhelming proportions that if a stagehand so much as placed a chair a quarter of an inch out of position he, Richard, would fly into a tantrum that couldn't be stilled until the whole company got together and not only volunteered to lynch the offender but assured Richard, who would then emerge pacific and smiling benignly, that never had there been such a wonderful genius as he and that if anything happened to him, God forbid, they would all commit suicide within three minutes after the unbearable catastrophe.

Asserting that he was unable to endure the vast and

hounding admiration of his public, Richard declined to stay at hotels and lived while on the road in a gaudy private railroad car, stacked with autographed photographs of himself which he would dispense, with magnificent, kingly gestures, to those backwoods dramatic critics who properly esteemed him. His valet was instructed always to refer to him, in the presence of visitors, as " the great Mr. Mansfield "; and it was the duty of his personal press-agents not only to indicate their respect for their Master by putting on full dress suits the moment the sun went down but, in addition, to stand in the rural theatre lobbies during his performances and regally give the nose to any customer who, coming out in an intermission, didn't display the proper audible enthusiasm.

The late Nat Goodwin ran a close second to Richard. It was Nat's custom to threaten any theatrical manager he didn't especially like that he would stop acting that very minute, thus ruining and putting out of business for all time not only the manager in question but the whole American theatre. If a critic gave him a bad notice, he would publicly proclaim that henceforth a likeness of the knave would be pasted on his favorite cuspidor. And if an actor in his company didn't please him, Nat would lie in waiting at the stagedoor after the matinée performance and loudly and witheringly condemn the poor fellow to the gathered art-lovers, mostly newsboys, corner bums and elderly maiden ladies, as a curse to a noble profession. Acknowledging the ensuing applause, he would then bow low and throw out kisses.

Richard Bennett was restrained from making curtain speeches denouncing audiences who didn't sufficiently indicate their appreciation of him only when his managers carefully included an injunction in his contracts. But the late Lowell Sherman allowed his speech-making temperament full play by rushing the barrier before managers thought up any such precaution. Lowell was a honey. If a customer so much as rattled a program, if an usher so much as coughed, or if a playgoer showed the first faint sign of dozing, he would wave an imperious hand to his fellow players, step to the footlights, and let go with a volley of sarcastic remarks. On one occasion — it was at the Hudson Theatre in New York — a customer took it upon himself to interrupt Lowell with a peremptory request to go to hell, which so upset Lowell that, in backing away from the footlights, he fell flat on his fanny, which in turn so abashed our hero that he suffered what was announced as " a nervous collapse " and couldn't resume his art for two whole days.

Julia Marlowe was so delicately full of artistic temperament that she was once forced to post a notice on the call-board requesting the members of her company kindly to refrain from speaking to her — even to the extent of a good-evening — lest the impact of their harsh voices on her ear disturb her histrionic equanimity. Lou Tellegen was also a hot dog when it came to the business. Lou, who fancied himself as a lady-killer compared with whom Casanova was Alf Landon, would foam at the mouth if the fates periodically so willed it that more men than women were in the down-front rows. On such occasions, Lou would become frenzied to the point of disgustedly turning his back on the audience, mumbling his lines, discharging nasty sotto voce cracks at all and sundry, and — when he turned around — even contemptuously disarranging the modish contour of his cravat.

It was rumored, though denied by her press-agents, that before her present tonic metamorphosis Katharine Hepburn — whose delight it used to be to smash the cameras of press photographers who tried to snap her precious picture — erected a screen backstage during the short run of *The Lake* to guard her path from dressing-room to stage, lest the other members of the company, including such novices as Blanche Bates and Frances Starr, annoy her with any gratuitous conversation. Mrs. Leslie Carter's rich artistic temperament took the form of shuddering at the thought of eating anything that wasn't served on rare chinaware and of breaking the

aforesaid chinaware to bits if anything displeased her. Mrs.
Pat Campbell, while in her histrionic flush, was pretty near
tops among the feminine contingent. Her own especial artistic temperament ran the gamut from telling George Bernard
Shaw how to write his plays to demands of theatre managers
that they treat her pet dog with a consideration, courtesy
and esteem equal to that which they showed Henry Irving.
And our own Arnold Daly, peace to his ashes, was in the
habit of expressing his artistic soul not only by loudly denouncing as a foul discredit to her profession any fair actress
in his company who declined to admit a reciprocal yen for
him but also by either biting her in the arm or poking her in
the slats just as she was on the point of making a stage entrance.

The buffos of today are altogether too well-behaved. In
a way, it's rather sad.

DEVAL.   If the critics were hospitable enough to pass on
plays for producers before their production, Jacques Deval's
Lorelei would never have been exhibited, and a lot of good
money might have been saved. The critics, as they subsequently and duly wrote, would quickly have discerned that
the script was vague and muddled to the point of silly confusion. They would also have been able to tell the producers
that you can't any longer persuade even the boobs that a play
is highly intellectual simply by labeling your hero a university dean, a world-famous biologist, and a Nobel Prize winner and having him indicate his cerebral puissance by breaking off suddenly in the middle of almost everything he says,
pausing studiously as if enceinte with a peculiarly profound
idea, and then proceeding with his initial vacuity. They
would further have pointed out that to relate the spiritual
torture and salvation of an honorable German of today in
terms of the old Lygia-Marcus Superbus hokum of *The Sign
of the Cross,* that to translate the conflicting Nazi and anti-
Nazi ideologies in terms of the old boy and cutie hokum of

Accent on Youth, and that to wind up the show with such facile hokum as confronting Hitlerism with the names and philosophies of Schiller, Goethe, Kant and Beethoven was to court vacant seats by the carload.

DONT'S FOR PRODUCERS. Followers of the profession of dramatic criticism frequently suffer the routine rebuke of theatrical producers that it is much easier to criticize than to contrive and that, if places were changed, they would in all probability make just as many mistakes as the producers themselves. It is, of course, possible, but I rather doubt if any critic of experience would do any such thing.

To a brash statement like this, the producers will unquestionably reply, not without an accompanying superior snicker, that it is mere supposition, and as such properly to be waved aside. But is it? As one practising critic of the theatre, here is what I would and would not do, by way of avoiding some of the errors the producers so often make, if I happened to find myself in their job.

In the first place, I would never produce a play with a punning title. If it had such a title, I'd change it, inasmuch as it disposes nine-tenths of the reviewers against the play long before the curtain goes up and inasmuch as their reviews subsequently betray their understandable impatience and prejudice. No play with such a title produced in the last ten years has received other than bad notices and all have failed. The list includes exhibits with captions like *The Cinderelative, Love, Honor and Betray, Little Orchid Annie, City Haul, Miss Gulliver Travels, Wife Insurance, The Sophisticrats, Double Dummy,* and *Where There's a Will.* Furthermore, aside from their titles, all were very poor plays, as one should know that any author who would name a play of his in this wise couldn't be much good to start with.

While on the subject of titles, if I were a producer I'd never invest a nickel in anything bearing some such pseudo-sophisticated title as *A Good Woman — Poor Thing, A Wom-*

an's a Fool — To Be Clever, or *Too True To Be Good*, even if the last named was by George Bernard Shaw. Nine times out of ten the plays are doomed to be failures. The reviewers always go to them with their fingers crossed.

Titles are often dangerous things. When Gilbert Miller announced that he was going to present a translation of Bourdet's *Le Sexe Faible* as *The Sex Fable*, the critics waxed privately derisive the moment they heard it. And other producers have my word for it that they did the same thing when they learned that plays were to be produced under such strainedly facetious titles as *The Sap Runs High, Bulls, Bears and Asses, The Unsophisticates, Let and Sub-Let*, and *Symphony in Two Flats*, or under such cheaply suggestive titles as *She Lived Next Door to the Firehouse, Foreign Affairs, She Means Business, Intimate Relations*, and *The Body Beautiful*.

I would produce no more plays dealing with Lesbianism. *The Captive*, a first-rate play, was the beginning and end of them. Two such plays flopped recently and several others that will doubtless be produced in the future will also flop. The reviewers are sick of them, and so, apparently, is the public.

Even if they were good, I would put on no more plays about Marie Antoinette. Marie has been done to death and almost everybody is theatrically pretty tired of her.

Any translation from the French involving a serious approach to the amours of middle-aged women I should hastily sidestep. I'd also give the prompt go-by to any serious French drama having to do with passionate triangles or ageing actresses who are jealous of their young daughters.

If I wished to make money, I should read at least twice any English play that had been a great success in London. Once in a while some such play succeeds over here, but more often it doesn't.

If I were a producer, I'd never denounce the reviewers or bar any of them from my theatre. They may occasionally deserve denouncing but I'd shut up nonetheless, however sore I was. In the long run, a producer who goes in for critic-baiting gets the worst of it. The reviewers will continue to give him a perfectly fair deal but, being human, they won't overlook oblique opportunities, when and if such opportunities arise, to mock him. Their reviews of his productions will not betray their personal attitude toward him, but when they are not reviewing and are writing of theatrical matters in general you will often find that they will lug in the producer and make him look just a little ridiculous, even though he doesn't always merit it.

If my opening night was a fashionable one, I'd never irritate the reviewers, who are always in their seats on time, by delaying the curtain until the fashionable belatedly moseyed in. A producer who does so is viewed as a snob and is regarded with humorous contempt.

I should put on no more British murder plays dealing with abnormal culprits, and no more American plays with radical parlor heroes or heroines.

If I were a producer, I should refrain from giving to the press announcements of my European voyages of discovery. Speaking of English producers, though the same thing holds true of several of our own, James Agate not long ago observed that every theatre manager brags eternally of such voyages of discovery, "which, being interpreted, means Buda-Pesth, which, being further interpreted, means that he is prepared to charter a private airplane, but has no notion of taking the public bus. Which, lastly and in the plainest English, means that he never dreams of going near Kew or Swiss Cottage (suburban London experimental play-houses) even when these theatres have a success."

"The truth," Agate continues, "is just that your theatre manager does not look for new plays. He is a luxurious person who does nothing but lunch. After his valet has dressed him, his chauffeur decants him at some restaurant à la mode, where he proceeds to lunch until some time after midnight, when his chauffeur calls for him and his valet pours him into bed, his arduous search for new plays being confined to the hope that while lunching somebody will tell him of a new version of *French Bats in Margaret's Belfry*."

If I were presenting a star actress, I should exercise pains to restrain her from making herself silly in the eyes of the critics with such newspaper interviews as Miss Grace George, for example, gave out last season. " I can't understand how a play like *Of Mice and Men* could get the Drama Critics' prize," said Miss George. " It was all right as a book but on the stage it is something else again. It is about degenerates and perverts. It's an unpleasant play about unpleasant people and yet it receives the prize! " I would take my star actress aside and confide to her that *Oedipus Rex*, Gorki's *Night Refuge*, and other of the world's admittedly great plays are also about degenerates and perverts and are also " unpleasant plays " about " unpleasant people ". Then I'd lay her across my knee and give her a good spanking.

In conclusion, if I were a producer and produced something like *Come Across, Waltz in Goosestep, Ringside Seat, Bright Rebel, Dear Octopus, Miss Swan Expects, The Happiest Days, The Brown Danube, Jeremiah* or *Please, Mrs. Garibaldi* I'd not put on a white tie and tails for the opening and stand proudly at the back of the auditorium as if it were something by O'Casey, O'Neill or some other first-rater.

E

ECSTASY. In this little E showcase, ladies and gentlemen, we observe the emotion of ecstasy as it is frequently interpreted in incidental dramatic dance numbers directed by such Professorinen as Madame Felicia Sorel. I fear that I cannot share your obvious pleasure and delight, as my idea of the expression of ecstasy presently calls for something a little more terpsichoreanly novel than a group of men and women suddenly sticking out their right legs, abruptly contracting their abdominal muscles and simultaneously throwing forward their necks and giving conspicuous play to their Adam's apples.

ENGLISH CRITICAL REBUS. There is one thing about my friends, the English dramatic critics, that I can't quite comprehend. That is their habit of coming over here and saying that the American theatre isn't much good when compared with their own theatre and then going back home and writing for the whole next year that their own theatre isn't any good at all.

Take, for instance, Ivor Brown, of the London *Observer*. Ivor, who is an all right fellow in every other respect and who justifiably jumps to the ceiling when some confounded American waiter puts ice in his whiskey and soda, visited us not long ago, attended the theatre studiously, and then announced it as his firm conviction that hardly anything he saw of ours, whether plays or actors, was worth a hoot. What is more, he further announced that all this talk about the freshness and vitality of our theatre was absurd and that the English theatre, when it came to that sort of thing, out-

distanced ours by several hundred miles. Of course, being
the politest people in the world, save perhaps only the Mo-
zambique Negroes, we didn't say anything, but just went on
quietly drinking our own whiskey-sodas (with ice), gulping
wistfully once in a while, and wondering.

Our wonder increased when Ivor got back to London.
There, he published several lengthy treatises heatedly arguing the truth of what he had told us when he was here, to
wit, that the American theatre and its plays were, for all the
increasing respect on the part of us Yankees, infinitely sour
and let no one who loved and admired the English theatre
be in the least deceived about it. Well, each critic to his own
judgment and who, except maybe all of us American critics,
shall call him wrong. But that isn't the point. The point is
this. Having duly delivered himself of his opinion, our friend
proceeded about his duties as a reviewer of the London
stage. In his very first criticism, published directly after the
articles peremptorily dismissing the American stage, he
wrote in his review of an English crook gimcrack as follows:
" If you must spend your evenings in Crookery Nook, well,
here is your occasion, and bang opposite that Yard (Scotland) *without which* (my italics) *English drama could nowadays hardly exist.*" A few days later and quick on the heels
of his critical disgust over the English theatre's absorption
in cheap mystery stuff, he began his review of a play by
James Bridie thus: " Of eighty per cent of London plays,
Much Ado about Nothing would be an accurate title." And
then, only a few days later, he gave one of the most enthusiastic notices he had written in many months to a presentation at the Apollo Theatre. The presentation was the American Robert Sherwood's American *Idiot's Delight.*

I herewith offer a grand prize of one dollar in cash to
anyone who can determine the logic in all that.

James Agate, critic for the London *Sunday Times,* is another of the English gentlemen who troubles my metaphysic.
Doubtless the best dramatic critic presently in nightly prac-

tice over there and certainly an otherwise highly intelligent, perceptive and amusing cock, James arrived here a short time before Ivor and also took a look at our theatre. Like Ivor, he couldn't see much of anything in it. It was, sad to relate, pretty blarsted, bloody bad. Its much-talked-of enterprise, courage, honesty and progress he couldn't at all agree to. Flat, he calls it, flat, and stale, and dull. " The most interesting thing about the theatre I've seen since I've been in New York," he confided to us, " is Mrs. Pat Campbell! " Being, as I have remarked, the politest people in the world, save perhaps only the Eskimos, we of course again said nothing, and again occupied ourselves with our refreshments, and again quietly wondered. Then, after sending back to England a series of articles telling his fellow-countrymen not to worry and that the English theatre was as right as the American was wrong, our friend James sailed for home.

Directly upon his arrival, he resumed his reviewing of the English theatre. In his review of a play called *The Last Straw,* by Edward Percy and Reginald Denham, he had this to say: " A modern English audience regards tragedy only as something happening a long time ago and in a foreign country." In his review of a play called *Satyr* he had this to say: " The play failed on the principle that the English are far too flippant-minded to tolerate a serious play." In his review of English acting in another play he had this to say: " Perhaps it is unfair that I came to this play hot-foot from seeing a film by and with Sacha Guitry. It doesn't matter what M. Guitry does or doesn't do; the play of his wristbands is more expressive than the by-play of your typical English light comedian who has no use for light or shade or fun or mimicry or the calling-up of a thousand absurd images, all of which is the essence of comic acting. Your British walking gentleman is a charming fellow who thinks his job is done when, attired in tennis trousers, he sinks back in a deck-chair and gracefully exhibits a pair of immaculate tennis shoes. Mr. Cyril Ritchard is of the British school; he composes a likable mask and sticks to the same kind of likability with the determination of a square of British infantrymen charged by French cavalry in a picture by Lady Butler."

In a review of another performance, our friend James had this to say: " Miss Ena Burrill is that odd thing on the English stage: a young actress who can act." In a review of a play called *The Painted Smile,* by William P. Templeton, he had this to say: " This piece is not worth the space I intend to devote to it. . . . The explanation is that this is the first play of a commencing (English) playwright. And of all (English) commencing playwrights two things may be firmly said: ninety per cent of them should never raise the curtain at all, and a hundred per cent drop it too late." He then proceeds: " (However) this play's lack of competence is far more interesting than much of that competence which has recently flooded the London stage. Its diffidence is more reassuring than the others' assurance. Consider the ways in which it avoids being (in comparison) bad. It is not inane. It is not entirely about the impuberal. It is not about ' necking '. There is no toying with telephones, siphons, cigarette and vanity cases. It contains neither deck-chairs nor tennis shoes. The play, in short, is not that play which during the last five years has so often nauseated us. I think it must have been Wilde who originally started this modern (British) green-sickness with that piece which he labeled ' a trivial comedy for serious people '. His aptest pupil, Mr. Coward, misread his master when in *The Vortex* he took to writing serious comedies about trivial people. But there is misreading and misreading, and those who have misread Mr. Coward do so by writing too trivial comedies about too trivial people." Reviewing a play which he admired, James wound up thuswise: " I advise every reader to see it, provided that it is still running when this account of it appears. (But) it is such big stuff that I cannot understand, playgoing taste being what it is, how the bats in this metaphysical belfry have survived to flit across the London sky for a second, third and even fourth evening." And in a review of *Banana Ridge,* by the popular Ben Travers, and of *Lady with Designs,* by Frank Gregory and Edgar Middleton, he had this disdainful say: "The commercial theatre this week offers two plays, one of which is so good in its own way and the other so poor in any way that there is nothing whatever to be remarked about either."

Figure out the anti-American-theatre logic in all that and you get a grand prize of *two* dollars! In fact, I raise it to three if you can get anywhere after James' further confessions that "T. S. Eliot's *Murder in the Cathedral* was successful in England only because it was, as one of our wittiest younger critics, Alan Dent, said, ' obstreperously dull ' "; that "Recent experience of English audiences shows that they take readily to two things only — unadulterated farce and sheer hugaboo, and by hugaboo I mean the T. S. Eliotish rhapsody. . . . In other words, what Mr. Polly called alternatively ' Eloquent Rapsodooce ' and ' Sesquippledan Verboojuice '. They like nonsense and they like uplift, and they hate anything in between, for a reason which, so far as I know, obtains in this nation alone — the reluctance to use brains in the theatre. Abroad things are different. . . . In the end, this laziness of ours must ruin our theatre, because any theatre which is to continue as a living force must mirror the world of which it is a part "; and that such trashy melodramas as Walter Hackett writes "will doubtless always be considered masterpieces in a country which talks of giving its potatoes assistance."

(*Key:* James antecedently derogates critic St. John Ervine for holding that *Punch* is extremely funny and quotes from it this joke:

Clergyman's Wife: Will you help the potatoes, dear?

Clergyman: Certainly, darling, of what assistance are they in need?)

Speaking of my good comrade, the talented St. John Ervine, there's another valued friend who doesn't think much of our theatre, although to give him his due he is more graciously generous toward it than either James or Ivor. Nevertheless, he seems decided in his conviction that it cannot be compared with the English theatre. Yet we find him writing in his London weekly journal that " These are melancholy times for the lover of the English drama, for it seems to become harder and harder for a dramatist to obtain performance for a play of more substantial quality than a macaroon." Nor must we overlook Charles Morgan, critic for the London *Times*. Charles is also no passionate lover of our theatre, preferring, it seems, the higher estate of that of his own land. And what is this theatre of his own land like? What and who is its most successful dramatist? Reach for the smelling-salts ere I quote Charles: " Miss Dodie Smith, formerly known in the theatre as C. L. Anthony and author of *Autumn Crocus, Service, Touch Wood, Dear Octopus,* and *Call It a Day,* is the most consistently successful playwright in England, and one to whom no one grudges her success ". Then — " Has she anything to say or must her plays always be, in effect, popular magazine stories adroitly told? "

While certainly not posing the proposition that the present-day American theatre, for all its vast improvement, is God's sole, true gift to the world of the stage — an opinion which my reading trade assuredly knows I hardly hold — I still believe there is something transparently phony in the attitude displayed toward it by the English critics. I can understand a possible chauvinism on their part that might arbitrarily impel them to denigrate it in favor of their own theatre, but I can't understand how immediately on the tail of that denigration they allow that their own theatre is contemptible. It doesn't make sense.

What is their present English theatre like? Charles Cochran, one of its foremost and most intelligent producers, returning to London after an admiring round of the American theatre, made this statement to an interviewer for the *Observer:* " You know, when I came back from America I went to a lot of theatres here — and how depressing it all was!" Every one of the English critics who has sneered at the American theatre and its drama recently went into ecstasies over O'Neill's *Mourning Becomes Electra* upon its production in London, stating that the play — which was produced here half a dozen years ago — was the finest new thing in the way of drama that the English theatre had seen in a very long time and a lesson to British dramatic pretensions. After writing when he was in America that he couldn't see anything in the American critical idea that Maxwell Anderson amounted to anything much, my good comrade Agate a little while after he got home saw a suburban London presentation of one of Anderson's inferior plays, *The Masque of Kings,* and wrote: "It is magnificently written, every line demanding and repaying attention. In other words, the evening is a grown-up one. Nevertheless I am persuaded that the piece will come to Shaftesbury Avenue, always provided that room can be found for it among the horde of titter-traps about twittermice." My good comrade Ivor Brown, on the other hand, arrives in America and disparages its drama almost in toto and then goes back and writes of the "richness and vitality" of that stick of English bubblegum, *George and Margaret.*

This *George and Margaret,* which the rapidly progressing American theatre ridiculed into quick failure and which is third-rate comedy frippery, lasted far into the second year of a palmy run in London. That other gob of bubblegum, *French without Tears,* which got only a short distance here, enjoyed the longest run of any play presented in London in its particular period; it totaled more than six hundred and eighty-five performances. *Housemaster,* a tepid boys' school frolic which was done here as *Bachelor Born* and was only fairly successful, ran for six hundred and ninety performances. *Black Limelight,* a dose of mystery rubbish which the American theatre would have none of, recently closed a run of more than a year in London. *Dear Octopus,* sentimental drivel that lasted for only a few weeks here, is at the writing moment in its London eleventh month. *Spring Meeting,* a commonplace little comedy that met locally turned down thumbs, went into its London second year. And so it goes. Meanwhile, the condescended-to New York theatre's successes in the same period have been such plays as *Tobacco Road, Of Mice and Men, Shadow and Substance, I'd Rather Be Right, The White Steed, The Little Foxes,* . . . *one-third of a nation,* and *Abe Lincoln in Illinois.* Even allowing for the success, also, of such things as *Susan and God* and *The Philadelphia Story,* the difference in standards must be clearly discernible to any honest English eye.

The dawning truth is that, although my British colleagues do not seem to realize it, they are obliquely going Yankee Doodle with a vengeance. For longer than we can remember, it was their aforenoted practice and pleasure to sneer at everything theatrically American and coincidentally, save in the instance of Bernard Shaw, to allow that everything about the English theatre was pretty close to tops. About a year ago, however, something began to happen. What that something was, I won't take it upon myself to know. It may have been a sudden burst of enlightenment, or a belated gagging at parochialism, or a left-handed propaganda calculated to draw us closer to England in its hours of deep national concern, or something else. But whatever it was, it witnessed such a turn-about as hasn't been matched since Italy last shifted to the Allies. Things have come to the point, indeed, where about the only thing American that doesn't now tickle most of the English critics half to death is this kind of comment on them.

Since first he began to write, Eugene O'Neill was regularly and airily waved aside by the London boys. Now, as I have pointed out, he is suddenly greeted as a world-genius and his *Mourning Becomes Electra* as a masterpiece of dramatic art. S. N. Behrman, who was sarcastically sent to the dump by them with his *Biography* and other plays, is now suddenly hailed as a matchless wit merely on the score of his adaptation of *Amphitryon 38*. Robert Sherwood, after years of superior sniffing, is now passionately enfolded in their embrace along with his *Idiot's Delight*. Clifford Odets, who was dubbed "a shilling Chekhov", is now huzzahed as a born great dramatist and his *Paradise Lost*, a poor play, is allowed to be "Better value for money, dramatically, emotionally, and in the scale of pure entertainment, than all of London's current successes put together". And John Steinbeck's *Of Mice and Men* is shortly thereafter heralded as being not only the finest play on the London stage and superior to all the English plays but better even than *Paradise Lost*.

The overnight admiration apparently knows no bounds. Wyndham Lewis, writing in the *Bystander*, goes on thus: "Personally we should say the good American play is nearly always one hundred percent better than ours. . . . The cretin generally finds less to please him on the New York stage than in London, where a Harley Street alienist once told us at least ninety percent of the regular playgoing public is in a state of arrested mental development and aged about fourteen." Alan Dent, writing in the Manchester *Guardian* and reviewing an American exhibit, allows that "wit, that rarest of birds in the London theatre, flies continuously to and fro over this production. . . . The shades of Apollodorus, Herodotus, Plautus, Molière and Dryden cannot but be gratified. That of Meredith will be enchanted". James Agate, writing in the *Sunday Times* about another Yankee exhibit, allows that "Add first-class direction and a furious energy of acting as though that art had just been invented, totally unlike the English duplication of esteemed successes, and we may perhaps be on the track of discovering why, to put it bluntly, the American theatre is so much more alive than the English." W. A. Darlington, in the *Daily Telegraph*, says of Sidney Howard's bad play, *Alien Corn*, that it is "obviously a good play", and Anthony Squire, in the

News-Chronicle, proclaims that " the author has dealt with the theme somewhat in the manner of Chekhov, and that's no unfair comparison with Chekhov." He adds: " The characters and the construction are superb, and the dialogue is one of the most moving I have heard in the theatre for years."

This sweeping love-feast, by way of adding to its booziness, has just as suddenly been accompanied by an even further high, wide and handsome derogation of the English stage. Up to very recently most American actors and actresses were abruptly dismissed as impossibly vulgar and uncouth. Now we have Mr. Agate slapping the whole English sisterhood by writing of one of them, Rosemary Scott, that " she possesses a quality which has almost disappeared from the English stage, that of being able to stand, sit, walk, talk, look, and listen like a lady ". Moreover, writes Mr. Agate, if the play in which the aforesaid Miss Scott is acting fails, it will be " because it contains a young lady *and* a young gentleman and, of course, no West End audience is going to stand for that! " Speaking of an American production, he proceeds to praise to the skies all the actors in it and then asks if there is any actor in England to match any one of them. " The answer," he concludes, " is three-fold. There isn't, there isn't anybody trying, and there are no plays to try in."

The Britishers, forsooth, are now employing for their own theatre an even lusher scorn than they until lately reserved for ours. " There is apparently nothing," writes Ivor Brown in the *Observer,* " which the British playgoer more relishes than the spectacle of first-rate artists putting a first-rate gloss on third-rate stuff." Speaking of a very bad English play, Agate observes that " Having almost every conceivable fault and no merits that I can discern, it will probably run a year, for if there is one thing on which the British public dotes it is poverty of idea richly dressed." Writing of the obligatory evening dress in London theatres, he says: " The

Englishman can never dress up his body without at the same time undressing his mind. Evening clothes connote a spree, and to him a theatrical spree connotes a musical comedy. For your Englishman cannot conceive an intellectual spree and would deny that such a thing exists. He's for a tale of larkishness or he sleeps, the most that he will concede being the half-way house of easy sentiment. That is why at any time of national crisis the only plays to thrive will have titles like *Dear Periwinkle, Rowdy Wedding,* and *Cheerio, Mr. Fish!* "

Hot-diggity-dog!

ENGLISH CROOK PLAYS IN AMERICA. The local curtain goes up on one of them. Being a crook play and English, you can readily from long experience predict the tone and flavor of the rest of the evening with your eyes shut, particularly when and if you note that it is an English crook play dealing with American crooks. You will know that the local producers have cautiously tried to conceal the usual dubious British characterization of American crooks by here and there altering such locutions as " Oh, I say, old man " to " Sez you, bo " or its equivalent. You will know that where in an American play of the same species the characters would all comport themselves like Dutch Schultz full of gin, it being an English one they will instead comport themselves for the most part like Basil Dean full of tea. You will know that the plot will be the Class-B movie wham which London Class-A audiences so highly esteem. You will know that the comedy dialogue will consist largely in the inability of the English characters to comprehend American slang, the inability of the American characters to comprehend British parlance, the request by the American characters that the British characters please speak English, and the customary jocosities about chewing gum and Chicago. And you will know that the authors read all the crook stories and saw all the crook plays that the late Edgar Wallace ever wrote and thought they were pretty wonderful.

ENGLISH RARE HUMOR.   Imported from England where it was a huge success, both critical and popular, M. J. Farrell's and John Perry's *Spring Meeting* [*vide English Critical Rebus*] once again made us wonder whether it is the English or ourselves who need the attention of a brain specialist. Hailed by the London critics as everything from " a superb character play " to " magnificent entertainment ", what we obtuse Yankees found was only a tepid little horsey comedy about the love tremors of a trio of Celts which began with a young woman crying out " Oo, darling, me that time! " when another, trying a dress on her, stuck a pin into her, which had its characters remarking either " I must have a look at the Solario colt " or " I must see the horses before they go out " whenever the authors wished to get them off the stage, which contained such familiar early-century comedy lines as " Michael's family are far too decent and respectable to think of marrying into ours " (Michael being a servant), and which ended, like nine out of ten school plays in Samuel T. French's catalogue, with three couples happily paired off and about to be married.

The company doing the play in London contained that admirable Irish comedian, Arthur Sinclair. As almost any play is likely to be amusing if it has Sinclair in it, this may in some part possibly account for the entertainment the English found it to be. But as Sinclair was unfortunately not in the local presentation, I continue bewilderedly to scratch my nose over the " rare humor " that the London critics discovered in the manuscript until I read, in another direction, Mr. James Agate's pleased citation of the best and most rib-busting joke heard at a recent Royal Command variety performance at the Coliseum. " Where's your old man? " asked Elsie Waters of Doris Waters. (" They lace an extraordinary talent for low comedy with genuine Cockney wit," writes Agate.) " At an identification parade," came the answer. "That won't take him long," declared the first speaker. And received the reply: "Last time it took him three months!"

I begin faintly to understand.

ENGLISH SPEECH. As an American theatrical commentator who last year had to take it on the chin from the English press for observing that many of the English actors who came over here suggested that they were blood relatives of as many leprechauns, and as one who the year before had to take it even harder on the jaw from the same press for reflecting on the atrociousness of many English actors' speech, it is both gratifying and critically flattering to note that that press is now belatedly finding itself in regretful agreement.

As to the dowdy speech of the English actors, St. John Ervine, critic for the London *Observer*, has led the British protest and has done a fine job of it. His indignation over the inaudibility of the Piccadilly and Shaftesbury avenue shape-jacks and his ridicule of what he designates as their "re-fayned" diction and popinjay manner of enunciation and articulation have made tasty reading. Week after week he has pursued the topic and week by week he has taken the absurd English mummers for an increasingly mortal and increasingly deserved ride. Ivor Brown, his critical associate on the *Observer*, has now brought up his artillery to assist in Ervine's campaign. I quote one pointed shot out of many. Discussing the English actor, James Mason, making his appearance in Dodie Smith's *Bonnet over the Windmill*, thus Critic Brown: "His diction was slovenly. Why call *not, nut,* and *Great Scot, Great Scart?*" From Mr. Brown's various critiques one gains the impression that the English stage is currently overrun with Masons and that it may not be long before they will have to import hitherto despised American actors to teach them how properly to speak their own language.

The dramatic critics, moreover, are not the only Englishmen who are beginning to sympathize with the American

animadversions on the manner in which English actors gar-
ble the English tongue. Mr. M. Gulick, Honorable Secretary
of the Association of Teachers of Speech and Drama, 32 Bel-
grave-road, London, S.W. 1, has rushed into the combat with
a message to one of the leading British journals admitting
that " We are a nation of mumblers. Members of this association have labored long and arduously to remove this reproach,
and have to some extent been successful. Much, however,
remains to be done. Surely more time ought to be devoted to
training speech as well as to improving the general physical
condition of the nation."

In many of the more recently imported English exhibits we have been presented with renewed evidence of the
dropped-squeak, chipped-tweet, elided and mottled British
actor locution. For years American audiences, still in a state
of ignorance and cheap snobbery, were given to a mistaking
or at least to an acceptance of such speech as very high-
toned and as the last word in worldly smartness. But today
they are on. They have come to realize that, so far as smartness goes, many English actors speak like valets and footmen,
especially when they are cast in the rôles of educated gentlemen, and they have come further to realize that what they
once mistook and accepted for something very genteel, well-
bred and extremely doggy is in actuality nothing more than
illiteracy, affectation, and crass ignorance.

As to the English critics' admission that many of their
native actors and even playwrights seem unmistakably to
have been born in the Grimms' inkpot, I have already recorded the reflections of Mr. George Munro, of the *Empire
News*. Now comes the *Era,* the London equivalent of our
own *Variety,* with a surprising paragraph implying concur-
rence. Now follow no less than a dozen published London
newspaper letters from British theatregoers complaining of
the peculiar fowl and lamenting the corruption of so much
of dramatic effect through their presence in various irreconcilable rôles. And now, lance flashing in the sun, lunges for-

ward the wittily merciless Mr. Agate himself with the free allowance that at least one of England's favorite young actors is apparently a little too much on the girlish side in speech, manner and comportment to do full justice to the tragic, masculine rôles he vaingloriously essays.

The New York newspapers recently carried a United Press cable telling of the attempted suicide in London of Russ Brown, an American actor, who was hissed by the English audience and denounced by certain English critics the week before at the opening performance of *Take It Easy* at the Palace Theatre. If Brown gets well, wishes to take another chance at the London theatre, and wants to get the applause of its audiences and fine notices from the certain critics aforesaid, I give him a suggestion. Let him begin at once to practice speaking the English language as if it were recorded on a rapidly revolving Berlitz phonograph disc which someone has promiscuously chipped with a scissors and then let him rehearse himself day and night until he can proficiently suggest that the maternity hospital nurse was something of a prevaricator when she breathlessly announced to his prematurely proud papa: " It's a boy! "

Entente Cordiale. In the case of Ian Hay's *Bachelor Born* [*vide Ibid.*] my critical colleagues indicated that they were doing their best to answer J. B. Priestley's prayer. Mr. Priestley, you recall, some time ago got down on his knees and, in the name of Jehovah and Neville Chamberlain, supplicated the local reviewers to accept English plays in the spirit in which the English themselves accept them and not loftily to dismiss them merely because their tone happens to be markedly different from the American product. The Hay comedy provided the first test of my colleagues' chivalry and, as noted, they responded with such politesse to the Priestley injunction that after the next distribution of court honors we may confidently expect to have to address them as Sirs, if not indeed Lords, Dukes, and Viscounts.

Nevertheless, in view of the quality of the Hay exhibit, it was not any too easy for them. In several instances their hedging was so extensive that it was hard to distinguish their reviewing from landscape gardening. And small wonder. For with the best will in the world and with hands across the sea giving each other the Elk, Shriner and even Brewers' Association grips, *Bachelor Born* presented a problem in international critical magnanimity. It was so infecund from any point of view, the reputable English included, that genially to state it wasn't was to slight the English intelligence and taste. In place of the picture of British public-school life which it pretended to be, it gave us chiefly the antics of three young women who invaded the academic premises and who, when they weren't effervescently hopping around in pajamas like so many Polly Chases in *The Liberty Belles,* were otherwise impressing the audience with their irrepressible youth by breathlessly jumping the cues of the older characters, indulging in so much eye blinking that one wasn't certain whether one was in a theatre or an optician's consulting room, and taking every exit as if it were a train rapidly pulling out of a station. The scholarly housemasters indulged in such locutionary morsels as " disassociate "; the general playwriting was of the species wherein an elderly man and woman meeting again after many years sentimentally observe to each other: " You haven't changed a bit "; and the humor consisted in hiding under beds, getting very drunk on one cocktail, dubiously smelling a proffered cigar and then pressing it to the ear to listen to it; and referring to one of the teachers as " Poop." I wager that Mr. Priestley himself, were he an American critic, would indite a more acescent report on such English mush than this relatively complacent one, for all the fact that the mush ran in London for nigh unto two years.

ENTERTAINMENT CURSE.   One of the most difficult things to find in any sizable American city today is a place where one

may get dinner or supper without a band, a singer, a per-
ambulating guitar player, or a whole floor-show getting into
one's soup. The difficulty, indeed, has extended in some
quarters to lunch. In Kansas City, for example, according to
report one restaurant actually offers with its thirty-five-cent
business men's lunch a strip-tease act. What's more, not even
breakfast is any longer safe. In certain hostelries in New
York — the Lombardy and Madison, for instance — your
breakfast on the week's one day of rest, Sunday, is accompanied by a pianist and the latest musical show ditties. And
what is still more, if you think you can catch a quiet sandwich in between times in one of the larger delicatessen
ateliers you are sadly mistaken. With it, you are pretty sure
to get a big dose of music from the newfangled mechanical
music-transmission machines.

The latest news from the Hollywood sector informs us
that various drive-in eateries, hamburgerstuben and hot-dog
stands have succumbed to the passion for ruining the national
digestion and have installed entertainment of one kind or
another with which to abuse their helpless and despairing
customers. And I have just received a circular letter apprising me that a restaurant chain is soon to be inaugurated in
Cleveland, Detroit, Chicago and other of the larger cities in
the Middle West which will bestow gratis in connection with
lunch, five o'clock tea, dinner and late supper a complete
one-ring circus, including a trained bear, a giraffe, and a baby
elephant. As yet, the drug-stores haven't put on shows at
their fountain counters, but the time probably isn't far off.

The curse of gratuitous entertainment saw its faint be-
ginnings some years ago, but it is only now that it has reached
its full bloom. You can't get away from it. It is everywhere.
Try to escape from it on a steamer and you run slam-bang up
against a carnival of joy from early morning until late at
night. If it isn't deck games, it is vaudeville concerts; if it
isn't band and orchestra music, it is gala fancy paper hat and
confetti doings; and if it isn't costume parties, it is horse races,

moving pictures and sailor parlor-performers. Try, in turn, to escape from it even on trains, which up to last year were perfectly and wholesomely safe, and on such as seasonally ply between Florida and the North you will find a whole car especially designed and devoted to entertaining people who would give ten dollars not to be entertained and to be left in peace. But nothing doing! No sooner have you got to the engrossing point in the latest novel where Scarlett Goldfarb tells Lord Aubrey Philpotts that she can't have anything to do with him until he gets a divorce from his paralytic wife than you are dragged off to the pleasure car and made either to listen to some bad piano playing or to play shuffleboard, quoits, ping-pong, and guessing games.

Even in such cases as you deliberately seek entertainment, like going to the theatre, for example, it is beginning to be so that they won't any longer allow you the old-time intermissions for a moment's surcease. If a string quartet isn't regaling your intermission cigarette with tzigane tunes, as at the Empire and several other theatres, still another string quartet, as at the Winter Garden, accompanies your entr'acte call of Nature in the lavatory with a rendition of such collateral melodies as *Flow, Shannon, Flow, River, Stay 'Way from My Door* and *Down Where the Würzburger Flows*. And at this same *Hellzapoppin* the entertainment tenaciously persists even after the show is over and you make a dash for home. In the outer lobby a gymnast entertains you with his efforts to get out of a strait jacket, a clown sits in a tree and strives to amuse you with various peculiar shouts and cries, and a bogus cop bids for your humors with facetious loud commands.

Several years ago, this business of entertaining you perforce went to the extreme, in the instance of one restaurant, of having a girl on a low-flung trapeze see how closely she could skim over your roast beef and Yorkshire pudding, to say nothing of your French fried potatoes, without dumping them onto your lap. At another, a trio of trick waiters, drafted from the old vaudeville ranks, was hired to give you the time of your life by dropping cigar ashes into your oyster cocktail, pouring ketchup onto your apple pie, and pulling your chair from under you. It was wonderful! Only the most irascible, crochety gourmet could be ungrateful and complain. And at still a third chowhouse up in East Eighty-third street a man with a cornet was employed to mosey about the tables and delight the diners no end by blowing fortissimo notes into their ears.

Last month, by way of clinical research and for the purposes of scientific exactitude, I selected seven different New York restaurants for dinner. I herewith append my report on what I got with my dinners:

At restaurant No. 1, a band, two rhumba dancers, a man who did card tricks, and a trained dog.

At restaurant No. 2, a jazz band, a floor-show with semi-nude damsels parading near my table, and a dance contest with prizes offered to the couple who did the best Cubanola Glide.

At restaurant No. 3, a migratory instrumentalist and singer who interrupted my fillet of sole, turnedos and coupe Champs Elysées with twangings and mewings.

At No. 4, my gustatory tranquillity was invaded by what was described as " A Versatile and Insouciant Little Chanteuse," to say nothing of by a male nightingale who warbled what were described as " Nostalgic Ballads " and a magician who performed his tricks within six inches of my sirloin steak.

At No. 5, I got a troupe of fancy ice skaters, a society débutante who discharged strange noises into a microphone, and an orchestra that played *This Can't Be Love* five times in one hour.

At No. 6, I was regaled from soup to nuts by a female Russian dagger-dancer, a gypsy trio, a pseudo-French cutie who sang something to the effect that she was in lowve wiz ze beeg strong Americain mens, and — as a grand finale —

a shower of toy balloons, two of which landed in my cherries Jubilee.

And at No. 7, they vouchsafed me three hill-billy singers, a female contortionist, a comic who sang *I Can't Dance, I Got Ants in My Pants,* and a performer who gave imitations of a bagpipe, sawmill, express locomotive whistle, and a pair of trousers ripping, not to mention a performing goat, a memory expert, a ventriloquist, and a Negro quartet.

In the future I shall either equip myself at the dinner hour with ear-muffs and dark goggles or stay at home, have my dinner served in, and as a slight concession to the prevailing fashion play my musical beer-mug.

ERIN GO BLAH. That the Irish voice is so beguiling that it can read even Dale Carnegie in a way to make us enthusiastically mistake him for Swinburne needs no restatement. But the infelicitous fact remains that, lovely and musical speech aside, the present Abbey Theatre company has put the dub in Dublin. Not so long ago one of the finest acting organizations in the world, it is now a caricature of its former self and, save when it offers itself in the more trivial comedies of its repertoire, as generally lack-lustre a theatrical outfit, whether in the way of group acting, stage direction, scenic and lighting skill, or compositional manuscript interpretation, as one may encounter this side of the fashionable London stage or the average summer cow-barn theatre.

Surely this is wet news, yet the truth of it must be apparent to anyone who has attended the company's more recent performances. What are the reasons? We all know, of course, that the greater Abbey actors and actresses — Fitzgerald, Sinclair, Allgood, O'Neill, *et al.* — deserted the company some time ago. And we have all heard how internal dissension and politics have contrived to weaken the once proud institution. But these reasons are not sufficient. After all, there are some competent actors and actresses still left — McCormick, Shields, Delany and Crowe among them — and, after all, the Abbey even in its heyday was never noted for the splendor of its scenic investiture or the virtuosity of its stage lighting. It must be something else. It is, and this is it.

First, Shields, who currently has the main hand in the direction of the company's productions, seemingly knows so little about stage direction, except in the most elementary sense, that when recently he was borrowed by Eddie Dowling to produce his fellow Irishman Paul Vincent Carroll's *Shadow and Substance,* due for an initial presentation in Pittsburgh, he proved himself so wholly unsatisfactory that Cedric Hardwicke and Sara Allgood, the latter of the eminent older Abbey company, rebelled against proceeding with rehearsals unless he were replaced. He was. Secondly, the Abbey company is obviously unable to control its fundamentally talented but personally over-cocky actress, Maureen Delany, and to prevent her from indulging in an outrageous overplaying, winking, snorting, and mugging that wreck any serious play she is in. And thirdly, the management most recently associated in the Abbey's local engagements has added further to the confusion by insisting that in the interests of audibility the players shout their lines like so many college yells and play so far down-stage that they are in imminent danger of tumbling into the orchestra pit. As a result, the once æsthetically adult Abbey family has become so excessively juvenile that we may expect any day now to hear that Patience, Richard and Johnny have joined up with it.

EVANS. Reading Maurice Evans' pronouncement in advance of the opening of *Henry IV* (Part 1) that he would portray Falstaff "as a gentleman and not as a bloated old drunk," one was seized with misgivings. One had the fear that he and Miss Webster, his director, had perchance lately come upon James Branch Cabell's admirable essay in defence of the plump knight which showed him in actuality to have been no mere roisterer, lecher, and tosspot but a man of many heroic qualities, a fellow of high and proud record, and a fine gallant withal. One had the further fear that they might have allowed too much research to go to their actor and director heads, that long delving o' nights might have entertained them with the merit of the idea that Falstaff should be played with an alleviating recollection of the libels that were originally charged to have been visited upon him and with various palliative intimations that the old souse possessed, hidden deep within him, traces of the more or less estimable historical personages from whom he was drawn: John Oldcastle, the holy martyr Cobham, and John Fastolfe himself. And one was particularly griped by the fear that all this, together with the modern actor and director passion for new interpretations willy-nilly — a passion that has given us everything from Ophelias who comport themselves like medieval Eva Tanguays to, in London recently, Malvolios who suggest impersonations of Ibsen by Leslie Henson — would lead to offering us a Falstaff that might conceivably be the flesh but surely neither the fowl nor good red marinierte herring of Shakespeare's design and intention.

Up, then, went the curtain at the St. James and proved our trepidations wholly groundless. For all Evans' pranky prefatory bulletin, Falstaff relievingly remained Shakespeare's own creation. Neither scholastic nor mummer freakishness had been permitted to work its vain whim upon him, and in the actor's shrewd and comprehending hands he lurched over the footlights not only for the every last, true ounce of his classic self but with an amiable clarity and beaming self-criticism that many actors who previously have battened on him have denied him. Under the Webster guidance, the brilliance of Evans in the rôle proceeded not from an obvious, periodic emphasis of the wisdom, the fundamental wit, the pervading humanity, and the healthy regard for self-interest, self-comfort and self-satisfaction that are imbedded in the character of the tun-bellied sot, but from the gradual internal establishment of those qualities and their confluence with the vapors of sack and rolling of ribald guts.

The portrait was hardly that of gentleman rather than that of a venerable stew, but it may at least be said for Evans' publicity preamble that it was what Shakespeare undoubtedly meant it to be: the portrait of one who was once a gentleman cajolingly vindicating his decline from grace with a boozy, contemptuous, and convincing hedonistic philosophy. It is to Evans' credit, and to Miss Webster's, that they didn't permit their portrait to go any farther than that. For foolishly to make this Falstaff a gentleman of the moment would even more foolishly be to make at least one of the indubitable gentlemen who surrounded him and mocked him a bounder. Which, in turn, would be to make the whole thing burlesque.

It is a double pleasure to American critics to see Evans, with his continuing excellent performances, reap from them his increasingly condign rewards. It is a double pleasure, I say, because aside from his professional merits he has conducted himself while amongst us with a decency, modesty, reserve, affection, and good-feeling indicated in the instance of very few English actors who come over here. Too many of these others, talented though they are, arrive with an ill-concealed condescension (God alone being able to figure out how come), publicly play and personally conduct themselves as if they were doing the United States an unheard-of favor, and duly depart jingling our gold in their jeans the while they sniffishly derogate the theatre and the audiences that magnanimously gave it to them. Evans isn't any such mackerel. He is giving the American theatre the best that is in him; he shows frankly that he is tickled to death that the American theatre likes him; and we gladly give him back what he well deserves.

EVERYMAN HIS OWN CRITIC. The lay theatregoer who hasn't time to read the professional reviewers' reports may readily spot a bad play for himself ten minutes after the first curtain has gone up. Herewith, some guide-posts:

1. If, shortly after the play starts, one of the characters,

usually an old woman with a quaver in her voice, shakes her head ominously and remarks with symbolic import that there's a storm brewing, whereupon a faint rumble of thunder is heard in the distance.

2. Immediately a young actor in a seven-dollar brown suit and with mussed hair, thus representing a Communist, enters the drawing-room of Brenda Van Hoogstratten, a rich society girl with a polo-playing fiancé.

3. When the curtain rises on an anti-Nazi drama and discloses a Jewish family of such angelic character that you don't know whether you're looking at a stage or at the ceiling of the Sistine Chapel.

4. The moment anyone puts anything into a drawer with a furtive look.

5. When in any French drama a married woman approaching forty looks wistfully out of the window and sighs.

6. If the rise of the curtain discloses (*a*) a group sitting around in flannels fingering tennis rackets; (*b*) an ingénue arranging flowers in a vase and happily humming to herself; (*c*) a butler taking a book from the bookcase; (*d*) a male character knocking at the door and, when no one answers, entering and, upon finding the room empty, wondering aloud if anyone is at home; or (*e*) a thirty-five-year-old woman secretary with her hair slapped severely back, wearing glasses, and speaking officiously into a desk telephone.

7. When, returning to his small home town, the first thing the sophisticated city fellow does is to take the photograph of his mother off the mantel, look at it a moment with smiling tenderness, and kiss it.

8. Any English comedy in which by 8:45 a lovable old daddy yowls that he has mislaid his glasses, which are on his forehead.

9. The instant you hear the line, " My dear, sit down. I want to talk to you. Things cannot continue this way."

10. The instant, even before hearing it, you anticipate the line, " You must give up this child! "

11. When Annie, the Irish servant girl, palpitatingly confides to a member of the household: "A man broke out of the pinitintiary last night, and they haven't found a trace of him yit."

12. In four cases out of five, when at the rise of the curtain the wife is writing a letter and the husband, in an easy chair, is reading a newspaper.

13. If the program announces that the action of the play is laid in 1980.

14. The moment any leading character uses the phrase, " 100 percent American ", without smiling.

15. When, as the curtain goes up, you hear newsboys shouting " Extra! " " Extra! "

16. If the scene is the home of a family in modest circumstances, if the son is discovered studying a racing form, and if a radio is conspicuously visible at upper stage center.

17. If it is a pacifist play, the minute a ghost of someone killed in the World War shows up.

18. Any comedy one of the leading characters in which you can instantly recognize as having been described in the script thus: " A faded blonde of forty, fluttery and superficial. She talks with exaggerated emphasis, interspersing her remarks with a slightly nervous laugh. Her clothes are in the extreme of fashion, a trifle too fussy and youthful."

19. Any mystery play in which, at the very start, someone remarks that the nearest house is two miles away.

20. If it is a rustic folk play, the second you hear Pa warn one of his kin: " Don't yuh go near my tin box 'til I'm dead! "

21. Any translation from the Hungarian in which the heroine is called the Countess Katinka.

22. Any exhibit in which the very beautiful young daughter of a rich and aristocratic family falls in love with the household butler or chauffeur who thereupon, like a damned fool, begins talking about the difference in their social positions.

23. As soon as you hear the line: " If a man kills a man, that's murder. Why isn't it then also murder if a man in uniform does the same thing. War is murder! "

24. The play with the old Boy-Meets-Father variation of the old Mother-Meets-Boy *Madame X* hokum. Papa and Mama are always criminals of one sort or another and come upon Sonny after all these years. At the finish, for which it is unnecessary for you to wait, tearful, self-sacrificing farewell.

25. The one about the timid little man who has a yen to be a hero.

EXIT EUROPA. Each successive season demonstrates more and more clearly that the American theatre has to be self-reliant in the matter of its new dramatic goods. With the European play market, war or no war, sinking year by year, our stage's life must depend increasingly upon the native product, which may be a good thing for the native product if not always for the native theatre. For, flag-waving aside, a theatre as large as ours cannot reasonably hope to keep its heels kicking high in the air without a little assistance now and then from outside writing hands. Nor can it reasonably expect that there be a sufficiency of American talent to fill its manifold stages with reasonable satisfaction for an entire season.

But that, with minor exception, it will valiantly have to try to go on its own becomes insistently apparent. Germany, once a source of valuable import with goods ranging all the way from Hauptmann tragedy and fantasy and Kaiser Expressionism to Fulda comedy and Blumenthal-Kadelberg farce, has been swastikad into sterility. Austria, once a goldmine of sentimental Schnitzleriana, waggish Bahriana and other such glittering theatrical minerals, has gone the way of Germany. Hungary, which supplied us with Molnár, Földes, Lengyel and so many others and whose playwrights were for the most part Semitic, has aryanized its drama to the vanishing point. The Czech drama, so far as it went, died with Karel Capek; the Spanish drama died the day after Franco put on his uniform; and the Italian drama, now that Pirandello is gone, has next to nothing to send overseas. France, once and for long a lively coaling-station for the American stage, has run pretty flat. Whereas in earlier years it could be counted on for at least a dozen available plays annually, today it seems able to hand over only an occasional practicable exhibit. In the last five seasons, ten out of the twelve French imports have been failures, and the two successes had to be very liberally adapted. Russia has given the local professional stage only one new play in the last half dozen seasons, and that one met with small success.

We come to England. Up until five or six years ago, the Mamaland was in the habit of supplying the American theatre with acceptable plays by the shipload. Things sometimes got to the point, indeed, where a New York playgoer could tell he wasn't in London only by recollecting that he would have to go around the corner if he wanted an entr'acte drink and by reinforcing his conclusion in finding he didn't have to pay for his program and in sniffing the circumambient C–N disinfectant. But presently and suddenly something snapped. Not only was it found that comparatively few English plays were longer suitable to the demands of the local platform but that most of those that were in one faithful quarter or another deemed suitable turned out to contradict and impoverish their apostles. Out of fifty-eight definitely English importations in the last five full seasons, fifty were failures, four got by only half-way and then by the skin of their teeth, and but four — *Victoria Regina, Tonight at 8:30, Call It a Day,* and *Bachelor Born* (in a very modest sense) — were successes.

It thus begins to look that unless things take another quick and surprising change our American playwriting boys and girls will have to take an extra-high hitch on their panties and get to work in wholesale fashion. Not only is Europe

— Ireland alone, praise to whom whence all blessings flow, excepted — largely either played out, dried up, shot, or in concentration camps, but even where it isn't, is unmistakably often a poor gambling market so far as our theatre is concerned. The standard, discrimination and taste of our theatre have advanced so signally in late years that foreign exhibits which once, in a more backward era, were swallowed whole are now summarily dispatched to the ashcan, and to the accompaniment of impolite hoots. The day when a popular American actor could pack a jejune and snobbish theatre simply by putting on a morning coat and an Ascot tie and posing as Lord Alastair Pishpiffle in a slice of Piccadilly smart junk has disappeared down the chute along with the day when the public would crowd the box-office to revel in the Gallic boulevard spectacle of several lascivious bald-headed actors hiding under a woman's bed. And with those days have vanished, too, the days when a Teutonic parsimony in respect to stage scenery was cleverly passed off on the local quack highbrows as an esoteric art called Impressionism, when a similar Russian economy in respect to stage lighting was equally cleverly passed off on them as profound Slav tragedy, and when a stage strewn with half a dozen corpses was esteemed not as 10–20–30 melodrama but as august Catalonian dramatic art simply on the score that the corpses were clad in boleros and mantillas instead of in cowboy, Indian and policemen's outfits.

EXPERIMENTATION AND ECONOMY.   That we are in for a lot of theatrical experiments has been evident since the Mercury group induced a potulent ecstasy in the critical fraternity by putting on *Julius Caesar* without scenery and costumes, and much as if Shakespeare were Sinclair Lewis lecturing on Fascism in Town Hall. No one is more in favor of experimentation than I am, but I begin to wonder from the evidence in hand if my critical brothers' enthusiasm for the specimens that have been recently revealed to us hasn't been based to a considerable degree upon the mere applaudable financial economy with which they have been accomplished. I am also in favor of financial economy, when it comes to that, provided only that something in the way of imagination and artistic quality goes along with it, but it seems to me that the economy disclosed by some of the theatrical experiments has not been confined entirely to the physical aspects of production and has been unnecessarily extended to the other attributes mentioned.

I am thinking in this connection not of *Julius Caesar*, but of some such experiment as, say, Marc Blitzstein's labor opera, *The Cradle Will Rock*. If Richard Strauss or someone like him (if there is anyone like him) wishes to write a labor opera or any other kind of opera, produce it without costumes and scenery, arrange the performers on several rows of kitchen chairs, and employ only a piano in place of an orchestra, it will be all right with me. But when Mr. Blitzstein or someone like him (and there are some like him) poses himself at such an enterprise, I pay myself the critical tribute of a large head-shake. It isn't that Mr. Blitzstein hasn't some cleverness. He has. But he hasn't enough cleverness and he certainly hasn't enough musical and libretto talent to make a satisfactory go of it, except perhaps in the estimation of drama critics whose knowledge of music does not go much farther than *Hail, Hail, the Gang's All Here* and *I've Been Working on the Railroad* or of excessive Labor sympathizers whose knowledge of lyrics, in turn, does not extend much beyond the *Internationale* and the verse in the *New Masses*. It isn't that I am casting undue aspersions upon *Hail, Hail, the Gang's All Here* and *I've Been Working on the Railroad*. I've sung them in my time along with the rest of the boys in a baritone noted perhaps less for its richness than for its loudness, and I've sung them with such exuberant and steadfast passion that it occasionally took as many as three bouncers to get me out of the place. Nor is it that the words of the *Internationale*, considered solely as

words, are not grammatical, literate and given to some eloquence. (I won't say anything about the verse in the *New
Masses.*) It is simply that Mr. Blitzstein's exhibit is so innocent of any musical importance, so completely obvious in its
libretto and, with one or two small exceptions, so unimaginative in its lyrics that only that species of criticism which translates the kick inherent in mere novelty as dynamic theatre and
drama can justifiably endorse it. *The Cradle Will Rock,* in
short, is interesting chiefly in the sense that we speak of a
woman in an " interesting " condition. But on this occasion,
for all the implicit potentialities and fond hopes, the final
result has been a miscarriage.

As in the instance of *Julius Caesar,* Blitzstein's opera *en
déshabillé* was celebrated by the critics for its " excitement ".
Defects, they here and there hesitantly allowed it had. But,
they proclaimed, what matter when, first and foremost, it
instilled in its auditors so great a degree of this excitement?
Now, no one likes excitement in the theatre more than I, but
it still seems to me that there are different kinds of dramatic
excitement and that the species engendered by Mr. Blitzstein is hardly to be distinguished, either critically or artistically, from a theatre cry of " Fire! "

That the exhibit, with its minstrel-show technique
adapted to pseudo-opera, is novel, we may agree. But novelty purely as novelty is exciting only to cub criticism. That
its defiant shout of labor propaganda from a stage apron
slam-bang against an audience's ears is aurally jouncing, we
may also agree. But excessive noise, whatever its quotient of
meaning, is exciting only to admirers of melodrama, jazz,
Negro revival meetings, aviation movies, and the novels of
Zane Grey. That it dismisses all the conventional accoutre-
ments of the musical-show stage, that it abandons scenery
and costumes, and that it confines itself to a single piano
played by its composer, we may further agree. But so did
the celebrated *London Follies* which, when shown at Weber's
theatre some years ago, got such a blast of ridicule from both

press and public that it was overnight driven in humiliation back to England. Surely, these things could not account in the reviewers' minds for its exciting quality. That its lyrics are in one or two instances fairly amusing, we may still further at least pretend to agree. But Lorenz Hart's and Ira Gershwin's lyrics are generally amusing in four or five instances, and I have yet to hear them called exciting.

We come to the singing and acting. It was, the reviewers agreed, eminently bad. We come to the score. It is, the one or two reviewers who know the slightest thing about music agreed, of no distinction; in point of fact, it is for the major part wholly obvious and alternately shoot-'em-in-the-ear and grease-'em-in-the-ear stuff. We come to the staging. It was, the reviewers agreed, of a charade cut and manner. We come to the words. They rely for their eloquence and punch solely upon their obstreperous articulation. We come, finally, to the theme: a battle cry of organized labor, familiar enough from a dozen or more recent plays. But, still insist the reviewers, it was all immensely exciting. You make that out; I can't. That is, I can't unless, as I have observed, a loud cry of " Fire! " constitutes a more critically and artistically exciting event in the theatre than something, quietly calm, like *Le Coq d'Or* or — if you want the greatest dramatic plea for labor ever written — Hauptmann's *The Weavers.* So far as *The Cradle Will Rock* goes, it strikes me as being little more than the kind of thing Cole Porter might have written if he had gone to N.Y.U. instead of Yale.

FAILURE. Twenty-two-year-old William Bowers' picture of fraternity life at a small Midwestern college, *Where Do We Go from Here?*, was a failure in the estimation of nine-tenths of the New York newspaper reviewers and the public that follows their verdicts. Yet it seemed to me a relatively worthier effort than either of those other school plays, *Brother Rat* and *What a Life*, upon which the same reviewers visited lavish praise and upon which the public that follows them visited lavish success. The point to be observed in this connection is the difference between theatrical criticism and dramatic criticism.

In the eyes of theatrical criticism, which is the genus dispensed by the daily reviewers, Bowers' play failed because it hadn't been given the mazda stage life with which a doctor-director like George Abbott infuses exhibits of a kidney, because it was deficient in plot, because it didn't gather its ends into a firm knot, and because in the reviewers' vocabulary it wasn't, finally, a " play ".

So far as popular theatrical criticism goes, the reviewers were largely correct. But so far as the species of dramatic criticism which doesn't reckon with popular taste and prejudice goes, Bowers' exhibit, while admittedly no important shakes, had many elements to commend it. Its close observation of its subject matter was first-rate. It didn't, save for a slight dose of unabashed hokum at its finish, compromise for a moment with Broadway, as both the heavily doctored and adulterated *Brother Rat* and *What a Life* continually did. Its characters were honestly drawn; its honestly simple and natural story was allowed its honest and natural simplicity and was not arbitrarily hocused into a fuller fraudulent dimension; and it presented its vague and baffled and foolish college boys not in terms of the slick grease-paint stage but in terms of their own muddled and absurd and natural selves. On the lesser levels of dramatic art, it is dishonesty that usually spells prosperity at the box-office. Bowers' failure lay in his honesty.

But even purely theatrical criticism, though it made some sound popular points against the play, was here and there confused in its derogation of it. Mr. Atkinson, for example, alluding to what he described as the interpolation of "the usual college comedy female complaint of incipient pregnancy", ironically observed: "No college play is complete without it, and the nobility it creates". If Mr. Atkinson can name more than one out of every ten college plays produced in the history of the modern theatre that contains the complaint, I shall present him, for the adornment of his estates, with a life-size marble fountain statue of Adolph S. Ochs. Mr. Atkinson continued: "To make it completely enjoyable, all they need is a play." Bowers' exhibit may not have been a play in the sense that Mr. Atkinson used the word, but, then, neither in the same sense, for that matter, were Gribble's *March Hares,* Lady Gregory's *Spreading the News,* and George M. Cohan's *The Tavern,* all of which, as Mr. Atkinson will freely grant, were completely enjoyable.

Mr. Watts, on the other hand, deplored the absence of plot in the Bowers' exhibit, to say nothing of the absence of "ideas." There was considerably more plot in Bowers' play than there is in Shaw's *Getting Married,* or in such popular exhibits as *The Better 'Ole* and *You Can't Take It with You,* and the lack of plot didn't materially dismay even theatrical criticism in these latter cases. In fact, the introduction of so much as a sliver of plot into the Kaufman-Hart play seriously discommoded the reviewers. As for the lack of "ideas", where are these so-called ideas in such hugely popular plays as *Sherlock Holmes, Charley's Aunt, Lightnin', Peg o' My*

Heart, Is Zat So?, or even *Tobacco Road?* Bowers' play, complained certain other reviewers, got nowhere. Well, where, exactly, do such loftier plays as Hauptmann's *The Weavers* and Galsworthy's *Strife* get? Or such popular plays as *Dinner at Eight, The Women,* or even, after more than four fairly prosperous centuries, *Much Ado about Nothing?*

FAIR PLAY.   A playwright's indefatigable determination to play fair with both sides of his problem too often results in tedium. Praiseworthy as his determination is, he should realize that the more everyone understands and sympathizes with one another in drama, the less drama there is.

FATA MORGANA.   Wishing by way of rest and change to get away from the theatre and all talk of the theatre, I not long ago got on a boat and headed for Puerto Rico, dulcet land of rum, Rositas and rhumba comfortably remote in the Indies. Once there, I knew I would be safe from everything associated with my trade and able completely for a spell to forget it. I appreciated, of course, that on the ship going down at least six female strangers, all past fifty and somewhat forbidding in aspect, would urge me to read plays they had written, that at least eight drunks in the smoking-room would solicit me confidentially to get Mary Martin's telephone number for them, and that an assortment of deck walkers, those ignominious fish, would accost me in search of enlightenment as to how the Lunt-Fontanne marriage was getting along — and I wasn't disappointed. But three and a quarter days isn't long and, after that, I was happy in the thought that it would be theatre good-bye.

Arrived at San Juan, the black boys who dive for coins tossed by passengers swarmed in the waters below the ship. I looked on, but tossed no coin. One of the boys was apparently disgusted with me. " Hey, hey," he yelled, " money, money! Loose up, Mister Shubert! " On the dock I was met by several Puerto Rican journalists. After the usual amenities and a brief interview on my health, plans, and opinion of the New Deal, one of them wanted to know when Eugene O'Neill's play cycle would be finished and why the Spanish dramatist, Benavente, had never succeeded with American audiences. Arriving at the cool and charming Condado, its lovely terrace garden washed by the blue sea by day and the saffron moon by night, the estimable host turned out to be no Manuel Gonzales or Ponce de Alvarez but an American named Pierce who inquired of me how the prospects for the next theatrical season looked and what had ever become of Lillian Lorraine. Also did I personally know Otis Skinner.

The maid who did my rooms, a bright-eyed young ebony chick, excitedly requested my autograph. I asked her what on earth she wanted *my* autograph for. It developed that she had seen a photograph of me in that morning's *El Mundo,* that the captions on it and on a photograph on the same page had got mixed, and that she thought I was Bojangles Robinson. The same evening I went to a supper party and dance given by that most urbane and felicitous of diplomats, Governor General Winship, at La Fortaleza, which, incidentally, under the nighttime starlit tropical sky presents a romantic picture unequaled anywhere in the world. Some three hundred guests were present. Among them were four young Puerto Rico belles who confided to me that it was their ambition to become actresses and could I tell them how best to go about it, an Englishman who wished to know just where I placed Ivor Novello in relation to Noël Coward, a gentleman from Haiti who bade me send him the score of *I Married an Angel* for his wife, who in her younger days was in the chorus of Victor Herbert's *The Fortune Teller,* and a French dowager who gave me a long lecture on the admirable new directorship of the Comédie Française.

The next day at luncheon at the Escambrón beach club whom should I run across but Jack Paton, the honey and coffee king, who had a copy of *Stage* magazine under his arm and showed me the pictures of various cuties in it while the waiter was fetching the Daiquiris. We were joined shortly by Señor Aguilez, a Puerto Rican magnifico, who over the Manzanilla Pepe Gallardo said it was his hope that one day San Juan might have a theatre of its own to offer competition to the present numerous film houses and could I tell him what plays to see when he and his wife came to New York in October.

Later in the afternoon I lay down for a siesta. I couldn't sleep, so I picked up a book from the table next to my bed. It was *The Life of Beerbohm Tree*.

FLAG-WAVING. George S. Kaufman's and Moss Hart's two hundred thousand dollars' worth of chronological flag-waving called *The American Way* and involving two hundred and fifty people (including a few actors and a brass band) was manufactured for the purpose of making a little money out of instilling patriotism in us. This, under present circumstances, may strike some of us like setting up business to sell us our own undershirts, but we'll skip that and pass on to a scrutiny of the specific cantharides with which the authors sought to heat us into a passionate admiration and yen for our country. I herewith list some of them:

1. The old song called *Goodbye Girls, I'm Through*.
2. The Hollywood movie actor, Fredric March.
3. A large photograph of William Jennings Bryan.
4. An even larger one of Herbert Hoover.
5. College graduates driven to work for the WPA.
6. The bank collapse and panic.
7. A man indignantly kicked out of a saloon for declaring whom he was going to vote for for President.
8. Several references to banana splits.
9. The spectacle of eager but jobless present-day youth.
10. A mandolin player.
11. The song, *I Picked a Lemon in the Garden of Love*.
12. The woman who won't dance any more with an awk-

ward partner because she says she wants to be able to walk in the future.

13. A scene in which half a hundred young American radicals fall upon and kill a poor old German.

14. The song, *Barney Google.*

15. A girl in a red, white and blue dress.

16. A funeral, with a coffin carried around the stage.

17. A radio crooner.

18. A run on a bank which subsequently fails and ruins a hard-working community.

19. A boy and girl who can't get married because the boy can't find work.

20. A large picnic without even a glass of beer.

21. The emergence in the nation of Fascist predilections and racial antagonisms.

22. A cautious suppression of any reference to the Spanish-American war.

23. The song, *There'll Be a Hot Time in the Old Town Tonight.*

24. An idiotic small-town mayor.

25. The introduction of double-feature movies.

26. The brass band.

There was, of course, also the inevitable parade of the boys in khaki returned from the World War, and it is significant that, serving as the big finale to the first of the two acts, it aroused the evening's highest enthusiasm in an audience which didn't stop to reflect that it celebrated by all odds the most fruitless and deplorable mistake ever made by our national government.

In a word, *The American Way,* however noble in its intention, seemed to me not only cheap hokum playwriting but, worse, juvenile jingoism. And it also, while we are on the subject, seemed to me that all those reviewers who hailed it as a great American patriotic document should, after consulting their pastors, begin to scratch their critical ears and reflect a little. It is these same critics who are loudest in their sardonic derogation of the open-and-shut propaganda drama in Germany and Russia. It is, they say, an insult to dramatic art. Yet it is these same critics, too, who yazoo for almost any American patriotic ballyhoo that comes along. They may not always endorse the plays themselves, but the chauvinistic propaganda nevertheless wins their hearty approval. If they move to save their faces in contradiction, show them such plays of the last season alone as *Abe Lincoln in Illinois, Knickerbocker Holiday, American Landscape, Everywhere I Roam* (bad in every other respect though they admitted it was), and this *The American Way.* If they still insist that propaganda doesn't fetch them, ask them how they responded to Victor Moore's kicking the Nazi ambassador in the belly, in *Leave It to Me!*; to the movie ridicule of Hitler and Mussolini in *Hellzapoppin;* to the spoken ditto of Hitler, Mussolini, Stalin and Hirohito in *Sing Out the News;* to the anti-dictator philosophy of *Danton's Death;* to the scene in the tripe called *Waltz in Goosestep* wherein Hitler is almost shot (the only thing in the junk that stimulated them); the heroic anti-Nazi sentiments of *Lorelei;* and the anti-authoritarian doctrine of *The White Steed.*

Let him who is without propaganda henceforth cast the first critical stone.

Eugene O'Neill some years ago remarked to me that anyone who would write an American historical panorama in terms of having a character pop in every once in a while shouting something like " Andrew Jackson has been elected President! " or " The *Maine* has been sunk! " was both a lazy and unimaginative loafer and a catchpenny playwright. O'Neill, to put it with wholesale politeness, wouldn't have cared for *The American Way.* For its authors rested content to indicate their chronology in the equivalent of just such terms, to say nothing of adding critical insult to dramatic injury by further dragging in as milestones the popular tunes of each era. But even this was not the half of it. Their effort to evolve a stimulating national pageant resolved itself into little more than an uninterrupted and languid parade of the most obvious stencils of theatredom, and was slightly embarrassing to any American with dignified national pride and dramatic taste. They missed none of them: the German immigrant who becomes so intensely and patriotically American that General Pershing seems in comparison a Japanese spy, the old German-American mother who tearfully at the outbreak of the World War beseeches her son not to go out and kill men who may be his blood relatives, the golden wedding anniversary with the gray-haired wife tenderly telling her gray-haired husband that it seems only such a little while that they have been married, the homecoming of the boys in khaki with the incidental all-stage embracings, the Hoover wheeze about the chicken in every pot and the two cars in every garage, the college graduates carrying picks and shovels for the WPA, the radio crooner who interrupts his broadcast to send a message of love to his dear old grandparents back in Mapleton, Ohio (a high-spot of the evening), the pipe-smoking ancients who sit in the garden at twilight sentimentally nodding their heads over the peace and contentment that their wives and children and grandchildren have brought them, and the final curtain with the stage bemeasled with American flags and everyone singing *The Star-Spangled Banner*. (I almost overlooked some forty stage children who were trotted out at intervals to enchant the customers with their cuteness, not to mention the excitement at the country club when news comes that Lindbergh has flown across the ocean, the introduction of *The Blue Danube* waltz with an old couple sentimentally trying to get into its rhythm, and the picnic interrupted by the inevitable rainstorm. Also such counterpoint chronological indices as mentions of Mary Miles Minter and other past movie stars, the indication of the advancing age of the leading characters by having them walk as if seized by gradually increasing and painful bellyaches, and the women in theoretically convulsing bygone bloomer bathing suits.)

Heil, Hitler! Heil, Mussolini! Heil, Göring, Göbbels, Ribbentrop, Stalin, the Chicago Fire, and the San Francisco Earthquake!

FLAPDOODLE.   We hear it constantly said that the two forenoted beloved dictators, MM. Hitler and Mussolini, are " great actors." This is nonsense. In the theatre, both would suffice only in cheap melodrama where stridency and overemphasis are the histrionic and dramatic requirement. In any form of drama calling for acting reserve, modulation and vocal shading they would be peremptorily dismissed as atrocious hams. Both, but Hitler in particular, are simply 10–20–30 villains playing at three dollars top.

FOUR-LETTER WORDS.   With its admirable production of Dekker's comedy, *The Shoemakers' Holiday,* the Mercury Theatre saw to it that the only two remaining four-letter words not yet spoken from the American stage duly received their belated hearing. Although the words in question did not in the least ruffle a Queen of England when the play was first done in her honor some three hundred years ago, they somewhat damaged the sensibilities of the contemporary polloi which embraces Park Avenue theatregoers, License Commissioner Moss, and our local producers of the classics, it being the conviction of these that what is eminently proper to literature is highly improper to drama and that it is much better to entertain and safeguard the taste, education, and morals of the public with the authors of *Mrs. O'Brien Entertains, Day in the Sun* and *Off to Buffalo* than with Ford, Jonson, Dekker, and Shakespeare.

The Mercury Theatre is to be congratulated on having had the taste and courage to allow to a piece of historical dramatic literature its inalienable right and privilege and at the same time on having made critical monkeys of such producers as McClintic, Howard, *et al.,* who have hypocritically and dunderheadedly tried to make even the greatest dramatist who ever lived conform to the pretty standards of the Broadway hacks. It is to be further congratulated on having had the shrewd sense to cut out all the Dekker redundancies and to give us a show that, lasting but little more than an hour, was enormously amusing whereas, uncut, it might have been proportionately tiresome. Let us, in the name of intelligent and satisfactory entertainment, have more of these one hour or one hour and a half plays. The two and one half hours regularly, arbitrarily, and foolishly imposed upon us have done much to hurt the theatre. Everything that the great majority of present-day playwrights have to say can be said fully and advantageously in an hour at the outside. To ask us to sit around for an additional hour and a half and listen to them either saying nothing or repeating what little they have said before is very impolite of them.

FRENCH FLAVOR. American revues with a presumptive French flavor generally follow more or less resolutely a hard and fast tradition. The scene in the Apache dive, the undressing scene in the chorus girls' dressing-room, the scene in front of the Café de la Paix with Americans struggling with the French language, the skit in which the young soldier, embracing the famous cocotte in her midnight boudoir, informs her he has won her for five francs in a lottery (they get that one out of an 1890 time capsule), and the sleek, gleaming toothed, accentful Gallic juvenile who sings about Rendezvous Time In Paris, We Live On Love, and (with a meaningful wink) The French Have A Word For It and who at the conclusion of the numbers bends one of the ladies over backward and bites her passionately in the neck — these are all or in part usually in evidence. And with them, too, are the number in which the chorus girls recite in unison the wickedness and delights of Gay Paree, the trio of thirty-year-old kids in short skirts who with wide baby stares sing of the dangers lurking for them in that same Gay Paree, the parading show girls in chartreuse mosquito netting, the scene at the passport photographer's, the saucy ditty called *History Is Made at Night* with seven or eight ladies of the ensemble indicating their particular contributions to the annals, the comical ditty about the indefatigable roué, and the ballet number called *Danger in the Dark,* sung by a tall blonde who throws her arms high in the air at her final vocal burst and danced by a quorum of girls who indicate their fears for their chastity by exposing nine-tenths of their anatomies through abbreviated gauzes.

GHOSTS. The late Karel Capek's *Mother* was a two and a half hour groan over cannon-fodder, peopled chiefly by actors representing ghosts. Right here I wish to register something about such stage ghosts. After many years of reviewing contact with them, I begin to wonder why directors can't at last vary them just the least bit. Having viewed scores of the bores, I am hungry to look at just one who won't stand so stiffly erect that he suggests his mundane body was frozen to death at the North Pole, who won't move about the stage as if his job during his lifetime had been understudying Charles Evans Hughes, who won't talk as if death arbitrarily imposed upon one the diction of Walter Hampden, and who won't have a baby spotlight follow him around the stage like a portable shower-bath.

GLAMOUR DECEASED. Give the average New Yorker over forty-five two drinks and he is pretty certain to deliver himself of the plaint that the theatre isn't as glamourous as it used to be. Give him three and he is equally certain to howl that it has lost all its glamour. And give him four and he will burst into tears over having profoundly convinced himself of the tragedy.

Our friend customarily bases his allegation on four points. First, he argues, the theatres themselves aren't what they were. Secondly, he contends, the actresses aren't what they used to be. Thirdly, he grunts, the audiences aren't of the old-time gala aspect. And fourthly, he moans, the plays aren't what they were. What the old fraud means, ten times out of ten, is simply that the girls aren't as pretty as they were in the past. But on this, as on his other points, I have the

honor to believe that he is what the pedants describe as
screwy.

When our venerable friend disparages the glamour of
today's theatre he commits the usual fallacy of over-sentimen-
talizing the impressions of his youth. It isn't that the theatre
has lost glamour so much as it is that he himself adheres
stubbornly to his juvenile concept and view of glamour. He
has not grown up with glamour and is still in the short-pants
glamour stage. And the older he gets, the more he seems to
persist in remaining in that stage.

Let us take up his laments in the order named. He believes, first, that the theatres as houses are no longer romantic. It is perfectly true that some of them aren't, but many
of them also weren't any more romantic back in the period
whose passing he deplores. A full third of the playhouses of
twenty and thirty years ago — and there were fewer theatres
then than now — were shabby, dirty and worn structures,
both inside and out, and were as physically glamourous as
so many provincial hotels. Daly's, the Bijou, the Madison
Square, the Princess, the Park, the Fifth Avenue, the Garden,
Wallack's and others cried for fresh paint, new upholstery
and a regiment of scrubwomen. They were frugally lighted
outside and in the lobbies; their ushers were slovenly; and
their drop curtains looked for the most part as if they had
been left out in the rain for a decade.

The actresses, our friend goes on to weep, aren't the
lookers they used to be. Where, he loudly demands, deaf-
ening the bartender, is there one to compare with Lotta
Faust, or Irene Bentley, or Sandol Milliken, or Edna Wallace,
or Marie Doro, or the Hengler sisters, or the young Ethel
Barrymore, or Irene Fenwick, or Vernona Jarbeau, or Eleanor
Mayo, or Lillian Russell, or Amy Ricard, or Pauline Fred-
erick? Or with such lulus as Gertrude Elliott, Katherine
Florence, Edna Chase, Camille D'Arville, Madge Crichton,
Mabelle Gillman, Edna Goodrich, Eleanora de Cisneros,
Mabel Barrison and Vashti Earle? Without assuredly in the

least reflecting upon the loveliness of many of these fair ladies, though a connoisseur exception may be taken in several instances, the theatre of our immediate day need not hesitate a moment to challenge them with a lengthy list of girls including Tallulah Bankhead, Katharine Hepburn, Frances Farmer, Grace McDonald, Martha Scott, Julie Haydon, Margot Stevenson, Sylvia Weld, Haila Stoddard, Helen Trenholme, Lillian Gish, Kitty Carlisle, Margaret Vyner, Claire Luce, Adele Longmire, Erin O'Brien-Moore, Jane Wyatt, Sylvia Sidney, Eleanor Lynn, Madge Evans, Constance Cummings, Rita Johnson, Ethel Barrymore Colt, June Knight, Lois Hall, Marcy Wescott, Uta Hagen, Marian Shockley, Doris Dudley, Betty Field, Gene Tierney, Mady Christians, Louise Platt, Joan Wetmore, Catherine Bailey, Joyce Beasley, Hope Manning, Lena Horne, and some two dozen or more others.

Our nostalgic friend's next cramp, relating to the disappearance of glamour in the audiences, has even less basis in fact. The representative audience of the days he wistfully reflects on regularly included in its composition wine-agents like George Kessler and Manny Chappelle, theatre managers like the Sire brothers, figures in the town's night life like Harry Thaw, Jackson and Aimée Gouraud, Billy Baxter, Fred Lewisohn, Fred Housman, restaurant operators like the Bustanobys, and hotel men like Regan of the Knickerbocker, along with a thick leaven of ladies of the chorus who were temporarily " at liberty ", Wall Street curb brokers, and shyster lawyers. One night in 1914 I made a list of the component elements of such an audience and placed it in the record. The occasion was a gay opening at the Casino Theatre. Herewith, the catalogue:

    28 Actresses out of work.
    31 Actors out of work.
    16 Chorus girls out of work.
     3 Wine agents.
     8 Song writers.

19 Maintained ladies.
19 Maintainers.
 1 Corset manufacturer.
 2 Scene painters.
14 Members of leading woman's family, or friends.
10 Members of leading man's family, or friends.
40 Friends or members of families of other actors in the company.
 1 Wife of orchestra leader.
 2 Stenographers in producer's office.
 4 Program, billboard and advertising men.
 3 Ticket speculators.
 2 Newspaper illustrators.
 2 Dressmakers
 2 Milliners.
 1 Wigmaker.
 2 Representatives Orange Costume Company.
 1 Representative Russell Uniform Company.
 4 Play-brokers.
 3 Other theatre managers.
 2 Broadway theatre doctors.
 6 Broadway lawyers.
 1 Hotel manager.
 3 Restaurant managers.
 2 Newspaper society reporters.
 4 Vaudeville booking agents.
 8 Members producing manager's staff.
 1 Producing manager's valet (in balcony).
 1 Theatrical photographer.
17 Stockbrokers.
 1 Florist (came to see how his flowers looked in the lobby).
 2 Press-agents.
 3 Producing manager's backers.
 4 Racetrack touts.
12 Steady Rector customers.
14 Newspaper and periodical critics.

Glamour my eye!

The plays, pipes our friend, aren't as good as they used to be. Let us compare the outstanding plays on view twenty-five and twenty-six years ago with those of these most recent two years. In the seasons of 1913 and 1914 the leading new plays, we find, were the following: *After Five,* by William and Cecil B. De Mille, *Are You a Crook?*, by William J. Hurlbut, *The Argyle Case,* by Harriet Ford and Harvey O'Higgins, *At Bay,* by George Scarborough, *The Auctioneer,* by Charles Klein and Lee Arthur, *Believe Me, Xantippe,* by Frederick Ballard, *Blackbirds,* by Henry James Smith, *The Escape,* by Paul Armstrong, *The Family Cupboard,* by Owen Davis, *Fine Feathers,* by Eugene Walter, *General John Regan,* by George Birmingham, *The Ghost Breaker,* by P. Dickey and C. Goddard, *A Good Little Devil,* by Austin Strong, *Grumpy,* by T. W. Percyval, *Indian Summer,* by Augustus Thomas, *Kiss Me Quick,* by Philip Bartholomae, *The Lure,* by George Scarborough, *Maggie Pepper,* by Charles Klein, *The Misleading Lady,* by P. Dickey and C. Goddard, *Patriots,* by Lennox Robinson, *Peg o' My Heart,* by J. Hartley Manners, *The Poor Little Rich Girl,* by Eleanor Gates, *Potash and Perlmutter,* by Jules Goodman, *Romance,* by Edward Sheldon, *September Morn,* by Alice E. Ives, *Stop Thief,* by Carlyle Moore, *Seven Keys to Baldpate,* by George M. Cohan, *Today,* by George Broadhurst, *The Unwritten Law,* by Edwin Milton Royle, *What Happened to Mary,* by Owen Davis, *Years of Discretion,* by the Hattons, *Children of Today,* by Samuel Shipman and Clara Lipman, *Daddy Longlegs,* by Jean Webster, *Experience,* by George V. Hobart, *He Comes up Smiling,* by Byron Ongley, *On Trial,* by Elmer Rice, *The Dummy,* by Harvey O'Higgins and Harriet Ford, *Twin Beds,* by Margaret Mayo and Salisbury Field, *The Miracle Man,* by George M. Cohan, *A Pair of Sixes,* by Edward Peple, *Under Cover,* by Roi Megrue, *The Yellow Ticket,* by Michael Morton, *It Pays to Advertise,* by Megrue, *A Perfect Lady,* by Channing Pollock and Rennold Wolf, *Apartment 12–K,* by Laurence Rising, *The Salamander,* by Owen Johnson, and *Kitty Mackay,* by Catherine Chisholm Cushing.

Compare that list with the list on view in the 1938 and

1939 years: *High Tor, You Can't Take It with You, The Women, Yes, My Darling Daughter, Room Service, Amphitryon 38, Golden Boy, I'd Rather Be Right, Father Malachy's Miracle, Of Mice and Men, The Cradle Will Rock, Time and the Conways,* . . . *one-third of a nation, Shadow and Substance, On Borrowed Time, Our Town, Haiti, Once Is Enough, Murder in the Cathedral, Wine of Choice, Whiteoaks, All the Living, Tobacco Road, Victoria Regina, Susan and God, What a Life, The Little Foxes, Abe Lincoln in Illinois, My Heart's in the Highlands, Oscar Wilde, Kiss the Boys Goodbye, Rocket to the Moon, Wake Up and Sing, Here Come the Clowns, Mamba's Daughters, The Primrose Path, The Gentle People, The White Steed, Family Portrait, The Philadelphia Story, No Time for Comedy, Danton's Death, Dame Nature, The Fabulous Invalid, The Time of Your Life, Key Largo, The Man Who Came To Dinner,* etc.

Well, protests our friend, " I don't know, but there was *something* about the theatre in those days, *something* that's disappeared! "

What has disappeared are such exceeding rare parcels of glamour as the hereinbefore noted Polaire, who made a sensation on the score of being advertised as the homeliest woman in the world; Cleo de Mérode, who made a sensation on the score of being reputed to have to wear her hair draped over her ears because her ears had been shot off; the Poillon sisters, who made a sensation by being advertised as quick to get even with any man who tried to get fresh with them; Nan Patterson, who made a sensation through having figured in a notorious murder trial; Polly Chase, who made a sensation by appearing in pink pajamas; and Mrs. Leslie Carter, who made a sensation because she had been a party to a sensational divorce suit and had the reddest hair this side of Jim Tully's late grandfather, Pat.

GLAMOUR REDIVIVUS. Coincidental with the tearful complaint that the theatre in recent years had lost its old-time glamour was for some time heard the tribute to the movies that they had captured it away from the theatre and made it their very own. The complaint and tribute now appear to have changed partners, for this last year has witnessed so sudden and surprising a metamorphosis that even Hollywood, loath though it may be, has been forced to admit it.

From at least a dozen Hollywood quondam die-hards have come symptoms of concern over the altered scene. Edgar Selwyn, of Metro-Goldwyn-Mayer, puts it this way to me: " There was hardly an actress in New York two years ago who wouldn't have given her very chemise to get into pictures. Today, there is hardly one in Hollywood who wouldn't give hers to get a chance in the theatre ". Even the swarms of young fish who not long ago viewed the movies as their dream of heaven — the girls and boys from the farms and villages and towns who saw Hollywood as fancy's purple goal — are beginning to turn their faces toward the East. It isn't that the theatre provides an easier chance for them; it provides, in fact, a much harder. It isn't that the Hollywood players themselves are losing their jobs and are looking to the theatre for new ones; many of them are among the screen's most successful performers. It isn't the mazuma hard-luck stories that have been publicized by the cinema bosses, or even the theatre's recent coming into renewed prosperity. It is none of these. It is, simply, that the gilt and tinsel which were once the popular property of the theatre and which the theatre once lost to the movies have now been lost to the movies in turn and revisited upon the theatre.

Many things have contributed to the phenomenon. Inasmuch as the popular interpretation of glamour is indistinguishable from a sardine's infatuation with a goldfish and has no more relation to realistic intelligence than the Wilsonian ideology, it all comes down principally to a matter of the imagination. It is true that such sentimentally romantic plays as *Victoria Regina* and *The Barretts of Wimpole Street*, romantically acted by such actresses as Helen

Hayes and Katharine Cornell, have swept up a valuable sentimental reaction to the theatre on their prosperous excursions through the country. And it is also true that the succession of bad movies and drab stories and unappetizing players has taken its toll of the film fans. But beyond and above these things there are various minor factors that have brought about the change.

In the first place, the screen has not been able to supply its public with more than one new male or female idol in several years, and its public has begun to grow tired of the old ones. It has been unsuccessful in finding more than one new man or woman to restimulate the romantic libido of its customers. In the second place, promiscuous marriages, cheap scandals and bad publicity have removed from many of the film players what bogus glamour the fans once attached to them. In the third place, the defection of so many players from the pictures and their mere hope to succeed in the theatre have been instrumental in arousing the movie public's skepticism as to its former belief in the innate glamourous importance of the Hollywood art. In the fourth place, the new stage girls have become prettier as the new screen girls have gone off in looks. With the single exception of Hedy Lamarr, Hollywood hasn't delivered a new agitating damsel in all of three years. Meanwhile, the theatre has uncovered at least two dozen girls available as magazine cover material. In the fifth place, the screen has proved that, even if it spends two million dollars on musical shows like the *Goldwyn Follies,* it can never capture the romantic beauty and charm of a relatively simple stage show like *I Married an Angel.* At bottom, it all remains the old story of the silk purse and the sow's ear.

GOOSEFLESH DRAMA.   The mystery story is the victim of one of our most popular fallacies. Four persons out of every five believe that of all literary forms, excepting only the story laid in the future, it is the easiest to write, and comfortably within the talents of the meanest vivandière of drugstore belles lettres. Nothing, of course, could be farther from fact. The number of first-rate such stories written in the last quarter century could be counted on less than the fingers of two hands. And the number of even passably good mystery plays in the same period could be counted on the fingers of one.

In the last eight full theatrical seasons, by way of illustration, there have been produced exactly fifty-eight attempts at mystery plays and the one and only one of the lot that got anywhere near to being fully satisfactory was George M. Cohan's dramatization of Earl Derr Biggers' *Seven Keys to Baldpate* — and that production was a revival from the season of 1913. In the season of 1931–32 thirteen mystery-spiels were shown, eleven of them excessively sour and only two, *Riddle Me This!* and *Whistling in the Dark,* approximating even the second-rate. In the season 1932–33 there were four tries, all poor and with *Criminal-at-Large* alone approximating even the third-rate. In the following season, 1933–34, we had eight specimens, seven of them pretty dreary and only *Ten Minute Alibi* proving faintly diverting. In 1934–35, there were ten displays, the Cohan revival referred to being the sole exception to the general depression. The next theatrical year, 1935–36, saw a like number of attempts and of the whole ten only one, *Blind Alley* (which did not, at that, too exactly fit into the mystery catalogue), turned out to be partly acceptable. In 1936–37 we had nine attempts, all bad. In 1937–38 there were four, similarly all bad; in point of fact, worse. And last season there were two, *Come Across* and *Ringside Seat,* that were worse still.

One of the recent particularly dour specimens, by way of general exemplification, was something called *Escape This Night*. Dealing with a couple of murders in the New York Public Library, it failed to engage the interest for the same reasons that most of these murder strudels do. In the theatre it is next to impossible to work up much concern over a done-in corpse unless the playwright has exercised the pre-

caution to interest us in the character of the corpse before it
is done in. If a character comes on and is popped off before
we in the least get to know him, it is dollars to free passes we
don't give much of a hang if he is murdered, who murders
him, or why he is murdered. An extremely skillful playwright maybe once in every two decades can prove the contrary, but there are few extremely skillful playwrights who
dissipate their efforts on such delicatessen. In the theatre,
further, it is disastrous, as the authors of *Escape This Night*
again did, to save up all the surprises until final curtain time.
It is all well and good to hold back the big secret until that
time, but dexterous mystery playwriting appreciates that it
is advisable in the business of jockeying suspense to spill at
least one or two little secrets on the way. Five exciting minutes at the close of a play were never sufficient to atone for
two antecedent placid hours. And in the theatre, further still,
it is important to the full prosperity of a mystery exhibit that
it be written — as this one assuredly wasn't — by someone
either humorously or solemnly pretending to be afflicted with
spinal epilepsy and *cutis anserina,* even if it be subsequently
directed and acted by a score of sclerotic William Gillettes.

GORDON.   For some reason that I have not been able to make
out, unless possibly it is because she is personally a thoroughly charming, witty and very popular young woman, it
has been the custom of the critical fraternity always to pull
its punches in reviewing the performances of Miss Ruth
Gordon. She has, true enough, given some first-rate accounts
of herself when the rôles have been down the alley of her
particular and idiosyncratic talents, and on such occasions
there has, of course, been no need to hold back. But there
have been other times when, her rôles unsuited to her, she
has left much to be desired, and such a punch-pulling has
been then in evidence as hasn't been recorded since the days
of Ad Wolgast and Kid Lavigne. With her recent appearance as Nora in *A Doll's House* we got the first intimation

that the long established chivalry of the lads was on the decline, although a sufficient number of stand-patters and let-
down-easyers were still in evidence.

Miss Gordon's Nora, still and fully allowing for her un-
questionable personal charm, wit and popularity, was from
almost any critical point of view a pretty disastrous affair.
Mistaking the doll of Ibsen's title to mean a creature stuffed
with sawdust and pulled into this emotion and that by greasepaint wires, she diverted — with her director's misguided aid
— the celebrated character from its proper innocent muddleheadedness and irresolution into a compound of Stair and
Havlin ingénue, Evans and Hoey soubrette and Heckscher
Children's Theatre character woman, the sum of which was
a cross between a congenital moron and an adscititious nitwit. The result was such a distortion of the play that when
finally she slammed the door on Helmer the audience had
all it could do to restrain itself from jumping up on the stage
and offering him its warm and hearty congratulations. Had
old Henrik been present to witness the performance he would
doubtless have rushed out at the end of the first act under
the impression that he had got into the wrong theatre by
mistake and was seeing not Nora in *A Doll's House* but
Lotta in *Family Jars*. If the old boy had remained for another act, he would have changed his mind. He would then
have become fully and absolutely convinced that what he
was looking at was Anna Laughlin in *Editha's Burglar*. And
if he had stayed for still another, he wouldn't have had any
mind left to change.

These, I appreciate, are graceless and indelicate words
to visit upon the professional performance of anyone personally so thoroughly charming, witty and deservedly popular as the actress in question. But criticism, after all, has
its ungallant duties even as its practitioner ex officio has his
gallant ones. And there is, in this opinion, no other honest
way to designate this particular Nora. Yet, as I have noted,
one still observed a considerable hemming and hawing on

the part of a considerable number of the reviewers. It hurt them, it seemed, to say too cross things about the charming Miss Gordon. That I can understand their feelings, I freely admit. For I also, to repeat, esteem Miss Gordon as a fair and charming person. But, were she a thousand times more fair and a thousand times more charming than she is, damme if I could persuade myself to go as far for her as our old critical sweetheart, Mr. Burns Mantle, went when, in a courtly and endearing effort easily to let down her performance, he wrote: " But though Ibsen might have squirmed his way out of the theatre watching Miss Gordon striving sincerely and with mighty effort to approximate his Nora, he could not have proved her entirely wrong in her conception. She could have answered him by saying that hers was an American and not a Scandinavian doll wife ".

Fancy that, Hedda!

GRAND PRIX. The *Grand Prix de Bel Paese Supérieur* for the year's gamiest slice of theatrical criticism is herewith bestowed upon Mr. Kyle Crichton, alias Robert Forsythe, for his *Is the Theatre a Waste of Time?*, published in the *New Masses*. I privilege you the honor of several luscious sniffings.

Whiff 1. — " If there are ten out of fifty possibly firstrate modern plays which can stand revival, they will be found among the works of two men: Shaw and Ibsen. For the rest — "

Deodorant. — Modern dramatists other than Ibsen and Shaw whose plays have been successfully revived in recent seasons: Strindberg, Synge, O'Casey, Chekhov, O'Neill, Maugham, Odets, Bruckner, Wilde, Rostand, Tolstoy, Rolland, Gogol, Barrie, Sierra, etc., not to mention such as Drinkwater, Eliot, Lawson, Robinson, Colton, Milne, Cohan, Vane, etc.

Whiff 2. — " In a manner, it (the theatre) may be compared with poetry . . . which unfortunately is so limited in its appeal that it may be disregarded as a literary force."

Deodorant referred to the kindergarten class.

Whiff 3. — " At the very instant when it is historically important for all men who have influence to use it where it will be the most effective, they have preferred to occupy themselves with an art which is as limited as a family corporation. . . . This myth of the theatre is obviously a hangover from the days when a play, even in this country, could have seven or eight companies acting it simultaneously. When that was true the playwright was justified in feeling that he was speaking to America."

Deodorant. — How many plays in past days were ever acted simultaneously by seven or eight companies? Please name them. *Charley's Aunt* was once acted, I believe, by four, but what great message did its author, Brandon Thomas, speak to America? Aside from *Uncle Tom's Cabin,* which was once played simultaneously by six or seven companies, I can recall no plays that were duplicated by more than four at most, and they were few, and all of them were trash that had better been left unspoken to America.

Whiff 4. — " *Abe Lincoln in Illinois* is wasting its efforts on sabled audiences who are neither amused nor convinced."

Deodorant. — *Abe Lincoln in Illinois* ran in New York alone for more than an entire year to large and enthusiastic popular audiences; it has reaped a small fortune from their deeply impressed reaction to it; it has received various awards for merit; it is, as I write, on a road tour through the eastern states; and it has impressed even Hollywood so deeply that Hollywood has paid another fortune for the movie rights and has put it on the screen.

Whiff 5. — " Last season the critic was beating the drums for *Shadow and Substance.* Unfortunately, I did not see the show but I am willing to accept judgment that it was the finest play of the year. That makes its fate all the harder. It played on Broadway and subsequently made the customary brief stops in Chicago, Philadelphia, etc., but for all practical purposes . . . it will have come and departed like an embarrassed and distant relative, fleetingly with us ", etc.

Deodorant. — *Shadow and Substance* ran for one hundred and sixty-nine performances on Broadway; a month (including a return engagement) in Philadelphia; four weeks in Boston; three in Chicago; and covered the country east of the Mississippi from Buffalo and Rochester to Dayton and Pittsburgh; from Detroit, Indianapolis and Cleveland to Toledo, Madison, Wisconsin, and St. Louis; from Ithaca, New York, to Fort Wayne and Cincinnati. It was subsequently played in the summer theatres; it is currently visible in the outlying stock company theatres; it is due to appear on the screen; and in book form it has had a uncommonly large sale.

Whiff 6. — " Imagine the difference if Sinclair Lewis had written *It Can't Happen Here* originally as a play. It would have had the usual Broadway run if he were lucky, and the pathetic road tour and that would have been the end."

Deodorant. — The dramatization, co-authored by Lewis, ran for almost one hundred performances at the Adelphi Theatre. It was then played simultaneously by the greatest number of companies in American theatrical history (18) in the Federal Theatre Project's houses throughout the land. It was thereafter played by summer stock companies and is now about to be made into a moving picture.

Whiff 7. — " The theatre in Russia is exciting because it gets to the people, productions having as many as a hundred simultaneous showings throughout the country."

Deodorant. — Names and dates, please.

Whiff 8. — " The situation becomes worse when one realizes that the young people even in New York are no longer attracted to the theatre."

Deodorant. — The young people even in New York are responsible for the Group Theatre, the Actors' Repertory

Company, the Mercury Theatre, the Labor Stage, the Play Room Group, the Studio Group, the Juvenile Art Theatre, the Children's Art Theatre, etc., etc., etc. The young people are responsible for most of the countless little theatres all over America. The young people are largely responsible for the extensive summer theatre circuit. There are so many youngsters set upon a professional acting career that the situation is as bad as that of the surplus thousands of extras in Hollywood. The dramatic schools and academies are full to the roofs with the kids. About every third young man or young woman you encounter these days is busy writing a play. And they have to put extra cops on duty at the New York theatres to shoo away the large, new mob of youthful autograph fiends.

GREASEPAINT POISON. In *Ends and Means,* his recent book, Aldous Huxley argues that the profession of acting ruins the character of any person who enters it. In other words, that whatever a man or woman may be like before, he or she is bound to be corrupted by contact with greasepaint. Is it true and, if so, what are the reasons?

As to its truth in nine cases out of ten, I think there is not much doubt. There are, of course, tenth cases and, as there are thousands upon thousands of actors, indignant maintainers of the opposite point of view may be assuaged with a relative sufficiency of exceptions. But it would take an expert and somewhat inebrious mathematician to increase the ratio. For anyone with even the most limited experience of player folk must readily appreciate that the acting business does something very peculiar to most of them. And what is more, it is understandable.

In the first place, the acting profession is the only one that demands of its practitioner that he pursue each day's work gazing more or less fondly at himself in a mirror for at least three-quarters of an hour. This naturally induces in him not only an extravagant self-consciousness but also, if he rather fancies himself (a phenomenon not unheard of among show folk), an exaggerated concern with the sublimity of his pan. It is, as well, the only profession that demands that its devotee paint his face. This in time also naturally insinuates a general artificiality into his concept of himself. And it is, further, the only profession that periodically speaks as its own the beautiful thoughts of other men and that, assisted by an analytical confusion on the part of the public, comes vaingloriously to believe that the beautiful words are its own.

In the second place, at least so far as a considerable share of the modern drama is concerned, the actor must largely play himself, be himself and look himself. It is, therefore, that criticism at bottom often deals with the actor as an individual rather than as a dramatic character. And it thus happens that the actor is the only professional creature extant who is considered critically for his carriage, his clothes, his manner, and his looks. A Heifetz may have one leg, wear rags, and doesn't have to look like a violin. A Paderewski may be a hunchback, come out stark naked, and doesn't have to look like a piano. But no matter; it is what and how they play that alone matters. Not so an actor. And it is because of this that personal vanity must inevitably be part and parcel of him and his work. It doesn't hurt an actor much if he has an intelligence quotient equal to that of a half-wit. But he is out of luck if a couple of his front teeth are missing, if he is knock-kneed, if he loses part of his nose in an accident, or if he can't see without glasses.

There is, as I have freely allowed, always the agreeable tenth exception, but the actor in general must — in the third place — be something of a hypocrite if he is to be popular in his profession and get along in it. The actor who would dare to tell the truth to other actors would promptly be an outcast. It is the tradition among actors that they must flatter one another's performances, however atrocious the latter may be. An actor may honestly believe that a brother mime's performance smells to heaven, but just the same it is professionally expected of him that he tell the other that he is nothing short of magnificent. He must, before an opening performance, send him a telegram predicting that he can't fail to drive all the critics crazy with joy and, after it, he must rush backstage and, even if the actor has been so bad that even the stagehands got colic, must warmly congratulate him on having given the performance of his life. If he fails in his accepted duty he will be put down as an envious bounder and other actors will decline to nod to him when they pass him on the street.

At least three plays out of every five that the modern actor is called upon to act in are pretty trashy affairs. Yet night in and night out, if they enjoy any sort of run, which alas they now and then do, he must devote himself interestedly and even passionately to cuckooing their idiotic lines, sentiments and emotions. Unless, therefore, an actor is fortunate enough to play in the dramas of the better and more literate playwrights — and there are few such lucky actors — he becomes in time like a layman condemned night in and night out to reading aloud a novel of Laura Jean Libbey's. Meditate the corruption of mind that must inevitably follow any such catastrophe!

In the fifth place, we have the clannishness of actors, an inheritance from days long past when the actor was a pariah and when clannishness was forced upon him. Although today he is free to mingle with persons outside the profession, in the great majority of cases he doesn't, preferring to associate with his fellows in the histrionic racket. This obviously narrows his interests, his experience, his breadth of vision, and even his conversation down to a civilized and cultural minimum. He thinks greasepaint, feels greasepaint, and talks greasepaint. And after a while he becomes simply another automaton in a little pink world of automatons.

Commenting on Huxley's animadversions and defending the actor against them, St. John Ervine has answered that, taking one with another, the character of actors is superior to that of, say, authors. You will not, he avers, find a meaner and more envious parcel of human beings on earth than a group of writers. Without venturing to contradict him, save to pause long enough to wonder just what kind of writers he has been associating with, it seems to me that he carefully, even painstakingly, elects to overlook one rather important point. Allowing for the sake of the argument that writers are so much vermin, it remains nevertheless that it isn't their profession that makes them so. If and when they are found to be vermin, Nature has beaten the literary profession to the job. They were lice before they wrote their first line. The actor, on the other hand, may be a relatively normal and meritorious fellow before he takes up the acting profession. It is the acting profession that does the damage to him.

Still another reason for this damage and corruption of character is the generic nature of the theatre itself. The theatre is the house of make-believe and actors are its boarders. They eat and drink make-believe year in and year out until almost all that is real and natural in them becomes gradually metamorphosed into artificiality. It may be charming artificiality, but it is artificiality nonetheless.

It is often said that one can spot an actor a block away, and with sound reason. There is something, however small, that quickly stamps him as an actor and as different from the generality of men. It may be a slightly histrionic walk; it may be a slight theatricality of dress; it may be nothing at all that one can exactly put one's finger on. But there is that about the fellow that gives out the unerring hint that he is an actor. A stranger to the American scene and not aware of their indentity might perhaps mistake Theodore Dreiser, Ernest Hemingway and Eugene O'Neill for Tammany politicians, street-car conductors, chiropractors or even Ku Kluxers, but he would certainly never mistake them for actors. But the same stranger encountering nine actors out of ten would surely never mistake them for anything but actors. I do not mean to imply that this is to the actors' discredit. It is simply that whereas other men's professions preserve to them their individuality, the acting profession tends to make most of its practitioners very much alike, if not in detail at least in general composition.

Once again, I repeat that there are honorable exceptions. But I have a feeling that in even the honorable exceptions there is a trace of the greasepaint poison.

H

HAMLET. We have seen many and various Hamlets in later years. In Fritz Leiber's interpretation the melancholy prince was a descendant of Robert B. Mantell who had matriculated at a Düsseldorf stock company theatre under the impression that it was the University of Wittenberg. In Walter Hampden's he was Professor William Lyon Phelps with a hangover. In John Barrymore's he was alternately Boris Karloff crossed with Henry E. Dixey and Papa Maurice Barrymore crossed with Richard Bennett. In Leslie Howard's he was the Duke of Windsor out to get Stanley Baldwin and wife, with Winston Churchill playing both Rosencrantz and Guildenstern. In John Gielgud's he was Lord Alfred Douglas having an exciting melodramatic cup of tea with Beverley Nichols. In Basil Sydney's modern dress version he had a considerable share of the intelligence that Maurice Evans gives him, and also a poise and power above the average. Sydney's interpretation, in point of fact, was critically pretty good. But, pretty good or not, there has been seen none, I think, on the latter-day American stage that comes anywhere near to matching Evans'.

In his unabridged presentation of the tragedy, this Evans' Hamlet abjures all the egregious devices and greasepaint colorings more usually associated with a performance of the rôle. Clearly and sharply, like a saw gradually and cruelly cutting through the character's icy intelligence, it slowly engenders the saw's incidental accretion of heat and gives us the perfect picture of a cold mentality sundered from its equilibrium by a hot emotionalism. The customary elocutionary exercises, the customary anatomical quivers, the customary struts and bounds, the customary stomachic growls and laryngeal gargles are missing. It is, in short, the best thought-out and the most thoroughly rounded-out and convincing Hamlet of our day.

If, parenthetically, anyone thinks that this is greasing an actor somewhat too voluptuously, I ask him to hang his head in shame when he makes comparison with the following, written some months ago about the late Robert Loraine by my distinguished brother, Mr. St. John Ervine, in the London *Observer:* " Who that was present on the terrible night at the Apollo, in 1927, when Loraine revived *Cyrano de Bergerac* in a succession of troubles, will ever forget the calmness — I had almost written the majesty — of the man when, as he prepared to die in the last act, the scenery fell and he had to interrupt his dying to hold it up? He went to the back of the stage and sustained the falling flats until the stagehands could repair them, and then he returned to his seat and died like a gentleman. No one laughed or indicated by a flicker of an eyelid that anything untoward had happened. Such was the authority of this extraordinary actor! "

If it was the authority of an extraordinary actor rather than the delicatesse and politeness of a fashionable London audience, to say nothing, surely, of a deficiency in irresistible if deplorable low humor, that was responsible for the absence of laughter and eyelid-flickering, I shall be glad to present you, my dear St. John, with skeleton keys to my wine closet, my safe deposit box, and my old clasp-album with the pictures of Lydia Thompson, Lillian Russell, Pauline Hall, Marie Jansen, Madge Lessing, and Marie Doro (that one will wobble you, old boy!) in tights.

HARLEM. Harlem, which for years engaged the attention of countless exotic thrill seekers, both American and foreign, has presently lapsed into so benign a chastity that its one and only remaining sensation is a revivalist clergyman. The road that began with Florence Mills has ended with Father Divine. Like Chinatown, the once famous Negro arrondissement of song and story is today largely a memory, and a sigh. Closed are most of the celebrated old hot spots; gone are most of the characters who gave the quarter its reputation; desolated is its air of the sounds of former revelry. Jazz has been supplanted by hymns; the rattle of clogging feet has been succeeded by the rattle of coins in revival collection plates; and wickedness has given way to virtue. And as virtue is hardly an expedient box-office magnet, the Quartier Nègre, except for a few left over spots that still struggle pathetically to work up echoes of the gay and saucy past, now wears the aspect of a blackface minstrel troupe forlornly looking around for a job and a place to sleep.

Harlem's death was brought about by several causes. In the first place, the curiosity of night-time prowling Stanleys and Livingstones as to Afro-American life and entertainment was dissipated by their gradual discovery that, while one naughty dance may be exhilaratingly naughty, two or three hundred naughty dances are likely to become depressingly tiresome. In the second place, the moving into Harlem of white capital and its conversion of the Negro night-clubs and dance dumps, formerly authentic, into cheap duplicates of the downtown Caucasian establishments removed all the atmosphere and color from them. In the third place, most of the best Harlem entertainers, finding that they could make more money elsewhere, moved downtown into the Broadway and other night-clubs and into various theatrical revues, and thus left Harlem to their inferior colleagues. And, in the fourth place, Europe itself had got such an overdose of imported colored entertainment that when Europeans, who once flocked to Harlem by the thousands, came over here they were only too happy to stay away from it.

The sight-seer who used to go to Harlem to see Ethel Waters now sees her at the fashionable Empire Theatre. The sight-seer who formerly wanted to get a popped eyeful of physical contortions at the old Cotton Club in Harlem can now get the same thing at the new Cotton Club at Broadway and Forty-eighth street. In a dozen downtown night-clubs and restaurants he can hear the colored jazz and swing bands that once he could hear only in Harlem. If it was good old mammy Southern fried chicken that he craved and used to find at Tilly's in Harlem, he knows that he can now get it in the very midst of the city, for Tilly has moved into the white district only a block or so away from the Guild Theatre, that residence of pale-face art. In point of fact, aside from the Father Divine mentioned, about the only conceivable things that might lure the sight-seer back to Harlem at the present moment are the Savoy Ballroom, a Negro dance hall where he may observe the colored lads and their best girls hoof rather more exuberantly than their white brothers and sisters at the Pierre or Biltmore, if rather less so than at the Havana-Madrid and Conga; a seedy cellar restaurant with its " Creole " chorus girls slightly less formal than the cream-skinned girls at the Paradise restaurant on Broadway; and one or two dingy holes in the wall where hired stock companies of colored ladies and gentlemen sit around looking very dreamy and faraway and smoke small Pittsburgh stogies which the dumps' ballyhooers whisperingly confide to the visiting boobs are marijuana.

Harlem, in short, is no longer Harlem because Harlem has scattered itself all over the rest of New York and Europe. The English get it in London, what with the night-clubs there full of erstwhile Harlem jazz artists and hoofers and warblers in swanky evening clothes, and Lew Leslie's theatrical presentations of Harlem colored revues, and more former Lenox Avenue piano pounders and blues singers than one can count. The French similarly get it in their Paris night-clubs and supper restaurants, as well as in any number of such stage shows as *Harlem Black Birds* playing at the Alcazar and unloading all the old Harlem stuff from Louis Douglas' fancy hoofing to imitations of Paul Robeson. And,

Americans get it in such large and surfeiting doses all over New York that at least one night-club proprietor last season made a lot of money by advertising " White Entertainers Only ".

Fifteen years ago, when Harlem was in its prime, it offered a novelty that only the Chinatown of San Francisco in its heyday could match. It was natural and unaffected then, and its racial dancing and singing and general deportment exercised all the strange effect that honest strangeness always does. There were scores of places to which one might go and where one might see such mad and untamed physical frenzy and hear such boisterous vocal performances as the white sections of the city had not known. But today what little remains of Harlem is like a white Broadway turkey show blacked up. The Negro entertainers sing the songs of the white man's Tin Pan Alley and of the Hollywood musical-film factories, dance strainful imitations of Fred Astaire, Ray Bolger and Eleanor Powell, drink mixtures tonily patterned after the formulæ of Racquet club and El Morocco cocktails, and perform in places decorated to look as much as possible like the white night-clubs and supper restaurants in the East Fifties. When one reflects that in recent years the only things about Harlem that caused any talk at all were a Negro production of *Macbeth* and another of *Androcles and the Lion*, both under the auspices of the Federal Theatre Project, one may appreciate the change that has come over the quarter. The next step, unless all signs fail, will probably be a Bach festival.

The old entertainment aristocracy of Harlem today has nothing to do with Harlem. It looks down upon it as something beneath its new position and affluence, and goes back, if it goes at all, only for an annual sentimental glimpse of the scenes of its childhood in the amusement world. Josephine Baker has become a Paris pet, has married an uncolored gentleman of title and, when she condescends to visit America, appears with magnificent snootiness in a Winter Garden show as an associate of Fannie Brice. Ethel Waters sings at fashionable parties, plays in a revue in which she is starred with Lady Peel, and acts in drama on the same stage once occupied by Maude Adams and Ethel Barrymore. Paul Robeson plays Shakespeare in London, even as John Gielgud, and sings at Town Hall in New York, and is a big-wig in Hollywood. Bill Robinson dances with Shirley Temple and engages in Gilbert and Sullivan. Gladys Bentley hobnobs with the high muckamucks in the Argentine. The Theatre Guild has put on a Negro folk opera that drafts all the good singing voices in Harlem that have not already been drafted elsewhere. And Johnny, the famous Johnny whose piano playing once held Harlem in thrall, got to Berlin years ahead of Hitler. It is that way with most all the rest. Small wonder that Carl Van Vechten nowadays goes to bed directly after dinner.

HAYES. There is something about Helen Hayes that most of our other actresses of her age and experience — indeed, of even more than her age and experience — completely miss. It may be an inner warm womanliness; it may be a dramatic heart beating in a theatrical mind; it may be that little-girl spirit that has ever been a vital asset to the world's best actresses of whatever vintage; it may be a natural and ex officio sincerity that siphons itself into her stage person; it may be any one or ten of a dozen things. That it is, above them all, a genuine acting talent we of course know. But it is these other qualities, too, that must surely and so brilliantly differentiate and distinguish her from the rank and file of director puppets, greasepaint crooners, big chest-tone purveyors, and superficially competent old war horses of all ages who so often drive us out into the cold alley to warm up.

HECHT. Ben Hecht is one of Hollywood's foremost citizens. Some years ago he promised to be something of a figure in American drama, but his immersion in film composition has apparently given his pristine talent the works. Like many another playwright who has sold himself down the Swinee river, Hecht celebrated his return to the theatre with an exhibit desperately calculated to persuade us that Hollywood hadn't made the slightest dent in him. With this purpose ferociously in view, he superciliously abjured the straightforward drama of conflict and action as something suitable only to the lowly screen and permitted himself the treat of going on an intellectual bender. The result was a play that, while a teetotaler in the matter of drama, was so boozy with rhetoric and so bibacious with Brown Derby animadversions on love, life, sex, politics, religion, and what not that even the most loyal theatregoer suffered a painful ringing in the ears before the evening was half over and battled with an impulse to get out, run around to a film parlor, and seek some less pretentious, less verbose, less postureful, and more relieving entertainment in one of Hecht's melodramatic Hollywood movies.

Hecht who, with Charles MacArthur, his frequent collaborator, has spent a considerable share of his life playing pranks at the expense of others, in this instance unwittingly played one on himself. It was called *To Quito and Back* and it gave Hecht not only the hot-foot, the hot-seat, and a large gob of itch-powder, but in addition dropped a hot penny down his collar and simultaneously gave him the old fraternity grip with a smear of Limburger in its hand. It happened this way. Hecht, as has been intimated, is the Bright Boy of Hollywood, the Schopenhauer of the Sam Goldwyn lot, the Voltaire of the Paramount studios and the Oscar Wilde of Astoria, who two years ago published a statement — after signing a fat new contract with Goldwyn — proclaiming that the theatre and its drama couldn't hope to compare with the matchless art of Mr. Goldwyn's movies. Having made the statement, he thereupon cockily set himself to the composition of a drama which, he felt certain, would prove that anyone could write a satisfactory, nay, even a relatively remarkable play for the theatre with one's left hand, whereas the writing of a good movie, for all the habitual sneers, was something else again and required the full-time genius of even such a genius as himself. It would, hee haw, be a corking joke at the theatre's expense, chuckled Hecht between a couple of mordant quotations from Remy de Gourmont, and wouldn't he have the time of his life, after his play proved it, derisively thumbing his nose at those who considered his statement, in view of his Goldwyn connection, both pretty apocryphal and ridiculous, hee, haw, ha!

This *To Quito and Back* was Hecht's cocksure challenge, his glove slapped across the theatre's face, and was *To Quito and Back* a pratt-fall! Unanimously dubbed pretentious blah by every critic, reviewer and even columnist in practice and setting its audience to such a loud snoring that the Guild Theatre on the opening night sounded like a cage of elephants to whom Charlie MacArthur had fed lighted cigarettes in lieu of peanuts, it eloquently attested to what Hollywood had done to Hecht, however indirectly. Trying vaingloriously to wrench himself away from his Hollywood moorings and, for all his posturing, trying with every ounce of his resources, he revealed himself as a writer who had apparently lost all his one-time understanding of the theatre and drama and who imagined that a good play for the metropolitan stage may be handily achieved simply by writing it over the heads of the Hollywood lowbrows. And then — following the prevalent principle of other highly paid Hollywood scenario writers who have returned to the theatre — by intimating a crested indifference to Sam Goldwyn and his big weekly salary checks, and incidentally persuading folk that he had not been contaminated by Hollywood mazuma, through an incorporation into his play of a defence of Communism. No, Ben, old fellow, it can't be done. *To Quito and Back* was merely the Hollywood idea of a very intellectual play and the New York idea of a very juvenile and very bad one.

These are hard words? Not at all. Hecht himself now indicates that he fully appreciates their truth by writing a second play for the theatre (in collaboration with his old buddy, MacArthur) that doesn't in the least even pretend to dramatic quality and that in every respect is frankly and entirely Hollywood. Its title is *Ladies and Gentlemen*. Hecht is himself again.

HELLMAN. Lillian Hellman's latest play, *The Little Foxes*, provides fresh evidence of its author's high position among American women writers for the stage. Both in *The Children's Hour* and in this exhibit — even, indeed, in certain phases of her defective *Days to Come* — she indicates a dramatic mind, an eye to character, a fundamental strength, and a complete and unremitting integrity that are rare among her native playwriting sex. Her dramaturgic equipment is infinitely superior to Susan Glaspell's, her surgery of and grip on character are infinitely superior to Lula Vollmer's, and compared with her Rachel Crothers is merely a shrewd old girl in a box-office dispensing prettily water-colored parlor tracts. Some of her other sisters enjoy pleasant little talents but there is none in the whole kit and caboodle whose work shows so courageous and unflinching an adherence to the higher and finer standards of drama. Once she has succeeded in mastering her present weaknesses — a periodic confusion of melodramatic bitterness with suggestive tragedy, intensified and unrelieved acerbity with mounting drama, and a skeletonization of episode with dramatic economy — she will find herself occupying a really distinguished critical place in our theatre.

Her most recent play is a scrutiny of social and economic changes in the South at the turn of the present century. Related in terms of a middle-class family of rapacious and conniving knaves bent upon outdoing not only one another but upon sacrificing all that is proud and fine in the tradition of the old southland to the new economic slavery and the new capitalistic greed, it may flippantly be described as a Dodie Smith nightmare. It may also be less flippantly described as the very best illustration of the difference between the current cheap and squashy family drama calculatedly manufactured by English female pastry cooks and the fond intention, at least, of American women like this Hellman to bring to the stage that inner inviolable dramatic vitality and thematic meat which London critics on brief excusions to these shores have often in the past so offendedly and patriotically minimized and derogated. From first to last, *The Little Foxes* betrays not an inch of compromise, not a sliver of a sop to the comfortable acquiescence of Broadway or Piccadilly, not the slightest token that its author has had anything in her purpose but writing the truest and most honest play on her theme that it was possible for her to write.

The central characters are a woman and her two brothers who individually and apart brook no interference with their selfish determinations to get for themselves what they want out of family, community, finance, and worldly position. The woman is hard, disillusioned, and merciless to the point of contributing to the death of her invalid husband in order to perch herself on top of the heap. The brothers descend to perjury, theft, and even to veiled threat of murder accusation to dislodge her from it. (In the handling of character, the ghost of Strindberg here and there unmistakably and occasionally a bit too obviously peers over Miss Hellman's shoulder as in the treatment of theme the ghost of Ibsen — momentarily, too, the ghost of the Pinero of *The Thunderbolt* — here and there edges the spook of Strindberg to one side.) The conclusion resolves itself into a temporary triumph for the wily, slate-hearted female but with the evil of the money-hungry brothers' machinations a cloud darkening her future. And out of the parable of boiling acid there emerges the disgust and defiance of a new, young generation that throws into the face of mankind the challenge of human decency, fairness, equity, and honor.

Where the play partly defeats its potential, proper, and full effect is in the grinding monotony of its emotional drive, in its periodic over-elaborate melodramatic countenance, and in its failure to invest its explosion with that complete sense of tragic purge which is the mark and nobility of the drama of Melpomene. It strikes the note of bitterness so steadily and loudly that, when the moment for purging exaltation comes, the psychic and emotional ear is too deadened to hear it even were it there. But just the same it is a play 'way above the general and a credit to its author and to American dramatic writing.

Hepburn. Katharine Hepburn, that anatomical honeysuckle, who was an acting disaster in *The Lake* and drew down upon herself the sneers of the critics, has now been proclaimed by them, on the score of her performance in Philip Barry's *The Philadelphia Story*, a genuine histrionic artiste. In this, we once again observe how much jazbo enters into the critical appraisal of acting talent. That Miss Hepburn is effective in her rôle is to be granted. But that she has overnight developed from the bad actress of *The Lake* into a highly gifted one is open to a large skepticism on the part of anyone who at one and the same time sharply appreciates the acting craft and is privy to the inside on Miss Hepburn's successful performance.

That inside is this: the Hepburn rôle was tailored to the actress by Barry in every last detail and particular. It was written and re-written, edited and re-edited, tricked and re-tricked with painstaking shrewdness so that each and every one of her acting shortcomings might be either eliminated or cleverly glossed over and so that her visual virtues might be thrust constantly into the foreground and help further to throw criticism off its guard. It is whispered to me that the playwright actually spent two months in close professional contact with the actress, noting carefully every attractive gesture she made, every awkwardly graceful movement of her body, every little odd quirk of her head and every effective dart of her eyes, and that he incorporated them all into the rôle he was writing for her. A line was interrupted to allow her to swing her lithe figure across the stage; another was so contrived that a toss of her lovely brown hair would pictorially embellish it; still another was so framed that it would permit her, while seated, relevantly to cross her knees and display her pretty legs to the critical professors out front. If her voice was found unable properly to cope with a line, it was altered until she could handle it nicely. If a scene might betray her acting weakness, it was tricked to conceal her limitations. The natural harshness of the actress' personality was converted into a dramatic virtue by dramatizing it in terms of a harsh stage character. Her personal metallic chill was made the character's metallic chill. Her " spoiled darling " air in her extra-stage manifestations, which had brought her an often hostile press, was metamorphosed into a spoiled darling dramatic character.

And so it went. The result was, naturally and almost automatically, sure-fire; but when it comes to hailing Miss Hepburn a remarkably developed and authentic actress on the score of it, one critic politely asks to be excused. A real actress does not have to rely upon the legerdemain of the cinema cutting-room and on a cameraman who affectionately and entirely concerns himself with her two or three photogenic angles.

However and nevertheless —

Miss Hepburn, while still not much in the way of an actress, is still an immensely decorative and attractive young woman, and one blessed to boot with the gift of fascinating the attention and making it her own. Although so far as being a Hepburn fan goes I have always been of the electric variety, with its attendant coolth, all this is nevertheless as it should be. Our stage is full of women who can act and in the process often bore the pantaloons off an audience, but it is pretty short of girls who, whatever their competence, can massage the eye and imagination into a melliferous and schnapsy reaction.

If, perchance, you think such remarks grievously uncritical and unbecoming to one whose profession it should be, among other things, to support the art of acting until hell freezes over, please to consider yourself something of a cad. Acting, whatever the academicians say, is, as I have hereinbefore oracled, anything that gets over satisfactorily to an audience, even though professional actors, sitting in judgment, may moan mygod and work themselves into an indignant fit. Miss Hepburn, who can't play even third fiddle to many an established actress, gets over thus satisfactorily, and that is all there is to it. What is more, she not only impresses the lay audiences and brings home the box-office bacon but apparently also deceives the reviewers (who like everybody else fall under the influence of evocative feminine attractiveness and appeal) into the conviction that, as a histrionic artiste, she is rather top stuff. One of them, happily possessed of a more enthusiastic appreciation of feminine oomph than most of his colleagues, actually now proclaims her as one " who must be placed among the important actresses on the American stage ". So far as your humble servant is concerned, she mustn't be placed among them at all, but just the same he would rather watch her than a number of the others who are acceptedly big potatoes.

Miss Hepburn's Barry-made vehicle is a shuffling and uncertain job of playmaking suggesting a series of card tricks by a parlor entertainer trying to imitate the digital virtuosity of a Nate Leipzig or Cardini, or — more dramatically relevant — of a Langdon Mitchell. The story, in brief, deals with a spoiled little daughter of the rich who gradually discerns her own hollowness, achieves a sounder set of standards by which to live, and comes into a warm and understanding womanhood. This story, hardly a virginal one, Barry relates in terms of characters hardly less familiar, the only relatively fresh one being a humorously sophisticated brat who, incidentally, bears a close resemblance to the saucy papoose conceived by Lillian Hellman seven years ago in the uncommonly amusing skits which she contributed to *The American Spectator*. The rest are largely out of a score of stage drawing-rooms: the aforementioned flighty society girl who is given the rough philosophical works by the homespun son of the working classes (the only fillip being that she doesn't once come on in a riding habit), the daughter of the working classes who best understands the aforesaid son of the working classes and to whom he returns in the end, the rich old papa who seeks romance away from his depressing fireside in the person of a Russian dancer, the snobbish fiancé who ultimately gets the mitten, the society girl's divorced husband who sits around biding his time until she comes to her senses and takes him again unto her bosom, and so on. It is Barry's sly dodge, however, to conceal the fundamental obviousness of these character stencils from his average customer by treating them elliptically and, further, by now and again causing them suddenly to act in a manner foreign to their natures, which any more honest, if duller, playwright would never permit. This chicanery, embellished with intermittent schnitzels of humor and the presence of Miss Hepburn's flying brown hair, comely features, swell figure, and beautiful Valentina dresses, goes to constitute a show for which the majority of the critics no less than the other boobs fell like a ton of bricks.

HINT TO AN AMBITIOUS YOUNG MAN. If I were a young man with a few dollars in my pocket and with an interest in the theatre who wished to make a name for himself and a lot of money, both with a minimum of effort, I should promptly become a theatrical producer. Becoming one, my procedure would be this. First, I would go around and see nine-tenths of the already practising producers. Second, I would determine from them the kind of plays they wouldn't touch with a ten-foot pole. Third, I would add up the total of such plays and determine which topped the list. Fourth, I would then go around and see the producers whose qualms and dislikes thus headed the list and would find out just how violent they were in their antipathy to the particular plays. Fifth, I would thereupon go back home and check the plays at the top of the list which had received their most emphatic blackballs. Sixth and finally, I would then immediately and without further ado produce those plays and thereafter sit back, smoke two-dollar cigars, take things easily, and live off the fat of the land.

The majority of our producers' ideas as to what will and what will not go with the public are and pretty nearly always have been the kind that the road to the poorhouse is paved with. And it has, accordingly, generally been either the young or contemptuous older producer who, with a mind of his own, has walked off with the money. Twenty-seven established New York producers peremptorily rejected *The Barretts of Wimpole Street* on the theory that the public would not be interested in a play about a couple of literary people, and poets at that, whereupon one put it on and made half a million dollars with it. Thirty-odd years before, all but one producer in New York argued that the public would never for a moment stand for a play that began with a funeral and ended with a suicide, and the one put it on — it was Clyde Fitch's *The Climbers* — and, though the other producers seemed to be right for the first two weeks of its engagement, eventually amplified his bank account with it.

You can't ever fool an audience and get away with 'it, his fellow producers warned George M. Cohan, so George wrote *Seven Keys to Baldpate* and made a small fortune. The American public doesn't care for an evening made up of one-act plays, they told Noël Coward, so Noël produced not one but three programs of one-acters and with his *Tonight at 8:30*, as he billed them, also garnered a small fortune. You can't get away with a heroine who is deliberately contrived to bore all the other characters on the stage to death because it is a theatrical axiom that she will also bore the audience to death, they informed Clare Boothe, so she gave her *Kiss the Boys Goodbye* with heavy misgivings to Brock Pemberton who said thehell with such bosh, put it on, and made all kinds of money out of it.

A play without suspense is destined to be a sure flop, say the producers. Thornton Wilder's *Our Town,* which has about as much suspense, in the accepted dramatic sense, as a baseball game played by two women's teams, thereupon confounded them by being a big hit. The producers shook their heads over a theme dealing with sexual perversion, and *The Children's Hour* came along and stood 'em up for six hundred and ninety-one performances. The public was sick of war plays and war plays no longer stood the ghost of a chance, they argued, and along came *Journey's End* at the very height of their positiveness and chalked up a hit of resounding proportions. The public, according to these same statisticians, had had so many plays about Hollywood that another one wouldn't stand the faintest chance, whereupon George Abbott put on *Boy Meets Girl* and it ran for six hundred and sixty-nine performances.

People, it was maintained by the wise men, don't like plays dealing with actors — and *The Royal Family* embarrassed the wise men by drawing the aforesaid people in large crowds. Vaudeville is dead, cuckooed the same wise men, and *Hellzapoppin,* which was vaudeville from start to finish, wowed the town. And *The Streets of Paris,* which followed it and which was similarly composed of vaudeville acts, discountenanced the sages further by attracting such mobs of customers that its producers, to clear the lobby, were compelled to raise the admission fee from the original three dollars and thirty cents to four dollars and forty cents.

It is dangerous, believed the producers, to attempt a love story between a very young girl and an old man; it is not only dangerous to the box-office, they argued, but slightly offensive to audiences. And then *Accent on Youth* proceeded to run prosperously for almost an entire season. Episodic plays are a bad gamble, confidently stated the masterminds — and *Victoria Regina* ran for so long that Burns Mantle, who keeps check on such theatrical figures, stopped counting. Plays about death are also a bad gamble, contended the producers, and rudely paying no heed to their wisdom *Death Takes a Holiday* and *On Borrowed Time* made all kinds of money. And then, further to discomfit them, *Outward Bound* contemptuously revived itself and was a huge success.

Mythological plays, bah!, sniffed the box-office savants, whereupon *Amphitryon 38* kept box-office employees busy for many months. Plays of sordid ugliness, bah! bah!, even more emphatically sniffed the Broadway brain trust, whereupon *Tobacco Road* started gaily on a five-year run that at this writing promises to break all existing American theatrical records. Beware of plays touching on Catholic matters, ominously warned the Aldiborontephocophornios, and Eugene O'Neill wrote and Arthur Hopkins produced *Anna Christie* to wide public acclaim. "What! An audience asked to go to the theatre at five o'clock and sit in it until 11:30. Crazy! " derided the producers. And *Strange Interlude,* disappointing them, took the town by storm. "Well," they reluctantly admitted, "maybe you can get away with it once as a stunt, but you can't repeat it." So O'Neill and the Theatre Guild practically repeated it with *Mourning Becomes Electra.* "The public apparently won't stomach a play in which a minister falls for a whore," moaned the producer of *Rain* while it was being tried out before sparse audiences at the Garrick Theatre in Philadelphia, " and anyone who wants a slice of it can buy it cheap." A week later *Rain* opened in New York, was a sensational success with the public, and ran for six hundred and forty-eight performances.

I could go on with dozens upon dozens of further examples, but I assume that by this time the young man I mentioned in the beginning has already opened up an office and is ready for business.

HOLLYWOOD ETHIC. Mr. Rupert Hughes is one of Hollywood's leading movie scenario writers. At an Authors' Club luncheon out there, the Los Angeles *Times* quotes him as having delivered himself of this statement: " The fact is, as every student of that literary era knows, that Shakespeare and half a dozen of his collaborators did almost precisely as Hollywood scenarists do now. Usually they began by stealing a story and then worked it out in conferences like our story conferences."

HOLLYWOOD LOGIC. That Hollywood does something to the minds and previous condition of education of even its more literate denizens is once again indicated in the case of Mr. Nunnally Johnson. This Nunnally is a fellow greatly superior to the general run of the herring out there, yet his protracted residence in the California film swamp has apparently taken its toll of him.

Katharine Cornell, it may be recalled, when not long ago told by a film producer, who was trying unsuccessfully to persuade her to do a movie, that the movies, unlike the stage, were a guarantee of immortality for a player, arched her eyebrows very prettily and sweetly inquired of him: " And how many five-year-old pictures have *you* seen lately? " His Hollywood pride and patriotism hurt by Miss Cornell's retort, Mr. Johnson, a loyal Hollywood son, galloped hot-foot to the movies' defence as follows: " Why didn't the movie producer ask her who is going to see her in *The Green Hat* these days? Or in *Alien Corn*? That is, if she was implying that the stage is the vehicle to immortality. Or, to cover a wider field, what five-year-old plays with anybody at all in them has Miss Cornell been seeing lately? "

Permit me to re-educate our Hollywood patriot. A few of the many five-year-old and very considerably more ancient plays (with anybody at all in them) that Miss Cornell and all the rest of us this side of Hollywood have been seeing lately are the following: *Hamlet, The Trojan Women, The Drunkard, Hedda Gabler, The Country Wife, Othello, King Richard II, An Enemy of the People, London Assurance, Candida* (with Miss Cornell herself in it), *St. Joan* (with Miss Cornell herself in it), *Romeo and Juliet* (with Miss Cornell herself in it), *Abie's Irish Rose, Damaged Goods, As You Like It, Henry IV, Amphitryon 38, Julius Caesar, Antony and Cleopatra, A Doll's House, The Shoemakers' Holiday, Jeremiah, The Bridal Crown, The Sea Gull, The Merry Wives of Windsor, The Wild Duck, The Circle, Heartbreak House, Outward Bound, Lightnin', Journey's End, They Knew What They Wanted, Danton's Death, Three Sisters,* and *The Importance of Being Earnest.* We've seen them all in the last three seasons.

Proceeds Mr. Johnson: " You've got to take it on faith that Garrick, the Booths, Mrs. Siddons, the Kembles, et al., were great artists. They have the surest of all immortalities, because nobody can check on them. It would be pretty embarrassing all around if by some miracle a reel of Edwin Booth emerged from the past and it turned out that he was the Edmund Lowe of his day."

One no more has to take the eminence of the great actors of the past on faith than one has to take that of the great dancers, singers, bull-fighters, jockeys, prize-fighters, orators, or even lovers. That is, unless, like Henry Ford, one believes all history is a liar. The impression the actors made on the greatest critics of their times, on the foremost writers of their times, and on journalists and novelists and dramatists generally are recorded in living type for all to read. And since when has the printed word of a Hazlitt, a Lewes, a Lamb, or a Coleridge been less acceptable evidence than an old Biograph, Vitagraph, Selig, Essanay, or Thanhouser film? As a matter of fact, if an actor's or actress' immortality depended not upon the stage but upon the screen, where would the persistent reputation of Sarah Bernhardt be today if the old Mercanton film, *Queen Elizabeth,* were to be offered as

evidence of her artistry? In point of truth, to look at any of
the old films of bygone dramatic actors is to be skeptical of
even the share of talent which the stage indicated they had.
If you doubt it, get them to run off for you James O'Neill's
film, *Monte Cristo,* or James K. Hackett's *The Prisoner of
Zenda,* or Mrs. Fiske's *Tess of the D'Urbervilles,* or William
H. Crane's *David Harum.* One or two of these mimes may
have been indifferent stage actors, true enough, but on the
screen they were revealed as the worst conceivable kind of
hams. Go to celebrated picture actors of the past themselves.
For all their registered films who today is substantially con-
scious of the histrionic immortality of Louise Glaum, Anna
Q. Nillson, Dorothy Dalton, Barbara La Marr, Maurice Cos-
tello, Agnes Ayres, Evalyn Brent, Francis X. Bushman, Lon
Chaney, Nils Asther, W. S. Hart, Ben Lyon, Bebe Daniels,
Billie Dove, Ethel Clayton, Corinne Griffith, Mary Miles
Minter, Alice Terry, Owen Moore, Olga Petrova, Wallace
Reid, Louise Fazenda, John Bunny, Pola Negri, Vilma
Banky, Flora Finch, Rod La Rocque, Norman Terry, Monroe
Salisbury, Earle Williams, Carlyle Blackwell, Alice Joyce,
Ormi Hawley, Blanche Sweet, J. Warren Kerrigan, Romaine
Fielding, James Cruze, Muriel Ostriche, Edith Storey, Lil-
lian Walker, or any of the rest of them, all one-time great
film audience favorites? Rudolf Valentino's films, not long
ago reshown around the country, drew derisory howls. Gloria
Swanson's, Norma Talmadge's, Mary Pickford's, Richard
Barthelmess' and John Gilbert's are safely buried from the
public gaze. *The Birth of a Nation,* long considered the
screen's greatest masterpiece, drew only loud laughs when
it was recently re-exhibited.

One may, in short, achieve immortality in a grave, but
hardly in a can. "It would be pretty embarrassing all around
if by some miracle a reel of Edwin Booth emerged from the
past and it turned out that he was the Edmund Lowe of his
day," says Mr. Johnson. It wouldn't be embarrassing at all.
It is a foregone fact that if a reel of Booth did miraculously

emerge from the past he would in all likelihood seem to have been the Edmund Lowe of his day. The screen, with the passing of even a relatively short time, has a way of making Edmund Lowes out of even the best actors.

HOLLYWOOD MIND. In *Yr Obedient Husband* of two seasons ago we had renewed evidence of the gulf that separates the theatre and Hollywood. Written by an illustrious movie scenario writer, staged by an illustrious movie director, acted by an illustrious movie actor, and produced with illustrious movie money, it got no nearer to the heart and soul and quality of the theatre than the greatest movie ever made gets to even the better grade second-rate drama. With the best of intentions, it still showed up the droll incompetence of Hollywood when Hollywood vaingloriously tries to climb to a more exalted art form. And it proved conclusively that what is signal talent in moviedom is only pretty poor side-street talent when it comes to the theatre.

The exhibit afforded a lovely cross section of the Hollywood mind. Desiring to show himself off on the stage, Mr. Fredric March obviously took stock of himself so: " Being a movie actor, I'll have to proceed with caution to protect myself. First, I must select a play with not the slightest suggestion of a movie smell. One dealing with celebrated figures in the world of literature should be safe. It will impress the theatre public with the fact that I am no mere movie actor but a lover of literature, a student of literary history, and a mind above the Hollywood general. I must have a rôle removed from the matinée-idol category, something entirely different from the movie rôles with which I have been identified. The drunken, quarreling, lecherous, bounderish — but mentally brilliant — Richard Steele, that's the ticket! They'll expect me to play an heroic combination of Errol Flynn, Gary Cooper and the other beautiful boys, and will I fool 'em! Secondly, I'll have my wife play opposite me. That'll persuade them of the high moral tone of Hollywood and will lend the proper note of respectability to things. And, thirdly, I'll steer clear of the Hollywood brand of publicity and hire a dignified theatrical press-agent like Richard Maney to give the enterprise the right air. It'll be a wow! "

So far, maybe so good. But then what happened? To write the play, our aspiring movie actor engaged one Jackson, whose previous dreams of dramatic art had been translated largely in terms of screen epics showing Napoleon falling for Greta Garbo and the good earth of China populated to a ponderable degree by Viennese cuties and New York East Side Jewish tragedians. To stage the play, our aspiring movie actor engaged one Cromwell, whose producing genius had long been consecrated to such spiritual exercises as shooting the legs of Marlene Dietrich, the ears of Clark Gable, the curls of Shirley Temple, and the posterior of Mae West. And to act the play, our aspiring movie actor cast for the leading rôle one Fredric March, himself, who for years had been relying upon Hollywood mechanical " mixers " to give his voice the proper modulations, upon carefully chalked stages to check and guard his physical movements, upon countless " retakes " to perfect his scenes, and upon the movie public's lack of knowledge of what constitutes real acting to give him histrionic status. The composite result was visible for a few days in the Broadhurst Theatre. It didn't belong there, even for a few days. Its place was on Sid Grauman's Hollywood screen, with ten thousand dazzling searchlights illuminating the heavens outside and with twenty thousand Hollywood art lovers tumbling all over themselves to get the great Mr. March's autograph.

Last season, having — strangely enough for a Hollywood actor — learned his lesson, Mr. March concluded to leave his subsequent stage career to the theatrical mind of Mr. George Kaufman. Mr. Kaufman put him in Mr. Kaufman's play, *The American Way*, and carefully showed him the difference between Hollywood and dramatic acting. Mr. March worked like a dog to learn the difference, learned it in small part, and gave what was at least a half-way satisfactory performance. And even a half-way satisfactory dramatic performance isn't so bad for even a full-way satisfactory Hollywood actor.

HONORS FOR EVERYBODY. Now that Eugene O'Neill, to the high and complete satisfaction of everyone from the head professor of classic drama at Harvard to the third assistant colored strip-teaser at the Apollo, now that Pearl Buck, to the high and complete satisfaction of the John Day Company, and now that Carl Anderson and Clinton J. Davisson, to the equal satisfaction of the few people who ever previously had heard of them, have been awarded Nobel prizes for literature and physics, everybody in America seems to have been taken care of in the way of prizes and we can sum up the grand total. It is possible that one or two persons, or even animals, have been overlooked in the big dispensation of cheques, ribbons, medals, buttons, sashes, certificates of merit, and gold and silver plaques and cups, but as they will probably have got theirs by the time this appears in print the statistics will be definitive.

It is estimated that in the last four years — when the American giving of prizes first got under way on a wholesale scale — no less than thirty-two million such awards have been bestowed upon Americans of all sorts for one reason or another, sometimes, indeed, for no apparent reason at all. To list the species of the prizes would require at least a half ton of paper and enough type to print *Anthony Adverse* even had it been written by Dreiser. There have been and are prizes for the best novel of the year, the best play of the year, the best poem, the loudest hog-caller, the marathon couple who can dance longest, the biggest pig in Missouri, the most beautiful girl in the scantiest bathing suit, the best tennis, golf, ping-pong and bridge players, the actor or actress who can speak the clearest English, the champion corn husker of Ohio, and the woman who has the most babies. There have been and are awards to the Sunday-school pupil who can recite the Lord's Prayer oftenest in fifteen minutes, the man who has presented more than three books gratis to the Bibliothèque Nationale (he gets the red ribbon of the Legion of Honor), the best short story writer of the year, the man who can ride a bicycle for six days and not fall off it more than eight times, the grower of the largest watermelon in Georgia, the hen that lays the most eggs, the Boy Scout who has never shown up at a meeting without his pants, the man who has bottled more than fifty-six varieties of pickles, and the child under ten who writes the best essay on peace and the utter impossibility of there ever being another war.

But that isn't all, not by any means. There are Congressional medals, honorary college degrees and large cups for bankers, students and sportsmen, blue ribbons for horses, cats and dogs, merit service stripes for policemen, firemen and railroad conductors, letters for athletes, cash awards for literary folk, badges of distinction for the growers of the biggest potatoes, buttons for expert tuna fishermen, laurel wreaths for pole vaulters, high divers and weight throwers, and honorary keys to the city for channel swimmers, aviators, dignitaries with sufficiently long whiskers, baseball players, prize-fighters, cinder track sprinters, and scores of others. There are banquets and eulogizing speeches, together with a handsome gold watch, for everybody who has written a book that has sold more than three thousand copies, for any actor who has played Shakespeare badly over a sufficient period of time, for after-dinner speakers who have managed to survive their fiftieth birthday, for any foreign visitor whose name has appeared in the newspapers half a dozen times and who is rumored to own a dress suit, and for the wives of celebrities who themselves wouldn't be caught dead at a banquet, whether in their honor or anybody else's.

Aside from the gold medals awarded at various fairs to the best ketchup, the best chili sauce and the best peanut butter, a fragmentary list of medals itching yearly to be awarded to someone or other includes the John Fritz medal, the Hoover medal, the Daniel Guggenheim medal, and the Edison, Washington, Spirit of St. Louis, Worcester Reed Warner, Norman, Croes, Douglas, Holley, Saunders, Rudolph Hering and other medals for mining, metallurgical, mechanical, electrical and civil engineers; the Nichols, Chandler, Perkin and Grasselli medals for chemical research; the Laetare medal of Notre Dame for anybody from an actress or an orator to a banker or a doctor; the Franklin, Cresson, Potts, Levy, Henderson, Wetherill and Longstreth medals for everything from discoveries in railroad engineering to essay writing; numerous architects' medals, geographical society medals, radio broadcasting announcers' medals, grape growers' and wine makers' medals, and medals, gold and silver, for greased-pole climbers, flag-pole sitters, potato-sack runners, automobile speed drivers, Holstein cows, wood choppers, hotel orchestras, magazine subscription getters, champion pie eaters, perfect thirty-sixes, rhumba dancers, movie directors, and demons at typewriting.

The craze for awards of all kinds seems to have reached its peak. If it hasn't, the peak must make the Matterhorn's look like an ant-hill's. It is true that the prize business is not peculiar to America. European countries also go in for it, and here and there on a considerable scale, as any Frenchman can tell you. But in no country in the world has it ever approached even remotely the recent gigantic American proportions. A passion on the part of someone to give someone else a ribbon, a button, a medal, or maybe even a big hunk of money for any reason at all seems to have swept the land. It has got to be so that it is next to impossible for a man to come home at night from his work and not find three men in frock coats waiting for him on the doorstep with an award of some kind for him. It may, of course, be little more than a scroll informing him that he has been honored with the post and royal purple sash of Grand Beglerbeg of the Exalted and Noble Order of Beglerbegs or a silk American flag attesting to the fact that he sold more tickets to the policemen's annual ball and oyster roast than anybody else, but it is an award, an honor, a mark of distinction, nonetheless. At least in the minds of the presenters and donors.

Americans who do not happen to have enough money to spare for a cup or even a ribbon to present to someone horn into the award business by composing lists of the ten best this and that. There are currently so many of such annual lists of ten bests that the only one thus far missing seems to be a list of the ten best makers of lists of ten bests. There are lists of the ten best plays, the ten best novels, the ten best dressed women, the ten best dressed men, the ten most beautiful women, the ten best short stories, the ten best restaurants, the ten best hostesses, the ten greatest gourmets, the ten best actors, the ten best actresses, the ten best movies, the ten best movie directors, the ten fastest automobile drivers, the ten best radio acts, the ten best radio announcers, the ten best northwestern apple growers, the ten best shaped girls in Miami, the ten best typographical works, the ten best bartenders, and the eleven best football players. If anyone hasn't been voted the best something or other by this time, he may just as well consider himself a rank failure in life. Even Dorothea Brande and Walter Pitkin won't be able to do anything for him.

Things have got to the point where almost every man you pass on the street has either a button or a ribbon in his coat lapel attesting to the fact that he has been honored for something, and is quite a magnifico. The house without at least one silver cup on the mantel signifying that paterfamilias or materfamilias or one of their children is a champion is a rarity. The chef in a public restaurant who hasn't a cordon bleu affidavit on the wall above the stove is ready for the Automat. The horse or dog or cat or cow who hasn't been awarded a ribbon, be it blue, yellow or some other color, hangs his head in shame. And the author, sculptor, painter, poet or architect who hasn't been singled out for an honor of some kind feels like taking the first ship out for Majorca.

Not a rich man myself, I have a suggestion to make to any rich man who wishes to perpetuate his name. Let him put aside in his will a fund of one hundred thousand dollars the annual income from which shall be bestowed as a mark of the greatest honor upon that American who, during the year, will have received no prize or award of any kind. If they can't at the end of the year find any such American, let the bequest go to that American who has given away so many prizes that he hasn't got any money left to eat.

HOPTOAD DRAMA.   It is something of a fact, as one of the shrewdest older actresses on our stage recently confided to an idealistic newcomer, that the two worst influences on our audiences, for all their other estimable attributes, are the Messrs. George S. Kaufman and George Abbott with their slam-bang, quick-step stage rodeos and their breathless, galloping directorial jinks. Trained to such hoptoad spectacles, the typical theatregoer has become out of patience with any play that doesn't move with the speed and racket of a Ringling Brothers' chariot race or Congressman Sirovich's tongue.

HOWARD.   It seems that when a whilom ambitious playwright who has sacrificed himself to cheap movie money becomes contrite and heads East and toward the sun again he buoyantly views the theatre as an escape from either Will Hayes or Darryl Zanuck, that is, as a liberation from moral censorship or from editorial restrictions. And it also seems that so askew has he become from his Hollywood confinement that he loses all his erstwhile conception of values, whether dramatic or personal.

Take the late Sidney Howard, for example. In *The Ghost of Yankee Doodle*, which marked his re-entrance into the theatre, he, like Hecht, imagined that he broke free from Hollywood and ingratiated himself with theatre audiences as a fellow of superior mind and culture by thickly raisining his exhibit with allusions to various writers, economists, philosophers, architects, poets, statesmen, and painters. Like someone haughtily putting Sam Briskin or Hal Roach in his place, he baronially tossed off in dazzling succession references to Thomas Jefferson and Karl Marx, quotations from Ruskin and Milton, citations of Socrates and Booth Tarkington, titbits about Mark Twain first editions and the etchings of George Bellows, casual remarks on Stanford White and *Othello*, etc., all in the unmistakable belief that such references were doubly valuable and impressive because if he tried to put them into a movie the studio bosses would throw him out on his ear. Like other of the returned prodigals, he sought further to attest to his divorce from Hollywood by incorporating into his play a lofty derogation of the movies, in this instance a slap at little Shirley Temple. He childishly tried to persuade his audience that he belonged heart and soul to the tradition of the theatre by sentimentally and nostalgically recalling a song sung by Julia Sanderson in *The Dollar Princess*. (More usually, it is Lillian Russell and *My Evening Star*.) He essayed, like Hecht and others before him, to prove that Hollywood, with its boy-meets-girl, divorcée-meets-first-husband and Zola-meets-an-Aryan-Dreyfus stories, had not diminished the pristine magnitude of his cerebrum by filling his play with so much talk about liberalism, Communism, Fascism, unemployment problems and other such topics that all that differentiated it from Union Square was its greater windiness. And he sought to hint that he was a very serious and sober fellow, even when in Hollywood, and that the Trocadero and the Clover Club knew naught of such as he by including in his exhibit at least one disdainful sneer at the kind of loafer who stoops to mundane pleasures and diversions, in this instance a diplomat who liked to dance. (Shades of Washington, Jefferson, and Hamilton!) As a consequence, his play, if only he knew it, was left-handed Hollywood with a vengeance.

I had a vague feeling that I knew what Howard was

driving at in his play, which seemed from the evidence to give me a slight edge on Howard himself, but my boasting began and ended there. After having given his exhibit my last ounce of close and studious attention, I found myself unable to clarify it any too satisfactorily for my customers. I could very easily tell them that in a general way it had to do with the plight of the liberal in the world of today and I could even tell them that there was in it a lot about jingoism, the problem of unemployment, the late World War, the next World War, mob hysteria, crooked journalism, Communism, the pathos of autumnal love, the narrowness of college thought, the proper manufacture of eggnog, the nut and bolt business, aviation, the lack of trees in Alaska, and the profusion of fairies in Florence, Italy, to say nothing of various references to the aforenoted Mark Twain, George Bellows, Shirley Temple, Fascism, Julia Sanderson, and Karl Marx. But to make it much clearer than that was beyond me. I knew that it had somewhere in it a love story involving a great newspaper-chain owner and a middle-aged woman who was once an actress, and also a love story involving her daughter and a young aviator, and I seem to have been able to decipher something about the newspaper owner's hope to plunge the country into war in order to save the nut and bolt factory, which supplied his beloved's income, from bankruptcy. But that was all they could expect from me.

For two and one half hours Howard came near to out-talking Hecht's *To Quito and Back,* and at the conclusion of the multiloquence everything was similarly just about where it was at the start, except a considerable portion of the audience. For Howard, like Hecht before him, very evidently believed that a pregnant play of ideas was to be achieved through a painstaking restatement of the platitudes of the late Herbert Croly indignantly crossed with those of young Mr. Corliss Lamont and periodically interrupted with a wistful quotation from Ruskin or Milton. Like Hecht, he didn't seem to appreciate that what resulted was infinitely less a play of ideas than a second-hand recital of the cogitations, philosophies and prejudices of various predecessors, the majority of whom most often had no ideas worth speaking of to begin with.

Mr. Howard set out to write an exhibit demonstrating the pickle of the liberal in the modern ferment. But as in the case of Hecht, who set out to write about the same subject, he entangled himself in so involved a thematic skein and got his feet caught in so many diversified strands that before long his tripping act rivalled that of Mr. Will Mahoney. Consider one point alone. The play opens " eighteen months after the commencement of the next World War." England, France, and Russia are opposed to Germany, Italy, and Japan. An American ship is torpedoed and sunk by a French submarine and American neutrality is threatened. The country is aroused by jingoes and is about to join the conflict. Yet though, jingoism or no jingoism, it is hardly likely that the United States could be hornswoggled into an alliance with the Fascist powers against England and France and though, further, the sinking of an American ship by a French submarine would hardly drive the country into a frenzied partisanship with France, Howard's young American aviator hero promptly decides to offer his services to the latter, presumably an enemy nation. You make that one out! I couldn't, unless the mumbling and gargling of the actors played havoc with the playwright's intention. But whether I heard correctly or not, one thing was obvious. The play in its entirety indicated anew that the place for playwrights who spend most of their time in Hollywood is still Hollywood.

Like Hecht, Howard started out as a playwright of promise. Then, like Hecht, he imagined that he could go to Hollywood and write movie scenarios with one hand and reputable plays with the other. And here, also like Hecht, he discovered — or if he didn't, all the rest of us did — that he imagined the apparently impossible. One can't drink one's swimming pool and have it.

But one point remains. It is to Howard's great credit that he seemed to appreciate what Hollywood, for all his desperate effort to beat its influence, had done to him. Asked if Hollywood had had any sinister effect on him — I here quote the New York *Times* — he said that it had, that the lack of an audience and a low standard of taste had exerted an impact on his own playwriting integrity. "It's the easy money, perhaps; I don't know," he said. "But it's true."

HUNGARIAN DRAMA. The Hungarians, both resident and refugee, are still writing the play about the immaculate butler in the high-toned household who indicates his intellectual superiority to his employers by pronouncing the first two syllables of *conscientious* as if they were an Englishman complaining of his bad eyesight and who is therefore fallen in love with by the proud daughter of the family. One of the latest to come forth with the knicknack is Bus-Fekete. It is known in its American version as *The Lady Has a Heart* and it amounts in essence to little more than the kind of thing which those eminent local Hungarians, Ladislas Tarkington and Fédor Bus-Wilson, used to grind out for popular consumption some twenty-five years ago. Bus-Fekete has added a bit of political commentary to the old dish, but for the rest it is simply William Hodge redivivus dressed up like the Broadway idea of a Hungarian butler, comporting himself after the stereotyped stage conception of butlers (which is generally a cross between Noël Coward afflicted with rigor mortis and A. E. Matthews conscious of the presence of a bad odor), and accordingly impressing to the point of amour the hitherto aloof and snobbish Olive Wyndham cast as the Countess Katinka.

The butler in the latest rehash was Vincent Price and the countess Elissa Landi, emerged for the occasion from the

California celluloid Corinth. Mr. Price, who bears something of a resemblance to a Chicago-company Brian Aherne, denoted the *soigné* austerity of the man-servant rôle by conducting himself throughout the evening like a slightly paralyzed six-foot icicle recently and very self-consciously graduated from Harvard and, when complimented by one of the characters on the precision of his French, promptly proceeded to demonstrate the propriety of the encomium by proclaiming, "Après moi le déllooj!" Miss Landi, a comely creature, haplessly betrayed her infection with the *streptococcus filmus* by acting the young countess like James Cagney dressed by Jay-Thorpe. One actor appeared with the other performers, Mr. Lumsden Hare.

I

I. The day on which I am writing this marks another milestone in my life. I have just received from my clipping service the six-thousandth cutting proclaiming that I don't like *anything*. It has been going on for years now. Just how the idea started I do not know, but it enjoys such a fecund vogue that I conclude there must be either a lamentably enormous number of people who don't read what I write or that many who do are sufferers from malignant myopia somewhat complicated with a proclivity for reading upside down. It is true that, when it comes to plays and players, I sometimes do not like what other critics like. But also sometimes I like what they do not like. When the former happens, the I-don't-like-anything complainants get going at me in a big way. And when the latter happens, it seems it is just a sign that I am arbitrarily contrary. It is all pretty hard to figure out.

Yet there must be something that has generated so wide a belief that I am inordinately difficult to please. What, we may wonder, is it? It is, I imagine, this: Whereas the critics on the daily newspapers and some of the periodicals are in the habit of reviewing a play in terms of the immediate theatrical moment, that is, in terms of today, it is my habit to review it rather in combined terms of yesterday, today and, more especially, tomorrow. What I try to do is to estimate it according to the best past standards in its particular category and further to estimate its possible residuum of quality after its momentary effect, sometimes so easy and dubious, has passed off. In other words, to consider it after the boozy effect of the drink on the house has gone and, upon regaining equilibrium, to speculate just what was in the Mickey Finn.

Any such critical procedure naturally arouses the distrust and disdain of many folk. Inasmuch as most of them view the theatre merely as a casual diversion and have no more interest in its artistic position, health, growth and pride than they have in the food with which they stuff their bellies or the liquor with which they try to forget and apologize for it, they resent any critic who has such an interest, just as they resent any interference with any other stupidity which adds to their personal complacency. If they see a second-rate play that entertains them, they do not wish a critic to tell them that if it had been a first-rate one it would have entertained them doubly. And if, because of their admiration for the second-rate, they do not know a fine play when they see one and are told that it nevertheless is a fine play, they are naturally insulted. The dislike of critics is thus based upon the aggrieved if unperceived inferiority of the people who read them. Tell the profoundest musical ignoramus that he knows nothing about music, and, though he appreciates that you are right, he will nevertheless abominate you for derogating him. Tell someone who had a wonderful time at *Abie's Irish Rose* — and there were a hundred thousand such — that to any instructed taste it was a slice of Brie, and he will put you down as either a deplorable dumbhead or a very offensive person.

I do not, of course, mean to posture any such vainglory as to insist that my own judgment of plays is always right and the one and only true judgment. Far from it. But, whatever its demerits and weaknesses — and I have made sufficient mistakes in my time — it is at least a judgment that tries humbly to base itself upon the firmest and highest of standards. It never considers box-office success or failure; it never gives a hang for " names "; it never gently lets down anything in the interest of good manners; it doesn't distinguish between personal friends and enemies; it is never influenced by outside considerations of any kind; and it says its say without polite and brummish circumlocution. If you think this is brag, you are mistaken. It is just one rooster's stubborn way of pursuing, for good or ill, the job he thirty-odd years ago chose for himself. And I may whisper confidentially that it is pretty sagacious.

The easiest thing in the world is to write the truth as you see it. It is also the most profitable. For people, however much they may resent you for pricking their pretensions, can't resist reading you. If you need proof, look at the letters sent in by readers of the various periodicals and newspaper syndicates I write for. Nine-tenths of them are folk who hotly denounce me for disagreeing with their own opinions and who urge the editors to consign me to the doghouse as quickly as possible. As the indignant letters continue to pour in month after month and year after year, however, it becomes plain that the indignantos go right on reading me in spite of themselves. And what is the result? The result is that if the editors foolishly cashiered me and took on in my stead some critic whose opinions coincided with those held by all the readers of the magazines and newspapers, it wouldn't be long before those readers would get so blamed tired wasting time reading what they already believed that they'd complain twenty times louder than they presently do. And what is the further result? The further result is that the editors, being sapient fellows, not only have to raise my wages every other month in order not to lose my precious services but every now and then, when they get worried, have to bribe me into not deserting them with cuff links, gold watches, cases of Rhine wine, and love letters.

I have a general feeling that what most of the yawpers object to in me is not that I don't like anything but that I often don't happen to like the things they like, and vice versa. If I were to like every single play produced during a season and my clients were to think they were one and all pretty terrible, you would hear a tenfold greater objection to me than you presently do. There is no disrelish so acute as that for a person, whether professional critic or layman, who enthusiastically admires something that you yourself have no use for.

Experience has taught me that, if nothing else. Let me like greatly a play that no one else likes and even my critical associates are not backward in slyly nominating me a combination of nitwit and lausbub on the one hand and a mélange of chronic dissentient, cavilling protestant and noncompliant horse's asterisk on the other.

It is, of course, the popular defect of my critical code that it prevents me from liking many plays that certain other less rigorously self-disciplined critics permit themselves to like. It may be too bad, but it can't be helped. For a critic of any probity at all can no more change his basic personal critical attitude than he can change the color of his eyes or the length of his innominate bone. So, God help me, I suppose there is nothing left for me to do but to resign myself for the rest of my life to go on reading my readers' same old potshots, same old kicks, and same old bellyachings.

IMPROVEMENT. American dramatic writing has improved enormously in one respect. Seldom any longer does it betray that assertive mental vanity characteristic of the uneducated which made so much of it whimsically ridiculous twenty and twenty-five years ago.

INTELLIGENCE IN MUSICAL SHOWS. Almost everyone, with the exception of Fritz Kuhn and the kind of dramatic critic who maintains that intelligence is the most vital requisite of a musical show, should like some such exhibit as *Leave It to Me!* Herr Kuhn wouldn't like it because Victor Moore, as an American Ambassador to Russia who wants to get back home to Kansas as quickly as possible, thinks he can accomplish his end by kicking the Nazi spokesman in the belly, only disgustedly to find that that is exactly what the whole world has been wanting to do and that, alas, he is a hero. The kind of critic who holds intelligence to be the most valuable asset of a musical show wouldn't, in turn, like it because, while it may seem a sufficiently intelligent show to the rest of us, it hasn't that peculiar brand of intelligence he especially cherishes, to wit, the brand which figures in such pedantic bores as *Knickerbocker Holiday*.

There is altogether too much talk about literate and intelligent musical shows for musical shows' good. The tribute " literate " is customarily reserved, we discover, for lyrics that sound as if they had been written by someone studying to be an assistant professor of English at some coeducational college with a championship chess team. And the tribute " intelligent " is usually visited upon shows which, if you deleted the girls and tunes from them, would be denounced by the same critics as dramatic stinkers. The person who venerates intelligence in a musical show is, in short, one who does not stop to realize that the chief ingredients of any such show, good or bad, are for the most part naturally and even violently irreconcilable with intelligence; that is, love, libido, combustible females, dancing, singing, merrymaking, low comedy, scant skirts, distracting lights and colors, and a general back-to-Maxim's spirit.

Leave It to Me! is an eminently satisfactory exhibit because it is intelligent only as a musical show properly should be intelligent. It doesn't make the silly mistake that the other so-called intelligent musicals make in trying at one and the same time to play itself straight and show. That is, simultaneously to contend with itself as a quasidramatic Seabiscuit and an Ed Wynn comedy nag. It is content to institute a prophylactic holiday from affected highbrowism by transferring its cerebrum to the region of the midriff and letting go with all pants and vest buttons. Paraphrasing their old farce-comedy, *Clear All Wires,* the droll Boy-Meets-Girl Spewack duo has contrived to extract a fresh, new humor from the familiar farcical idea of the man who despairingly essays one thing and in the act prosperously accomplishes another and quite different thing. The formula has had many changes rung on it since the time of *Brewster's Millions* and before, and this is one of the more jovial. I have but one complaint.

Can't we soon be through with musical-show titles with exclamation marks? There have been so many of them in recent years that even something like *Knickerbocker Holiday,* which comes along peaceably with no scarifying punctuation, is a kind of relief. It seems that the moment anyone gets hold of an exclamation point these days, he promptly sits down and writes a musical show around it. If I succeed in this campaign, I shall immediately proceed to pursue the putsch into the book field. If one more book appears with something like *Goodbye, Mr. Chips!, My Son, My Son!* or *Listen! the Wind* on the cover, I am going to start a one-man revolution for *Mother Goose!!*

IRISH DRAMA. While, with minor exception, the English are devoting themselves assiduously to the composition of ducky little parlorspiels and psychoneurotic murder-mystery shockers; the Germans restrictively to schmalz acceptable to Leni Riefensthal's boy-friend; the French to 1890 sexual rogueries in modern dress; the Russians to hallelujahs to steam locomotives, threshing machines, and open plumbing; the Hungarians to boiler-plates in which butlers are uniformly presented as being more literate and sapient than their masters; and the Americans to largely arbitrary hoots and derisions of the philosophies of the American playwrights who directly preceded them, the Irish are trying to do something about the art of the drama. More and more it becomes evident that it is to Ireland we must look for plays of merit and repute or, if not directly to Ireland, at least to some stray in another land with some trace in his veins of the blood of St. Patrick.

It isn't, certainly, that all the plays that are coming out of the Celtic soil are masterpieces. Very far from that. But in even the poorest of them one finds a probity, a passionate undertone, a brave resolve, and a hint of spiritual music that one all too infrequently encounters in the present dramaturgy of other peoples. And in the finer plays there is a poetic sweep, a surgery of human emotions, and a warm golden glow that even the best drama of other countries most often lacks. The current English seldom plumb the human heart much beneath the fashionable Jermyn Street waistcoat that covers it. The French, with not more than two exceptions at most, traditionally and habitually seem to confuse it with an organ socially somewhat less ecclesiastical. The Germans of the present day identify its beat with that of a swastika drum. The Russians politically and loftily dismiss it; the Hungarians seem to imagine that its pulse beats invariably in three-quarter time; and the Americans interpret it either in terms of the baton of a swing band or a perfumed dime valentine, or crack jokes about it. The Irish alone as a playwriting nation appear to know it for what, in all its strange and various moods, it is, and the Irish alone with a shameless beauty and a singing candor permit it to tell its true and often aching story.

In so much of the Irish drama one thus detects a dramatic mind and heart infinitely superior to most of the minds and hearts that go into the creation of the plays we commonly get in the theatre. These other minds concern themselves chiefly with such exalted matters as who is intent upon sleeping with whom, who murdered the actor whose body has been discovered under the spittoon, and who will marry the young Park Avenue society girl whom no one in real life outside a Keeley Cure would marry on a bet. And these other hearts palpitate principally with such emotions as are induced by tea-table Communism, the acute unhappiness that is the corollary of the possession of money, the woe that comes to a child when its drunken father who never enters the house without falling on his ear and breaking a leg deserts its mother, and the impossibility of preserving the high ideals inculcated in one by Hollywood amid the fleshpots of New York and points South.

In the Irish drama in question the minds inquire into no such dowdy box-office goods but into the vague and puzzled

inner spirits of men and women, and the hearts beat com-
passionately for the tortures and the little glories of mankind
unending. Above its keyboard there sound the misty overtones of unarticulated melodies, and one takes with one out
of the theatre not merely the play one has seen and listened
to but the play that lies under and above and beyond it.
With the average play that the theatre gives us, the only
things one carries with one out of the theatre are the thoughts
that three dollars and thirty cents was a devil of a price to
have been nicked for it, that for the three dollars and thirty
cents one could have got romantically, imaginatively and dramatically tight on six glasses of first-rate schnaps and could
have had thirty cents left over for the waiter, who could
therewith have reciprocally exalted himself with at least one
drink over on Tenth Avenue, and that in all probability one
is now going to get one's feet wet and contract a very bad
cold, and maybe pneumonia.

The feeling of the Irish drama, furthermore and in conclusion, is not, as we more often find, reserved solely for its
actors, but trickles out into its audiences and sweeps them up
into its own embrace. Its sentiment is not the mixture of
marmalade and correspondence-school love letters of the
usual play, but something that proceeds from intelligent emotions filtered through understandable minds. Its drama is not
derived from the conventional dime dramaturgical acrobat-
ics but from all the doubts that man is heir to, and the final
impression it imparts is akin to having been honorably moved
by good music, good literature, or good wine.

IRISH PETARD. This talent of the Irish is, however, getting
to be as much a critical embarrassment as it is an obvious
theatrical blessing. For some years now they have been im-
pudently writing better plays than almost anyone else and
the fact is so palpable that it would take a critic married to
Hitler's aunt, in love with Göring's sister-in-law and carrying
on with Göbbels' cook to deny it. Thus, naturally, few have

denied it and the few have been confined to such Nazi critics as are officially forbidden to praise any playwright save he argue that it was Horst Wessel the three wise men discovered in the manger at Bethlehem, such English critics as believe that any American importation in which a man enamored of a girl says " I love your damned guts, kid," is immeasurably superior artistically and realistically to any English play in which he expresses his ardor somewhat less intestinally, and such Americans as are persuaded that there is something undramatic about any speech that runs over three sentences, has in it the feel of beautiful literature, and doesn't end up either with an injunction to go to hell or please not to slam the door as you go out. The great majority of other critics, properly appreciating the Irish eminence and duly and regularly setting it down in print, have gradually and disturbingly found themselves hoist by the Celtic petard. The necessity of indulging in so much unremitting praise has not only made their writings monotonous, but, to that ample body of monkeydonkeys who detect in too much commendation a suspicion of crooked prejudice, has implied a deficiency in critical balance, adjudication, and even economic and anatomical chastity.

It is difficult in the critical business to go on boosting any one thing for long, however patently it deserves to be boosted, without having people nod their heads significantly and pass out a meaningful wink or two. To gain and preserve a reputation for complete honesty and integrity a critic has to be something of a cheat and swindler, as the public has a set of rules upon which its idea of complete honesty and integrity is predicated and as the aforesaid set of rules can be obeyed and followed only by a critic who is dishonest and without integrity. The honest critic who, if he is jake enough to bother about such matters, wishes to conciliate the public and achieve its admiration, accordingly has a hard time of it, and usually winds up around the age of forty either by being kicked out of his job by some editor whose girl is in the chorus

of some musical show, reads Nietzsche, has a superior contempt for the public and tells her beau that his critic is a slice
of cheesecake, or, worse still, by sticking to his sad juggling
post until he is eighty and becoming a laughing-stock not
only to his boss and his boss' girl but to himself.

The only way for a critic to get on in the world is to roast
the living tar out of everything that calls for such roasting
and never stop for a minute and to praise the living roses
back into everything that calls for such praise and likewise
never stop for a minute. One procedure is of course as tedious to his customers as the other, but what the odds? The
public has never yet made a critic's reputation for him and it
never will. It has, true enough, made bogus reputations for
bogus critics and it has, in the making, made them popular
and made them rich, just as it has — with equal sapience and
soundness — made names and fortunes for such similarly acceptable, soothing and agreeable, if similarly dubious, things
as Swedish massage, Buchmanism, Alexander cocktails, and
Lloyd C. Douglas. But it has not and it cannot give him any
true and decent standing unless, first, he has that standing in
himself and unless, secondly, he forces it against its will, as
Shaw, Brandes and certain others have forced it, to recognize him for what he is.

What all this hubbub leads up to is the disconcerting
news that Paul Vincent Carroll, whose *Shadow and Substance* got so much critical praise that *Variety* argued some
of us must have had money in the show, last season came
along with a follow-up, *The White Steed,* which once again
made us unloose nosegays on its behalf and which once
again, accordingly, induced some kippers to conclude that
there must be some niggers in the critical wood-pile. It was
too bad for us, but there was nothing we could do about it.
For this *The White Steed* was and is not only in every respect
up to the mark of the antecedent play but, in many, very considerably superior to it.

Carroll's theme is a not particularly fresh one. It has already been presented to us a number of times in Irish novels, short stories and essays, notably by Liam O'Flaherty and Sean O'Faoláin. The latter has also written a play concerned with it, called *She Had to Do Something*, which is currently going the rounds in search of a producer. But neither O'Flaherty nor certainly O'Faoláin, whose play is feeble and often hackneyed, has given the theme the drive and agitating eloquence that Carroll has brought to it. That theme is the bigotry of the Irish priesthood that would suppress all freedom and beauty in Irish life and that seeks to underline all of Erin with a stringent and vicious moral code. Against this bigotry Carroll aligns a Canon of the older liberal school and a young woman who, like a Celtic Joan of Arc, contemptuously challenges the weakness and poltroonery of the men about her and herself goes forth defiantly to flout the enemy.

In the mouths of these two characters the dramatist lodges his ammunition. At Father Shaughnessy, Carroll's symbol of churchly dogmatism and intolerance, Canon Matt Lavelle hurls this in retort to Shaughnessy's "You say that to me because I feel conscientiously there are many abuses in this parish that should be stamped out":

"I say it to you because you are looking for mathematical exactitudes in the spiritual and you'll not get them here so long as the Irish mind re-echoes back to the oak tree and the wishing-well. In this country of ours, with all respect to your psychology and ethics, in spite of governments and laws, the people are fundamentally free. What you want is to replace their old wayward love of God, that is splattered with mud and blood and crudities, with a shrinking fear of God that'll knock all the life out of them. If you want that sort of thing, go and live in Scotland, where the people have measured every word in the Bible with a screw-gauge and knocked every ounce of beauty out of their national life, and what have they achieved? Merely a reputation for the Bible amongst intelligent people as the most volatile and dangerous book ever written."

And again:

"What is the use? I won't agree with anything you say. I don't agree with this new tide of ideas. I am human enough to want like all ordinary people a little sugar in my tea, a little soda in my whiskey, a wee bit of coaxing in my dogma, and a hot bottle in my bed on a frosty night. I hate anything in the raw from raw poteen to raw men like Calvin, whom I'd have strangled out of a sense of decency to the humanity Christ died for. If our Lord had never been human, had never drunk wine, had never allowed a woman's hair to clean his feet, had never pitied a miserable little bitch selling herself in a narrow street, half the people who now believe in Him would have sput on Him long ago. No, Shaughnessy, I am not with you, I am agin you. You can laugh at me when I call my servant Rosieanne instead of Rose, when I go mad for fresh vegetables and mashed potatoes, or when I read *The Independent,* but I believe that when I go down on my knees on the stone floor of that old Church out there, and ask God in my own way to forgive the human weaknesses of these poor slaves of ours, that I am doing more good than all the Calvinistic seekin'-out and spyin' and Vigilance Committees you propose. There now, I have had my say, and in me heart I'm agin you."

To the girl Nora, a character that leaves an impression as profound and as touching and as phosphorescent as the Brigid of *Shadow and Substance,* Father Shaughnessy observes, "The evil you assimilated in a pagan land is deep in you, woman"; whereupon this challenging answer: "What I have in me that won't let me stoop I didn't get in England, for England hasn't got it to give. I got it here. It was in Aideen when she rode by Oscar's side at the battle of the Garva. It was in Cu Chulainn when he tied himself to a pillar before he'd stoop to death. It was in Ossian when he rode back on Niam's white horse and found the land full of priests like you and little men like that poor schoolmaster there, and it's in me now, making me refuse to come to your council table and swallow the ancient draught of humility." And at the play's conclusion, when the old Canon gently says to her, " It's the music of the rebellious world you hear, my child, the music of the new deadly sirens. Ulysses tied himself to the mast, do you remember? Your mast is a sensible little man like Denis and the flag of the Church on top of it. Dreams, Nora, should be left on the right side of the blankets. You're not going back to England, I hope," — it is so she replies:

" No, I will never leave Ireland again. There's something here that is nowhere else. It's away back far and away deep down. A man going down a moonlit road from a fair may know it, or a child reading on a broken window sill of Niam or Aideen or Maeve, but they will tell you no name for it. They will look away from you and the tears will come with a sudden wild rush, but the cry is within them forever, and neither money nor mating will make them happy. I am like that, Canon. It's my only sin, and this is my only true confession. There's great loveliness in a child, you say. Do you think I don't know? But I'd destroy him from his beginning. I'd call him Finn or Ossian and want him to grow into a man that would drive a sword into the heart of all that law and custom have blessed. Would you have that, Canon? . . . I must find out. I must follow the steed till I see that face that is turned away, and then I will know. If you want the firelight, Denis, go to it. I must be away. I must see the face of the queen that rides it, and find out who she is — if she is Niam or Aideen or Brigid or the Mother of God, or all of them in one. Then I will know and love. Oh, the ruin that's in you, Denis, and the falling down, and the whole horrible shame of the little black men. . . ."

In these few quoted speeches you get the force, the flavor and the flower of the play, a play that edges its indignation with an alleviating humor and that dramatizes its colloquies into at least two scenes — one at the end of the second act, the other at the climax of the fourth — that shake the emotion out of any audience that witnesses them.

There are minor faults in the play, for example the slight overdoing of allusions to the legend of the white steed and the playwright's love for stage directions that call upon his characters every ten minutes or so to " sit dejectedly, face buried in hands ". But small matter. *The White Steed* is still another credit to the Irish drama and this dissertation, whether it bores you or not, is of necessity still another testimonial to the becoming monotonous Irish genius.

Just by way of giving you a little novelty for your money, however, I may confide to you that Carroll's one-act play, *Coggerers,* isn't anything to tell the boys at the pub about. Employing the familiar device of statues come to life, in this instance those of Parnell, Emmet, Tone, Mitchell and Fitzgerald, it resolves itself into little more than a rather damply sardonic titbit involving an old scrubwoman whose son is killed in the cause of Irish freedom. But — and here is where we return to the old recurrent motif — if you are looking for a one-act masterpiece in low-comedy, I suggest you consult *The End of the Beginning,* by that best of all Irish stage writers, Sean O'Casey. If a funnier, bellybustinger, whiskerticklinger, riproaringer short play has ever been written by anyone at any time anywhere, I don't know of it. The spectacle of a couple of rummy old codgers trying to run a house in the absence of the wife of one of them is, as O'Casey shows it to us, the grandest piece of hilarity that has come the way of the theatre in a coon's age. I have read the script half a dozen times and each time have laughed louder and more obstreperously than the time before. When it gets to the stage, if they hire a couple of good Irish comedians to play it, I warn the management they had better for everybody's comfort's sake leave six seats vacant on either side of and in front of and behind me.

J

JAPANESE STENCIL. Most of our American stage directors indulge themselves in the whimsical notion that all young Englishwomen of the early nineteenth century never under any circumstances walked like their forbears but invariably pitapatted around like geishas.

JOHN CHOLMONDELY BULL. Arising in all the splendor of silk knee-breeches in the House of Commons, Mr. Sydney F. Markham, M.P., recently expressed his Oxonian horror at the inroads being made into the British kingdom by our vulgar American speech. "Through radio and films," he moaned, " we are acquiring what might almost be described as a transatlantic idiom." With cheeks flushed with indignation, he thereupon continued: " I saw in a recent American grammar that great phrase, *Sez you*, raised to the dignity of being described as ' a doubting affirmative '. It may be that the First Commissioner of Works will in time label this Aye lobby as the Sez You lobby. It is certain that the tongue of Shakespeare has had many strange twists put upon it by our transatlantic cousins in the past few years! "

It grieves me sorely to have to point out to the distinguished Mr. Markham that he is by way of being a bit noodled and that, for all his vaunted scholarship, he apparently knows next to nothing of the tongue of Shakespeare about which he has so overwisely speechified. If he did, he would know that " Says you," or at least its closest equivalent, was used by the old boy himself.

Various other items concerned with the tongue of Shakespeare, which he so proudly esteems, might further interest if not entirely enchant and gratify him. If Mr. Markham, M.P., deplores our American lingo, what will he think when I take the liberty of informing him that a great deal of that contemptible lingo derives directly from the worshipped Bard?

Is he, for example, aware that *lousy* is the Bard's? Must we acquaint him with the facts that *stewed, pash, all wet, crack* and *peach* (for blab) are Shakespeare's own, and that *blob* itself no less is? It may further pain him to learn that the American usage of *dump, goat, dame* and *punk* derives from the great William, as does that of *nut, daisy, piece of cheese* and the indelicate and humiliating *goose.* It was Old Bill, as well, who provided us with the inspiration for *stiff, bum, whale* and *rap,* to say nothing of *cuckoo, lemon, bite, rat* and *bow-wow.* And one might go on with a considerably more extended and embarrassing catalogue.

This whole general British sneer at our American speech is getting to be just the least bit tiresome. So, by way of an amusing change, let us do a little sneering in return.

In one of the most successful of present-day London plays recently also produced in New York, we encounter such sweet locutions as these: *I'm quite poopsie, It's grand by me, It's the cat's whiskers, It looks like a sitter for you, It's an absolute pinger, A nice suck-in,* and *I'm whistled* (for drunk). If this sort of thing keeps up, someone should get up in our House of Representatives, with or without knee-breeches, and complain that the speech of Nathaniel Hawthorne has had altogether too many strange twists put upon it by our transatlantic cousins.

What's more and worse, it does keep up. Here, by way of illustration, are a few choice samples culled from other recent English plays: *buzz off* (leave), *scrimshanker* (knave), *I'll crime you* (punish), *me should tell you!, Crikey!* (apparently a paraphrased ejaculation of the name of the Saviour), *poppet* (father), *swashingly ripping* (extremely good), *tippingly topping* (ditto), *bags I this one* (I get this), *faldalaldy* (highfalutin), *nip along* (hurry), *in the flummox* (trouble), *conked out* (light-headed), *hi-oo* (and Mr. Markham can't stomach *hi-yah!*), *chuck us a moist* (kiss me), *ghastly washout* (bore), *talk your say* (proceed with the conversation), *amn't I?*, *aren't I?*, *I'm done in* (knocked out), etc.

It's time to say aloha.

Returning briefly to the Member of Parliament's indignation over the American ejaculation, *Sez you!*, is it, aside from its corrupted spelling, essentially much more ridiculous than the ubiquitous English ejaculation, *I say!* Inasmuch, further, as it is employed chiefly by the American equivalent of the London Cockney, is it, spelling and all, any more objectionable than the Cockney *I sy!* Let us go on. If the objection of Mr. Markham is to the phonetic spelling of the *sez,* is it any more deplorable than the lack of phonetic spelling, on the part of his fellow countrymen, of some such name, say, as Wriothesley (third Earl of Southampton) which is pronounced Rotsli, or Beauchamp (Earl of Warwick) which is pronounced Beecham, or Mainwaring which is pronounced Mannering? Let us still go on. If it is *says,* however it be spelled, that the Member of Parliament doesn't relish and demands *say,* however it be spelled, in its stead, what does he say or sez to such Phil May and George Belcher British locutions as *I says to the bloke,* *You says to me* and *We says to the blighter?*

One can only hope the distinguished Member of Parliament never takes a trip over to Ireland. What he heard there would doubtless bring him to get up again in all the glory of his silk knee-breeches and demand that Erin be ceded at once and without delay to Hitler.

When the English find fault with our American speech they invariably put themselves in the position of the pot calling the kettle black. They wax sarcastic when they hear a gangster in a Hollywood movie use some such expression as *Cheese it, Joe, the cops!* and yet remain self-satisfiedly calm when they hear Lord Balderdash in one of their own drawing-room spiels use some such expression as *Dash it, Jeeves, where's my spot?* They throw up their hands in horror when an American radio comedian says *No soap,* meaning nothing doing, and delight themselves no end when an English ditto says *Nabsolutely nutterly,* meaning the same thing. They shrink from the vulgarity of an American revue that employs such locutions as *Peddle me you, kid!* and gleefully accept an English one that substitutes such as *Givee the googoo, sweet!*

The truth of the matter probably is that we are both pretty bad when it comes to the English, or what passes for the English, language. If they say *cemetry* for *cemetery, secretry* for *secretary* and *rayally* for *really,* we say *reelly* for *really, South-hampton* for *Southampton* and *Scotch* for *whiskey.* They call it *lift* and we call it *elevator,* even when it's going down. They confidently say *Cheerio!* and we confidently say *Here's how!* and both nevertheless suffer a foul hangover the next morning. They pronounce *Cholmondely Chumly* and we pronounce *Arkansas Arkansaw.* However, we at least both agree on one thing. We both say, *it stinks!*

JOHNSTON. Denis Johnston's latest contribution to the theatre is a play called *The Golden Cuckoo.* It reveals the author of the memorable *The Moon in the Yellow River* in one of his prankier and more capricious moods. What he here attempts is the humorous mountain-molehill sort of thing made familiar by various modern playwrights from Lady Gregory to Bruno Frank and James Bridie, that is, the forcing of a triviality into a theatrical hot-house plant. This particular tempest in a tea-cup and storm over Patsy passes in its three acts from the converted stable residence of its central figure, Mr. Dotheright, " an author ", to a newspaper office, thence to a suburban post-office, thence back to the newspaper office, on to a police court, and finally back to the Dotheright residence. The first act introduces us to Mrs. Vanderbilt, who is Mr. Dotheright's profane household servant with a penchant for stealing everything from a bag of beans to a goat; Mr. Pull, a jitney corporation official; Mr. Pennywise, a quack lawyer; Mr. Haybottle, a cabman; and Mrs. Golightly, a hussy given to drink. The point at issue is who is going to pay the cabman for a ride to a cemetery. This point is argued at length with all the grave pomposity of a session of the House of Lords and comes down finally to the discovery that no one has any money, due chiefly to the circumstance that Mr. Dotheright, whose authorship is confined to writing obituary notices for the local paper, has unfortunately composed one about a man who isn't dead and hence can't collect the usual honorarium.

The second act witnesses the pilgrimage of Mr. Dotheright, the cabby and the others to the newspaper office in quest of the fee owing the charioteer, who by this time is getting pretty sore about the whole business. With a pomposity that has now developed into a magnitude surpassing that of the House of Lords and approximating that of the headwaiter at the French Pavilion at the New York World's Fair, Mr. Dotheright and his friends debate the delicate subject with the distraught editor, Mr. Lowd, who is on the point of kicking them all out when Mr. Dotheright proceeds to a sly bit of blackmail that drives Mr. Lowd foaming at the mouth to broadcast by telephone the information that Mr. Dotheright is crazy and should be carefully watched by the authorities.

To the street outside the post-office Mr. Dotheright, the cabman, and the latter's debtors now indignantly march. After a protracted series of big speeches on a variety of topics that only at odd moments touch upon the matter at issue, Mr. Dotheright, who has worked himself up to an explosive indignation over the injustice of the modern world, declares that he will inaugurate a one-man world revolution. Won by his eloquence, his several friends, together with the cabman, conclude that they may as well string along with him and set the world right. There is only one hint of hesitation, and it comes from Mr. Pull. " But we haven't got any swords," he protests. This annoys Mr. Dotheright no end. " But we have got words," he orates, "words that battle — big-bellied words billowing like galleons out of Espanola! That is why we have assembled here at a Public Telephone Box." The telephone box, however, is inside and that presents a problem. Mr. Dotheright ably meets it. " Let's occupy the Post-Office! " he cries, echoing the challenge of a lady souse who has joined the revolutionists. "All rebellions have to occupy the Post-Office! " They duly occupy the Post-Office and are promptly collared by a disgusted cop and hauled off to the hoosegow.

The third act is taken up with the efforts of Mr. Lowd to extricate himself from the multiplication of woes growing out of Mr. Dotheright's blackmail tactics, the difficulties of Mr. Dotheright's Revolutionary Party with the law, the payment of the honorarium due Mr. Dotheright for his obituary notice of an alive man who in the interim has conciliatingly died, and the pacification of the creditor cabby. As the curtain falls, Mr. Dotheright is delivering a severe reprimand to God and Mr. Dotheright's pet rooster is clucking loudly and adding to the general nuttiness by laying an egg.

Like most of the other playwrights who have tried to dramatize molehills into two and one-half hour humorous mountains, Johnston doesn't any too happily manage the feat beyond the first act. And as in most of these plays, one thereafter has difficulty in seeing the mountain because of the molehill that constantly, assertively and all too obviously gets in the way. The materials in this case are serviceable enough, but repetition and consequent monotony dim their flavors.

JOURNALISTIC CRITICISM. It is the piquant custom of *Variety,* the theatrical weekly, to publish at the conclusion of every season its idea of the year's best New York newspaper dramatic critic. It arrives at this conclusion by making a tabulation of the number of plays each critic has reviewed, the number of times he has been right in his predictions as to a play's success or failure at the box-office, and the number of times he has been wrong. Obviously, we should at this point properly conclude this section with the word *Pfui*, but in the interests of the higher journalism let us append a few further remarks.

That a sound critic has no concern with the success or failure of a play at the box-office, anyone with an intelligence quotient slightly more elevated than that of a Hollywood mastermind sufficiently knows. The commercial success or failure of a play should have no more to do with dramatic criticism than the financial success or failure of a book has to do with literary criticism, or the amount of real money an expert counterfeiter garners has to do with anything but his aptitude as a swindler. Thus, the theory that a critic who didn't like some such thoroughly reputable if rather evasive play as *Katie Roche* and correctly predicted its collapse at the dunderheaded box-office and who in turn admired some such juvenile dish as *What a Life* and correctly predicted its prosperity at the same box-office — the theory that such a fellow is a wizard in the critical art is enough to make Mr. Mack Sennett roll over in his bed and muse sadly on a misspent sober career.

The better to appreciate the imbecility of theatrical journalism of this species, let us assume that you are a critic and that the following two groups of ten plays each were to be presented to you for review:

1. *East Is West, The Old Maid, The Star-Wagon, Seventh Heaven, Brother Rat, Abie's Irish Rose, Peg o' My Heart, Dinner at Eight, Design for Living,* and *The Shanghai Gesture.*

2. *The White-Headed Boy, Daughters of Atreus, Within the Gates, Richard of Bordeaux, The Moon in the Yellow River, General John Regan, The Man with a Load of Mischief, The Man Who Ate the Popomack, The Glass Slipper,* and *The Master.*

You would, naturally enough if you had any critical training, say that none of the plays in the first group deserved the consideration of serious criticism, and you would thereupon dismiss them with the observation that, if they did succeed at the box-office, it would be too bad for the interests of really reputable drama. In the case of the second group, you would say that the plays were worthy plays and that, if they didn't succeed, it would be a gosh-darned dirty shame. Inasmuch as the first lot prospered highly and the second prospered hardly at all, you would be voted by *Variety* a critical numskull and would be placed at the foot of the class. If, on the other hand, you were to say that, while you couldn't stomach the plays in the first group, they would surely be box-office whales and that, while you admired those in the second, they would in all likelihood be failures, you would, in *Variety's* estimate, be pretty good. But if, still further, you declared flatly and finally that the first group was wonderful stuff both in and out of the box-office and the second awful trash anywhere, *Variety* would vote you the world's critical champion.

It is thus that the bible of show folk instructs them in the art of criticism. Now that dramatic criticism in America has advanced so greatly in the last dozen years, small wonder show folk have so little respect for it.

K

KAUFMAN, HART AND PRINTERS' ALLEY. When *I'd Rather Be Right*, the exuberantly amusing lampoon of F. D. Roosevelt and Co., opened for a tryout in Boston, the editors of the various New York newspapers ordered that it be covered as a news event, it being their conviction that it was the first time that living government officials had been displayed and caricatured on the stage under their own names. This recalled the late Frank Munsey's prayer that he might one day find an editor for one of his New York papers who didn't live in Morristown, New Jersey, and who might accordingly know a little more about what was going on in New York. The average metropolitan newspaper editor, as Munsey appreciated, may know all that is necessary about Sam Seabury, Sam Leibowitz, Sam Koenig, Sam Ordway, Sam Untermyer, Sam Levy, Sam Foley and Sam Dickstein, but when it comes to anyone or anything divorced from politics, law, crime or mazuma and having to do with one or another of the arts — the theatre in great particular — he usually knows less than his own office-boy or even his star editorial writer. He may conceivably be faintly aware that Sam Harris isn't the late Sam T. Jack and that the late Sam Shipman maybe wasn't Sam Behrman, but it is good betting that he is not entirely sure whether Sidney Howard was or wasn't Willie Howard's brother, whether Eugene O'Neill or George O'Neil wrote *Bound East for Cardiff*, whether Claire Luce is the actress and Clare Luce the author of *The Women*, or whether Marc Connelly is an actor and Walter Connolly a playwright, or vice versa. Things have got to the point where the editor of the *World-Telegram*, whose acquaintance with the drama evidently began and ended the night Stanford White was shot in the Madison Square Garden roof theatre, recently decided that the theatre was at all times a news event or nothing and ordered that it be treated as such, with the result that his appointed reviewer, a former reporter, is gradually going crazy hoping for a murder or at least a good fire at every dramatic première, or a wholesale criminal assault on the ladies of the ensemble at the musical show openings.

The newspaper editor attitude toward the theatre, born of a commuter indifference or the city-slicker belief that a Tammany Hall Irishman named Dooling is a more important personage than an Abbey Theatre Irishman named O'Casey, has persisted for years. I well remember that many years ago, in the days of my novitiate on the James Gordon Bennett New York *Herald,* when I was assigned to the dramatic department as a sub-play reviewer it was the injunction of my editorial chief to give space to a new play in proportion to the fashionable eminence of the audience. One night, I recall, I was sent to review the opening of a melodrama in the old Fourteenth Street Theatre. It turned out to be, I thought, an excellent specimen of its kind, and before setting to the writing of my critical piece on it I reported as much to my boss. "A stick will do," he stipulated. But why? I wanted to know. "No one of any importance is ever in a Fourteenth Street audience!" was his firm reply.

The news about the Kaufman-Hart exhibit, *I'd Rather Be Right,* was and is that it was a very good show, which in its particular theatrical season was, God knows, news indeed. But the newspaper editors' notion that it was news because of its great novelty and extreme daring in presenting living government officials under their own names only once again attests to the noted fact that, when it comes to the theatre and drama, they know just as little as they do about the worlds of music, opera, ballet, literature, poetry, painting, sculpture, architecture, or even illustrious journalism. (As to the last named deficiency, certain Pulitzer Prize awards made on the recommendation of the Advisory Board of the School of Journalism at Columbia provide sufficient proof.)

It may be of some interest to our friends, the newspaper editors, to be told that the great novelty and the extreme daring which so impressed their news-noses in the instance of the Kaufman-Hart show have been familiar to American audiences for quite a few years — in point of fact, for about one hundred and fifty, or since the time directly following the American Revolution. John Leacock's *The Fall of British Tyranny* in that period daringly offered by name as one of its characters the living George Washington, the leading figure in the new government. Nor was Leacock an innovator even then. Directly preceding him, Mrs. Mercy Warren put onto the stage in her two lampoons, *The Group* and *The Blockheads,* several celebrities in the political, military, and social life of the day, and under names that their own fathers, mothers, and creditors could immediately recognize. In our own theatrical day, it doesn't take much of a memory to recall the numerous musical shows and revues that offered us, during his lifetime and faithfully christened, the combination of sombrero, gold eye-glasses, heavy watch chain, buck teeth, and " Dee-lighted " that went by the name of Teddy Roosevelt. And three or four years ago, Moss Hart, co-author of *I'd Rather Be Right,* anticipated the " novelty " and " daring " of his exhibit in his co-authorship of *As Thousands Cheer,* which lampooned not only Herbert Hoover under his own name but Mrs. Hoover under hers. (The then alive John D. Rockefeller, along with John D., Jr., also came in for literal spoofing.)

It would be easy to amplify the index. The attention of the newspaper editors might even be called, public stage or no public stage, to the Gridiron, Inner Circle, and Dutch Treat Club shows and, certainly, they might be informed of Rip, the best known and most amusing revue writer of the Paris theatre, who for the last twenty-five years has been mercilessly lampooning the leading living personages of the various French governments under their own names. But it is difficult to teach some old dogs even old tricks, and they will doubtless still go on considering it news that it was George M. Cohan who introduced the patriotic flag-waving hokum in *George Washington, Jr.* in 1906 when Mordecai M. Noah anticipated him by exactly eighty-three years in *She Would Be a Soldier*, that *The Girl of the Golden West* was the first American box-office play on an American subject to be converted into an opera libretto when so long ago as 1808 the same thing was done with James Nelson Barker's *The Indian Princess*, and that the Minsky brothers were the fathers of the condemned strip-tease and the Misses Ann Corio and Gypsy Rose Lee its first exponents when Oscar Hammerstein beat them all to it, with a houri named Charmion and without police interference, at least thirty years before.

A number of the editors of the dramatic departments of the metropolitan newspapers would seem to be Morristown neighbors of the editors of the news departments. Consider them in connection with George Abbott. Mr. Abbott, it will be remembered, was lucky enough to produce four plays in the several years in point that turned out to be hits. They were *Three Men on a Horse, Boy Meets Girl, Brother Rat,* and *Room Service*. Following their established conviction that after a producer has one hit he is a public figure, after two a wonder-boy, after three a genius, and after four a miracle man, the drama editors proceeded to give over their supplements to eulogies of Mr. Abbott as a producer whose touch invariably and inevitably converted everything into pure gold and who could not possibly fail, the implication being that his producing record was a long and unbroken succession of remarkable successes. Then, no sooner had the ink on the testimonials dried than Mr. Abbott produced *Angel Island,* a murder-mystery sausage which shocked the drama editors no end by being a deadly and very prompt failure. They couldn't understand how it came about. Their hero had betrayed them.

If, however, they spent less time in their metaphorical Morristowns and spent a little more in acquainting themselves with theatrical statistics, their surprise might have been considerably lessened. Mr. Abbott, they would have known, has been far from being a uniformly successful producer. In the last ten or more years he has had fully as many bad failures as hits. *Kill That Story!* was a failure. *Ladies' Money* was a failure. *John Brown* was a failure. *Sweet River* was a failure. *The Fall Guy* was a failure. *A Holy Terror* was a failure. *Love 'Em and Leave 'Em* was anything but a real success. *Spread Eagle* was a failure. *Four Walls* was another. *Lily Turner* was a failure. So was *Those We Love.* *The Ragged Edge* lasted just eleven nights and wrecked the Chicago Play-Producing Company. These are examples; there have been others, equally failures, in which Mr. Abbott has had, on the quiet, a directing hand. *Angel Island* was thus no particularly startling exception to the Abbott rule, whatever the drama department editors believed to the contrary. Should, furthermore, the matter come up again in the future, the editors may be instructed that additional Abbott failures since *Angel Island* include *Brown Sugar*, *All That Glitters*, and *Mrs. O'Brien Entertains.*

Footnote. *I'd Rather Be Right* provided the biggest opening since the Grand Canyon. Coming on the night of the New York Mayoralty election, it so overshadowed that event in metropolitan theatredom that the enormous audience inside and outside the Alvin doubtless still hasn't the faintest idea who won, unless maybe it was George M. Cohan. Offers for a pair of tickets ran as high as one hundred and fifty dollars, one gentleman loudly proclaiming that in addition to that sum he would throw in his Stock Exchange seat, thereby killing any chance of making a deal. Seventeen hundred autograph maniacs blocked the street and sidewalks in their delirium to achieve the treasured hancocks of such attendant great notabilities as Mr. Arnold Reuben, the three-decker sandwich impresario, and Mr. George Raft, the movie actor. Two squadrons of mounted police were effaced in the shuffle, haven't been heard from since, and are now known to the press as the Lost Battalion.

The occasion for all this excitement was a musical show that, as has been noted, called its actors by the names of the chief functionaries of the national government. Why the idea of calling George M. Cohan Franklin D. Roosevelt should have engendered so intense an interest I can't figure out, unless it was because Franklin D. Roosevelt, on the other hand, has been called everything under the sun but George M. Cohan. However that may be, the fact remains that no theatrical exhibit within memory has piqued such an exuberant antecedent curiosity. And the second and more important fact remains that, though the curiosity may have been of the generic New York hayseed fiber, the show, once the curtain went up, proved itself so often gay and sprightly a beanfeast and one so frequently rich in amiable monkeyshines that it wouldn't have mattered awfully if Mr. Cohan, instead of being dubbed Franklin Roosevelt, had been called Lee Shubert, Louis Untermeyer, or even Lizzie Borden. In point of fact, it might have been better all around to call him simply George M. Cohan, for there was infinitely more Cohan than Roosevelt to the evening, whatever the authors tried to assure us to the contrary. Which, certainly even the most chauvinistic Democrat would agree, helped a lot.

The chief criticism heard of the show was that it wasn't as good as *Of Thee I Sing*. It wasn't and isn't. But neither is *Macbeth* as good as *Hamlet*, which doesn't altogether damn *Macbeth*. The show had its dull passages, notably when the authors stopped talking, pushed Mr. Cohan aside, and allowed Charles Weidman's choreographers to occupy the stage with their arty nonsense. But in the main it applied a droll and delightful slapstick to the seat of government and amounted to about as happy sport as the theatre had provided in some time. It may all have been somewhat more Gilbert and Miller than Gilbert and Sullivan, though in two spots the inspiration of the latter was clearly detectable; its endless balancing-the-budget gabble may have become a trifle tedious; and such of its numbers as *Spring in Vienna* may have been more aptly suited to the Krimsky Music Hall than to a political lampoon. But small matter. It was, to repeat, a very amusing show.

KINEMATIC ADJUDICATION. The motion picture screen, with all its lovely girls, has still to produce its beauty legend as the stage has done. That is, women who will persist in the minds of men (and also of women) as enduring symbols of feminine beauty. The screen has yet to suggest a woman who in coming years will share the pedestal of enduring popular imagination with such stage Venuses as Mary Anderson, Lily Langtry, Cora Urquhart Potter, Lillian Russell, Lantelme, Maxine Elliott, and even Lotta Faust. But, demand the devotees of the films, what of Garbo? Well, Garbo is primarily the adoration of the women customers of the films and the memory of beauty is perpetuated never by women but always by men. Thus, though I may be a poor clairvoyant, I doubt if even those women who now estimate the Garbo as sister to the Trojan Helen will remember and venerate her as a beauty longer than it takes Shirley Temple to reach the age of fifteen.

KUMMER. Clare Kummer most lately went the whole hog in an attempt to cater to the current fad of reducing the drama to its bare elementals. We have had plays without scenery. We have had plays without costumes. We have had operas without an orchestra. We have had plays acted entirely by one person. But these, apparently, were merely the beginning. Mme. Kummer in an exhibit called *Spring Thaw* gave us no play at all. By way of topping her imaginative triumph she also contrived to have her dramatic vacuum not acted. And, topping her top, she further saw to it that her absentee play and absentee acting were climaxed by absentee stage direction.

In the matter of contemporary theatrical Ersatz this *Spring Thaw* not only took the cake but ate it and still had it. The only thing about it that suggested one was in a theatre was the presence of an audience, and even that suggestion largely disappeared after the opening night. Mme. Kummer's substitute for dialogue assumed the uninterrupted two-hour form of having one stage dummy make some such remark as " My spirit is gone " and having another look at an empty whiskey bottle and say, " So I observe." Also by having still another say " It's raining outside " and having another still retort, " Strange, I thought it usually rained inside." The hypothetical star of the hypothetical play, Mr. Roland Young, along with several of the other hypothetical performers, substituted a kind of sleeping sickness complicated with pernicious anemia, suppressed respiration, and rigor mortis for acting. And Mr. Arthur Hopkins, the hypothetical director, contributed his share to the novel experiment by inducing into the proceedings a comprehensive anæsthesia dolorosa. What *Spring Thaw,* doubtless intended as a genial bit of vernal cuckooism, needed, in short, was a whole lot more Printemps and even more Harry.

L

LEFT PROPAGANDISTS. Seldom a week goes by that any critic who peculiarly believes *King Lear* is a somewhat better play than, say, John Howard Lawson's *The Internationale* doesn't get half a dozen letters denouncing him for his arbitrary prejudice against the proletarian drama. Or if he doesn't get them, his editor does. The assiduity of the Left propagandists is remarkable, which is more than may be said for their intelligence. For I have yet to read one of their letters or hear one of their arguments that contained the faintest modicum of critical sense. And I have yet to meet and talk with one of the gentlemen who wasn't, when it came down to tacks, something in the line of a Quintus Roscius.

Despite the apparent conviction of these Leninnies, I am no more opposed to the Left Wing drama than I am to the Right Wing. I am opposed to both when they are bad, and to an equal degree. But I have never yet been able to persuade myself that a bad Left play was better than a bad Right play simply because it was a Left play, which is evidently the consummation the proletarian boys devoutly wish. The truth is that a good nine-tenths of these Left plays which have been put on the local stage in the last five or six years have been not only critically worthless but have done the cause or causes they championed a hurt rather than a benefit. For they have been, above everything else and above the possible validity of their themes, badly designed, badly written, badly articulated, and woefully dreary, and one can't gain sympathy and make converts under such circumstances. Paradoxically absurd though it may seem, *You Can't Take It with You* remains a much more convincing argument against capitalism than the most vociferous diatribe produced during the life of the radical Theatre Union, as *I'd Rather Be Right* constitutes a fundamentally sharper criticism of our present form of government than half the Communist plays that have tried to yell us onto their side.

The fault of the proletarian boys is that they believe the only way you can make an argument impressive is to put it into a sandbag and hit the other fellow over the head with it. As a result, the plays they write and the plays they endorse are largely indistinguishable from so many holdups. To persuade an audience fully, the weapons must be equally distributed between the play and the audience. A play can't hold a pistol against an audience's head and command it to give up. The audience also wishes to have a little say about that. So silly have the Lefts been that even their own side is beginning gradually to recognize it. Not long ago, Mr. Louis Schaffer, executive director of the Labor Stage, cordially admitted as much when he stated that the endless succession of pickle-faced exhibits dealing with revolution, strikes, and the Soviet grandeur, what with their desperate lack of humor, gave him, for one, something of a pain. It was, incidentally, by way of slightly alleviating the pain that he helped to produce *Pins and Needles*, which has shrewdly and successfully laughed its propaganda into its audiences' benignity.

It is too bad that the other boys of whom I have been speaking do not share at least a measure of Mr. Schaffer's winning sagacity. But even if they did, there is one point that they, in their wholesale indignation and in their faith in the mission of the Left drama, overlook. It is this: For all we hear to the contrary, the drama, whether Left or Right and even at its best, exercises little or no positive influence upon people. They may be affected by it momentarily, but after a very short time it evaporates from their consciousness, that is, in so far as anything of importance or relative importance it may have to say goes. It may, at its best, somewhat improve their cultural taste; it may add to their stock of apt quotations; and it may for the fleeting moment enrich their hearts and spirits. But in any other graver directions and for any greater length of time it does not in the least alter and change them. All the Communist plays written since Lenin's day haven't made any more converts to Communism than all the Capitalist plays written since Taft's have made converts to Capitalism. Such plays merely reconvert the already converted. An audience may take a new emotion out of a theatre but it rarely takes a new thought or philosophy. In the whole history of the more modern drama, the number of plays that have even faintly exercised any influence upon persons other than playwrights and critics or upon institutions other than the theatre itself may be counted on the fingers of one hand. Beaumarchais' *The Marriage of Figaro,* 'way back in 1784, was one; Hugo's *Hernani,* 'way back in 1830, was another; Ibsen's *A Doll's House,* 'way back in 1879, was possibly another; Brieux's trashy *Damaged Goods,* back in 1902, was momentarily another; and Bernstein's almost equally trashy *Après Moi,* nine years later, was possibly still another. That about completes the catalogue, unless my memory tricks me. The drama in the last one hundred and fifty years, in short, has not in its entirety had any substantial public after-effect comparable to even such a single boom-boom novel as Harriet Stowe's *Uncle Tom's Cabin* or Upton Sinclair's *The Jungle,* to even such a single war-whooping song as George M. Cohan's *Over There,* or to even such a single evangelical Elk grip as Frank M. Buchman's handshake with God.

A century and a half of the theatre's history has demonstrated that if it has any influence at all, that influence is confined largely — apart from the specific directions already noted — to matters of a supreme cosmic unimportance. A Cleo de Mérode may be instrumental in persuading women to alter the manner in which they dress their hair; a *The Red Robe* may cause several Paris professional letter-to-the-editor inditers to yowl, entirely without effect and result, against the methods of French jurisprudence; or a Sheldon's *The Nigger* may bring some of our more excitable colored fellow-citizens to protest, unsuccessfully, against the use of the derogatory term in its title. But, by and large and otherwise, except in the occasional and oblique matter of idiotic moral censorship, its influence is nil. After half a century, the countless audiences of the anti-drink propaganda drama, *The Drunkard,* are still going out and getting happily boiled to the ears and the countless audiences of the scareful *Ghosts* are still, if we may believe the recently revealed and staggering statistics, going out and merrily contracting syphilis. *Tobacco Road* can run ten more years and it will doubtless not persuade anyone who sees the picture of misery it presents to lift a finger on behalf of the wretched and pitiable Southern cracker folk. It seems to be the fate of the drama that audiences will frequently accept and abide by its artistic and cultural injunctions but seldom, if ever, by its political, social, religious, or economic.

It is, accordingly, ridiculous for the champions of the proletariat to work themselves up to a lather in their contemplation of the current dramatic scene. But even if it were not, the fact should be recalled to them that they themselves and those who ardently sympathize with them do not seem to be sufficiently interested and numerical to make the Left drama, when it does appear, a paying or even a partly going proposition. And certainly the general public with its very thorough and obvious indifference isn't helping them any. The Theatre Union, which sought to institute a home for the proletarian drama in Fourteenth Street and which charged so little that any interested worker could easily afford to be a customer, failed after a brief try and was forced to close down. The Left play, *Marching Song,* produced in the Bayes Theatre, was a quick financial failure; the Left play, *Steel,* was a similar financial failure; and so were other such uptown presentations as *1931–, Wolves, We, the People, Judgment Day, Between Two Worlds, Gentlewoman, The*

Pure in Heart, Paradise Lost, Panic, Parade, Paths of Glory, Squaring the Circle, Let Freedom Ring, Weep for the Virgins, Searching for the Sun, Case of Clyde Griffiths, And Stars Remain, Ten Million Ghosts, Days to Come, But for the Grace of God, Tide Rising, To Quito and Back, Siege, Sunup to Sundown, Everywhere I Roam, et al.

All these plays fall either directly or roughly into the Left category; all have been shown in the last half-dozen seasons; some were produced by Right Wing producers; the Theatre Guild sponsored four of them; yet none of them drew enough customers to make it pay. There weren't enough Lefts, apparently, to keep them going, and there was no public to augment the handful of Lefts. The few proletarian plays that managed to survive and prosper, e.g., Odets' *Awake and Sing* and *Rocket to the Moon* and Kingsley's *Dead End,* contrived to attract audiences not so much because of their themes as because of either their comedy element or their spectacular staging. More people surely went to Odets' plays to be amused than to give hot ear to their Left sympathies, as more probably went to Kingsley's to see Norman Bel Geddes' remarkably realistic and widely advertised stage setting than to listen to its plea for slum children.

Let the Left boys, as I have intimated, soothe themselves with the thought that what they bitterly denounce as the contemptible popular Right drama is in reality often much more effectively and popularly Left than the Left drama itself. The question of any critical quality completely aside, where will they find in the recent professionally Left drama a more persuading argument against the waster rich than in the popular box-office *Dinner at Eight,* against the present order of civilization than in *The Petrified Forest,* against the present order of democratic government than in *Both Your Houses,* against anti-Semitism than in *Having Wonderful Time,* against aristocratic snobbery than in *Rain from Heaven,* against property and capitalism than in *High Tor,* against constituted monarchy than in *The Masque of Kings,* against Sacco-Vanzetti injustice than in *Winterset*, against oppression of the poor and humble than in *Excursion*, or against the woe of war than in *For Services Rendered*?

LE GALLIENNE. There are two schools of thought about Miss Eva Le Gallienne. One, embracing a number of other reviewers, is headed by my esteemed colleague, Mr. Brooks Atkinson of the *Times*, along with the man who writes the "Who's Who in the Cast" notes in the back of Miss Le Gallienne's programs. Of Miss Le Gallienne's performance in *Madame Capet*, Mr. Atkinson wrote that it was "beautifully modulated; her acting as the stricken queen is superb; she acts . . . with stunning authority." Of Miss Le Gallienne herself, the man who writes the notes in the back of the program said that soon after she first stepped upon the local stage, "there was no longer any question as to her genius. Eva Le Gallienne was universally recognized as one of the leading actresses of our day. Every producer wanted her; every playwright was inspired to write for her; the theatre-going public could not obtain tickets quick enough."

The other school is headed by one or two of my equally esteemed colleagues, along with my less esteemed self. They, like myself, suffer the belief that not only was Miss Le Gallienne's performance in *Madame Capet* pretty bad, but that the man who writes the notes in the back of her program was kidding somebody. Being impolite, if rigorously statistical, souls, they also like myself were motivated to chuckles when bidden to read of the cosmic acceptance of Miss Le Gallienne as a great acting genius, of the despair of Stanislavski, Danchenko, Meyerhold, Reinhardt, Jessner, Gémier, Antoine and all other such producers when they couldn't capture her for their own, of all the playwrights in the world from Rostand to Shaw, Pirandello to O'Neill, and Hauptmann to Yeats frenziedly composing plays for her, and of a theatre public that could not obtain tickets quick enough for such of her fiascos as *Hannele, Jeanne d'Arc* (by Mercedes de Acosta), *The Call*

of Life, and *The Master Builder*, to say nothing of her subsequent Civic Repertory company which lost $40,000 in a
single season.

It may be possible that I know nothing about acting,
that, whatever I may think, there is nothing in Edith Evans,
or Marie Tempest, or Helen Hayes, or any other such players,
and that Miss Le Gallienne is a truly remarkable artiste. It
may be possible. But if it is and if what Miss Le Gallienne
offered in *Madame Capet* was competent acting, I have
blamed little respect for acting. Her Marie Antoinette
seemed to me to be enlisted in the March of the Wooden
Soldiers. Her emotional equipment was confined largely to
her dilator naris and intercostal muscles, and her almost con-
tinuous reliance upon gestures and gesticulations implied a
self-appreciated deficiency in the inner projectional attributes of her craft. Her diction was good, but her periodic
elaborate affectation in such pronunciations as *eteequette,
Meerrrabeau,* and *reclees* for *recluse* (remember, the play
was an English translation of the French) was ridiculous.
And her attempt at song was embarrassing. Except for a single brief moment in the final scene when she prepares for
death, her Antoinette, in short, needed only a camera and
some film to make it a serviceable Grade-C double-feature
neighborhood movie.

As for the play, adapted from the already dull French
of Marcelle Maurette by George Middleton and pick-ax, it
presented itself as an absurdly sentimentalized and amateurish chronicle of the queen's life from her profligate days at
Versailles to the cell in the Conciergerie that led to the guil-
lotine. It was full of stuff close to a vain actress' heart. It
permitted her to display herself, seriatim, as a gay, reckless,
and capricious girl (interpreted by throwing imaginary forward passes to herself all around the furniture); as the hot
passion of a handsome Count (interpreted reciprocally by
the bestowal of a cautious buss on his upstage cheek, lest her

coiffure become disarranged); later as one in whom the depths of mother love have been stirred (interpreted by patting a small child actor on the tochus); subsequently as a queenly being who treats her solicitous court counselor with lofty disdain (interpreted by sniffing thrice through the right nostril and impatiently tapping the left leg with a riding crop); again as a harrassed and brave woman stoically on trial for her life (interpreted by smearing her face with white talcum and gazing expressionless at Mrs. Katzenberg in Row A); and finally as one heroically indifferent in the presence of death (interpreted by keeping the executioner waiting while she changes into a pretty white dress).

One cannot, however, help admiring the theatrical pertinacity of Miss Le Gallienne — as one cannot help deploring the churlishness of a critic who yearly calls attention to it. But criticism, unfortunately, has nothing to do with gallantry — save in the instance of young critics who still have not outgrown their sentimentality for ladies of the stage regardless and of old ones who fear an actress may be a friend of the boss' wife and who do not, at their age, wish to put themselves to any discomfiture — and so it is that one between the two groups finds himself in the same old infelicitous spot. For the fact persists that Miss Le Gallienne, seemly and ambitious, literate and highly purposed as she is, is a very gamy actress and one whose efforts to soar like an eagle with only a pair of cuckoo wings at her command provide a severe tax on chivalrous reporting.

In this last exhibit, as in almost every other play she has appeared in since her early epiphany in the purely pictorial rôle of *The Swan*, Miss Le Gallienne disclosed herself devoid of most of the attributes that go to constitute not only a sound, but even a moderately effective, actress. Her emotional scenes again suggested that she feels nothing below her larynx. Her gestures — she uses half a dozen in the course of a single line — often have little or no relation to what she is saying and are apparently employed merely, in her idea, to give "life" and "movement" to her interpretation. What they give, I fear, is rather the picture of an actress who, like the rest of us, admires Gertrude Lawrence but who, attempting to duplicate her method, has somehow got Miss Lawrence mixed up with Hugh Herbert.

In the matter of speech, Miss Le Gallienne has certain virtues. She speaks well and clearly, but here, too, she invalidates the good impression, as I have noted, by an intermittent preciousness of pronunciation that suggests a Berlitz pupil trying to get in big with teacher. I appreciate that Miss Le Gallienne knows French better than most American actresses, but why must she always so superiorly and disturbingly seek to impress us with the fact? Her bearing, when she stands still, is admirable, but her carriage when she moves, except when she moves in a straight line, is jerky, forced and awkward, suggesting a very proficient but unfortunately slightly arthritic Delsartian. And, though it is evident she has a good head and knows fully the meaning of the lines she speaks, she cannot for the life of her fuse them with the least sincerity.

LESBIANISM. I neither saw nor read Aimée and Philip Stuart's *Love of Women* in its original London version, so I may not know what I am talking about, but there are many indications that it dealt with the Mytilene divertissement commonly called Lesbianism. In the version produced in America by the Messrs. Shubert, however, the Lesbian motif was moralized into something that seemed to be a commixtion of an older woman's motherly love for a young girl and the desire of two females to pursue their collaborative literary work without interruption by men and love. Inasmuch as the whole play, for all this timorous dodging of its only possible authentic intent, was obviously and patently either about Lesbianism or nothing, the public and critics naturally spoofed it into the wastebasket and incidentally treated the Messrs. Shubert to some very luscious raspberries for their old-fashioned moral qualms.

Up to about four years ago, there was among the magazines which I served as drama critic one, a very doggy periodical, whose editor, a punctilious gentleman, refused to allow any contributor to use such terms as *Lesbian, whore, syphilis* or *abortion* in his pages and who, on the theory that they would shock and offend his readers, was in the invariable habit of altering them respectively to *classic inamorata, fille de joie, blood disease,* and *illegal surgery.* I recall the amusement I privileged myself, in a first-night review of *The Captive,* in fooling him by writing that the play dealt with a couple of women who were members of the famous *Les Biens* troupe in Paris, which he doubtless thought was something on the order of the *Les Gymnastes* troupe at the Cirque Medrano or the *Les Jackson Girls* at the Folies Bergère. The magazine, which hadn't realized that the world had changed a lot and that people who were now reading D. H. Lawrence and Ernest Hemingway were the same who not so very long before were reading Anthony Hope and Fannie Hurst, naturally failed. And the failure of the Stuarts' play was due to the same absurd hesitation and equivoque. In a day when such subjects as Lesbianism, homosexuality and the more romantic forms of fornication are the favorite topics of polite society and when syphilis, abortion and rape are headlined in the daily family newspapers, a magazine or play that evades direct statement and employs euphemisms of one kind or another simply makes a monkey of itself. And it makes a double monkey of itself when, like this *Love of Women,* it thematically argues that the late World War, which saw in England the taking over of men's tasks by women, had the effect of masculinizing women, when further it presents two such he-female exhibits, and when then it cheats the truth by drolly contending that they are still capable of dismissing sex of any kind from their lives. Tell that to the Marines — or to the Eldorado and Monokol girls in Berlin!

LIBERTIES. At the New York opening of the Federal Theatre's Negro swing version of *The Mikado* there were periodic minor hisses from several parts of the auditorium. They apparently came from the omnipresent species of squintsconce who esteems it his arbitrary duty to protest against any liberties that may be taken with the stage's classics. It was, however, gratifying to read the subsequent newspaper appraisals of the production and to observe that the reviewers not only didn't share in the objection but went to the extreme of complaining that even more liberties should have been taken and that the exhibit should have been swung a heap more than it was.

I say it was gratifying because up to very recent years even certain of these same reviewers, when it came to the classics, were of the mind and attitude of the opening night grumblers. Any freedom taken with Shakespeare, however theatrically valuable, irritated them no end. Any editing of Molière or Sheridan aroused their punditical indignation. And any deviation, however slight, from the Gilbert line made them pretty boiling mad. The change that has come over them is a critically welcome one, and all to the good.

One of the silliest attitudes of a critic or any other person with sufficient dramatic experience behind him is the rigorous opposition to any free play, however intelligent, with a classic (which everyone knows by heart) that may lend it a fresh breeze, novelty, and added entertainment. Shakespeare in modern dress was long a bitter pill to the severe classicist, as was Ibsen staged in the contemporary idiom and the Goethe of *Faust* brought into the key and tone of the later-day dramatic expression. But time and reflection have coated the pill with sugar and it is only the intellectual mountebank who today gets on his ear over such matters. Take this question of *The Mikado*. Is it any greater distortion of its values to cast its Japanese with Negroes than it is to cast them, as conventionally, with English? Is directing several of its dance numbers in the Negro rhythm any more absurd than directing them in the old-time, established mincing pitter-patter which stage tradition has bogusly associated with all Nipponese terpsichorean movement? Further, is the shifting of the scene to an island in the southern Pacific and the substitution of tropical costume for the familiar kimonos any more malapropos and questionable than Shakespeare's own shifting of an ancient Danish court to what is unmistakably, if unadmittedly, the England of centuries later or the wholesale substitution of kimonos for the more generally Jap affected Western costume in such English-Japanese operettas as *San Toy* and *The Geisha?* And, in a general way, if George Bernard Shaw can be made more popularly amusing by tuning him up in *The Chocolate Soldier* and Shakespeare by tuning him up in *The Boys from Syracuse,* why may not Gilbert and Sullivan also be zipped up with swing, goona-goona wobbles and cake-walks?

LIGHTER ENTERTAINMENT. The so-called lighter entertainments, whether musical comedy, revue or farce, have often been more critically important in reflecting American life, the American attitude and the American idiosyncrasy than the run of so-called more serious plays. Charles Hoyt's farces are an infinitely more accurate and more illuminating picture of the America of their time than three-fourths of all the sober plays written during the same period. George Ade's roughhouse comedies told and still tell us more about the America of the time, its habits, predilections, humors, prejudices and comportment, than all of the dramas written in those years by the long-faced playwrights. George Cohan's farces, musical shows and revues are better guide-books to their American years than nine-tenths of the plays manufactured by Charles Klein, Augustus Thomas, George Broadhurst, Eugene Walter and David Belasco. Perhaps it isn't so strange that it should be so. Let us not overlook the fact that there is a much juicier reflection of the English mind, heart, psyche and attitude in the light left-handed appraisals of W. S. Gilbert than in the combined heavier right hands of all the Victorian dramatists.

LILLIE. The old contention that the English are deficient in a sense of humor finds some support in the circumstance that they do not sufficiently appreciate their own best musical show comédienne, Beatrice Lillie. Just a year ago, in fact, they so loftily refrained from being amused by her that the show she was in went soon into the discard. It has remained for us loafers over here to size her up for her own great humorous worth and to reward her with the diamonds she so richly deserves.

The Lillie was lately on American view again in a Noël Coward revue called *Set to Music*. Inasmuch as the revue without her would have been something more than feeble, Mr. Coward should chip in handsomely on those diamonds. For it is she who took its indifferent materials and with her own genius for healthy low comedy converted them into gay and bouncing sport. When she lay hold of some such overly familiar victual as a travesty of a fashionable charity pageant, it became in her hands a fresh and rip-roaring feast. When she tackled the old Russian spy hoopdedoodle, it turned into the tastiest kind of buffoonery. When she went into the *marron* about the bored actress haughtily spurning her admirer's jewels, the while she manages to keep them securely in her fist, she made the whole business just about as gala as even the frostiest-faced critic might have wished. She is, it seems, one of the few persons in the entertainment world who doesn't need material with which to work. She can apparently make it up as she goes along. With one dart of her eye she can spare a skit writer a dozen lines; with one little affectionate pat on her rear and one little vocal squeak she can save the management royalties on the most desired blackout sketch. The girl is, in short, pretty hot stuff.

Mr. Coward's contribution to the evening was, as intimated, no particular shakes. It represented songs and skits largely gathered together from various of his London ventures and frequently gave off an unmistakable aroma of yesterday. A number called *The Stately Homes of England* was fair satirical fun and another, *A Fragonard Impression*, with Miss Lillie entering a delicate boudoir on a white horse was authentic hilarity, but on the whole the Coward humor indicated a fatigued return to such motifs as *Children of the Ritz* (you know all about that one from the title), *Three White Feathers* (you immediately know it's the one about the vulgarian on her way to presentation at Court), *Mad About the Boy* (in which you guess several different types of women will variously indicate their amorous reactions to a movie idol), and — you knew it was coming with your eyes shut — the number detailing the idiosyncrasies of Elsie Mendl, Laura Corrigan, Daisy Fellowes, and other such figures in the Riviera heeg leef.

LINCOLN.   It has long been argued that no actor can fail as Hamlet. This, of course, is nonsense, as the records duly attest. It might, however, be argued with considerably more truth that not only is it extremely difficult for an actor to fail as Lincoln but that it is equally difficult for any play about Lincoln not to impress its audiences. The mere spectacle of an actor made up to look like Abe seems to do something to people. The old melodramas of the Hal Reid period in which Lincoln, implored by the lad's old mother, used regularly to pardon Langhorne Roanoke, the young Confederate spy, brought cheers from all over the house. Movies from *The Birth of a Nation* to *Wells Fargo* have found in Lincoln the surest of sure-fire hokum. And in the whole history of the later American drama I can think of only one

Lincoln exhibit, *If Booth Had Missed,* which didn't fully jounce its customers, undoubtedly because they appreciated that it presented a Lincoln who was pure fiction. But show audiences an Abe they already know, and they are yours. The ready-made effect that was once implicit in Mother, Baby, and the Flag remains as invincibly implicit in Lincoln as in Cinderella, the Saviour, and a tiny illuminated train winding along a backdrop in the dark distance.

In the legitimate theatre, in short, Lincoln continues to be as hokumissimo as Teddy Roosevelt with a big Indian club in his fist or a chorus dressed in leafy South Sea Island skirts used to be in the musical show theatre. Or as the sketch in which Pat, asked by the waiter what he wanted, elaborately indicated a passing bosomy young blonde and replied " breast of chicken " invariably was in the old burlesque theatre. It is thus that Robert Sherwood's *Abe Lincoln in Illinois,* which keeps Lincoln on the stage throughout its entire course, naturally and inevitably moves such of its audiences as bring their emotions and reactions, already resolved, into a theatre rather than such as prefer to take them, surprised and affected, out of one.

In his play, Mr. Sherwood has pictured Lincoln honestly and with playwriting dignity, but with an imagination that lacks the elasticity and flower to translate the historic literal into the dramatic literary. We get a record, often automatically eloquent by virtue of the nature of its basic materials, rather than an inspired interpretation of a record. We get, in short, the " tortured soul," " the gaunt, lonely man " and all the other clichés that Lincoln in the designation of writers and critics on end was — and we get him with a measure of theatrical vividness — but we do not finally get a Lincoln who, from any imaginatively penetrating level of dramatic criticism, is much other than John Drinkwater in a black Prince Albert, plug hat and whiskers, relieved only by a couple of American drinks under his belt.

Not only, however and nevertheless, did Raymond Massey, who played Abe, naturally and consistently make the hit of his acting life, but when Massey took a holiday and was succeeded in the rôle by his understudy, one Gaines, this Gaines too made in turn the hit of his.

LONSDALE. It is one of the merits of any play by Frederick Lonsdale that the theatregoer can pretty well tell what it is going to be like from a preliminary glance at the program. In a day when one often has to wait patiently until the curtain has been up for five minutes to realize that a play isn't at all going to be to one's taste, this is a luxurious virtue, granting, of course, that the theatregoer is a glutton for somewhat rococo polite comedy. Such a one, Mr. Lonsdale seldom disappoints. The English house party, one is reassured by the program, will again be in evidence. So, too, will be the Duchess of Laurajean, familiarly known as Libbi, and her husband, the Duke, familiarly known as Boohoo. The weekend guests are sure to include Lord Somerset, familiarly known as Stinky, who will growl when hauled off by Lady Maugham for a round of golf; Lord Vandruten, familiarly known as Wobbles, who will growl when Atkinson, the eighth footman, fails to show up with the port; the stodgy Lord Pinero, familiarly known as Hokum, who will growl when his young wife, Lady Pinero, familiarly known as Pinchy-winchy, complains that he takes her to Ciro's only five times a week; and Lord Haddonchambers, familiarly known as Toodles, who will periodically plump himself down in the armchair near the fireplace and growl epigrams either to the effect that love dies when the heart stops beating or that the heart stops beating when love dies.

It will also presently and duly appear that the Duke is carrying on in camera with young Lady Pinero, and it will not be long afterward that the Duchess will become privy to the situation. But will the Duchess get sore? No, you well know, the Duchess will not get sore. The Duchess is a wise girl. She will have seen enough such English plays in her time to appreciate that all that will be necessary to win the Duke back will be to throw him into the arms of his charmer and then sit back and knit until the little rascal comes to recognize that his inamorata is a flighty bore. And along about ten minutes to eleven you are pleasantly confident that, hand in hand, the sagacious Duchess and her repentant spouse will be on their reconciled way up to her bedroom, stopping but briefly en route for a tender look at their two sleeping children. Sometimes, a bit of novelty will be injected into the proceedings by having Lady Sidneygrundy, who is broke, filch a pearl necklace and by having Watts, the impeccable butler, who is also broke, turn out to be in cahoots with Her Ladyship. But in general the pattern will not be much changed.

If, however, you conclude from all this that Lord Nathan, familiarly known as Grouser, is altogether displeased with the Lonsdale theatre, please to consider yourself faintly mistaken. It is, certainly, an ancestral and very trivial theatre and one beneath criticism in its more elevated and serious flights, but it is also occasionally an agreeably witty and graceful and literate theatre. And that, in any day, is not too superiorly to be sneezed at. If Mr. Lonsdale has nothing of importance to say, he at least says it charmingly and often with considerable humor.

LOVABLE RÔLE.   A recent evanescent little turkey called *Day in the Sun,* by the Messrs. Sammis and Heyn, provided Mr. Taylor Holmes with an opportunity to display himself briefly in the species of rôle so often fatuously yearned for by ageing actors desirous of re-wooing a no longer affectionate box-office. The rôle in question, which you have experienced on an average of at least twice a year for the last four decades, is of the kidney habitually described by everybody but the man in the box-office and the few paying customers as " lovable." That is to say, it presents some old actor, once and long ago a favorite, as a character who bores everyone on the stage and almost everyone in the auditorium to death with his wholesale warm-heartedness and oppressive geniality but who, in the actor's private vanity and the eyes of congenital theatrical sentimentalists, theoretically reflects the theoretically noble spirit that is the actor himself in person.

The rôle, while always fundamentally the same, takes on several superficial variations. Often it is that of a gentle old idler with an absurd hobby of one sort or another who sorely tries the patience of the family with his habit of coming to dinner without his shoes on and of hiding his bottle in the cuckoo clock but who finally, to his own and everyone else's surprise, contrives to lift the mortgage on the house by outwitting Ichabod Perkins, the shyster lawyer. Sometimes it is that of an old waster, chronically wozzled with gin, who drives his old-maid sister and his young daughter half-crazy with his fool inventions, one of which, however, turns out in the last act to be worth eight million dollars. And on occasion, particularly if it be confected by an English playwright, it is that of a white-haired old codger who was something of a gay dog in his earlier days, who still dons full evening dress even when dining alone, who offers frequent tender toasts in rich old port to the portraits in oil of his deceased sweetheart, Lady Diana Fitzgoldberg, and of Flying Heels, his favorite jumper, and who — without letting her know he is her father — beneficently looks after the future well-being of his beautiful young ward Daphne.

Lunts. It was a lucky day for the Theatre Guild when Eugene O'Neill first communicated to its board of directors the news of the advent in the southmost reaches of Georgia of Prof. Orville P. Mosedinck. This Prof. Mosedinck, O'Neill discovered, was a hypnotist extraordinaire; nothing like him, said O'Neill, had ever been seen anywhere; his powers were magic itself. "Get into touch with him at once," O'Neill urged. "He may, if he sufficiently exerts himself, be able to hypnotize a few good actors into the Guild service. He may, indeed, if you give him enough rope, even succeed in at last hypnotizing a good play into your hands."

The rest, of course, is history. Although the Prof.'s hypnotic virtuosity does not seem to have worked so well in the case of plays, his great feat in persuading the Lunts, while under the influence, to ally themselves with the Guild is commonly appreciated. (There is no truth in the scandalous rumor that, in order to persuade the Lunts, the Guild directorate had to supplement the illustrious Prof.'s efforts with several gallons of vodka and a variety of hypodermic needles.) The credit is entirely, wholly and completely Prof. Orville P. Mosedinck's. If it had not been for him, the Guild would still be going around with even more holes in its socks than it already has. For it is a well-known fact that, after it has annually put on its customary play by a Hollywood movie scenario writer, its customary feeble little gesture in Left Wing drama, its dramatization of some rococo novel, and its proud revelation of the first work of some Grade-G genius, it is the Lunts who have had to come to its rescue and make up enough of the deficit at least to pay for the postage stamps on the press department's bulletins telling how good the Guild used to be.

The two life-savers, Alf and wife, never more valiantly performed their services on behalf of the sorely stricken Guild than in the instance of S. N. Behrman's adaptation of Giraudoux's *Amphitryon 38*. As the Jupiter who is sufficiently Latin to appreciate the Italian proverb that angels may be all right in their place but not in bed and who craves for a change in the person of the mortal Alkmena, Lunt employed that oddly cajoling voice of his, which always suggests a throat lozenge mocking a tenor, to admirable dry comedy effect. And as the married morsel whom he covets, Miss Fontanne stooged it handsomely for him throughout the evening. The play itself was slight stuff but it provided a sufficient share of agreeable and witty boulevard entertainment, all the more welcome in a season that seemed to promise so much and that, at least in its earlier phases, for the most part haplessly resolved itself into a series of such denicotinized dramatic cheroots as the hitherto applaudable Maxwell Anderson's three-decker combination of ham, cheese and boloney that with infinitely more relevance might have been called *The Dog-Wagon* and Rachel Crothers' fossilized fable of the separated married couple reunited by their child and attemptedly given a touch of modernity by making the wife guilty of Buchmanism instead of adultery. Into such a scene *Amphitryon 38* came as comparative manna. Liberally and wisely deleted of its verbose philosophical disquisitions and converted by Behrman into livelier theatrical material through a shrewd suppression of its original bookish flavor, its retelling of the familiar legend in terms of Sacha Guitry crossed with a little Shaw was to be recommended to all such theatregoers, Guild and otherwise, as were beginning to become discouraged over the thought that the season would be devoted largely to proving that wit and humor were lost attributes of the drama and to substituting in place of them the species of dead-pan greasepaint literature which distils the emotions of the witless and humorless with flashbacks showing gray-wigged and dejected old folk in their happy, picnicking youth and with close-ups and long-shots of disconsolate intellectuals searching for their souls and for the meaning of life in the bodies of cuties.

In their subsequent financially auspicious revival of *The Sea Gull*, however, there were moments when one felt that the Lunts had unwittingly confused Chekhov with Molnár. This was not wholly because they often invested the Russian's Trigorin and Irina with something closely bordering upon a boulevard lightness of touch. We have become used to such capers in the revivals of various classics, as it seems to be the fashion to imagine that a theatrical modernity may be injected into almost any classic by lightening its more somber aspects, or at least gingerly avoiding a complete and thorough histrionic statement of the author's full-blooded tragic intention. We are thus periodically regaled with Iagos whose mordant cunning is here and there identifiable with Sacha Guitry's esoteric winks, Heddas who comport themselves like the heroine of a Hollywood *Gold-Diggers of 1937* film, and Portias whose trial scenes need only Bobby Clark lying leg cocked in air on the judge's bench to make them critically acceptable.

The Molnár impression was induced rather more, and helplessly, by the apparent increasing inability on the part of the Lunts to suppress those acting idiosyncrasies which have so joyously in the past embellished the lighter plays that have been their greatest successes. These idiosyncrasies, both vocal and deportmental, have become so deeply ingrained in them that, try as they will, they cannot conquer them in the interests of the more sober and serious drama, and the result in a play like *The Sea Gull* is that the characters they are playing become to a considerable degree disturbingly Lunts instead of the Lunts becoming coalescently them. The Trigorin of the present occasion, accordingly, stepped more or less recalcitrantly out of *The Play's the Thing*, as the Irina stepped out of *The Guardsman*. Both performances were absolutely first-rate Molnár, but when it came to Chekhov it was another matter.

The character of Nina, the lovelorn, heartsick girl, is, of course and incidentally, the dream of almost every younger actress' ambition, and with good reason. It is one of the sure-fire rôles of drama and it is next to impossible completely to fail in it. If anyone has failed completely in it, I am not privy to the news. Surely in none of the many productions of the play that I have seen in the Western world have I observed a Nina who didn't get out of the rôle most of its facile, ready-made effect. Even if the actress is not entirely satisfactory, one must shrewdly guard one's criticism of her, as Chekhov (who was in love with the character) alleviates what amateur traces there may possibly be in the actress and performance with a cleverly calculated extenuation in a later-act passage. Uta Hagen, the Nina in the Lunt exhibit, was considerably better, considerably more convincing, and certainly much more charming than a number I have engaged, but I wish her director would have confided to her that eager youthfulness isn't always best to be suggested by constantly throwing back the head and ecstatically tossing it.

M

MACOWAN. Norman Macowan's *Glorious Morning* offered
as its villain a totalitarian state that prohibited a belief in God
and as its heroine a young woman who beheld a vision and
thereupon conspired in defiance of the authorities to bring
God back onto the job. Without God, she maintained, the
people were doomed to misery; with Him, they would be so
happy they could hardly stand it. Without venturing into the
integrity of the author's philosophy, save perhaps to speculate worriedly on the relative ecstasy of Stalin and a Baptist
Georgia cracker with a hole in his pants, no shoes and pel-
lagra, what I couldn't help recalling during the progress of
the play was a buffoonery written almost twenty years ago
by two very clever young men and called *Heliogabalus*. The
villain in that case was a saintly wench who began preaching the Gospel in the gay and merry infidel Rome of the
hedonistic Helio and who, gaining converts, damn nigh
wrecked the happiness of the whole community. The hero
was the Emperor who finally got up the courage to boot her
out and thus restore some peace and joy to his country.
Without venturing, in turn, into the integrity of the two very
clever young men's philosophy, I still am persuaded that it
made a lot better show.

Both the heroine of *Glorious Morning* and the villain of
Heliogabalus were of a piece. The latter, true enough, was
intended as a comic figure and the former, true enough, as a
serious one. But the former was sort o' funny just the same.
As Mr. Macowan gave her to us, she was nothing but our old
hokum girl-friend, Lygia, out of all the *Quo Vadises, Signs of
the Cross* and other such holy delicatessen since Wilson Bar-

rett was tied into his first diaper. Mr. Macowan simply took off her familiar old white nightgown and put her in a modern street dress. There she was, nevertheless, as we have seen and known and been bored by her since originally she ambled out onto a stage long years ago, gazed intently and unceasingly at the peanut gallery (thus indicating her aloof otherworldliness), and slowly brought the Light into the life of the infidel lion tamer, chariot driver and pet of the Nubian dancing girls, Odius Maximus of Benzedrine, both of them at eleven o'clock moving nobly hand in hand, to the accompaniment of some very bad Palestrina, to their deaths in the arena. The white nightgown, as I say, was gone and the arena lions were now a firing squad, but the rest was essentially not much different, except that here there was a quorum of Odiuses in place of the old-time solo ham.

Adding materially to the unintentional humorous aspect of the exhibit was the heroine's description of the vision that led her to espouse the Lord's cause. Some day a playwright, conjuring up a picture of Heaven and the Almighty, is going to imagine God as sometimes doing something other than sitting on an old gilt Richelieu storehouse throne or, more often, walking up and down a great flight of steps (customarily described as closely resembling the staircase of the old Parker House in St. Louis), but it won't, I fear, be Mr. Macowan.

"Seldom," wrote Mr. Sydney W. Carroll in the *Daily Telegraph* when the exhibit was shown in London, "have we in our playhouses so distinguished . . . so imaginative a play!"

MATRIMONY AND THE ACTRESS. In a recent editorial, a prominent metropolitan newspaper delivered itself thus: "To cynical aphorisms must disillusioned males resort in these dark hours of reflection upon the marriage of lovely Vera Zorina. Now, say it if you can, she is Mrs. Balanchivadze. Romantic, eh wot? Gloom in the offices of those critics who described the star of *I Married an Angel* as ' something of a treasure ', ' heaven-sent ', ' graceful and exquisite ', etc., etc. Lucky is Zorina if she can draw such enthusiastic praises henceforth. True, all the critics couldn't have married the angel even had Zorina's fancies veered toward typewriters rather than terpsichore. But, so long as she remained an unmarried angel — they could all hope! "

That the editorial has something there, even if it too narrowly and absurdly confines itself to the reactions merely of critics, is plain. And what it says about the fair Zorina is true about most actresses of any allure whatsoever. Not only critics but men in the mass disrelish the idea of such plums giving themselves to the prosaic ball and chain. It corrupts illusion; it disturbingly mixes up the fragrant picture with a husband who often, judging from his published photographs, bears a close resemblance to a Brazilian dentist; it somehow all seems to be traitorous to that fabled world of gilt and tinsel and starry song that is the theatre.

In the case of a certain catalogue of actresses, it doesn't of course matter. If a comédienne or funny girl marries, she doesn't in the least discommode the fancy of her public, as nothing is so unromantic in the first place as a woman, whatever she looks like, who either publicly or privately goes in in a big way for humor. If a genuine histrionic artiste, whether beautiful or with a face like an ax, takes unto herself a spouse, it also doesn't matter, since a great actress remains a great actress whatever she does, even to the point of committing bigamy or eating garlic. But between the female clowns on the one hand and the dyed-in-the-wool geniuses on the other, with the piefaces thrown in for good measure, it is better for any stage girl this side of forty to keep away from the altar.

Art may be art, but when all is said and done the women of the stage remain women in the public concept rather than actresses. They are — aside from the exceptional prodigies amongst them — creatures to be sentimentally regarded, dolls to be looked at, living cigarette pictures to be collected by the boys who never grow up, lovely and glamourful items on the drab laundry list of life. It may be childish; it may be foolish; it may be even asinine; but that is the way it is and that is the way it has been for centuries. And when one of the imaginatively desirable lulus marries, it immediately puts her, in the public's estimation and disappointment, into the humdrum, routine and prosy category of all the other women in the world.

The late Charles Frohman, one of the shrewdest theatrical men who ever lived, duly appreciated all this and forbade his young women to enter into the state of connubial wet-blanket. When and if, against his will and better judgment, they did, he lost all interest in them and let them pass to other managements. That he was right, furthermore, was indicated in the fact that when the three fair young actresses whom he had built into public idols disobeyed him and married, all three soon went into the public discard. A fourth, who also failed to heed his injunction, had a hard time of it for years and regained her public only after she was considerably older and went in for character rôles.

The wiser young actresses themselves often duly realize the danger that their marriages must inevitably offer to their careers and, rather than risk it, abandon the footlights. It is thus that the stage has unfortunately lost some of its choicest ornaments. Anna Wheaton, one of the most promising of musical comedy actresses, married and wouldn't any longer take a chance colliding with the public's prejudice. Martha Bryan-Allen, a young dramatic actress of more than usual talent, did the same. Constance Binney, Shirley O'Hara, Adele Astaire, Ruth Findlay, Lois Moran in more recent years and Helen Hale, Erminie Clark, Marguerite Clark, Mary Duncan in somewhat earlier also sapiently did the same.

It would not be tactful to list the names of a considerable group of actresses who have married, who have continued on the stage, and who have lost a considerable share of their former grip upon the public's romantic affection. But anyone who is at all closely acquainted with the present stage may easily identify them. What is more, it is equally easy to summon to mind the names of several young women who began their careers with great success so little as three years ago, who have got themselves married, and who since then have had a hard time trying to get jobs from producers who appreciate that, so far as the public reaction is concerned, they have done themselves wrong.

Many things have conspired to do dirt to the stage girl who marries in these days. Gossip columns, miscellaneous interviews, honky-tonk personal press agency, the biographical notes in the theatre programs and a dozen and one other such intrusive publicity engines have combined to make of such a girl's marriage a cross between a street fair and a free delicatessen. There was a time when an actress could get more or less quietly married and go her stage way thereafter more or less in peace. But hardly so any longer. And the result, in many cases, has been to make out the married young actress of today as pretty much a stale sock.

Newspaper articles and interviews, embellished with pictures, betray to all and sundry the inside on last night's ethereal princess. She likes nothing better after the show, it appears, than to take off her shoes and cook a big dish of calves' livers and onions for herself and hubby, a photograph duly exhibiting the happy couple with their schnozzles deep in their chow. The princess' husband, it also appears from the photograph, hasn't shaved for several days and is rather bald on top, to say nothing of being seemingly averse, when at home, to wearing a collar. From the biographical note in the program, one learns that the fair princess' spouse, who was previously married to a soft-shoe hoofer on the Pantages circuit, is the actor who originally played the valet in the road company of *Up in Mabel's Room* and who since that time has been appearing in radio sketches sponsored by the Superbo Soup Co. Some other glamourous will-o'-the-wisp, it seems, is married to Jake Wasserbauer, of Wasserbauer's

Kozy-Fit Chemises, Inc. Her hobby is cooking (it is remarkable how all the girls immediately develop a hobby for cooking the moment they get married), and her pet dish is Königsbergerklops, which her Jake adores. There are photographs showing the loving couple sitting in front of their fireplace, the will-o'-the-wisp in a wifely house-wrapper and Jake with his feet on the mantel. "My husband, my home and my Königsbergerklops are all that really matter to me," sighs the will-o'-the-wisp.

And so it goes. Sometimes we see the moonlit princess of men's dreams seated on a couch in her flat with her arms around the neck of a husband who looks suspiciously like a fairy. Sometimes we see another such dear creature of fancy in a pair of seedy old breeches shoveling manure on her summer farm in company with a husband who is indistinguishable from the other hired help. And at other times we read of still some other starlit virgin who has two grown sons, one of them in reform school and the other studying to be a veterinary surgeon, and whose husband is vice-president of an exterminator company.

No, it won't do. Marriage may be a noble institution, but Juliet and Kathie and the Princess Flavia aren't the same to their customers once they have entered into it. The public doesn't pay three dollars to dream of proficient cooks of pigs' knuckles and bed-partners of presidents of glue factories.

MAUGHAM. The recent revival of W. S. Maugham's *The Circle* is at once the occasion for pleasure and regret. It is the first because after these many seasons it remains one of the brightest comedies to have come to the English-speaking stage in our time. It is the second because it once more forces into our consciousness the sad fact of its talented author's defection from the theatre. About a year ago I asked him if he was determined never again, as was his declaration, to write plays. "I have said that I shall write no more plays," he answered. "But" — and his right eye maneuvered something resembling a wink — " I have left myself a loop-hole. If ever I get an idea that doesn't fit into a novel and that is essentially theatre, I may change my mind." So there is still hope.

The gift that Maugham brought to later-day British comedy was a three-fold one. Not only is he one of the most skillful writers of his period and not only is he an expert in the handling of character, but in almost everything he does there is discernible the force of an independent and richly fertile personality. It is the common allegation against him that he is arbitrarily cynical and bitter. Nothing could be more ridiculous. No one who has read him closely or who closely has scrutinized his plays can fail to perceive that he is cynical and bitter only when a particular theme is itself naturally cynical and bitter and when any other treatment of it would be false and corrupt. And even when he engages such a theme there is plenty of evidence that the unruly sentiment that may be at the bottom of even the profoundest cynic gets its free and gracious and liberal play from him.

Take, for a single example, this *The Circle*. Stamped by nine critics out of ten a cynical excursion into comedy, it actually contains quite as much sentiment as the average exhibit by the average English sugar-teat confectioner. It would not, indeed, be too much of an exaggeration to say that this widely accepted specimen of Maugham cynicism is one of the most romantic comedies of the modern British theatre. Cynical? Bitter? Bosh. It smiles sympathetically with love on the wing. It cries into its beer over the lost stage beauties of an earlier day — Mrs. Langtry, Ellen Terry, Mary Anderson. It devotes itself to the considerate tenderness of love grown old. It plays wistfully with old albums and it is gentle with the mistakes of even those who have done us grievous wrong. It moons over the beauty of first loves and sighs for the loveliness of places where long ago one had been happy. It flatters old age in men and even momentarily extenuates it in women. It is, in a word, one long laugh at cynicism, only at rare intervals punctuated with the relieving injection of a little acid.

Further proof? Maugham, the reputed sourball, makes his young hero a business man, insists he is purely a business man, and then makes him, contrary to popular cynicism, at the same time a heroic and romantic lover. He pursues the hokum romantic point of view by causing his sagacious old Champion-Cheney, quondam member of Parliament, to be outwitted by a young woman. He goes in for such sentiments as: " When I drive about in a Callot frock and a Rolls-Royce I envy the shopgirl in a coat and skirt whom I see jumping on the tailboard of a bus." He argues with a perfectly straight face that the best way to make a woman love a man is for him to give her a black eye, surely the conviction of dyed-in-the-wool sentimentalists determined to hide their sentimentality. He evokes sentimental pictures with passages about cocoanut trees, azaleas, camellias, winding coast lines, and blue seas. His heart is in such purple song as: " The moon's shining, Elizabeth. We'll drive all through the night. We'll drive through the dawn and through the sunrise." And at the conclusion he cheers his young lovers through the gates and on to the warm tropics with (I quote) their blue skies and palm trees all along the beach.

Maugham a cynic? In your hat!

MODERNIZATIONS. Certainly, one who like myself has impertinently amused himself revaluing and modernizing the classics and who even now is fooling with the job of editing Ibsen's *Ghosts* in the light of later-day findings on syphilis should be the last to complain when others indulge in a similar diversion. Nor, equally certainly, do I complain. In point of fact, I rejoice. That is, I rejoice when a Hauptmann rewrites *Hamlet,* when a Shaw rewrites *Cymbeline,* when a St. John Ervine writes a sequel to *The Merchant of Venice,* when a clever Russian reconstructs *Antony and Cleopatra,* or when anyone else with humor, wit, and dexterity brings a sound critical prankishness to the business. What I lament, however, is the periodic and very foolish attempt to lay hold of some classic drama that has become thematically sterile and to seek to give it a bogus life on the modern stage by leaving its theme unaltered and intact but by bringing the dramaturgy and dialogue somewhat closer to the present-day theatrical idiom. That is what Thornton Wilder has recently done with A Doll's House and what results, as might have been expected, is a whimsical hybrid, neither fish, flesh, fowl, nor good red Louis K. Anspacher.

The only way in which A Doll's House might be modernized would be to make Helmer so disgustedly irritated with his silly wife's presumption to a plane of masculine equality that it was he who did the final door-slamming. To bid an audience today to be sympathetically exercised on behalf of a female squintsconce who has forged a note and then loftily deserts her children and her husband merely because the latter, who is head of a bank, doesn't heroically accept the ruin it might readily have brought upon him, is asking a little too much. And any such effort as Mr. Wilder's externally to doll up Ibsen's telling of the tale contrives only further to make things ridiculous. You can't make an antique seat less an antique seat by putting a flapper on it. And you can't make a modern play out of a rococo one simply by having Helmer call Nora " darling " instead of " little bird " and " squirrel " and by here and there changing the Ibsen dramaturgic technique to Clemence Dane's. It is much better to leave such things be. One can no more successfully modernize A Doll's House without revising it internally from head to heel than one can modernize Pride and Prejudice, Uncle Tom's Cabin, or Herbert Hoover.

Revised or unrevised, however, A Doll's House must depend largely in the theatre upon the actress who plays Nora, and Miss Ruth Gordon, who was the present Nora, dropped the play under her. Like a stage magician who has spent his life assiduously perfecting himself in the palming and passing of coins and who can no longer put a dime into his pocket without first flicking it up his sleeve, Miss Gordon has apparently got to the point where her overelaborated acting technique prevents her from doing anything simply, forthrightly, and naturally. As a consequence, she is given to so many tricks that one momentarily expected her Nora to step to the footlights and sustain the illusion by requesting someone to lend her a silk hat and thereupon pulling out of it a rabbit, a chromo of Elisabeth Bergner, and a good notice from a London dramatic critic.

MORALITY AND BURLESQUE. Censorship in the case of burlesque agitates itself solely about sexual morality. It believes that once it has abolished strip-teasing and nudity it has done its duty by the public and preserved the latter's well-being. The cheapness and vulgarity, the illiteracy and the shabby mentality of burlesque never, on the other hand, engage censorship's attention for a moment. It apparently holds that it is quite all right to debase the mind and taste of the public to the lowest degree just so long as you don't encourage its libido. In other words, to carry its conviction to the extreme, that a nation of morons would be infinitely more desirable than one given to an expansive demonstration of its amatory virility.

MORGAN. I should like to admire Charles Morgan's play, *The Flashing Stream*, more than I do, for several reasons. In the first place, Mr. Morgan is a fellow dramatic critic, serving the London *Times*, and when a dramatic critic writes a play I should prefer that it be an admittedly superior one, if only for the sake of not having to hear again the old nonsense about " he who can, does; he who can't, preaches " — which, incidentally, is a slightly gratuitous criticism of, among others, Kant, Darwin, and Jesus Christ.

In the second place, I dislike to find fault with a play by a fellow critic because it lays me open to the common allega-

tion against critics in such instances, to wit, that they resent
a colleague's taking up playwriting, particularly in proportion as he is popularly successful at it. If the allegation had
no truth in it, it wouldn't have occurred to me in this connection, but, unfortunately, it has. Dramatic critics are a mean
lot with one another. Save alone in France, where any play
written by one, however bad it may be, is boosted to the skies
by his fellows as a world-shaking masterpiece, the critic who
is foolhardy enough to write a play bares his bosom to his
brothers' arbitrary bean-shooters. Shaw found it out early
when Archer and certain others blandly assured him he
should forsake playwriting, as he would never be any good
at it. And many another lesser critic has similarly discovered it.

In the third place, Mr. Morgan has in his play (his first
effort) at least set himself to give the present-day English
theatre something that it is sadly in need of: drama of a
higher fiber than that concerned with country house weekend antics, perverts with a passion for slicing up old ladies
and arsonizing the household governesses, and actorgenic
rôles for old stage favorites in the last stages of amnesia. And
in the fourth place, I expect to be often again in London and
I should like again, as in the past, to enjoy pleasant social
intercourse, uncorrupted by hard looks, with my creditable
and engaging confrere.

I have told myself all this and have even gone to the extent of offering myself a bribe of five dollars to win myself
over to a state of fraternal acquiescence, but with no success.
That Morgan's play has a few commendable qualities, I am
delighted to acknowledge. It reveals, at least in its first act,
a fairly apt hand at dramaturgic preparation. It has dignity
of intent throughout, and never descends to cheapness. Its
dialogue, in several places, is adroitly managed. And, as I
have observed, its aim is assuredly loftier than three-fourths
of the suave sauerkraut that passes for drama in the London

theatre of the moment. But it ends up, nevertheless, as a very unsatisfactory play, and for various reasons in turn.

The first six or seven of these are betrayed by Morgan himself in the foreword and introductory essay which he has written for the play in its published form. Therein, he makes it apparent that he believes himself to be at once a super-shrewd audience-reaction critic, a deeply original dramatic thinker, and an audacious pioneer. I quote him, appending some possibly discouraging program notes:

1. "If the play fails, it will fail because the audience, collectively slower in mind than the individuals who compose it, feel that its thought and passion are over-compressed. . . . This peril attends all modern dramatists whose subject is complex or challenging."

Note: The over-compression of thought and passion in certain of the complex and challenging plays of O'Neill (*The Great God Brown*, for example, which ran for seven months in New York) of Pirandello (*As You Desire Me*, for example, which turned 'em away in Rome and Naples) of Wedekind (*The Awakening of Spring*, for example, which enjoyed success in Berlin), and of divers other modern playwrights, including Mr. Morgan himself (*The Flashing Stream* ran for six prosperous months in London), implies no such peril as Mr. Morgan argues. Parenthetically, Selznick-International was so impressed that it has even bought *The Flashing Stream* for a movie, which — when it comes to Mr. Morgan's contention — amounts to a pretty sardonic piece of critical nose-fingering. The whole point is not over-compression of thought and passion but the quality of thought and passion in question. I shall come to this, in Mr. Morgan's case, presently.

2. "The one thing certain in the theatre," continues Morgan, "was that no romantic heroine who confessed to Juliet's warmth of feeling could hope to retain the sympathy of her audience. This convention persists, and Karen Selby,

challenges it. The play may well disappoint the box-office for that reason."

Note: (*a*) See above. (*b*) Juliet's exceptional warmth of feeling, Mr. Morgan should know, is carefully qualified by her expressed demand that Romeo have honorable intentions. (*c*) Bosh. Many romantic heroines in the past theatre confessed doubly to Juliet's warmth of feeling and retained the wholesale sympathy of their audiences. For example, Marguerite Gautier, Iris, Joyzelle most certainly, etc. (*d*) The convention does not persist. *E.g.* Miriamne (*Winterset*), Irma (*The Glass Slipper*), Mary (*The Masque of Kings*), etc. (*e*) Morgan's heroine challenges it. How? Turn on a protectively cooling electric fan as you listen to a few samples of Karen's scorching warmth:

Schnitzel 1.

Ferrers: "Put a circle round this moment too. . . . Why do you say no? "

Karen: "Not now. Not yet. It would blind us."

Schnitzel 2.

Ferrers (*taking hold of her*): "Will you stop talking. Stop. Stop."

Karen: "Your hands! You are hurting! "

Schnitzel 3.

Ferrers: "Come here. Let me look at you. Inside you, what are you thinking? "

Karen: "Of your suffering."

Schnitzel 4.

Ferrers: "But if this job goes wrong, we shall never marry. Do you understand that? "

Karen: "No."

Schnitzel 5.

Karen: "I thought *I* was arrogant — but you frighten me."

Ferrers: "That's why you love me."

Karen: "Is that why? "

Schnitzel 6.

Karen: " There's only one real misery in life — to be entangled."

Schnitzel 7.

Ferrers (*takes her passionately*): " You know what would happen? "

Karen: " What would happen? "

Schnitzel 8.

Ferrers (*violently*): " Kiss me."

Karen: " Oh my God! "

3. Proceeds Mr. Morgan: " The truth which she (Karen) admits openly is one that has not hitherto been recognized in the modern theatre. It is remarkable that the theatre should still conventionally hide it . . . namely, that many women have pleasure in the experience of sex . . . yet to acknowledge its truth in what is called the heroine of a play is almost revolutionary."

Note: Is it possible that Mr. Morgan cannot have heard of such modern plays as Stanley Houghton's *Hindle Wakes,* Korfiz Holm's *Mary's Big Heart,* Hjalmar Bergström's *Karen Borneman,* etc.?

Subsidiary note: Herewith, the revolutionary manner in which Mr. Morgan's revolutionary heroine does the revolutionary open admitting:

Brissing: " Kiss me again! "

Karen: " As much as you like."

Brissing: " And you? "

Karen: " Very well. As much as *I* like."

Brissing: " How much, Karen? Enough? "

Karen: " I suppose so."

Brissing: " Tonight? Don't turn your face away — Look at me. Answer me." (*She quietly releases herself.*)

Karen: " What *are* we? "

(*Enter Denham with tea*)

After tea, as Brissing starts to go:

Karen (*calling him back*): " Peter! "

Brissing: " What? "

Karen: " There will be no answer."

Brissing: " No answer? "

Karen: " To the question you asked. There can be no answer. There could never have been. Do you understand? "

4. " She (Karen)," proudly re-emphasizes Mr. Morgan, " says openly what has, I think, not been said in the theatre for over a hundred years and not by an honorable character since the Elizabethans — that she desires men."

Note: It is a matter for regret that Mr. Morgan has not had time to familiarize himself with various modern plays ranging from Artzybasheff's *Enemies* (1917) to Lynn Riggs' *Russet Mantle* (1936).

Subsidiary note: Herewith, the revolutionary manner in which Mr. Morgan's revolutionary character says it:

Ferrers: " You are a woman men desire. That's the danger."

Karen: " I desire men. That's the safety."

5. " For saying this," continues Mr. Morgan, " she will be reviled, but it seemed to me necessary, after watching more than two thousand plays, that so simple and, outside the theatre, so unrevolutionary a truth about women should be re-stated on the stage."

Note: Far from reviling her, critics in both England and America who have, like Mr. Morgan, watched more than two thousand plays but who, apparently unlike Mr. Morgan, have kept their ears open, have passively and leisurely accepted her as being a little bit of old-hat.

6. Mr. Morgan makes an extended ado over the novelty of his play's central theme: " singleness of mind." He presents it as something quite as dramatically original and revolutionary as his sex concepts. By singleness of mind, to which he devotes his long prefatory essay, he means a strict and unyielding adherence to purpose and end, an absolute and

undeviating integrity in determination — in short, the endeavor to march to one's goal in a straight and unswerving line, with no extrinsic interruptions or corruptive influences permitted to horn in.

Note: It must be confided to Mr. Morgan that his singleness of mind theme has long been familiar to the drama and is by way of being pretty stale stuff. Does he forget Ibsen's *Brand?* Has he never seen Githa Sowerby's *Rutherford and Son?* Or Wedekind's *Hidalla?* Or Octave Mirbeau's *Business Is Business?* Or numerous plays in the more recent theatre, ranging from John Wexley's *The Last Mile* (if ever a dramatic character was possessed of singleness of mind, Killer John Mears is) to Lillian Hellman's *The Little Foxes* (compared with Regina Giddens, both Morgan's Ferrers and Karen are irresolute, vacillating dilettantes).

Let us come to the play as we directly engage it upon the stage. Having delivered himself in his prefatory essay of the remarkable opinion that the great trouble with Shakespeare was that he lacked all sense of humor, we find Mr. Morgan offering as his own idea of authentic humor such passages as these:

1. " But it do give people a turn to say their watch is slow. May think you're a liar, but they can't be that sure. It's like winkin' the eye about a man's girl. She may be an angel with knobs on, but it makes him look slippy."

2. " I can't find my tie."

" It's in the loop of your shirt."

" Where? "

" Hanging down your back."

" Damn! (*Finds it.*) One of the disadvantages of a celibate life is that there are no mirrors."

3. " I decided you were a perfectly good bluestocking."

" I can assure you she's neither."

" Neither? "

" A bluestocking — nor perfectly good."

4. " Imagine her in trousers, my dear Ferrers. In deal-

ing with women, I have found it a useful exercise. God so made a woman that in trousers a part of her truth conspicuously appears."

5. "I should adore that. Like having a tame tiger. Or would you eat me? I should adore that too. I've always thought the lady of Riga had it both ways."

(*Laughing*) "Granted a Freudian tiger."

6. "Are mathematics Freudian, Miss Selby? Until this evening, I thought they were completely sexless."

"But I thought you said, Lady Helston, you were good at them at school."

"I expect those were what Edward calls pure mathematics."

7. "You wouldn't ask a musician to learn ours (language)."

"And why not? . . . Except that most of them seem to be Poles — or mad."

8. "Damn it, sir, I made the thing. It's my child."

"A mother isn't always the best judge of her own child."

"That wasn't Solomon's opinion, sir." (*Stage direction: They laugh. It is a relief.*)

9. "Do you lie awake at nights wishing you could go back to the bridge table and play a hand again? "

"Why, do you? "

"I don't play bridge."

"You are an extraordinary woman! "

10. "A cigarette, sir? "

"A pipe if I may. It persuades the newspapers that, though uninspiring, one is English at heart. For the same reason, if statesmen must go to France, it's advisable for them to cut out Paris and go straight to Aix-les-Bains."

11. "It's dangerous in England to give an impression that you like the French for their own sake. It throws suspicion on your morals."

12. "I haven't a daughter, sir."

" Few men can be sure of that; and they perhaps are not to be envied."

It is, as I have remarked before, clearly apparent from Mr. Morgan's foreword and introductory essay to his play that he is firmly convinced it explores new ground in the drama. In the play itself we have this passage, along with its stage direction:

" A woman is a personal animal . . . But this particular job needs — "

" Go on, Ferrers. What does it need? "

(*Stage direction: This carries the whole emphasis of the play and is spoken very slowly, clearly, quietly.*) " I think the rarest thing in the world, sir — impersonal passion."

The theme of female impersonal passion, Mr. Morgan surely must recall, if only he will scratch his head a little, is a not unfamiliar one in the drama. What, for example, in one direction, of some of the plays treating of Joan of Arc and Florence Nightingale? Or, in another, of Rubin's *Women Go on Forever*, Barry's *The Animal Kingdom*, Barnes' and Sheldon's *Jenny*, Daviot's *The Laughing Woman*, etc.? The theme is so familiar, indeed, that by way of freshening it up a little, farce writers have had a go at it as, for example, in Pascal's *The Amorous Antic*.

While it obviously is not always fair to argue that a dramatist's hero or heroine expresses his own personal convictions, it seems reasonable to believe — in view of Mr. Morgan's prefatory confessions — that in this case both his sadistically intellectual hero and heroine do.

Let us glance at a few of their expressed convictions:

1. To the First Lord's expansion of the hero's above-quoted statement on impersonal passion: " Do you suggest, Ferrers, that women haven't the capacity for impersonal passion? No religieuses? No artists? No women of science? . . . Come," Ferrers categorically and dismissingly replies, " They may be capable of it in relation to a God they worship."

Suggested research for Mr. Morgan: George Sand (after 1831), Emily Dickinson, Jane Addams, Madame Curie, Sophie Brzeska, et al.

2. In reply to Ferrers' remark that he and Karen in later years, upon recalling a quarrel they have had, may remember it, " but we shan't recognize ourselves in the remembrance," Karen rejoins: " I think that must be true of murderers — they don't recognize themselves in the remembrance."

Suggested reading for Mr. Morgan: the written and published confessions of some of the world's most notorious murderers. For one example, the gleeful memoirs of Eugene Weidmann, Parisian butcher de luxe.

3. Ferrers to Karen: " Oh it *is* true that one thinks and feels and wants two things at the same time. People who write won't allow that."

Suggested reading for Mr. Morgan, sufficiently varied: Dostoevsky and Clifford Odets, Balzac and Hermann Bahr, George Eliot and George Kelly, Ouida and George M. Cohan, D. H. Lawrence and Gerhart Hauptmann, De Quincey and Owen Davis, Blasco Ibáñez and Pirandello, George Gissing and Vincent Lawrence, Robert Hichens and Brieux, etc., etc.

But enough of all clinical criticism. What, in the end, does Mr. Morgan's momentous play — to say nothing of his momentous foreword and prefatory essay — come down to?

It comes down simply to this: a man working on a big job finds himself in love with and desirous of a woman but, feeling that any physical monkey-business would interfere with his mission, refrains from cohabitation until the job is finished.

Suggested thematically identical and momentous play-going for Mr. Morgan: Lincoln J. Carter's 10–20–30 gallery gods' delight, *Bedford's Hope*.

The difficulty with Mr. Morgan is three-fold. Highly esteeming himself as a sexual realist, he is in fact an arch-sentimentalist who dramatically suggests an offspring of Henry Arthur Jones and Dodie Smith. Equally highly esteeming himself as a dramatist of revolutionary ideas, he actually presents himself as something of a theatrical antiquarian. And even more highly venerating himself as a connoisseur of words, he writes the species of dramatic dialogue that periodically gives his actor-spokesmen the air of having swallowed a mixture of ground stained glass and Fowler.

His play purveys the thesis that without positive singleness of mind and complete celibacy the work of genius must inevitably be hamstrung. Yet, though stoutly defending his thesis, he allows his two mathematical masterminds constantly to invade their work with chatter on their love for each other and splendid abnegation, which impairs their singleness of purpose a deal more than if they had shut up talking, surrendered anatomically to each other, and got the whole thing profitably out of their minds and systems. He further unconsciously ridicules his concept by making his heroine at one and the same time a somewhat miscellaneous amorist and one of the admittedly greatest mathematicians in the world. In addition, he allows us refractorily to speculate (despite Balzac's animadversion) when in history celibacy has been the categorical imperative in genius' accomplishment.

Rid of its superficial embroideries, Morgan's exhibit amounts to rather stale business. He gives us once again little more than the venerable fable of the man of high purpose torn between his task and the urge of the flesh, familiar to us in more plays than one can remember. And, dovetailed with this old stuff, he trots out again the equally venerable literary and dramatic fable of the disturbance caused by the appearance of a woman in a far-flung masculine retreat (*vide* a score of stories like Molnár's *Snow* and two score plays like Willard Robertson's *Big Game*). The verbiage with which he has embellished this recognizable greasepaint amalgam, save in isolated praiseworthy instances, frequently varies between an uneasy colloquialism hoisted literarily on stilts and a painstaking, and plainly distasteful, theatrical compromise with

such low bourgeois lingo as " Where the hell are those cigarettes? ", " Dry up! ", and " That's why you're a slut." His
literary fastidiousness shocked and mortified by such grievous lapses, our friend thereupon speedily seeks absolution in
quotations from Pope, allusions to Beethoven's Fifth, references to Charles Lamb, and recapitulations of what Pompey
said to Menas. The English acting company's characteristi-
cally studious overprecision of diction added to the general
impression of artificiality. Margaret Rawlings, ordinarily an
actress of distinction, further succumbed to the fault of confusing intonation with lyricism, in which confusion Godfrey
Tearle handsomely backed her up with the inference that he
must have had a Wurlitzer for dinner.

MOVIE ACTOR AS CRITIC.   Mr. Charles Laughton in a recent
interview, after allowing that " an actor is the worst critic of
his own work, but he may be the best critic of his job," proceeded to a eulogy of his movie director, one McCarey. Said
Laughton: " I worked with McCarey years ago and saw what
a brilliant director he was. The time will come when he will
be recognized by everybody. You know, it took people fifteen years to see that Chaplin was a genius. It will probably
take them years to see that McCarey is a great comic mind! "
Pausing a moment in awe of the great man, Laughton then
continued: " You saw his film, *The Awful Truth*? A brilliant
film! You remember the scene where the husband calls to
see his wife at the musician's house and tries to force his way
in. The Japanese butler throws him in the fireplace and says,
' I do ju-jitsu.' Well, the audience laughs; that is the ordinary
gag. But McCarey builds up on that. The husband gets up
and throws the Japanese butler in the fireplace and says, ' I
do ju-jitsu too.' That is where McCarey is so clever and
great; he makes the ordinary gag original."

Without in the least wishing to diminish Mr. Laughton's
enthusiasm for Mr. McCarey's great and original genius —
as who gives a hoot the one way or the other? — I neverthe-

less must inform him that that self-same built-up gag was in evidence exactly thirty-six years ago in the burlesque-house skit called *On the Yukon,* featuring that best of all the old burlesque low-comedy trios, Watson, Bickel and Wrothe.

MOVIEGOING.   Whenever I go to the movies and wherever I sit, it always seems that the person sitting either next to me or directly behind me has a bad cold. This bad cold is invariably accompanied by an obbligato of sneezing which contrives to render either the side of my collar or the back of my hair so moist that I am contemplating taking a bath-towel along in the future. The person with the bad cold, furthermore, in nine cases out of ten appears to be convinced that any kind of candy, if only it be wrapped in paper which in the process of opening sounds like a Chinese New Year's celebration, is wonderful for colds. He seemingly is also persuaded that part of the cure consists either in crossing his legs so that one of his feet may handily insert itself into your side trouser pocket or in pressing his knees hard against the back of your chair and periodically and suddenly pushing them so that you are propelled half-way out of your seat.

The moment I have at length accustomed myself to all this and prepared myself to give attention to the screen, an usher parades down the aisle and turns a bright pocket-flashlight into my eyes, blinding me for at least two minutes. He then also blinds everybody in my vicinity, after which he slowly walks up the aisle with his flashlight and blinds everybody else. He must consider this fun, as he keeps walking up and down the aisle at intervals of every seven or eight minutes doing the same thing, all under the innocent guise of determining what vacant seats there may be or pretending to watch out for someone who has perchance lit a cigarette.

Seated on the other side of me from the person with the cold or next to the sufferer behind me there is sure to be a very small boy. This small boy evidently comes to the movies for the sole purpose, if he is beside me, of tangling himself up in

his seat like a pretzel and kicking my elbow off the arm of
my chair or, if he is behind me, leaning over the back of my
seat and breathing furiously in my ear. However, I can stand
this, as I get a respite every three minutes when he goes out
to the washroom.

All the people around me at a movie seem to be great
conversationalists. Since I have never mastered the trick of
dissociating what is coming in my left ear from what is coming in my right, I thus constantly am confused as to whether
Mr. Clark Gable is telling Miss Carole Lombard that he loves
her or whether it is all about what remarkable stockings he
can get at Macy's for forty-nine cents. Not long ago I went
to a Western picture and I could have sworn that it had to
do with a cowboy whose Uncle Moe was having an awful
time with his haberdashery store on Amsterdam Ave., whose
cousin Minnie who lived in Paterson, New Jersey, had an in-
growing toe-nail, and who was thinking of spending his summer vacation in Atlantic City.

Adjacent to or in close juxtaposition to a movie theatre
there always seems to be a nut shop and no sound-track yet
invented has succeeded in triumphing over it. These nut
shops, judging from the deafening crackling noises emanat-
ing from their merchandise, must do an enormous business.
Things have got to the point where you can tell the difference
between a drawing-room comedy and a Western only by
closely watching the clothes the actors have on. A short time
ago I went to see what I thought was Tyrone Power in *Jesse
James* and, blinded by the usher's flashlight, thought the gun-
fire in it pretty exciting, only to learn the next day that what
I had been at was a Deanna Durbin picture.

In the winter season, I generally find an elderly lady in
my proximity who wears at least six coats, to say nothing of
enough scarves, mufflers and overshoes to stock an Army and
Navy store. The old girl proceeds gradually to go through a
strip-tease that begins at the first reel of the feature picture
and isn't concluded until the Fitzpatrick travelogue comes

on. During the strip-tease, she bangs you on the head a couple of times, one of her cast-aside coats tumbles over your eyes, another knocks off your glasses, a muffler brushes your hat off your lap, a scarf gets wound around your elbow, a rubber-shoe smears its mud all over your socks, and the old baby herself, when finally she sits down, sits down not in her seat but on top of you. By then, the only thing left for you to see is the announcement of next week's picture and you can't even see that because now she has got up again, is standing half in front of you, and is taking off a seventh coat which she had previously overlooked.

A movie theatre also has a peculiar concept of ventilation. I suppose there are exceptions, but not in the case of the movie theatres I seem to go to. These theatres apparently work on two principles. Either they think that no ventilation at all is desirable, with the result that they smell like a Russian herring cannery, or they abruptly and simultaneously open a door out front and one back stage, with the result that you either get pneumonia or are blown slam-bang forward up against Edna May Oliver. (If it was Hedy Lamarr, it wouldn't be so bad, pneumonia or no pneumonia.) Certain other theatres which have been honored by my patronage steer a middle course. They have installed so-called fresh-air systems which always seem to be placed in such wise that they funnel the cold air directly down into your collar, with the result that after you have sat through a full-length feature you find yourself with a stiff neck, threatened sinus trouble, and backside chilblains.

Film houses with girl ushers present another embarrassment. Many of the girls aren't bad-looking and seem to be acutely aware of it. When you hand one your ticket stub, she looks you over in a rather coy, if theoretically impersonal, manner, winks her impression, if even remotely gratified, to her usher girl-friend, and escorts you to your seat with something of a saucy wave of the bustle. It thereupon suddenly in some strange way occurs to you that you will want something to eat before you go to bed that night, though you hitherto have never wanted anything to eat before going to bed, and you accordingly invite her to have a bit of supper with you. That is where the embarrassment enters. She can't. She is sorry, but she has a date. With whom? you indignantly demand. With her boy-friend, she replies. And who may your boy-friend be, my pigeon?, you blandly inquire. But even before she answers, you know. The boy-friend of every good-looking movie usher is invariably either the young man who presides over the candy-stand in the lobby or the resplendently uniformed bean-pole whose post is near the ticket-window and whose duty it is to lie about plenty of good seats inside.

If you have ever tried the loges in the more elaborate movie theatres, I needn't tell you what you are up against. You pay double the regular admission fee for the hypothetical pleasure and comfort of seeing a picture in quiet and peace, and what do you get? To one side of you, you unfailingly get a man smoking a cigar evidently made of Port du Salut cheese wrapped in alpaca. To the other side, you regularly get a hand-holding couple who devote the evening to arguing where they are going and what the girl is or, more usually, is not willing to do when the show is over, the colloquy generally ending in a quarrel and the stumbling of the couple over you on the way out in the middle of the picture. And to the back of you, you are pretty certain to get someone who has evidently mistaken the loge for a bedroom at the Hotel Taft and who snores and grunts so loudly that you can't hear even Victor McLaglen.

But the little cinema art theatres present the most embarrassing problem of all. They are so small and the screen is so close to you that you can't tell whether it is Charles Boyer or yourself who is in bed with Danielle Darrieux.

MOVIES AND STAGE.   So long as the theatre can produce plays like John Steinbeck's *Of Mice and Men* and Brian Doherty's

Father Malachy's Miracle it may humorously finger its nose at the notion that the moving picture can ever offer it any real and threatening competition. The movies, Will Hays or no Will Hays, would no more dare to risk such things intact, save suddenly they were taken over by some bravo who courted popular and financial suicide, than they would dare to risk revealing the glamourous Garbo in the altogether or Mr. Johnny Weissmuller fully clothed. Steinbeck's stripped emotions and Doherty's ironically decked-out ecclesiastical hypocrisies would, in the first instance, bring down the wrath of every women's club in the land were they retailed from the screen and, in the second, would cause the hierophants, doubtless including even the Rt. Rev. Father Divine Himself, to let out such a bellow that Sam Goldwyn, Adolph Zukor, and Sol Wurtzel would fearfully and promptly book passage to Tel Aviv.

Not to be arbitrarily condescending toward the movies, let it be frankly confessed that the theatre itself is not always too confident when it undertakes such departures from the usual. At the preview performance of Steinbeck's drama, I am reliably informed that a considerable portion of the invited audience left their seats in disrelish and indignation before the play was half over — just as a third of the first-night audience some years ago did in the case of *Tobacco Road* — and that the management and the actors were certain they had a failure on their hands. And so worried and doubtful was the producer of Doherty's play after consulting various persons connected with the theatre (to say nothing of listening idiotically to Metro-Goldwyn-Mayer's New York theatre-scout), that he actually dismissed the acting company, called the production off, and subsequently and finally persuaded himself to go ahead with it again only when two other managements who had had a look at a performance given gratis for them by the undaunted and resentful actors put in offers to take over the play. It is, however, to the theatre's great and everlasting credit that it almost always triumphs over its misgivings in instances like these, that its producers regain their courage, that the show, in the old saying, goes on, let the chips fall where they may, and that the new and more intelligent theatre public and the new and more intelligent drama criticism put their combined shoulders to the wheel in support of the enterprises.

Steinbeck's play, made from his familiar novel of the same name, is as powerful an exercise in unabashed realism, as beautifully honest a scrutiny of speech, act, emotion, and character, and at the same time as paradoxically gentle and tender a scraping off of the quicksilver on the back of the mirror it holds up to nature as the stage in some years has given us. It catches every last value of the novel and lends it a third dimension. In its author we have, I think, a genuinely significant new American dramatic talent. There surely has been no native newcomer into the field of drama in a number of years — and that includes Odets and others whom the critical diocesans have overnight anointed — who indicates so convincing a competence, whether in the writing of dialogue, insight into character, grasp of dramatic situation, or orchestration of emotional effect.

The characters in most of the plays we get in the theatre these days are the sort who would look comfortable on the top of a cake. They are fashioned out of so much confectionery for the popular sweet tooth, and they melt into nothingness, profusely dripping glucose, after fifteen or twenty minutes in the footlights' hot, realistic glare. Steinbeck, on the other hand, gives us in his two barley-binding bums no less than in his other stage figures not only vital humanity without cheat and without equivoque, but beings so unashamedly forthright and vulgar and true that all the ache of their hearts finds an echo in those of his auditors. The story you know. Briefly, it is the tale of a Damon and Pythias of the nether world, the one, a little fellow rational and strong, steadfastly protecting from those who do not understand him the other, large and weak and bewildered. If you have lost faith in the power of the stage, regard this play. Not all the movies made since the days of *The Great Train Robbery* have in them one-fiftieth the cacophonous but moving music of the human spirit that it has.

The very considerably less important *Father Malachy's Miracle,* similarly the dramatization of a novel, is a genial spoofing of the timidities and inner alarms of organized religion, and brings into the theatre the kind of thing Chesterton might have made of his play *Magic* if he had not been quite so professionally conscious a member of the Church of Rome, and the kind of thing Dunsany's rare gift for poetic expression might have converted into something genuinely important and lasting if he could master the three-act play form as he has the one-act. The tale of a little monk who challenges Anglican doubt by performing with God's polite help a miracle and the trouble it gets him into, the play is unquestionably for those more particularized and cultivated audiences who prefer to laugh with their wits rather than with their pharynxes and bellies. And it is, accordingly and to boot, a welcome and happy gift to a stage that generally believes it has commented on theology and religion very trenchantly and conclusively if it shows an actor with chalked, hollow cheeks in an Inverness cloak and vaguely identified with the Saviour having a hard time of it with modern mortals, or a chariot race during which a sudden shaft of light from the flies and symbolically identified with Jehovah miraculously breaks the axle on the chariot driven by the Roman infidel and allows the race to be won by the devout young Jew, Ben Hurwitz. Al Shean, quondam vaudeville partner of the late lamented Gallagher, had the rôle of the prestidigitating monk and, to the reviewers' unwarranted surprise, acquitted himself very creditably. Do not the reviewers know that vaudeville and burlesque have always been admirable preparatory schools for wistful, tender, and affectionate acting? Have they forgotten Denman Thompson, Dave Warfield, Lew Fields, Ben Welch, George Sidney,

Frank Bacon, Alexander Carr, and George M. Cohan, among others? Also, they may remember, there is a little fellow named Charlie Chaplin.

One of my more esteemed critical colleagues found fault with the play because, he complained, " the conclusion is apparent at the beginning of the second act." Let us agree that this is true. But let us at the same time politely inquire how many conclusions of the better plays are, oddly enough, not equally apparent at the beginning — or at least by the middle — of their second acts? In the main, it would seem that only the conclusions of the trashier plays — murder mysteries, detective sprees, English gimcracks such as *French without Tears,* and the like — are *not* apparent, even to a critic, at the beginning of the second acts.

MUSICAL SHOWS.   Some fifteen or more years ago the late Arthur Bingham Walkley and William Archer, celebrated English dramatic critics, gave a dinner for me, on a visit to London, at the Garrick Club. A number of the younger British critics, along with a group of theatrical illuminati, were present and there were speeches. When it came my turn I got up and proceeded at the behest of my hosts to expatiate on the American theatre. " The recent tendency in American drama — " I gravely began. " The devil with the recent tendency in American drama," howled Walkley and Archer in unison. " What we want to hear about is the Ziegfeld *Follies!* "

Walkley and Archer, the two most seriously minded critics of their London day, were not unlike most seriously minded and unaffected men when it comes to the theatre. For however soberly such men may regard and venerate the drama there persists in them that wayward leaven that irresistibly tugs their coattails in the direction of tune and toe shows. These shows are to the theatre what wines are to a substantial dinner. They are, to pursue the alcoholic analogy, the froth on the beer, for, while the froth is itself not especially nourishing and may be airily blown off, no beer is really good unless it has it. Down at the bottom of every man, be he a theoretically solemn and owlish fellow or one given frankly to the superficial doings of life, there is in gay melodies, pretty girls, lovely colors and vicarious romance something soothing to his psyche, inasmuch as it is a rare rooster who doesn't in his lonely vainglory romantically conceive of himself as a bright colored silk handkerchief looking wistfully for a pocket.

NADIR NUANCE. It is good news that the Theatre Guild, that once important but latterly insignificant organization, has at last taken stock of its ills and begun to go about doing something about them. The first step it has made is to get rid of its board conferences, which were well on the way to landing it in the poorhouse (after already landing it on the artistic dump), and to lodge its dramatic control in the hands of two persons. As the set-up now stands, Lawrence Langner and Theresa Helburn will run the works, with Worthington Miner after one season's service in the discard, with Alfred Lunt as hitherto operating independently, and with the primeval quartet, Philip Moeller, Lee Simonson, Maurice Wertheim and Helen Westley, made to stand in a corner with their faces to the wall.

What Mr. Langner and Miss Helburn will succeed in doing remains to be seen. But whether they succeed or fail, the vesting of power in them may conceivably prove that two heads are sometimes better than seven. Mr. Langner, a prosperous patent lawyer by profession, is probably, for all his periodic blunders like *Jeremiah,* the sharpest judge of play scripts around the Guild — in fact, the only one who has seemed to have any slightest critical taste and perception — and Miss Helburn should surely by this time have sufficiently learned the lesson of her silly little-girl theatrical theories to launch her vigor in a fresh and more pragmatic stream.

Things had got to the point where playwrights of standing hesitated any longer to submit their plays to the Guild. Once, the organization had practically the first call on scripts, but in recent years writers had become so disgusted with its regular rejection of reputable manuscripts and hearty acceptance of shoddy that they submitted their wares only after they had been turned down in most other quarters. Actors and actresses, too, began to give the Guild a wide berth, not being able to stomach Miss Helburn's Bryn Mawr theory that the best and only way to test a player's personality, competence, charm, and fitness for a rôle was to bid him or her without preparation to stand next to the water-cooler in the Guild's business office, to gaze admiringly at Miss Helburn, Lee Simonson and the rest of the directors, and — while Warren Munsell was dictating letters to Lee Shubert and the Imperial Office-Supply Towel Co. — to read, with all the wild passion and longing in the world, a playwright's apostrophe to the Caribbean moon or the stars over Lake Como. The initial moves of the new duo should be, first, to stop all such nonsense at once, inasmuch as the casting proceeding from it has often made the Guild stage ridiculous and, secondly, to constitute Mr. Langner the sole vote on play scripts.

In the meantime, the duo, while cautiously feeling its way, displays sense in allying itself with outside producers who are able to recognize good scripts when they get them, who are in the good graces of the better playwrights, and who are able happily to cast the scripts without driving a lot of poor actors crazy with a lot of asinine office recitations. Working with such men, Mr. Langner and Miss Helburn will be enabled to bring to the Guild subscribers, that long suffering clan, the kind of plays they have been patiently waiting for and will coincidentally, through a share of the spoils, help to put some money again in the Guild breeches pocket, which in recent years has suffered a pretty big hole.

It will be unfortunate in the long run, nevertheless, if the twain convert the Guild into a mere booking office for other producers, however gratifying the artistic, dramatic and financial results. The Guild, once its new guides have found themselves, should ultimately reseek its original independence and reconstitute itself a worthy producing unit. The temptation to take things easily and get a slice of soft money by leaning on other shoulders will probably be hard to resist, but the Guild owes something to its first principles and its early tradition and it is up to Mr. Langner and Miss Helburn eventually to bring it back into the sun. It will not be a simple job; it will be a very difficult one. But if Mr. Langner and Miss Helburn will brusquely shoo away the vitiating humbug that in late years has enveloped the organization there is no reason why they shouldn't eventually maneuver it.

NAZI GREASEPAINT. Oliver H. P. Garrett's *Waltz in Goose-step,* like all the anti-Hitler plays that preceded it, was both a critical and a commercial fiasco. Such plays invariably fail at the box-office because it seems to be a general rule that, while audiences are willing to lay out three dollars and thirty cents to relove a public or historical figure whom they already esteem, they are loath to lay out three dollars and thirty cents to rehate one whom they already despise. Thus, to charge people for disliking Hitler and what he stands for is theatrically akin to paying them for liking Lincoln.

But were this philosophy false, Garrett's play was such an all-round, all-fired bad one that it couldn't have succeeded even had it dealt with Beethoven, Admiral Dewey, or Eleanor Holm. Think of a playwright who asked us to accept seriously an anti-Nazi propaganda exhibit whose characters were given such Weber and Field names as Schmutzi (tr. Dirty), Sprecher (tr. Talker), Sturm (tr. Storm), Straub (tr. Bristle), and Masch (tr. Stitch), to say nothing of a general christened Straffen (tr., less an *f,* Punish) and of a homosexual called Laidi. Think of a playwright, even one who like Garrett has been smeared with the tarbrush of Hollywood, at this day paraphrasing again the old scene from **Bernstein's** *Israel* and any number of subsequent plays in which the Jew-hater finds that he has an illegitimate son by an early Jewish mistress, and then visiting the venerable hokum on Hitler. And think finally, if you are not tired of the whole thing already, of anyone writing an anti-Nazi play and employing as the closest approximation to an anti-Nazi hero a frank pervert who, in addition, is something of a blackmailer, physical coward, and sublime blockhead.

But, again, even had the play been much better than it was, some of the casting, acting, and staging would have stymied it. Whatever one's view of Our Adolf may be, it must be allowed that his words have been heard around the world, whereas those of the mummer playing him couldn't be deciphered back of Row D. Unfortunately, further, for the grave intention of the play, the actor who had the rôle of the Führer's chief aide made himself up to look embarrassingly like Sam Goldwyn. The actor who played Rudolf, the confidential German servant of the conniving anti-Hitler mastermind (the mastermind, it appeared, had never bothered to learn his confidential servant's last name!), came straight out of Lonsdale. And, so far as the production went, the unremitting up and down movement of the clouds in the first act suggested that the Führer and his party were not in the elaborate cabin plane we were asked to imagine them in, but rather in a dinky rowboat on a rocky sea.

NEGRO DRAMA. The Heywards' play, *Mamba's Daughters*, a dramatization of Du Bois Heyward's novel of the same name, transmutes what honest perception of the Negro the novel contained into something which is largely and merely a theatrical tale of a white mother-love played in black-face. The second half of the exhibit manages to achieve some stage kick on the score of its rape and murder gymnastics, but for the most part the evening is devoted to the clichés (including the aforesaid rape and murder) of the drama of the species. All the familiar chemicals are present: the revival meeting with the spirituals mounting gradually to epilepsy, the dressy, lecherous Negro who seduces the modest little high yaller, the deaf matriarch hobbling around on a cane and demanding periodically to know what it is all about, the smashed lamp and the fight in the darkened room, the cheap purple silk dress coveted by the poor married Negress who is willing to sell her soul for it, the courtroom episode with the inarticulate witness on the stand, etc.

Nostalgia.   The Farjeons' operetta, *The Two Bouquets,* is based upon the popular modern theatrical prejudice that the people of the Victorian era, save only the Queen herself, Disraeli, and possibly — though not positively — Lord Melbourne and the Archbishop of Canterbury, were morons. This, in the theatre, makes for what the critics call charm. It also seems to make for what they call nostalgic appeal. I am sorry that I cannot agree with them. It makes rather for what I call extreme dullness. It also, as I see it, makes infinitely less for nostalgic appeal than for an overpowering longing for the relative intelligence of even an exhibit involving Ed Wynn.

These, I appreciate, are harsh words and unbecoming a commentator otherwise so given to sentimental reaction that he cries copiously into his lager over the sophomoric nostalgia implicit in such things as *Old Heidelberg, The Belle of New York,* or any show laid in old Vienna in which the ladies of the ballet dance behind a scrim curtain to the tune of a Strauss waltz. But they nevertheless betray what is the sad fact. I can discern nothing in the least charming and certainly nothing that arouses any nostalgic emotion in me in a spectacle whose characters comport themselves like coy imbeciles and who reflect the customs and manners of the Victorian period much less than those regularly associated with it in the old summer beer-garden production of any entertainment laid in the 1880's in which the actresses wore bustles, shrank with horrified maidenly modesty when anyone mentioned a leg, an actress or childbirth, and fell in a dead faint when the handsome young Lieutenant Twickenham, their sister's beau, proposed marriage to them.

In some such more honest and unadulterated exhibit as *Victoria Regina* or *Pride and Prejudice* there may be a genuine charm and even a measure of nostalgic invocation. But I have difficulty in determining just where the charm is in something like this *The Two Bouquets,* which goes to the length of further travestying what in its composition is already travesty and which asks us to be wistfully affected by a picture of the past that makes mock of the past. The only hope for a presentation of this specific kind lies in its being neither charming nor nostalgic but frankly comical, and *The Two Bouquets* reaches its humorous pinnacle in such puns as " in vino libertas " and in the spectacle of a suitor in the act of wooing falling flat on his rear.

When we hear the word charm miscellaneously applied to these pieces we are assured that what people really mean is simply that the old-fashioned costumes are attractive, that one or two of the actresses are pretty, that the exhibit contains nothing in the least emotionally exciting, and that the drowsiness which hovers over it is as comfortably restful as a lazy siesta on a sultry afternoon. If all this constitutes charm, then the Farjeons' operetta may be granted to be charming.

NOSTALGIC THEATRE GLAMOUR. The Kaufman-Hart tribute to the nostalgic glamour and immortality of the theatre, *The Fabulous Invalid,* missed fire for two reasons. First, because most of the persons in its audience knew nothing or very little of the bygone plays which the authors selected to suggest and establish the nostalgic glamour and, secondly, because you can't work up any particular reminiscential heartburn by having a woman who looks like Apple Mary and who can't act impersonate Mrs. Fiske, or a girl with knees like cauliflowers pass herself off for Ann Pennington. Even if an

audience-imagination succeeds in remitting its judgment in
such directions, the authors and producer find themselves so
far up a tree that they can never get down when they further
demand of that imagination that it accept any substitute at
all for girls like Lotta Faust, Marilyn Miller and Adele
Astaire. I myself, a fellow whose imagination is so notoriously hospitable that it has gone to the length even of ac-
cepting Olga Nethersole as such a sexual tornado as never
had been seen in the world before and Mrs. Leslie Carter
as an actress, couldn't get myself, though fortified with half
a dozen Daiquiris, to go *that* far.

This business of impersonations, save it be handled by
someone like Cissie Loftus or Ruth Draper, or possibly even
Cornelia Otis Skinner, is always dangerous. And even the
ladies in question, very considerably talented though they
grantedly are, are wholly unimpressive when called upon to
suggest the youth and beauty of certain of those young
women of the past they may elect to try to personify. (It is
to their credit that, wise women that they are, they rarely attempt it.) You may handily mimic mannerisms, vocal inflec-
tions, carriage, gestures and other such attributes and pecul-
iarities, but there are some things the greatest mimic living
— and certainly the forty-dollar-a-week mimics of *The Fabulous Invalid* — can never mimic, and those things are the
inner spirits, the natural excitement of youth and the visual
loveliness of the theatre's girls of yesterday who are tucked
securely away in the memories of audiences.

But even were these defects absent, there is another reason for the Messrs. Kaufman's and Hart's critical failure.
Skillful and ingenious though they admittedly are, the one
thing they apparently are neither skillful nor ingenious at is
fantasy. Their attempt at it in the exhibit in point was accordingly disastrous. At moments it became downright embarrassing, as when the ghosts of two long defunct actors
stood in the balcony boxes and moaned for the return of the

dear old bygone theatre and as when the Holy Ghost, dressed in an LL.D gown and closely resembling Bernie Baruch, moseyed backstage and tried to persuade the two spooks to come back to heaven. There were several passages in the play that were not bad, and the whole, for all its obvious faults, exercised a measure of the automatic sentimental effect implicit in such analogous hokum as the sound of a distant steamboat whistle at night or the silent tears of a child. But the whole, too, disclosed its authors as having unfittingly selected for dramatization a Dresden doll in the hope that, when they squeezed it, it would say " Papa " and finding, when their heavy hands did, it only squeaked.

NOVELTY. The fact that we had two swing *Mikados* within a few weeks of each other attests to the poverty of imagination and lack of originality of our theatre people in their current avid search for novelty. Whoever first evolved the idea of agitating the Gilbert and Sullivan bodily structure, taking in the anatomy from toe to Titipu, deserves what credit is due him. But those who have duplicated the idea are a somewhat unresourceful lot.

Surely, a child or even the average theatrical producer shouldn't have overmuch difficulty in concocting novelties that might have an appeal not only to the more critical element in the public but also, in all probability, to the box-office. Being at the moment with just such a child cast of mind, I toss out a few possibly available suggestions:

1. A production of one of the Shakespearean comedies, say *As You Like It*, after the Elizabethan casting method, that is, with young men in the women rôles. It would be critically legitimate, and it would in this day be doubly amusing.

2. A production of Maurice Donnay's highly entertaining paraphrase of *Lysistrata*, the rôles cast not conventionally with older actors and actresses, but with young ones.

This, also, would be critically legitimate, thoroughly in key with the script, and similarly the source of a doubled amusement.

3. Some years ago, Rip, the cleverest of the French revue writers, confected a revue which began with a man and his sweetheart separating after a quarrel. The man, heartsick, thereupon proceeded on a voyage in quest of forgetfulness in the persons of other girls. But every girl who captured his mind and fancy, he found, looked like and was the girl he had left behind him. This idea, to wit, that a man's taste generally runs to the same type of woman, might be visited upon Schnitzler's *Anatol* with droll effect. Let all the various women who fascinate Anatol be played not by different actresses as usual, but by the same actress. I herewith put in my order for two seats.

4. A one-act play theatre not consisting, as is the more general rule, of a bill containing a dramatic playlet, a comedy playlet, a fantasy, and still another dramatic playlet, most of which are often bores, but one called The One-Act Play Laugh Theatre and devoted solely to estimable belly-laughter. I nominate the opening bill: Sean O'Casey's *The End of the Beginning*, as I have already observed one of the funniest one-acters ever written; Romain Coolus' *Mirette Has Her Reasons*, a gaily risqué little farce; Max Maurey's *The Benefactress*, which should give even Olsen and Johnson a guffaw; and, certainly, something we have all been crying for, a revival of the late Ring Lardner's howl to end howls: that one-acter done years ago by the Forty-niners dealing with three men gravely rowing a boat in a drawing-room and called, if memory serves, *The Tridget of Greva*. I herewith put in my order for half a dozen seats.

5. A new dramatization of Max Beerbohm's delightful *The Happy Hypocrite*, not with a score, as in England, by some attenuated Piccadilly Chopin, but by either Richard Rodgers or Cole Porter.

6. A dramatization, with its inherent present-day im-

plications, of Gorky's admirable story, *Twenty-six Men and a Girl,* written in 1899. A capital play should result. I nominate Lillian Hellman for the job.

7. If, finally, we must have more swing versions, why not one of *The Merry Widow*? Swinging it, in a modern revival, would be intrinsically justifiable and would lend it a new brio. Think what you could do with the Maxim's scene!

O'CASEY. The two worst influences on present-day play-wrights are, very often, Strindberg and Communism. Strindberg, for example, did all kinds of things to Paul Vincent Carroll before he reformed, as his *Things That Are Caesar's* sufficiently attested. And Communism, one fears, has now adversely affected Sean O'Casey as a dramatic artist, as a perusal of his latest play, *The Star Turns Red*, disturbingly hints. I content myself critically in presenting a mere synopsis of the exhibit and allowing you to judge for yourself.

The action takes place during the last few hours of a Christmas Eve. The period is "tomorrow, or the next day." The first of the four acts is laid in the home of an aged couple. Through the window can be seen the silhouette of a towering church-spire, and to the left of it a large, shining silver star. It soon develops that the two sons of the old couple are to define the coming drama. One is a Fascist, the other a Communist. Word filters in that trouble is brewing on many fronts: workers arming, the Saffron Shirts and Christian Front holding themselves ready, secret Red meetings at the Hall, the police and militia at their posts. The sons spit their bitter challenges in each other's faces, as from without, as obbligato, comes the sound of Christmas carols. The brothers are enjoined to hold the peace for this lone night of peace, but the thunder rolls dimly on. Despite the pleas and the logic, despite the fanciful dreams and the oily optimism of the Lord Mayor, the young girl Julia, the hypocritical Joybell, the Brown Priest and the Red Priest, the thunder still rolls dimly on. Enter presently a leader of the Saffron Shirts. "Take that star from your coat," he commands of the Communist son. The boy refuses. " For the sake of the brother who serves in the Circle, we warn you! " cries the leader. Still the boy refuses. The girl Julia's father pushes pale and frantic into the room. He has heard they have hauled off his daughter, who has offended the leader, for punishment. He demands her whereabouts and, rebuffed, rushes at the Fascist, whereupon the Saffron Shirt son of the household shoots him down. " Now, my arm," he whispers, dying, to the Communist son, " raise it, lift it high! Lift it up, lift it up in the face of these murdering bastards — the clenched fist! "

The second act takes place in the headquarters of the General Workers' Union and consists in a comprehensive record of the workers' estate. The third act returns to the scene of Act I. Outside, the thunder of conflicting elements rolls still louder on. Strange folk come to the house — a young man with a cough, a young woman with a withered baby in her arms, a hunchback — and debate the worth of Communism. " A world to gain — aye, and at the same time lose the dignity and loveliness the priests say poverty gives the poor," says the hunchback. But still the thunder rolls. The priests enter with their chants for the dead father of the girl Julia. The girl and the Communist son fling their scorn at them and order them out. One of the priests pauses: " Let the fair greeting given to Communism by virtuous men be the greeting of ball and bayonet, that we may sit safe and high over this cozy scum of the world's wickedness; that we may be delivered from these racketeers of the souls of the faithful; that we may be free from these restless red rats who seize a high holy day for the loudest slaughter and the richest rape." The stalking in of Red Jim, the leader of the workers, interrupts him. " Strike up the drums! " he yells to the mob outside the windows. " Take up our dead comrade, and strike up the drums! " The mob echoes his shout and sings, " Red star, arise the wide world over! "

The last act passes in the Lounge Room of the Mansion House and proceeds from a satirical spoofing of the Lord

Mayor, the Lady Mayoress, and others of the pseudo-gentry to the closer and still closer approach of the thunder. The *Internationale* is presently heard down the street, then the sound of galloping horses, then the sound of firing, then the wild sound of sirens. Hell has broken loose. The soldiers have joined the workers. The Fascisti have given in. The Red Guard enters and takes over. The Communist son has died for his faith. To the weeping young Julia who loved him, Red Jim speaks the final words: " You'll nurse now a far greater thing than a darling dead man. Up, young woman, and join in the glowing hour your lover died to fashion. He fought for life, for life is all — and death is nothing! "

The silver star seen in the heavens at the beginning of the play has turned to red, and slowly it grows bigger and bigger.

ODETS.   Clifford Odets continues to disappoint those critics who over-estimated him in the first place. One must relieve Mr. Odets of most of the blame in this connection, as one may not justly expect a playwright to meet and live up to a quality which was too excitedly and erroneously imagined into him and which he did not possess. That this Odets is a very talented fellow, no one can deny. But that his talent, whether hitherto or at present, touches the borderland of genius, as his rapt admirers somehow believe, is plausibly controvertible.

In *Rocket to the Moon*, his most recent play, Odets — departing for the nonce from his blanket concern with the political ills of the world — turns his mind to the emotion described by the poets as love. His mind, however, penetrates into no particularly new facets of the subject and what we get from him is little more than a restatement, in rather pompous terms, of what we have got from hundreds of playwrights before him, often better expressed. In an interview not long ago, Mr. Odets berated the modern theatre and said that it had so little to say that he seldom, if ever, paid it the honor of his attendance. This is something of a pity for, if he went to the theatre oftener, he would have known that what in this instance he regarded as something fresh in the way of sexual and marital philosophy had been done to death in the theatre and was almost as stale, whatever its rephrasing, as *A Trip to Chinatown*. Thus, though he is self-satisfiedly unaware of it, his *Rocket to the Moon* amounts in substance to a belated parroting of the meditations and emotions of a whole catalogue of plays beginning with Porto-Riche's *Amoureuse,* which is one of the best ever written on the subject, and ending with the more recent half-ton of hackspiels in which an aberrant husband, still touched by the memory of his inamorata, dutifully, if a bit sick at heart, returns to his wife.

It isn't, of course, that I am criticizing Odets simply because he uses old basic materials but rather because he treats them in much the old way. If he had something new and vital to embroider them with, I surely would not complain. But consider the nature of his cerebral contributions:

1. A very young girl can have little in common with a man old enough to be her father, however rich he may be.

2. Modern conditions are hostile to the perpetuation of true love.

3. Only by carefully nurturing love may love be made to flourish and endure.

4. Marriage must be an understanding partnership.

5. A marriage blessed by children is happier and more permanent than one not so blessed.

6. Emotional and sexual experience broadens one and makes one's life fuller.

7. What a young woman seeks is true love and in her search she is often frustrated.

8. Extremely hot weather is not especially conducive to sexual activity.

9. And so on.

Add to such revolutionary cerebrations, a plot that

slowly resolves itself into the familiar triangle idea, a climactic scene paraphrased from *Candida* in which two men state the nature of their offerings to the woman both love, the largely gratuitous sudden introduction of a paraphrase of O'Casey's sewing-machine salesman (in this instance an automobile tire salesman), the familiar elderly beau with an eye to the girls out of a hundred and one French boulevard exhibits, the lecherous Hollywood movie director, the wife neglected and left alone by her busy husband, and items of a piece, and you get a rough picture of the whole. Intermittent snatches of the dialogue are good, and here and there a flash of real character drawing emerges. But, judging from this play, Odets is going down rather than up.

Odets' directly antecedent play, *Golden Boy*, though it gets much closer to valid character and while some of its dialogue dances even more gaily to its author's ribald swing music, is in the main also an unsatisfactory job. It starts out with the exuberance of a man who has had three drinks and ends, like the same man after an undue attempt to prolong his mood with ten, with its head on the table. Some of its episodes are capital, but the weaving of them into a dramaturgic whole is not successfully accomplished. A play about a prize-fighter, it often suggests one who, after delivering each smashing blow, skips back into his corner, sits down, and privileges himself a comfortable breathing spell. Furthermore, while I am not one of those critics who arbitrarily find fault with a suicide ending on the idiotic ground that it is always an amateur's easiest dodge to get out of the difficult solution of a complex character problem, and while I believe that suicide is sometimes, as sound dramatists have occasionally proved to us, a more honest and profound dramatic solution to personal chaos than any twenty minutes of philosophical rhetoric that a Shaw may write — or any dozen self-banishments to Rhodesia or Australian sheep ranches or any two dozen marriages with healthy servant girls that lesser playwrights may apologetically fall back upon — while

I do not believe the one and do believe the other, I still believe that the suicide note on which Odets ends his play supports the view of the otherwise debatable critics whom I have mentioned. It may be logical and it may be true, but Odets here lacks the skill to persuade us that it is. It may be the sweet bell of surcease but it is dramatically jangled out of tune. Its suddenness may be justifiable in terms of life, but it is no more, for all its possible truth in that actual direction, dramatically logical and theatrically convincing than the equally sometimes lifelike but dramatically questionable expedient of suddenly bringing on the Marines in the nick of time or of looking at a watch, observing that a character is due at any moment, and causing him at that instant to ring the doorbell.

It isn't that Odets does not know the theatre. He knows it better, I daresay, than most of the other younger Americans writing for today's stage, even though his knowledge, as before recorded, may be Topsy-born. It is simply that, knowing it as well as he does, he indicates a measure of contempt for it. Nor is his contempt, as contempt sometimes proves itself, a sound and tonic one. It is bred not from superiority but from an impudent haste and an assertive impatience with deliberative calm and studious craftsmanship. He has the enormous self-confidence and self-surety of a little boy whose first girl has told him that she loves him. He has the same little boy's distrust of the sagacity of his elders. All of which is all right for a little boy. But the drama he seeks to serve waits patiently for him to grow up and to learn that only geniuses and imbeciles, in neither of which class he finds himself, can flout all the rules and regulations.

It is thus that Odets, while he possibly wouldn't for a moment consider closely imitating life to the extent of having, say, a dinner on the stage last for an hour and a half, still closely, brashly, carelessly and self-defeatingly imitates it with an extemporaneous, impromptu and dramaless suicide. It is thus that, in almost all his plays, he reduces the epic of life to a " quickie ", and the deliberations of mankind to a series of " rushes ". He can write scenes, beautiful scenes, but the noisy express train that is his drama steams past them so furiously that one recalls only a quick and insufficient glimpse of them. And all that remains in the critical memory is the loud chug-chugging of the locomotive, the loud rattle of the wheels, an occasional startling whistle — and an endless succession of telegraph poles without any connecting wires.

It has for some time been written of Odets by his critics, including myself, that he is wholly devoid of the art of self-criticism and that the aforesaid deficiency is his greatest fault. His critics may now content themselves that he has at last demonstrated that he has mastered it. He doesn't, true enough, appear in the slightest to be aware of the fact, but though it is clearly unintentional it is none the less obvious. For this *Golden Boy* constitutes in its plot outlines the best automatic criticism of its own author that has yet been indited.

The play tells the story of a young man possessed of an incipient competence in one of the arts. This young man, overpowered by a desire to gain sudden wealth and a flashy acclaim, abandons his studies, listens to the advice of dubious friends, and projects himself headlong into the prize ring. In short order he wins some facile triumphs and is hailed as a White Hope. But gradually, after he has broken one of his hands, he grows more and more befuddled and, though lucky success continues with him, his bewilderment increases. And in the end it drives him, disconcerted, tortured and defeated, to suicide. If that isn't first-rate self-criticism, I don't know what self-criticism is. In that story you have Odets' own impatience with close study of and critical application to his dramatic writings, his wish to make a sudden flash in the world, his ready ear to flatterers, his desire for money (quickly obtainable in Hollywood), his several plays, facilely contrived, that brought him too soon to be hailed as a White Hope, his damaged dramaturgic hand, his increased befuddlement, and — if not yet by any means his artistic suicide — something that, unless he quickly gets hold of himself, may eventually lead to it.

Golden Boy combines all the good qualities and all the very bad ones which have on each occasion been made visible to us when a curtain has gone up on one of Odets' plays. He can catch the sharp glints of character; he can write intermittent passages of dialogue that steam with life and reality; and he indicates a knowledge of dramatic tricks that few of his young contemporaries can match. But he shows that he lacks a feeling for form; he alternates diggingly true dialogue with stuff that sounds as if it had been written to order for a movie studio; he mixes an observant and telling humor with such vaudeville banality as causing a character repeatedly to attribute to Schopenhauer some humdrum cliché; and he in general presents himself in the light of a writer who composes Grade-A interludes for otherwise Grade-B pictures. So perhaps the critics remain right after all in that matter of self-criticism.

O'NEILL. When Eugene O'Neill was awarded the first of his three Pulitzer prizes, he expressed himself in a polite grunt. When he was awarded the second, he delivered himself of two polite grunts. When he was awarded the third, he exerted himself to the extent of three. When, during the process of grunting, he was elected to membership in the American Institute of Arts and Letters and subsequently elevated to the American Academy, he put the beribboned button attesting to the honor in the drawer with his socks. When, some time later, he was elected a member of the Irish Academy, his sole comment was that he was vexed that a splendiferous green sash of the species worn in St. Patrick's Day parades didn't go along with it. And when he was awarded the Nobel Prize, his answer to the press inquiries as to how he felt about it was: " Like a horse that's got a blue ribbon."

O'Neill cares even less for prizes, decorations and honors than George Bernard Shaw although, unlike Shaw, he is too mannerly and punctilious a fellow either rudely to decline what others graciously intend as the highest tribute within their means and power or vainly to advertise himself with some such Shavian retort as " No one can bestow the Order of Merit upon me, as I have already bestowed it upon myself." Not only is O'Neill unmoved the one way or the other by such accolades, save perhaps now and then to issue a quiet snicker in camera at his own expense; he is not even faintly interested in what the world, with almost negligible exception, thinks of the virtues or infirmities of his work. If he is praised by someone whose opinion he respects, he will vouchsafe the eulogist a proficient histrionic imitation of an enormously pleased smile and will thank him with all the grace of a suave headwaiter, and if he is denounced as a no-account he will manufacture, with all the art of his late matinée idol father James, a look upon his features that will indicate that the criticism has broken his heart — but all the while, in either case, he has only vaguely heard and not at all digested what has been said, as his thoughts, then as almost always, will be a thousand miles away from the immediate moment.

I have been a close friend of O'Neill's for now more than twenty years — and long before that, quite incidentally, my mother and his mother had been together at the same convent at Notre Dame in Indiana and an uncle of mine, a dramatic critic, had never missed a chance to take a fall out of his father — and in all that time I know of just four things in connection with his work that ever drew a small gratified peep out of him. One was a set of " stills " of the scenes and actors in the production of one of his plays in Stockholm. He was tickled that the faces of two of the actors looked something like the characters he had imagined. Another was the way the Russian Tairov's wife played the scene at the table in the Paris performance of *All God's Chillun Got Wings*. A third was a review in Polish of a play of his that had been shown in Warsaw; he couldn't read it and hadn't the remotest inkling as to what it said, but the long clipping in the exotic type-face fascinated him. And the fourth, paradoxically enough in view of his already noted usual attitude, was the news that he had been elected a member of the American Philosophical Society. The idea that he was regarded as a philosopher even by philosophers whom he had never heard of and doubtless wouldn't have recognized if he had was melliferous to him. Nevertheless — I happened to be with him when he got the news — he couldn't suppress a bit of an ironic smile. That quizzical smile never entirely deserts him. When Yale honored him with the degree of Litt.D., he whimsically allowed that it was unquestionably Yale's way of showing its appreciation and relief that he had gone, instead, to Princeton and Harvard.

The popular impression of O'Neill, gained from his plays, photographs and the books written about him by professors both in and out of college, is as inexact as a romantic spinster's conception of the smell of Venice by moonlight (or for that matter any other light) or the average man's idea of the workings of the acoustic altimeter. Because his plays, with minor exception, are chock full of murders, suicides, hangings, incest, insanity, sex frustration, spiritual torture, disease and despair generally, he is guessed to be a morbid and darksome creature, something of a cross between Cesare Borgia and the Second Grave Digger on the one hand and Dracula and Leopold and Loeb on the other. Because his photographs, at least those released for public use, almost invariably present him with a brooding and melancholy scowl, he is thought to be a somewhat sour amalgam of a German mathematics professor with a touch of dysentery and a cannibal suffering from a slight touch of trophoneurotic leprosy. And because the books written about him are by men who know him chiefly from his plays and his photographs, he is pictured by their readers as one who runs madly back into the house if the sun comes out even for a moment and comfortably buries himself in a dark cellar perusing volume after volume of abnormal psychology, along with the obituary columns in the newspapers, pictures of the more horrible tortures visited upon the inmates of Chinese prisons, the complete works of Krafft-Ebing and Stekel, and the statistics on the spread of malignant cancer in New Zealand, South Africa and the Straits Settlement.

The real O'Neill is no more like the public's generally accepted view of him than the real George Washington or Gaby Deslys was in turn like the pictures of them. While it is true that he reads everything bearing upon the nature of whatever play he happens to be working on, his chief reading pleasure, indulged in at least once a day even when he is working hardest, consists in detective and mystery novels (he averages no less than six or seven a week), in the hardly psychopathic stories of Damon Runyon, whose slang is a source of supreme enjoyment to him, and in the sports pages of any and every newspaper he can lay his hands on. So far as conversation goes, he would rather talk about prize-fighters and prize-fighting than about ten herd of Freuds and Strindbergs. He likes nothing better than to sprawl beside his swimming-pool in the sun after a long swim, to monkey around for hours in a garden (he rather fancies himself as a superior hedge-clipper and bush-shaver), to listen to a phonograph play Dwight Fiske's saucier records, to drop a nickel into his private mechanical piano (retrieved from an old New Orleans bawdy house and christened by him "Rosie") and with some male crony to accompany it vocally, at the top of his lungs, in a brewery rendition of *Alexander's Ragtime Band, That Mysterious Rag, Dardanella* or any other melody of similar vintage, and to have retailed to him, since he hardly ever goes to the theatre, the latest low jokes of the musical show clowns. He would trade in fifteen Shakespearean actors any day for one Jimmy Durante and he would supplement the fifteen with ten head of Ibsen actresses for one Bobby Clark. He has listened to Jack Benny over the radio and he enjoyed Benny's loud burlesque of *Ah, Wilderness!* so much that he'd probably throw in, if it came to a deal for Benny, a couple of Comédie Française stars to boot.

O'Neill smokes but doesn't drink; he gave up anything stronger than beer some years ago and two years ago gave up beer. He likes expensive clothes, fine linen, soft silks and hand-sewn British boots and has a wardrobe that a movie leading man might envy, although he usually goes about in a jersey and slacks when he isn't lounging in a dark Japanese kimono. He can eat anything, and does. He often draws the designs for his own stage settings in order to make sure of the exact stage proportions, and before he begins actual work on a play writes what amounts to a full-length novel covering the genealogy, history, habits, prejudices, tastes and everything else concerned with his characters, down to and including the kind of underwear, if any, that they wear, what side of the bed they crawl into at night, and what their preferences are in the way of literature, gods, spittoons, and ladies of color. He is privately and personally next to Sinclair Lewis, his American predecessor in the Nobel award, the happiest, most contented and most genial practitioner of belles lettres that I know. And, excepting only Lewis, he can laugh louder and longer when occasion warrants.

Such, the nature of the man who the public has been led to imagine is a jeroboam of acetic acid.

OPENING PLAYS. It seems to be a theatrical tradition that, however excellent a season may promise and subsequently turn out to be, it pretty nearly always begins with an exhibit that is far from a posy. Take the last ten years as examples. The 1929 season introduced itself with *Now-a-Days,* a wea-

sel; 1930 bowed with a beanbag called *Dancing Partner;*
1931 got under way with some cold gravy called *Three Times
the Hour;* 1932 made its début with the Gallic pap, *Domino;*
1933 entered the campaign with a dreadful fromage called
Love and Babies; 1934 got off with a tacky musical, *Keep
Moving,* and showed as its first dramatic offering *Kill That
Story!,* which even George Abbott's galloping staging
couldn't keep from being a periwinkle; 1935, following a
musical schnickelfritz called *Smile at Me,* toasted its birth
with that memorable huckleberry, *Moon over Mulberry
Street;* 1936, even with Jed Harris as initial master of ceremonies, could do no better than depress its opening customers with the jitney comedy called *Spring Dance;* 1937
raised its curtain with the musical meatball, *Virginia,* and its
first dramatic gift, though Arthur Hopkins was the entre-
preneur, was the turkey, *Blow, Ye Winds;* 1938 lifted and
perforce rapidly dropped its initial curtain on an onerous
mystery shindig called *Come Across;* 1939 baptized itself
with *See My Lawyer.*

ORIGINALITY.   The adjective " original " is one of the most
misused and misapplied in the critical vocabulary. Reading
of the fresh originality of this and that play, show or situation, one is often constrained to reach for the smelling-salts.
In the last three seasons, for example, the adjective has been
pleasingly and miscellaneously visited upon, among others,
the following:

1. Jacques Deval's *Tovarich,* which is an obvious liberal
paraphrase of the English comedy of several seasons before,
The Man in Possession, which, in turn, Deval had translated
and adapted for the French stage.

2. *Hellzapoppin,* which follows the formula familiar to
anyone who has seen the " Crazy Gang " shows at the Pal-
ladium in London, among them *These Foolish Things.* The
" Crazy Gang," in case you don't know, consists of the low
comedians Nervo and Knox, Flanagan and Allen, and

Naughton and Gold. And the shows in which they figure, in case you aren't acquainted with them, are much the same wild roughhouse as the Olsen and Johnson exhibit, with hell breaking loose all over the house, with mad nonsense smearing itself all over the stage, and with the audience frequently gathered in as part of the nutty proceedings.

3. *The Greatest Show in the World,* which treated of animals as human beings and which not only harked all the way back to Aristophanes for its basic inspiration but which had such inspirational antecedents as the Capeks' *Insect Comedy,* Pixley's and Luders' *Woodland,* Rostand's *Chantecler,* Avery Hopwood's *Dogs' Heaven,* William C. De Mille's *The Forest Ring,* Haynes Trebor's children's comedy, *The Amazing Adventures of Wiffles and Felisa,* Emma Gelders Sterne's children's fantasy, *The Reluctant Dragon,* Martha P. Munger's *The Tale of Cockalorum,* the marionette show *Peter and the Purple Pearl,* the various Peter Rabbit Sunday School plays, etc., etc.

4. Noël Coward's one-acter *Fumed Oak* in the series *Tonight at 8:30,* which is identical in theme to W. S. Maugham's play, *The Breadwinner.*

5. The sketch called *The Rest Cure* in *The Streets of Paris,* which is built upon the same idea as Gertrude Jennings' old and well-known London curtain-raiser similarly called *The Rest Cure,* once acted by, among others, Jack Buchanan.

6. *If I Were You,* by Paul Hervey Fox and Benn W. Levy, the idea of which was duly credited to a novel by Thorne Smith (also hailed as "very original") and which was familiar to New York theatregoers of twenty-five years ago in Avery Hopwood's translation of Wilhelm Von Scholtz's farce, *Borrowed Souls.*

7. *Family Portrait,* the fundamental concept of which figured in a short play written by Wilbur Daniel Steele years ago, the best and most favorably commented upon episode in which was a clear borrowing from Anatole France, and the modern treatment of whose materials was anticipated in

John Drinkwater's *A Man's House*, produced at the Malvern Festival in 1934.

8. The scene in *The Little Foxes* wherein a woman assists in hastening a man's death by refraining from providing him with an imperatively needed medicine, which, if memory serves, also figured in the scheme of W. S. Maugham's play, *The Sacred Flame*.

9. The device in *George and Margaret* wherein the two most talked of characters are always about to appear but never do, which — in the instance of one character — has been made familiar by Jean-Jacques Bernard, and which was utilized long before in both *The Duchess of Elba* and its operetta derivative, *His Majesty's Levee*, to say nothing of in Louis N. Parker's *Queen Victoria*, Louis Verneuil's *Jealousy*, etc., etc.

10. The character of Bill Jones in *Lightnin'*, revived last season, which is practically the same character which amused past generations for years in the celebrated *Tennessee's Pardner*.

11. Clare Boothe's *The Women*, acclaimed as highly original in that its cast was made up entirely of females. Previous plays containing only women: Rodney Ackland's stage adaptation of Hugh Walpole's novel *The Old Ladies* and called *Night in the House*, Cyril Campion's *Ladies in Waiting*, Alice Gerstenberg's *Glee Plays the Game* (it was this same Miss Gerstenberg who wrote the short play, *Overtones*, which anticipated Eugene O'Neill's dual personality drama device in *Days without End*), Christa Winslowe's *Girls in Uniform*, Aimée and Philip Stuart's *Nine Till Six*, Harold Brighouse's *Smoke Screens*, Zona Gale's *The Clouds*, several short plays by Gertrude Jennings, among them *The Bride, I'm Sorry — It's Out!*, and *Pearly Gates*, Walter Prichard Eaton's *Romance and Rummage*, Ellis Parker Butler's little comedy *The Revolt*, Elizabeth Brace's *Quite a Remarkable Person*, Vera Caspary's and Winifred Lenihan's *Blind Mice*, etc., etc.

P

PERVERTS. Leslie and Sewell Stokes' *Oscar Wilde*, imported
from England, aroused a degree of moral mortification in
certain local quarters because it treated, naturally and obviously enough, with homosexuals. To write a play about
Oscar and leave out homosexuality would plainly be like
writing a play about Buffalo Bill and putting it in. But,
aside from the moral aspect of the thing, the point, argued
the sensitive ones, is that the spectacle of male phoebes is
offensive, distasteful, and disgusting.

This seems to me to be defective criticism. That the
sons of swish may not *in facie curiae* constitute an endearing picture, it takes no heated argument to prove. But in a
world drama that has freely presented almost every other
form of abnormal and perverted humanity, most often without objection, they may — if treated honestly and without
cheap sensationalism — be allowed their clinical place. In
Oscar Wilde they are treated thus frankly, honestly and with
no attempt at cheap sensationalism, and it is the rankest kind
of hypocrisy to protest against their presentation. If they
are, as the moralists insist, offensive, distasteful and disgusting, that is the moralists' business. But it has nothing to do
with their dramatic validity or the validity of the playwrights'
effort and purpose. One may properly denounce as offensive,
distasteful and disgusting some such sensationalized Broadway androgyne fritter as Mae West's *The Virgin Man* of
blarsted memory, but it is hard to reconcile any such attitude toward the Stokes' sincerely contrived play with the free
moral acceptance of plays containing characters that in themselves smell to heaven with an equal abnormality. A theatre

that tolerates without a whimper everything from the incest of *Electra* to the degenerate pathological blood lust of *Rope's End* and *Night Must Fall,* from the Jack-the-Ripperism of *The Box of Pandora* to the Lesbianism of *Wise Tomorrow,* and from the sadism of *The Jest* to the masochism of *Countess Julie* and the algolagnia of *The Dance of Death,* has little right to be squeamish over the anatomical divertissements of Oscar Wilde and Co.

PICCADILLYDALLY.   Sean O'Casey has written of the latter-day English theatre that " it is the English theatre of yesterday, only a great deal more trivial, a great deal more tired, and a lot worse." By way of proving it, our American producers frequently and patriotically go to the expense of importing some of its outstanding dramatic specimens. It would be easy gently to let down these negligible British imports. It would also be polite. But at least one critic can't see how that might assist the native American stage to get anywhere. If our stage, whatever its present shortage of sound native dramatists, is to be helped to its goal, there should be small critical hospitality for these tepid little amusement peanuts of a tepid little overseas stage. Complaints of critical chauvinism and even parochialism are silly. There is no chauvinism or parochialism about the matter. It is simply a question of safeguarding the future of the developing American theatre by objecting to the unloading upon it, purely in the trust of easy box-office gain, of the down-at-the-heel and destitute immigrant drama. And not only such immigrant drama but also any drama of home manufacture that cheapens a stage in the eager and reputable making.

Whether the *George and Margarets, French without Tears, Spring Meetings, Dear Octopuses* and the popomacks like them are imported from England or are born on Broadway, it should be one and the same thing to any critic who believes that the hope for the American theatre lies in the efforts of such Americans as O'Neill, Steinbeck, Saroyan and their kind and in the lessons that have in the past been vouchsafed to it by, among other Europeans, such Englishmen as Shaw, Galsworthy and Maugham, and not — most certainly not — in the infiltration of such knicknacks as Savory's, Rattigan's, Smith's and similar Piccadilly parlor-scribblers.

PIONEER PLAYS. The American pioneer has been responsible for a large assortment of bad plays, bad novels, and bad films. It often seems that the stronger the character, the weaker the author attracted to him. We engaged the latest example in one Carlson who, in an exhibit called *Western Waters*, essayed to depict the pioneer on his way to the farming lands down the Ohio River at the close of the seventeenth century. What resulted was largely the familiar grease-paint compound of biblical quotations and hymn singing alternating with cuss words, rough-and-tumble fighting alternating with love making, and copious whiskey drinking alternating with loose looks at the females on the premises. Mr. Carlson also added for good measure the usual minor Paul Bunyan, the child awaiting birth in the difficult wilderness, and the crooked land agent.

PLAYWRIGHT DROUGHT. Worse than the country's once need of that good five-cent cigar is its present need of good three-dollar playwrights. What it is that has happened to the playwriting crowd is pretty hard to nose out, but the fact remains that, with a few honorable and obvious exceptions, even the quondam good three-dollar writers are turning out stuff that wouldn't be a bargain at two bits. And as for most of the others, I hope I may not be deemed too rude if I venture that an honorarium of three dollars might reasonably be demanded for attendance upon the greater part of their output.

When all is said and done, particularly done, a theatre without valid playwrights is like a bull-ring without a bull. You can give it the best actors, the best scene designers, the best directors, the best costumerie, and the best of everything and anything else and it will still be in the position of a man with a million dollars in his jeans on a beautiful desert island. And that, save for an occasional two or three months' visiting and relieving steamer, its whistle tooting rescue and salvation, is just where our theatre is today. It has the million dollars in its pocket; it is ready and eager to give itself a grand fling; the interest and sympathy of the birds that sing in the trees are its portion; but it is too often and long marooned on dry and lonely dramatic sands.

It isn't that the playwriting fraternity in general has temporarily either abandoned or lost interest in the theatre. A sufficient number of them, good and bad alike, are writing their heads off. But what they are writing is in the main, whether they are artists or hacks, inferior to what they have written before. As I say, I do not know the reason or reasons behind the prevailing slip and slide, but I allow myself a few guesses, all very possibly wrong. Here, nevertheless, they are:

Guess No. 1. Dramatic critics and others have for some time now been insisting to the playwrights that there is no, or at best small, place in the theatre any longer for plays without at least a measure of present-day significance. With the world presently in the state it is, they insist to the dramatists that plays, however good, which evade a consciousness of immediate conditions and philosophies are unwelcome. Foolishly giving heed to the critics and the others, playwrights who in the past have contrived eminently satisfactory plays in their different kind have become worried and, often without the ability to handle the demanded controversial themes, have still set themselves to the task by way of placating the critics. Naturally, since they are not adapted to this neo-thematic drama, their plays turn out to be of little value, whereas if the critics and other outsiders left them alone they might write plays which would provide pleasure and enjoyment, and which would be sounder stuff in every artistic and critical respect than the pseudo-profound liquors in which they now hopefully dunk themselves.

This demand that the drama identify itself with present-day significances is a gratuitous insult to the drama as an art, and the theatrical critics who make it should have their trousers taken down and be paddled. No critic, however asinine, argues that present-day painting can be of no importance unless it show Hitler simultaneously giving the Nazi salute and being kicked in the rear by Henry Morgenthau, or save it depict Stalin with a halo around his head and J. P. Morgan, in the upper left-hand corner, freezing in the breadline. No critic, however imbecile, in turn contends that all modern musical compositions should, if they hope for important acceptance, inevitably and arbitrarily include a few strains of either the *Internationale,* the Horst Wessel song, or *Yankee Doodle.* No critic, however much a sheep's-head he may be otherwise, further believes that today's architecture, to achieve full critical approval, must include a weather vane atop it showing a figure of Neville Chamberlain being chased around in a circle by Joachim von Ribbentrop, or vice versa, or that the parlor should be in the shape of a fleur-de-lis and the joe in that of a swastika, or vice versa. And so with sculpture, the ballet, and every other art, including belles lettres (despite, in connection with the latter, the minor wolf-cub howls of the boys on the *New Masses* and others who cannot persuade themselves to regard as literature anything that isn't awfully sore at itself).

But even some of the critics who esteem the drama as an art apparently decline to allow it currently the privileges and liberty which they allow to its sister and brother arts. And it is thus that we get from playwrights hospitable to their donkeyism the present smear of bastard dramaturgy. Let the playwrights recapture their former independence, tell the critics to go to, and write what plays they will. And by way of giving them a little confidence from one critic, let them be reminded that some such play as *Candida* is still a more estimable play than all the propaganda plays written in Fourteenth Street since Luchow's abolished its free lunch, that some such as *Juno and the Paycock* is worth all the American, English and French anti-Nazi or German pro-Nazi plays written since Adolf last ate a matzoth under the horrible impression that it was a chowder cracker, and that a play like *Old Heidelberg,* though critically it amounts to little, will for time on end nevertheless and doubtless continue to warm the hearts of the critics, especially such as loudly demand "significance" in their plays, more than all the significant plays thus far written by Elmer Rice (all of which the self-same critics subsequently loudly denounce).

Guess No. 2. A strained struggle for new dramatic forms has debilitated a lot of playwrights who, if they worked in the more conventional forms, might produce something better than what they are presently turning out. O'Neill is to blame for much of this, at least in the case of our American writers. His curiosity in the matter of new forms and the high critical and popular position he subsequently achieved have led his inferiors to believe that they, too, may gain such position by applying themselves to a similar activity. Inasmuch, however, as they do not enjoy O'Neill's uncommon dramatic virtuosity, the results have often been quite as embarrassing to themselves as to the theatre.

Experiment is a valuable thing, but before you indulge yourself in it you must have a thorough grounding in the established principles of your craft. And any number of our present experimenters haven't. They present themselves in the light of avid laboratory workers minus only the apparatus and instruments. They give us the experiments but fail to give us the necessary and essential dramatic accompaniment. We thus get from them, at their worst, dramatic vacuums filigreed with such experimental nonsense as movie soundtracks; at their second-best, what would conventionally be third acts played as second acts; and, at their best, so to speak, old-time minstrel show interlocutors in white-face leisurely smoking pipes and telling the audience what the audience should tell itself.

Guess No. 3.   The turmoil in which the world presently finds itself has naturally and understandably troubled the psyche of our playwrights, as it has most of the rest of us. One of its effects has been to convert many formerly aloof and snooty craftsmen, here and there without their being fully conscious of the fact, into propagandists of one kind or another. Sometimes, true enough, this propaganda is cast in an oblique mold and sometimes it is concealed in the shadows of dramaturgy, but it is propaganda nonetheless and, whatever its intrinsic merits, as ill fits into the specific dramatists' art as a bugle into Filina's *A maraviglia.*

It isn't that I argue against propaganda.   It is simply that some dramatists are suited to it and others are not.   And it is these others who currently essay it whose plays are sorely boggled by it.   The plays, as a consequence, give the impression of having awkwardly swallowed a dose of bitter castor oil to purge the consciences of their authors of a feeling of guilt at having hitherto sat in ivory, or more usually celluloid, towers.

There are, of course, two species of dramatic propaganda.   One, directed against something or other, is frankly labeled as such.   But the other, implying that what is opposite to that which the former attacks is automatically virtuous and desirable, often sneaks under the wire as something of sweeter and softer name.   Yet both are in essence one and the same thing.   Our lesser playwrights favor the first species; our better, the second.   And it is these better playwrights — slyly trying to deceive us, no less than themselves, that they are not to be classified as propagandists — who succeed only in confecting exhibits that are often neither the fish nor flesh of their antecedent plays but not even the good red Bismarck herring, however smelly, of the anti-Nazi dramatic claptrap.

We note in the instance of a number of our better American playwrights the apparent credo that a play filled with a democratic fervor may be good dramatic art, whereas one presently written in Germany filled with a totalitarian fervor can only be contemptible propaganda. God knows, any such German play, judging from the two dozen or so samples I have read and allowing free play to perfectly fair and unbiased dramatic criticism, is junk all right; but no less junk, allowing free play to similarly fair and unbiased criticism, is the conviction of the American playwrights in question. What is more, if there is any doubt about it, all save one of their plays written in the last three years prove it.

Guess No. 4.   In recent years, we have observed a tendency on the part of playwrights to consider it a great idea to show the other, less well-known and theoretically surprising side of this or that celebrated historical or semi-legendary personage. The playwright with the great idea generally hits upon a figure who has and is still popularly regarded as something of a sonofabitch and then, smiling to himself over his sagacious originality, proceeds to show that the sonofabitch wasn't so bad after all, that he (or she) had some gold in his (or her) heart, and that even if he (or she) murdered people by the wholesale in the daytime, when night came it was home sweet home by the cozy old fireside with the kids sitting on his (or her) lap and the family cat snoozing peacefully under the old armchair.

So far, maybe so good. But there is a practical dramatic hitch to the business. Any such celebrated sonofabitch is celebrated (and interesting) solely because he was a sonofabitch and when we are bidden to a play about him we don't want to see him depicted, albeit with a measure of truth and honesty, as a couple of other fellows from the old home town. We don't want it any more, in fact, than we want to see a play devoted, on the other hand, to some saint like Florence Nightingale and showing, maybe also with a measure of truth and honesty, her frequently irascible and acidulous temper, her bad legs, her dislike of hair shampoos, and her inverted libido. What we want, whether for good or ill, are our illusions, embrace they saints or sonofabitches. For if the theatre can't preserve them to us, what can? It is thus that when some foolish woman playwright gives us that good, old, riproaring, hell-shooting, cussing buzzard, Jesse James, and shows him to us as a cross between a Sunday School superintendent and a kleptomaniac at Woolworth's we give her in turn the Bronx cheer and warn her that if ever she shows us — with a certain equal, relative factual justification — either Wild Bill Hickok mortally afraid of spiders or Mozart fond of the ocarina, we shall not be responsible for our actions.

Guess No. 5. Let us skip the spirochete Hollywood, despite its unquestioned corruptive influence, as somewhat too old hat, pausing only briefly to entertain ourselves with still another recent example of what the æsthetic dump does to the minds of writers. Challenging Theodore Dreiser's statement out there that "I believe Hollywood is a world which authors should avoid, except as visitors; the author who lives for the kind of work he does — who strives for reality and sincerity — cannot remain too long in this atmosphere and retain his standards", Mr. Rupert Hughes launched forth as follows. "When Shakespeare lived, he and his associates were looked on as a lot of carousing bums who had to live on the wrong side of the river and were not allowed to present their plays on the right side!" exploded M. Hughes. "The literary critics of the day scorned them. I believe that three hundred years from now students of drama will look back to this period, when a new method of bringing beauty and inspiration and thrill to millions of people throughout the world was discovered and made permanent, as one comparable to the Elizabethan era in literary history!"

Returning to civilization, it is my fifth guess that the increasingly high standards of present-day dramatic criticism have operated in an unfortunate manner in the case of many playwrights possessed of a relatively minor, though far from despicable, talent. These have been influenced by the pressure of criticism to try their small wings in flights too lofty for them, and have found themselves sorely crippled. Not content to do the little things which they formerly did well, they have allowed themselves to be persuaded by the more exalted critical standards to do bigger things extremely badly. The theatre has thus lost a lot of very good minor entertainment and has gained in its stead only a lot of very bad dramatic art.

The critics have insisted upon " imagination," and the Philip Barry of several amusing little light comedies has hearkened to them and turned out such defective flights of fancy as *Hotel Universe* and *Here Come the Clowns*. The critics have emphasized " significance " and the Elmer Rice of such valid entertainment as *Street Scene* and *The Left Bank* has met their demand with such defective dramatic argumentation as *Between Two Worlds, We, the People* and *American Landscape*. The critics have proclaimed a desire for drama that Says Something, and the Ben Hecht of such gay and jolly stuff as *The Front Page* and *Twentieth Century* drives himself to confect such tinsel dialectic as *To Quito and Back*. Sidney Howard was brought to desert the satisfactory minor drama for such things as *The Ghost of Yankee Doodle,* which get nowhere in any direction, critical or otherwise. A young Robert Ardrey has been made to abandon the promising frolic of *Star-Spangled* for the juvenile sociology of *How to Get Tough about It*. Even the authentically talented Lillian Hellman, after the admirable *The Children's Hour,* listened to the critics and manufactured the dull labor problem play, *Days to Come*. (Then, providentially, she learned her lesson, stopped listening, and wrote the welcome *The Little Foxes*.) Robert Turney, after his first-rate classical paraphrase, *Daughters of Atreus,* was influenced to write a load of " modern significance " in *American Eagle,* so poor that no one, apparently, will produce it. And so it has gone.

Consider the case of the critics versus Maxwell Anderson. A little story here has its point. An Irishman, who for long years had been a cripple, heard of the miracles that were being performed on behalf of cripples such as he at the Shrine of St. Anne de Beaupré. Thither he betook himself and at the shrine for five weeks, daily, at the behest of the attending holy man, he paid his devotions and fervently prayed that he might be made well. At the end of the five weeks the holy man bade him discard his crutches and observe the miracle's wonder. "First," commanded the holy man, "throw aside your left crutch." The Irishman obeyed. "Now, throw aside your right crutch," commanded the holy man. Again, the Irishman obeyed. "And now," proclaimed the holy man, "behold!"

"And what happened then?" his friends asked of the Irishman.

"Then," said the Irishman, "Oi fell flat on me tail."

Those theatrical holy men, the critics, including myself, had for some time been commanding Anderson to throw aside his two crutches: the one, the arbitrary and often dubious blank verse designed to serve as a prop for his intermittently crippled dramaturgy; the other, the arbitrary tendency to see poetry in everything, whether it was there or not, in turn designed to support a deficiency in clear, realistic vision. Like the Irishman, Mr. Anderson obeyed the injunctions of the theatrical presbyters and, also like the Irishman, fell flat on his rear. The title of the tumble was *The Star-Wagon* and the thud was painfully loud. For not only was *The Star-Wagon* the frequently worthy Anderson's worst performance; it would have been a sorry performance from even one of the lowly Broadway box-office scribblers.

Abandoning blank verse and his wholesale poetic squirtgun and attempting to prove to the critics that he could accept their challenge and successfully throw it back into their faces, Anderson surprised and shocked even the least of his quondam admirers by writing a play that for complete banality, mushy and factitious sentiment, lack of imagination and muddled, juvenile philosophy had not been matched by any half-way aspiring playwright in some considerable time. It was difficult to believe that Anderson, who is a writer of integrity and hard resolve and who has as great a pride in himself as in the theatre, could conceivably have manufactured such a piece of shoddy. It was out of character and all logic. Resorting to one of the stalest devices of the popular hokum stage, to wit, the projection of his leading characters back into a past period, and maneuvering the mothy business with H. G. Wells' old "time-machine" substituting for the more usually employed and equally old dream, soothsayer's glass ball, doze in front of an open fireplace, or magic potion of Hanlon and Drury Lane extravaganza, he evolved an exhibit that, scene by scene, consistently and ploddingly followed closely the pattern of the most routine dramatic imaginings and phrasings of the venerable conceit. Nothing was missing. The unhappy old married couple who speculate on what might have happened had each married someone else and who are brought beatifically to realize, through various dramatic camera shots of the past, that with all their troubles and poverty they are better off than if one of them had married John D. Rockefeller and the other Mistinguett, were duly on deck again. So was the flashback to the days of bicycles, bloomers, straw sailor hats, horseless buggies and gay church picnics. So was the invention that finally makes the poor old inventor rich. So was the philosophy that the possession of money inevitably makes one very miserable. So was the flashback to 1902 in which the same characters who in the present 1930's talk easily, naturally and strainlessly, now that they are in the clothes and dress of the period talk like a costume party. The theory that rich women are always essentially bitches and that success in the world invariably makes men sons of them was again in evidence. So, too, were the young lovers who indicate their spiritual ecstasy by not looking each other directly in the eyes but by exaltedly fixing their vision intently above each other's heads. And so on.

The Star-Wagon, in short, was Anderson's sorest and bluest bottom-bruise.

A glutton for self-punishment, however, Mr. Anderson did not stop there in his effort to placate the critics. His genial answer to those who accused him of " defeatism," " morbidity " and " lack of humor," the very qualities that helped to make some of his earlier plays the meritorious dramas they were, took the impudent form of a musical comedy no less — *Knickerbocker Holiday* its name. And what was the result? This *Knickerbocker Holiday* gave off the impression of a dancing bear. Whatever Mr. Anderson's other gifts, the composition of a lively musical comedy book was apparently far from being down his alley. His attempts to be waggishly ironic in the drawing of certain parallels between the philosophies, customs and attitudes of the past and those of the present were not greatly superior to the English music hall standard, which usually takes its highest form in having a comedian dressed as a knight in armor unloose himself with a zipper or to the old local vaudeville stage standard in turn, which knocked 'em dead with Christopher Columbus' prediction that someday he would discover Columbus, Ohio, a stooge thereupon rejoining that so long as it wasn't Philadelphia everything was O.K.

Mr. Anderson's book in general further relied upon humorous devices whose staleness indicated that his knowledge of the musical comedy stage was very slight indeed. He brought in at this late day the episode in which the man twice about to be hanged, the rope around his belly, is dangled in the air for a while, sputteringly wriggles around like a Balaban and Katz German comedian, and is then abruptly pardoned. (The only thing lacking in *Knickerbocker Holiday* was that, when he was brought down, he didn't drolly brush off his knees.) We were also vouchsafed the paleozoic episode in which a young woman pulled through a small, narrow window lands on the stage minus her skirts. The arrow that hits a man in the seat of his pants, with the appropriate contortions on the part of the victim, was likewise again trotted out, as was the number in which Indians dance a Harlem Negro breakdown, the item in which a peg-legged man (Peter Stuyvesant) dances with a line of the chorus (shades of *The Burgomaster;* shades of 1901!), and the joke about a democracy being a government run by amateurs (regards to Finley Peter Dunne and Mr. Dooley). Nor was Mr. Anderson's lyric invention more vernal. I offer you the titles and themes of several of his songs: *Will You Remember Me?* (sung by the young lovers), *Young People Think about Love* (ditto), *Ve Vouldn't Gonto Do It* (Sam Bernard please write), *Romance and Musketeer* (Dennis King ditto), and *We Are Cut in Twain,* sung by the young lovers upon being forcibly separated (*vide* first act finale of 1,458 musical shows).

POLITE COMEDY.   Recent seasons have indicated one thing more or less definitely and that — though an exception may periodically and momentarily dispute the rule — is that English polite comedy of the species long made familiar by MM. Carton, Chambers, *et al.,* and their direct British offspring is rapidly passing out of American favor. Frederick Lonsdale's *Once Is Enough* was the latest imported specimen and the latest failure. But even had it succeeded, I believe that it would not have proved that such plays stand much of a chance in the future, unless perhaps they happen to be written by Maugham and are acted by a cast headed by Marie Tempest, the Duchess of Windsor, Elsa Maxwell, Robert Benchley and Noël Coward, with John Gielgud as the butler and Jessie Matthews as the maid. The average specimen, what with its Dukes, Duchesses, Lords and Ladies all airily comporting themselves like Michael Arlen trying to be Sacha Guitry and rather impressing everybody as Sacha Guitry distressingly being Michael Arlen, is quickly galloping toward the bonevard where lie buried the farces in which the rich bachelor uncle from South America returned unexpectedly and no end embarrassed the young married couple who had told him they had a baby, the problem plays in which the young waster son of the proud household got the maid in a family way, the melodramas in which the Italian organ-grinder turned out to be a Pinkerton detective and rounded up the wop counterfeiting ring that was holding Baby Marie, the banker's little daughter, for ransom, and the musical comedies in which the chorus at the finale excitedly described a horse race which was apparently being run around the back of the auditorium, thus imperilling the safety of George Lederer, Morris Gest, J. J. Shubert and the ushers, and which apparently finished off-stage at upper right in front of Diamond Jim Brady and Foxhall Keene, who were waiting patiently outside the dressing-rooms of Mazie Follette and Vera Maxwell.

What has minimized local interest in the polite English comedies is their failure over a period of thirty years to depart perceptibly from an established pattern. I have seen almost all of them produced in that time and my stream of consciousness about them is surely not different from that of anyone else who has had a similar protracted experience of them. With apologies to James Joyce, here it is:

Lord Whitehall (Reggie) Lord Pinkhall (Archie) Lord Mauvehall (Dickie) Jenks Jeeves Jarvis ten footmen port whiskey soda Lady Whitehall (Bimbo) Lady Pinkhall (Rimbo) Lady Mauvehall (Limbo) Ciro's Ritz Riviera Rhodesia the Bushwah country in South Africa golf tennis but I say old man the Pig and Whistle Rolls Royce Hispano Suiza the Gaiety Sybil Tremaine Lord Luddington (Wawa) Lady Luddington (Weewee) Oakes Doakes Hoakes eight footmen brandy soda tea tea sex is the duty of the poor the diversion of the rich you old blighter heigh-ho a little bit of all right old dear old darling Nigel has got to the point where he has no point dinner is served miladi I could never like *Siegfried* it so cuts into one's supper Claridge's the Carlton those strange Americans the Earl of Essussex (Choochoo) Hipps manservant as Rémy de Gourmont observed sir as Balzac observed sir as Schopenhauer observed sir Tony may be what you say darling but he is charming and he understands women Lord Barradine (Nicky) Lady Barradine (Nooki) bitch Sir Donald Heathcote M.P. Sir Aubrey Heathcote K.C. Sir Esme Heathcote M.P.K.C. Paris the Meurice Biarritz Rudge Mudge Fudge seven footmen whiskey soda port tea tea Derek Pettigrew Diana Pettigrew the Marchioness of Devon (Moxie) Mayfair Belgravia little restaurant in Soho sex is the multiplication of the poor and the subtraction of the rich I'm bored bored bored my dear I shall go mad Ramon Rolando gigolo polo the Duchess of Highgate (Mokus) the Duke of Highgate (Tokus) Lewes Hewes Pewes six footmen tea tea tea whiskey soda whiskey soda Sir Neville Lemoyne Bart. Mrs. Cortelyou bitch bounder bell-cord Ellean really my dear just a child my head's splitting *cachet fièvre* Duke of Westminster's yacht those strange Americans Berengaria Aquitania Capri Rome Como *pension* Bruce Ardale ducky I say I say checked one of those horrid mutinies in India broken heart Lady Gilfillian (Baba) so you knew Capt. Du Maurier in Cairo moonlight Nile whiskey soda dinner is served miladi a bit of a prig my dear Ronnie Hilary Daphne Phyllis there's no question of forgiveness in these things one loves or one doesn't love it's quite simple really pushes bell Phyllis Daphne Hilary Ronnie do you really love me so much that you think of me before breakfast that's the real test of love whether or not one thinks of one before breakfast one one one one one one one Lord Frothingham (Ham) Lady Frothingham (Dodo) no but I always *felt* unfaithful to you Perkins Firkins twelve footmen San Moritz Venice Shepheard's Monte Carlo Perrier Jouet whiskey soda tea tea Lady Wynton (Birdie) Lord Dilling (Winkie) she is either a very good woman Robin or very nervous port infidelity tell her ladyship I am not at home whiskey soda he's quite another kind young rich attractive clever but he has allowed life to spoil him tea port he has a reputation with women that is extremely bad consequently as hope is a quality possessed whiskey soda by all women tea brandy soda women ask him everywhere fourteen footmen Napier dear ring the bell will you gaol blighter beast brute Bond street really really you horrid men my sweet —

But enough.

Among the Englishmen who are still dissipating their efforts on this kind of thing Lonsdale, as I have remarked before, is one of the most adroit. He has a wit superior to most of the others, Maugham always emphatically excepted; he writes with flowing ease and style and skill; and he has a sharp and amusing eye to the foibles of the trivial people and trivial events with which he deals. But it all remains a polite zero.

One of the chief differences between this English and American polite comedy is that where in the former you are in four instances out of every five pretty certain to have a scene in which Lady Somethingorother quietly confronts and even more quietly outwits the hussy with whom her spouse is infatuated, in the latter you are equally certain to get one in which Van Rensselaer Somethingorother and Irving Feinbusch, the one a capitalist and the other an idealistic Communist, loudly confront each other in the presence of the coveted leading actress, who subsequently quietly outwits the playwright and the more intelligent members of the audience by going to bed with Irving, who in turn in the next act tells her she is only a rich loafer, slaps her face, and brusquely leaves her to follow, alone and unimpeded, the Moscow dream of uplifting humanity on a diet of smoked herring and no baths.

S. N. Behrman who, despite his several recent lapses, remains our best native writer of polite comedy, in *Wine of Choice* again vouchsafed us the rubber-stamp Van Rensselaer, Irving, hay-ride and slap, just as Lonsdale again vouchsafed us the business of the two girls getting in and out

of each other's hair. Lonsdale, with all his literary dexterity
and all his wit, couldn't, as I have noted, get much more out
of the rattling of the old bones than the same old drawing-
room minstrelsy, nor did Behrman, with all his ditto, succeed
any better. A British friend of mine, Terence Philip, describes these English exhibits of the Lonsdale school as too
much caviar and too little toast. They are a whole lot of
Theodores without a Ritz. The American exhibits of the
Behrman school, on the other hand, may be described as
Clyde Fitch editions of the *New Masses*.

It is, as I have already indicated, a weakness of so much
of American dramatic writing today that playwrights seem to
think it arbitrarily incumbent upon them to make their plays
" say something ", whether that saying-something has a natural place in their plays or not. Like almost everyone else, of
course, I prefer plays that really say something to plays that
do not. Yet so many of our playwrights who set themselves
to Say Something not only have nothing to say but, even in
the rare cases when they have, believe it absolutely necessary
that, whatever the rest of their plays may be like, they must
irrespectively say it about Capitalism, Communism, or My
God What Is Going To Become of Civilization. It has thus
come about that one can no longer go to even a good old rous-
ing detective play safe from the feeling that at quarter past
ten Inspector Mulligan will not pause a moment and thereupon proceed into a fifteen or twenty minute disquisition on
the futility of wars, the need for a new spiritual renaissance
on the part of mankind, and the ignominious shame of the
Corn Exchange Bank's having all that money when Bronxo
Martini and his brood of ten living in the slums haven't got
enough for more than a meagre dozen escallopini a day. And
it thus also doubtless will not be long before they will be incorporating into farces like *Room Service* various profound
meditations on the evils of Fascism, the doom of Democracy
and the fate of the liberal in the world of today (probably just
before and after Philip Loeb hustles Eddie Albert into the

bathroom), or before they will have Al Gordon's dogs come out in something like *Hooray for What!* with placards inscribed with the doctrines of Karl Marx on their necks and with caricatures of J. P. Morgan, Myron Taylor and Walter Chrysler, Jr., on their tails.

Just before Clare Boothe's play, *The Women,* was to be produced, I happened to run across her and discerned a forlorn look on her face. "What's up?" I asked. "My play doesn't stand a chance of success, I'm afraid," she said. "Why?" I wanted to know. "Because," she returned, "it doesn't say anything. It's just a play and there isn't a line in it about Communism or Collective Security or the Decline of Idealism or any other of those things that you seem to have to have in a play these days." I tried to console her with the thought that maybe that was exactly what a lot of people wanted just for a change nowadays and that, further, if she would bother to look up the records she would find that not one single successful play on the New York stage at that moment had the least thing to say of such problems as weekly drive the editors of the *Nation* and the *New Republic* half crazy but that — let the proletarian critics yell all they wanted to — they dealt instead with a couple of nobles turned servants, a cutie who had a hard time getting a job in the theatre, a family who made roman candles in the cellar, and kindred cosmic profundities. *The Women,* whose big scene showed a girl in the altogether sitting in a bathtub, opened in New York on the night of December 26, 1936. It thereupon proceeded to run at the same theatre for something like seven hundred performances.

Mr. Behrman appears more and more to be succumbing to the critical guff that plays, whatever their intrinsic nature, must unavoidably Say Something, even though many of them would be very much better plays if they didn't and if they contented themselves rather with being themselves. Some of the finest plays ever written have had and have no more to say than what was and is in their simple hearts. In both his

End of Summer and his *Wine of Choice* Behrman has strain-
fully lugged in his big Say like a piano-mover and dumped
it kerflop into his comedies with such a bang that it has frightened the wits, to say nothing of the happy and graceful tranquillity, out of them. If what he had to say was ringingly new
and philosophically, politically, economically or sociologically fresh, there would be small complaint. But, despite the
ingratiating manner in which he says his say, it isn't. And it
is because of this, no doubt, that when in these exhibits of
his I observe him suddenly invading their humorous pattern
with his disjunctive, portentous expatiations I am obstinately
reminded of the old burlesque shows in which — in the middle of the second act — the lights were impressively dimmed
to an oriental greenish purple, in which the orchestra began
to play sensual Turkish music, in which the chorus came
slowly out salaaming to the left upper stage entrance, and
when then there majestically entered once again Otto Bier-
heister, the German comedian, the only difference being that
this time he had on a stovepipe hat.

Pox Vobiscum.   The deplorable reticence which once enveloped the mention of syphilis has been succeeded by an
equally deplorable volubility. Suddenly released from the
moralistic vocabulary restriction, maiden aunts and others
who hitherto shrank modestly from the articulation of even
such a word as bellyache currently permit themselves the
spirochete pallida as a favorite topic of conversation. Family
and ladies' magazines that formerly considered it the height
of daring to print terms like breast, thigh, virgin or concubine
presently interrupt their articles on Shirley Temple's home
life and Bishop Manning's petunias with lengthy treatises on
Wassermann and Kahn tests and the desirability of making
certain three times a day that one's knee reflexes are in good
working order, along with the latest market quotations on
Salvarsan. It has got to the point where even breakfast-table

talk is often so occupied with the subject that you are lucky to get a breathing spell in which to down a demitasse.

The Federal Theatre just before its demise joined in the promiscuous gabble with a slice of its Living Newspaper called *Spirochete*. Confected by one Sundgaard, it traced the spread of the disease from its first appearances among the sailors under Christopher Columbus in 1493, the battle of such men as Fracastoro, Hunter, Schaudinn, Bordet, Metchnikoff, Wassermann, Ehrlich and others to get at its nature and check its course, and the moral hostility that so long hindered an open fight against it and that latterly has been broken down and conquered. While the presentation obviously exercised its facile effect upon all such persons as were once agitated by the white-slave films, it impressed the more instructed as little else but a crudely amateurish outline of a profound scientific record, with not one-fiftieth the dramatic power of some such capably contrived play as that study of yellow fever shown five years ago under the title of *Yellow Jack* and with not one-twenty-fifth of even that proficient claptrap on its own theme, Brieux's *Damaged Goods*.

The force automatically and naturally resident in his subject matter Mr. Sundgaard dissipated with some of the most juvenile writing heard outside a high-school dramatic society. To give ear to the great Dr. Bordet speaking in such phrases as " That's where I come in; I've got a hunch my test will detect it," to listen to such clichés as " I was innocent, but it was Spring," " I must tell them at the coffee house about it," " He would go through fire and water for me," and " You look beautiful; your mother's wedding gown and that lovely veil; it should be a beautiful wedding," and to drink in such prose as " Yes, doctor, we'll find him together, you with your science and I with my love will see him through! " — to absorb such stuff was to long avidly once again for the literary splendors of the drama of Charles Klein, Samuel Shipman, and Rida Johnson Young.

PRATT-FALL. When you read the advance announcement of any play laid in the Kentucky mountain region, the Tennessee hill country, or the back reaches of one of the Southern states, you are generally pretty safe in assuming that it will concern itself with the advent into the territory of one or more persons from some other locality who will be alluded to as furriners by the suspicious natives, most of whom will stand around for the first half hour grimly sucking straws and warning the intruders to gate the hell outn' heeyah and the rest of the evening supplementing their admonition with shotguns. The latest specimen bears the title, *Big Blow;* its author is Theodore Pratt; and its variations on the theme are fairly slight.

Mr. Pratt's locale is the inland Florida cracker country; his furriners hail from Nebraska; and for the resolution and reconciliation of his feud he dismisses the customary betrothal of the son and daughter of the warring clans, the falling of bitter old Lem Hatfield off a cliff, or the spiritual generosity that overcomes the chief revenooer in favor of a therapeutic hurricane. Yet even this minor variation is not too fragrant with dramatic novelty, as phenomena of nature have long since taken their place in the hokum category as plot and character catalyzers. Now, as in *The Deluge,* it is a flood; then, as in *Glory, Hallelujah,* it is a comet that presages the end of the world; again, as in the old Lincoln J. Carter melodrama, it is a forest fire or an avalanche; and still again, as in *The Storm* of gala Nubi-me-bad-girl memory, it is a big blow, just as it is in the present exhibit. Some of Mr. Pratt's incidental melodrama isn't so bad, but his play in the main is little more than a ten-twenty-thirty tub-thumper laboriously leading up to a $10,000 wind machine borrowed from a $2,000,-000 Sam Goldwyn movie. Nevertheless, I still can't persuade myself that it wasn't better for the government to dissipate its money on the theatre, even this kind of theatre, than on a vast Maine hydraulic development that wouldn't satisfy a Waldorf-Astoria bathtub, guides to New York apprising visitors where they can get a three-decker club sandwich for twenty cents, and parks in Altoona, Pa., splendorized with statues of Pocahontas and Chester A. Arthur.

PRIESTLEY. When J. B. Priestley was over here in connection with the production of his play, *Time and the Conways,* I was introduced to him one evening by Cass Canfield, his publisher. The first thing he asked me, rather truculently it seemed to me, was whether I had read Dunne's book on time, from which he had derived the theory on which his play was based. " Yes," I answered. " Did you understand it? " he challenged. " No," I replied. " Did you? " I returned, with heavy sarcasm. " No," he genially answered.

Now that his second play on the time theory, in this instance based on Ouspensky's *A New Model of the Universe* and called *I Have Been Here Before,* has seen local production, I am, while fully aware that he has read the book, tempted to ask *him* if *he* understood it and, whatever his reply, prepared once again to tell him that, so far as I am concerned, I didn't. Furthermore, appreciating his winning candor, I have an idea that his answer to the question would not be altogether unlike mine. Nor can you entirely blame either of us. These time theories dealing with static, recurrence and spirality, whether evolved by a Dunne or an Ouspensky, are superficially and easily assimilable in the sense that the time plots of such facile theatrical hokum as *The Road to Yesterday* and *Berkeley Square* are. But a scientific comprehension of them pretty heavily taxes the lay mind. What is more, if you will excuse my impertinence, I should hate to put the same question Priestley asked me and I in turn asked him to the MM. Dunne and Ouspensky themselves.

Under the circumstances, it is not surprising that this second Priestley chronologyklatsch is no more dramatically convincing than his first, particularly as the author augments self-doubt with self-doubt by confessing that " while I accept full responsibility for the free use I have made of these (Ouspensky's) borrowed ideas, it does not follow because I make use of them that I necessarily accept them." This skepticism, or bepuzzlement, or evasion, or whatever you wish to call it, badly debilitates his play, which resolves itself finally into little more than a sneaking apology for half-way believing an already controvertible scientific hypothesis.

Aside from this aspect of the exhibit, Priestley's dramaturgy leaves as much to be desired as his philosophical and scientific cerebrations. He again, as in his antecedent play, seems at periods to confuse the stage electrician's light-dimmer with spiritual mystification and bewilderment. He again seeks to interpret his characters' scientific perplexity and doubt by having them very slowly and ominously remark " I've been wondering — " and by having them " closely consider " each other after long pauses, stare at one another " strangely," eye each other " puzzledly," look " terrifiedly " at one another, and " curiously " scrutinize each other. Priestley's scientific exposition, indeed, frequently impresses one as being primarily ocular. As in *Time and the Conways,* he further sentimentally and ingenuously makes the leading actress his scientific mystic and Little Bright-eyes medium. " Don't think you know it all, and she knows nothing. She knows more about what's going on in this crazy universe than you or I do. She doesn't get it out of books, because it isn't in books. [Now is that nice, J. B., what with your debt to Dunne and Ouspensky?] But she can guess right now and then, and we can't." And how does Priestley indicate the sweet one's remarkable sapience? So: Janet (*struggling with her thought*), " I don't know. I wish I did. But there's something — some sort of influence — behind all that we do and say here — ."

Passing graciously over the playwright's introduction of his play with a woman fixing flowers in a room and, as she finishes her task, standing admiringly back and ejaculating, " That looks a bit better! ", thereby establishing our wholesale critical generosity, we come to his independent philosophical speculations. Although you may believe I am waxing facetious and making it up as I go along, I assure you that I quote our playwright literally:

1. " It's not really worth much — being rich. Half the time there's a thick glass wall between you and most of the fun and friendliness of the world. There's something devilishly dull about most of the rich. Too much money seems to take the taste and color out of things."

2. " You believe we have only this one existence? Of course? We all know that now. It is so obvious. But what a pity — if we are brutes that perish — we have not the dim feelings of brutes that perish. To have this one short existence and to spend it being tortured by cancer — to be given delicate nerves and consciousness only to feel pain — that would be a terrible cruelty. It would be better that nobody should be born at all." To this, another character replies, " I've thought so many a time." The first character, Dr. Görtler, whom Priestley employs as a mouthpiece, retorts, " Because you do not understand the long drama of the soul. To suffer like that, then to die young, that is not easy nor pleasant, but it is a rôle, a part, like any other brief appearance here — ." The second character then replies harshly, " That may mean something to you. It means nothing to me. Just so many fine, useless words." Whereupon, Dr. Görtler-Priestley with (stage direction) " authority and dignity ": " You will please remember, Mr. Ormund, that all my life I have been a man of science, and then a philosopher. I am not a political orator. *My fine words mean something!* "

3. " The point is, we're acting rationally and according to our own code, but our so-called consciences were made for us — during childhood — before we could make our own code . . . And that's what's the matter with us."

4. " All my life, I've had a haunted sort of feeling . . . as if, just around the corner, there'd be a sudden blotting out of everything. During the War I thought it meant I was going to be killed, so I didn't give a damn what I did and they

thought I was a brave fellow and pinned medals on me."

5. "Every summer I used to walk on the Thuringian Mountains. These high places have never been settled by men, so they are still innocent. There is not about them any accumulation of evil. Where men have lived a long time, the very stones are saturated in evil memories."

6. "Work, too, is a kind of escape."

At this point, asking the kindergarten class to remain in its seats just a little longer, we return briefly to Priestley's scientific, psychological and ratiocinative commentaries. Aside from the characters' periodic "incredulous" looks at one another, along with that electrician's dimmer, we are entertained by such rich sample lucubrations as these:

1. "I can tell him what Time is. It's a woman's greatest enemy."

2. "Perhaps I'm too impatient with that easy, optimistic half-thinking, but it does seem to me to be poor stuff in itself and to get in the way of real thought."

3. "We're like children groping about in the dark."

4. "I believe that a man and woman, feeling as Janet and I do, have a perfect right to do what we're doing. But somewhere in the back of my mind I've still to contend against centuries of belief that what we're doing is wrong."

5. "It is knowledge alone that gives us freedom."

6. "I believe that the very grooves in which our lives run are created by our feeling, imagination and will. If we know and then make the effort, we can change our lives."

7. "I tell you there is more truth to the fundamental nature of things in the most foolish fairy tales than there is in any of your complaints against life."

8. "All events are shaped in the end by magic. Yes. The creative magic of our feeling, imagination, and will. These are the realities — and all our histories are their dreams."

9. "We learn, but always too late. By the time we are forty, we know how to behave at twenty."

The kindergarten class is herewith dismissed.

No, J. B., it won't do. These time theories are not for such undernourished dialectics and Piccadilly playwriting. They call, if they call at all, for prolonged analytical deliberation and for the most painstaking dramaturgy. It is easy for a man of your considerable talents to write, as you do write, half a dozen novels a year, if the novels are like your *The Doomsday Men,* and half a dozen plays in the same year, if the plays are like this *I Have Been Here Before.* In point of fact, there's nothing to prevent a man of your aforesaid considerable talents from easily writing a dozen such novels and a dozen such plays a year. But the play that *I Have Been Here Before* might and should have been could not be contrived in the few weeks or so you probably allotted to it. It takes that long for a Eugene O'Neill even to sharpen his lead pencils.

In an English popular drama currently as idealess and devoid of imagination as Los Angeles journalism, Irish stew, and Verdi's *Aïda,* it is, however, not altogether surprising that, in the view of its critics, Priestley should stand out with the eminence of John Stuart Mill's breadbasket. His ideas and imagination, they duly appreciate, are frequently borrowed from others, but he at least borrows them from men of the stature of Ouspensky, Dunne, Blake, Wordsworth and Proust rather than — as in the case of many of his London contemporaries — from Cosmo Gordon-Lennox, Henry Guy Carleton and Noël Coward. And it is this discrimination in the matter of selection that marks him apart in the esteem of the Piccadilly saintebeuves.

I have a suspicion that Priestley, for all his public tributes to himself as a great thinker and notable dramatic artist and for all the contumely he regularly visits upon any critic who doesn't enthusiastically venerate his talents, is nevertheless secretly and no doubt smilingly privy to himself as a sly dramatic shenanigan merchant. His intelligence is surely sufficient to have imbued him with the critical wisdom which appreciates that when the drama on rare occasions ventures a relatively original philosophical or scientific idea, it most often makes a laughing-stock of itself, inasmuch as in the theatre the aforesaid philosophical nugget must be reduced to the mouth of an actor who usually looks as if he never had an idea of any kind in his life and as if he hadn't the faintest notion of what the playwright was driving at and as all scientific profundities must, further, be reduced either to childish stage props with blinking purple lights in them and which explode with a shower of electric sparks at the big metaphysical moment, to a gauze cut-out in the backdrop which when illuminated purveys the life on Mars, or to a laboratory consisting entirely of phials resembling Pilsner glasses and in a constant and inscrutable state of Bromo Seltzer eruption. He unquestionably recognizes all this. And he recognizes, as well, that, except perhaps for Shaw in his earlier days and Pirandello in his later, the drama has astutely refrained from even the simulacra of original ideas, preferring — because of the theatre's constricted two hours which allow insufficient time for the average audience to assimilate any save the very oldest and most familiar ideas — simply and effectively to relate the more accepted ideas in a new and fresh emotional manner. It is thus that, when nitwits speak of new ideas in the drama, what they really mean are not ideas associated with the mind but with the nervous system, not cerebral ideas so much as anatomical. If Einstein had been a dramatist and had sought to incorporate his original theory of relativity into a play, the show, however great its merits, would doubtless not have run longer than a few nights, even if all the dramatic critics in Christendom, none of whom would have understood it, lauded it to the skies and even if, to boot, Maurice Evans, the Lunts, and Butterfly McQueen played the leading rôles.

To persuade and convince an audience, and to succeed in the theatre, a scientific idea, however sound, must either be deprecated and ridiculed by every character in the play except the leading man or woman, who — if the play is to be a big success — must also shake his or her head skeptically at least six times during the evening, or it must be presented in the guise of fantasy and must argue its truth in terms of the highly improbable. As for genuine philosophical ideas, their sole small hope in the theatre, presuming their adventitious epiphany in that strange quarter, lies in the shrewdness of a dramatist who will appreciate that he must bequeath them to that male character whom the leading lady will contemptuously jilt in favor of the handsome bonehead polo player and so satisfy all save the customers in the balcony that they are not only rather foolish but slightly objectionable and offensive.

In both *Time and the Conways* and *I Have Been Here Before* Priestley, as noted, goes principally to the time twins, Dunne and Ouspensky, for his ideas. But, very shrewdly, as also noted, he abstains from the dramatic danger of too direct restatement and contents himself with the merest implication and suggestion. He foxily translates scientific inquiry into emotional answer and thus contrives a brace of plays which, for all their overtone of scientific importance, are essentially no more scientific than *Berkeley Square* or *Up in Mabel's Room,* but which, like the lights in far farmhouse windows on winter nights, romantically emotionalize the cynicism of the beholder into dismissing the unquestionably sparse and rickety aspect of their interiors.

In his own England, Priestley, as I have said, is regarded by the critics as a very original and profound fellow. In my own America, I prefer to regard him as merely a cannily superficial and cleverly posturing box-office playwright. As for his dramatic originality, when one of the English critics demands, " Is it not, for example, new to say that feelings, imagination and will are the only realities? ", I fear that I shall have to answer impolitely, " No — unless you have never heard of Pirandello." And as for his profundity, profundity seems to me to consist in something more than a mere quoting of Blake to the effect that joy and woe are woven fine in the woof of life, an emotional paraphrase of the Dunne theory of time, and the dropping of a final curtain on an unresolved scientific chord, with his mouthpiece meeting the avid scientific curiosity of his heroine with the grease-paint dash-strewn, hokum evasion: "There will be — something — I can tell you — one day. I'll try — I promise."

It is Priestley's pet dramatic dodge either profoundly to predict, in a scene laid in the past, something that the audience recognizes as having since occurred or profoundly to dispute the possibility of something that the audience in turn duly recognizes as having not occurred. In his earlier plays he has taken full responsibility for such ex post facto clairvoyance, but now, in his more recent time plays, he enlists Dunne, Ouspensky and Co. to share part of the burden. And what we finally and accordingly get is generally little more than the familiar plays which peep into the future but which here substitute a scientific metaphor for the more usual stage clairvoyant props and which achieve a bogus awesomeness and importance through the employment of the words "physics," "mathematics," and "science," a periodic ominous dousing of the stage lights, an exchange of incredulous and apprehensive glances on the part of the characters, and allusions to Euclid, Einstein, and the University of London. Whether or not a sound play may be made out of the Dunne or Ouspensky theories, I do not know, but if one can I have grave doubt that Priestley is the man to make it. My doubt is based upon many counts, but I content myself with specifying one. Such scientific hypotheses, I feel, cannot meet their sufficient dramatic interpeter in a playwright who composes such metaphysical dialogue as this:

Janet (*slowly*): I've been wondering —
Dr. Görtler (*as she hesitates*): Yes?

Janet: I was only wondering if I could have been here when I was a very small child.

(*She breaks off, and looks at him, and then away from him. Pause.*)

PRODUCERS VERSUS CRITICS. Following the bad notices and prompt failure of his production, *Everywhere I Roam*, written by Arnold Sundgaard and himself, Mr. Marc Connelly rushed into print to say that the critics were all dunderpates and didn't know what they were talking about. Following the bad notices and prompt failure of his directly antecedent production, *The Two Bouquets*, he exercised himself similarly. Let us assume that Mr. Connelly is right and that the critics are asses and don't know what they are talking about, which in the two instances in question, considering the particular exhibits, is a pretty big order. But let us graciously assume it anyway. Duly assuming it, we discover that the critics whom Mr. Connelly denounces are, with a single, solitary exception, the very same critics who in the recent past loudly praised his production of *Having Wonderful Time*, his collaboration, *The Farmer Takes a Wife*, and his dramatization, *The Green Pastures*. Also, that the solitary exception, a newcomer to the critical ranks, actually treated both *Everywhere I Roam* and *The Two Bouquets* quite cordially, God forgive him. If, therefore, the critics whom Mr. Connelly regards as imbeciles are — assuming Mr. Connelly correct — imbeciles, he must logically and inevitably entertain a supreme contempt for them for so greatly esteeming those productions and plays of his which they have esteemed. Can it be that he is right? I myself rather doubt it, at least in the matter of *The Green Pastures*, but who is a dunce of a critic to contradict him?

Some persons may argue that Mr. Connelly and others like him who, failing by sole virtue of their own shortcomings, seek to relieve their faces by blaming everyone but themselves, are simply soreheads and bad sports, and as such to be given the contumelious nose. That there is something to be said for their argument, I have no doubt. But just the same, though the critics themselves, whatever their short-comings in turn, are hardly soreheads and bad sports when it comes to their own fraternity, we nevertheless every once in a while find them denouncing one another as donkeys quite as Mr. Connelly has done.

By way of illustration, I hope I betray no secret when I tell you that seldom have you heard such ragging as many of his colleagues visited upon one New York critic who went to town in a big way for the supremely dull English comedy, *Spring Meeting*, endorsing it as "an evening full of rich chuckles." Or when I confide to you that another, who has apparently somehow confused the drama with Hennessy brandy and who awards Sutton Vane and Dodie Smith four and three stars respectively and Sean O'Casey and Paul Vincent Carroll two, has been made by his confreres to have his Critics' Circle dinner in the washroom. Or when I further apprize you of the fact that still another was ribbed out of countenance for eulogizing the mush called *The Star-Wagon*, to say nothing of for whooping it up, Heaven forbid, for *The Merchant of Yonkers*.

Maybe, after all, Mr. Connelly is doubly right. Maybe the critics are even greater oafs when they praise than when they condemn, that is, if Mr. Connelly is the logical fellow I (albeit reluctantly in view of some of his past efforts which I myself have dumbly also liked) am forced to think he is.

Speaking of myself, I find that when I don't care for a play most of my critical colleagues usually also don't seem to care for it. It is when I do care for one and praise it that I often find them eyeing me with a dubious Connelly eye and tapping their temples with a misgiving and significant finger. When, at the annual award congress of the Critics' Circle, I opined that Robert Turney's *Daughters of Atreus* was a worthy contender for the prize, Mr. Connelly would have had his belief in my critical imbecility more than substantiated by the untoward and deplorable actions of the other critics present, including even the relatively sober ones. When I praised Teresa Deevy's *Katie Roche*, Mr. Connelly, if he read all the other reviews, would have been justified in calling up Matteawan and requesting that a couple of guards be dispatched immediately to fetch me. The same in the instances of *Richard of Bordeaux, The Moon in the Yellow River* and *Within the Gates*. Again, when last season I discovered some merit in *Where Do We Go from Here?* and not more than one of my colleagues found in it anything but a stunning mediocrity, Mr. Connelly might have laughed himself blue in the face over my ignorance. Still again, when also last season I seemed to find virtues in *The Gentle People,* where the other critical masters saw none at all, Mr. Connelly might have become finally and firmly convinced either that I certainly was not the sort of critic whose judgment could be trusted to deal with such true gems as *The Two Bouquets* and *Everywhere I Roam* or, to make the problem even more confusing, that all the other critics were. To add confusion to confusion, however, not only all these other critics but I, too, thought both *The Two Bouquets* and *Everywhere I Roam* pretty poor stuff. And to add confusion to confusion to confusion, we all, as I have said before, thought some of Mr. Connelly's earlier efforts pretty good. Maybe the answer is that the critics and Mr. Connelly are all crackpots and don't know what they are talking about.

However, I am still taking the other end of the 50–50 bet.

I have mentioned Irwin Shaw's *The Gentle People* and I have a magnanimous, if turncoat, feeling that I ought to make those odds at least 40–60. Although the program clearly stated that the play was designed as a fable, every reviewer in New York condemned Mr. Harold Clurman's direction, which appropriately sought to stage the play for what it was. The reviewers lamented in particular, as being devoid of the strength of realism, the scene toward the end of the play in which the old men in a small boat murder a racketeer with rather gentle clouts from a gaspipe. It was, they said, ridiculous; you can't kill a man, certainly not a Brooklyn mugg, in any such pianissimo and fanciful manner. The reviewers evidently overlooked not only the point that the play was deliberately cast in the mold of semi-fantasy but that the very title emphasized the word " gentle ". Such criticism of it as they made, accordingly, would demand the realism of steel as opposed to papier-mâché spears in *Königskinder,* a wolf especially imported from Siberia for *Little Red Riding Hood,* and Al Capone as the lead in Dunsany's *The Queen's Enemies.*

You're welcome, Marcus.

PROGNOSTICATION. However greatly the American theatre may have progressed, it is still reasonably certain that every other season will continue to reveal the following phenomena:

1. An imitation and paraphrase of *You Can't Take It with You* whose author will imagine that he has captured the flavor of that success by cluttering up the scene with a wild assortment of wall decorations, by having one of the characters go to sleep in the grand piano, and by causing another, the aged grandmother, to slide down the banister.

2. At least one play written by someone afflicted with the conviction that poetry is merely a matter of putting down some such sentence as " The tomato crop in Iowa this year was completely destroyed by bugs " thuswise:

> The tomato crop
> in Iowa
> this year was
> completely destroyed
> by bugs.

When the critics loudly proclaim that the play is a lot of pretentious boloney, the producer will get his press department to insinuate a piece into the Sunday dramatic sections asserting that his proud aim is to produce only uncommercial plays that the other managers are too cowardly to touch. This, as usual, will make the other managers laugh so hard they'll get cramps.

3. Three or four English comedies, all great successes in London, will be brought over by American producers who have persuaded Hollywood money that they are natural goldmines. All but one of the comedies will contain a character named Alan, played by a nancy young English actor with no chin, who is craved by a luscious, irresistible and passionately alluring young adventuress named Diana, played by an American actress of forty-five whose two husbands divorced her for frigidity. The exception will contain a character named Keith, played by a nancy young English actor with no chin, who is a fearless explorer, hunter of big game and leader of men, who has had to leave England because of a certain matter involving cards and the wife of Lord Beerbohm-Trevelyan, and who encounters the Lord, in his cups and in the company of the half-caste girl Matsu Tomato (half-Jewish, half-Japanese) in the establishment of Madam Topaze in Saigon, where, after taking whimsical stock of the past situation, the two men, to say nothing of Matsu, become fast friends. When the plays fail, the Hollywood backers will say that it all just goes to show that people are tired of the theatre and that the motion pictures have killed it. They will then produce the plays in the motion pictures.

4. George Abbott will produce a farce which will contain cracks about Grover Whalen, Billy Rose, Congressman Dickstein and Mayor La Guardia and which will accordingly be hailed by the critics for its up-to-the-minute freshness, vitality and verve.

5. There will, of course, be a number of Shakespearean productions in which the leading actors, however good they may be, will be compared unfavorably to Maurice Evans by the critics and unfavorably to John Gielgud by reviewers who went to Harvard.

6. Max Reinhardt's press-agent will work overtime promising a wonderful new production by Max, but Max will hug close to Hollywood, where the mazuma is.

7. Three young Left Wing playwrights will come forth with dramas in which either a capitalist boss prevails upon his hired strike-breakers to put rat-poison in the milk of the workers' babies or a big steel-mill owner, an effete graduate of the Sorbonne with a magnificent villa at Sheepshead Bay and with fourteen mistresses, demands the Price of the Bohemian foreman's Polack wife if she doesn't want her husband to be discharged. When the uptown theatrical trade turns thumbs down on the exhibits, the Left Wingers will claim that it unmistakably goes to prove that the American theatre as it exists today wants only the ignominious pap of such writers as O'Neill, Sherwood, and the weak-kneed like.

8. Brock Pemberton will put on a feeble but agreeably naughty little comedy which will get grand notices from the critics, whereupon he will concernedly hustle to get his press-agent to send out statements arguing that he was shamefully misquoted that time when he was made to say that the critics didn't ever know what they were talking about and that they always praised the bum plays and condemned the good ones.

9. Observant of the great success of Noël Coward's autobiography, several actors who similarly have never done anything of any importance in the theatre will emulate his technique and also elaborately admit that they have never done anything of any importance in the theatre, which will make a fine impression upon readers who, though they fully realize that the autobiographers have never done anything of any importance in the theatre, will admire them because they haven't and brag about it.

10. As no one ever seems to be able to do anything about it, there will be another play about the clergyman in the small town who gets a whiff of romance in the person of his young secretary and who is on the point of leaving his humdrum wife and running off with her when his little son Ferdinand

is run over by a fire engine (symbolic of the vengeance of Hell).

11. Some lyric writer will present a contribution to the musical show stage in which he will rhyme " Schenectady " with " appendectomy ". He will be hailed as a genius.

12. Three plays which made big hits on the cow-and-chicken summer theatre circuit will be brought into New York by confident rural producers and will cultivate a rich crop of urban raspberries.

13. A Hollywood scenario writer will have a play produced in which he will seek to demonstrate that he is not guilty of a movie mind by incorporating into it learned allusions to Schopenhauer, the Brothers Goncourt, and James Hilton.

14. You may confidently expect at least two biographical dramas in which some actor who was last cast for type as " Blinky " Petullo, an East Side mobster, will be beheld occupying the rôle of King George II, or in which some actress who had previously played and accurately looked the rôle of a South Carolina hillbilly's aunt will be displayed as either Marie Antoinette or Lola Montez.

15. Concluding that the public is now finally fed up with realism, some producer is certain to try to cash in with a romantic play which will in essence turn out to be little more than something like *Three Men on a Horse* in hoopskirts and bustles.

16. Convinced that revivals of the classics are the order of the day, some exhibitor will go in for the staler Ibsen and, when it doesn't click at the box-office, will assert that the public are a lot of boneheads who won't patronize anything but jazz shows and vulgar farces.

PROGRAM NOTES. This business of printing in the play programs short and revealing biographies of the actors and actresses frequently has its disconcerting elements. I give you one suggestive example out of many.

In the closing months of last season, we had an exhibit called *The Happiest Days*. Its leading feminine character was a very young girl innocently and completely unversed in the matter of sex, which led to her sentimental and tragic suicide. The entire effect of the evening depended upon the illusion of her unworldliness. Yet staring at the audience in the program was the news that the actress playing the character had got herself married a couple of months before to a Broadway actor and was in the seventh heaven of bliss with him. To the professional critic and the more sophisticated lay theatregoer, it wouldn't, couldn't and didn't make the slightest bit of difference. But if you tell me it didn't kill the illusion for eight other customers out of every ten, I tell you that you do not know what you are talking about. It may be unreasonable in the face of the actress' competent performance; it may even be downright silly; but it is regrettably true nonetheless.

PROMISE.   In almost every theatrical season there emerges a playwright who impresses us with his promise and who in almost every next season or so makes us doubtfully shake our heads. In the more recent seasons we have been forced to engage in such a wealth of this head shaking that our heads begin to take on the appearance of Ringling trapezes.

There was, for example, Robert Ardrey, a young man who several years ago heaved onto the scene with an exhibit called *Star-Spangled* and who struck us as a fellow who had in him rare comic juices. Then what happened? A little time passed and again he appeared before us with a brace of exhibits, *How to Get Tough about It* and *Casey Jones,* which indicated that not only had he apparently lost all sense of humor but all competence in playwriting to boot. There was, for further example, Robert Turney, who got us all steamed up with his *Daughters of Atreus* and who, since the fireworks we set off in his honor, has manufactured two scripts, *Witch of Salem* and *American Eagle,* over which those who have read them sadly wrinkle their brows. And there was, for still further example, Leopold Atlas, whose *Wednesday's Child* persuaded many that he would prove somebody to be reckoned with and who then, in *But for the Grace of God,* turned in a play that doubtless discouraged even his Aunt Stella, who loves him. Alan Scott, in *Goodbye Again,* demonstrated a fruitful humor that his subsequent *In Clover* completely contradicted. George O'Neil persuaded any number of his customers that *American Dream* hinted at a talent beyond the ordinary and thereupon proceeded to indite several plays that no one seems to have taken sufficient interest in to produce.

These are just a few who lately have come into the theatre with flags flying and who, after their little day in court, have slid unhappily down the cellar door. What is it that causes their decline? What happened, some time before, to Edwin Justus Mayer, who wrote the estimable *Children of Darkness* and then fell flat on his tail-feathers? Or to Maurine Watkins after her gay satiric farce, *Chicago?* Or to Bartlett Cormack after *The Racket,* Sophie Treadwell after *Machinal,* Preston Sturges after *Strictly Dishonorable,* and Rose Franken after *Another Language?* Go on. Why has John Wexley never come within hailing distance of his *The Last Mile?* Whatever happened to the Gilbert Emery who wrote the commendable *The Hero* and lesser *Tarnish?* Where is Frederick Ballard, who in *Young America* suggested an interesting future, and Vincent Lawrence, who promised at one time to be a writer of high comedy of whom the American theatre might be proud? What has become of the competence that once was theirs? What has happened to Arthur Richman's (he entered the lists with *Ambush* that promised so much), and to Rachel Barton Butler's (she seemed to have something as a writer of comedy), and to Harry Wagstaff Gribble's (remember *March Hares?*), and to Hugh Stange's (his *Veneer* had all his future in it), and to so many others'?

The ability to write one good play, we of course know, demands talent. But the ability to write two, it seems, demands genius.

After all, however, just what about this business of " playwrights with promise "? In critical circles it is often simply the way of diplomatically letting down a relatively defective play that one rather likes in spite of oneself. It also usually has hardly any sound meaning. In the earliest plays of men who finally amount to something they often show no promise at all, or at best very little. It is commonly the eventual second-rater who in his first efforts suggests whirlwind potentialities. Björnson's *Between the Battles* in no wise hinted at the later Björnson, any more than Strindberg's *The Wanderer* predicted the great Strindberg to come. Heijerman's *Dora Kremer* gave no more clue to his later position than Ibsen's *Katilina,* which was so bad he issued it under a pseudonym, gave to his. Racine's earliest work, *Amasie,* is reputed to have been a peculiar little stinker, and the great Aeschylus' *Aetnæans* wouldn't have wobbled even a Boston dramatic critic. In our own day, O'Neill's very earliest plays might have been written by Sam Shipman in his prime. On the other hand, the first plays of dozens of our boys and girls like William Hurlbut, Zoë Akins, William Jourdan Rapp, Daniel Rubin, Laurence Stallings, Albert Bein, Mary Kennedy, Frank Mandel, Lynn Starling, Rita Wellman, Julian Thompson, et al., have suggested all kinds of promise — and look at them now.

PROTEAN ARTISTS. The so-called protean artists, those performers who jump behind screens every other minute, quickly change their makeup and costume, and then emerge and do nothing further whatsoever except to take a bow, always impress me as the most futile of all the specimens of genus jambon. I can never resist comparing them with the letters laboriously written by small children who have been given paint-boxes for Christmas and who elaborately and variously color the initial letter of each maundering and meaningless paragraph in the fond hope that grandma will be so impressed she will send them a present.

PULITZER PRIZE AND OTHERS.   A close consideration of the various prizes, awards and citations which are annually bestowed at the seasons' ends may be undertaken with some possible profit.

First, the Pulitzer prize, not — surely — because it possesses the slightest authentic importance, but because it is more widely known in the hinterland than most of the others. In New York and the other larger cities, it is of course recognized for exactly what it is, which is to say an award which, though without integrity and most often also without the slightest critical sense, has its occasional advertising and box-office value, particularly with regard to such fauna as are impelled to buy ketchup, chow-chow and anything else in bottles and cans in proportion to the number of World's Fair and African Colonial Exposition medals reproduced on the labels and as are further impressed by the endorsements of that miscellaneous critical Pollyanna, William Lyon Phelps, and the austerity of Nicholas Murray Butler's dress-shirt launderer.

The value of the Pulitzer prize as a gauge of merit is nil. That at least one committee of recommendation, composed of the Messrs. Walter Prichard Eaton, Clayton Hamilton and Austin Strong, resigned in complete disgust because its suggestion as to a play that merited the prize was dismissed in favor of a considerably less worthy one, is sufficiently known. That on at least one occasion the decision of the upper board was overridden by a single member who insisted the prize be given to one of his old pet students at Columbia, is also known. And that the rules governing the award have been altered so often in the last decade that a committee of Bronx lawyers has to be called in each successive year to interpret them to the awarders is common gossip.

As if in despair at all this, the award board some years ago apparently made up its collective mind comfortably and safely to forget all about questions of merit and simply bestow the prize upon some play that had made a particularly good box-office showing during the year and that seemed to please most of the people, of whatever nature, who had seen it. Thus, five seasons ago the prize was given to that dish of mush, *The Old Maid,* already a big box-office hit; four seasons ago to the melodrama, *Idiot's Delight,* already a sellout; three seasons ago to *You Can't Take It with You,* an amusing and commercially very successful farce-comedy that couldn't even momentarily have been considered for an award by anyone possessed of the faintest æsthetic critical sense; two seasons ago to *Our Town,* a safe and moral dose of sentiment which had met with safe and moral popular approval — and in a year that witnessed the production of John Steinbeck's notable *Of Mice and Men,* which, however, had a few disturbing cuss words in it, to say nothing of a blonde in a short skirt; and last season to *Abe Lincoln in Illinois,* an immensely popular patriotic exhibit which had packed the box-office and giving a prize to which was as popularly safe as giving one to the Dionne quintuplets. All this, however, persuades the dumber section of the public to view the Pulitzer judges as very acute critics, inasmuch as the judges' opinions coincide with its own. Watch this present season's Pulitzer award and see if the same kind of logic isn't pursued by the committee. The whole business is as comical as trying to make a critical name for oneself by giving a prize for architecture to that bank building which has the most money in it.

This practice of arbitrarily handing out the Pulitzer grand to best-sellers has also seemingly extended to the novel and biography. This last year the money was distributed to Marjorie Rawlings' *The Yearling,* which topped the fiction best-seller list and to Carl Van Doren's *Benjamin Franklin,* which topped the biography best-seller list. In previous years, it has been peddled to such best-selling novels as John Marquand's *The Late George Apley*, Margaret Mitchell's circus-seller, *Gone with the Wind*, Caroline Miller's *Lamb in His Bosom*, Pearl Buck's *The Good Earth* and Margaret Ayer Barnes' *Years of Grace*. And among the biographies there have been such fancy sellers as Henry Pringle's *Theodore Roosevelt*, Allan Nevins' *Grover Cleveland*, Douglas Freeman's *R. E. Lee*, Odell Shepard's *Bronson Alcott*, and Tyler Dennett's *John Hay*.

So self-conscious are the Pulitzer people about the criticism of their awards, particularly in the case of the drama, that they refuse to make public the names of the persons who at present constitute their play-recommending committees. Were they to make the names public, the laugh in all probability would be even more callithumpian than it is. For it is rumored that most of the appropriate gentlemen who have been approached to serve on the committees have abruptly declined and that in desperation a group of amateur stand-ins has been drafted into service. Stark Young, drama critic for the *New Republic*, for example, thumbed his nose derisively at a renewal of the invitation, and Gilbert Gabriel, former drama critic of the New York *American*, sent in his equally sardonic regrets. Last season's committee, it is reported, was accordingly made up of that hardy perennial, Billy Phelps, who has been steadily committeeing on the Pulitzer and other prix bodies since before Della Fox was born, Miss Phoebe Danzinger, who teaches drama classes at the Washington Irving High School, and Owen Davis, Jr., actor and son of the author of *Bertha the Sewing Machine Girl, Marry the Poor Girl, The Haunted House, Beware of Widows*, and *Gentle Grafters*. This and committees like it suggest the prize winner to still another and advisory committee which deliberates the recommendations and either follows them or independently follows its own sweet whim.

And then this advisory committee passes on its suggestions to the trustees of Columbia University, who dog-like publicize them.

Consider, if you will, the personnel of the advisory board in especial connection with the drama award. Its members are the following: R. L. O'Brien, former publisher of the Boston *Herald;* until his recent death, Ralph Pulitzer, sportsman; Nicholas Murray Butler; Joseph Pulitzer, publisher of the St. Louis *Post-Dispatch;* A. M. Howe, once an editor in Brooklyn; Julian Harris, of the Chattanooga *Times;* William Allen White; Kent Cooper, of the Associated Press; S. H. Perry, publisher of the Adrian, Mich., *Telegram;* Frank Kent, political columnist of the Baltimore *Sun;* H. S. Pollard, editorial writer on the New York *World-Telegram;* Walter Harrison, of the Oklahoma City *Oklahoman;* and S. Brown, of the Providence, R. I., *Journal.* All thoroughly estimable gentlemen, to be sure, but what they know of the theatre and drama might comfortably be put into a quinine capsule, with plenty of room left to spare for a copy of the Lord's Prayer, a tinted photograph of Major Bowes, and one of Anna Held's pink garters.

Moreover, this advisory board which commonly dispenses the Pulitzer drama prize apparently has so little interest in the theatre that neither collectively nor singly does it ever bother itself much with theatre attendance. Extended and careful investigation reveals the appended entire scope of playgoing on the part of its members during the last theatrical season:

R. L. O'Brien saw just three shows during the whole year: *Abe Lincoln in Illinois, Hellzapoppin,* and the Maurice Evans *Hamlet.*

Ralph Pulitzer, the most active theatregoer on the board, saw the following nine: *Hellzapoppin, Abe Lincoln in Illinois, Leave It to Me!, The Boys from Syracuse, Kiss the Boys Goodbye, Oscar Wilde, Knickerbocker Holiday, One for the Money,* and *Outward Bound.* (Five musical shows, that is, one revival, one farce-comedy, one English importation, and the play to which he voted the family prix.)

Nicholas Murray Butler saw seven out of a total of eighty-odd productions. They were *Abe Lincoln, Hamlet,* the D'Oyly Carte *Pinafore,* the musical *Hot Mikado,* the revival of *Outward Bound,* the paraphrase of an old farce, *The Merchant of Yonkers,* and the patriotic spectacle *The American Way.*

Joseph Pulitzer attended the theatre six times and saw *Abe Lincoln, Hellzapoppin* (twice), Beatrice Lillie in *Set to Music,* the musical *Knickerbocker Holiday,* and the Jimmy Durante–Ethel Merman tune show, *Stars in Your Eyes.*

A. M. Howe got around just twice, to *Hellzapoppin* and *Abe Lincoln.*

Julian Harris, so far as my agents have been able to determine, saw only *Hellzapoppin* and let it go at that.

William Allen White got to four shows: the inevitable *Hellzapoppin, Leave It to Me!,* Frank Fay's vaudeville show, and *The Swing Mikado.* No dramas, so far as the reports go.

Kent Cooper saw *Hellzapoppin, Abe Lincoln,* Beatrice Lillie, Jimmy Durante, *The Boys from Syracuse,* and Ethel Waters in *Mamba's Daughters.*

S. H. Perry contented his critical soul with *Hellzapoppin* and a couple of Merle Oberon movies.

Frank Kent called it a day with *Hellzapoppin, Abe Lincoln, Knickerbocker Holiday,* and another trip to *Hellzapoppin.*

H. S. Pollard made a better showing and saw not only *Hellzapoppin,* but *Abe Lincoln, The Little Foxes, The Boys from Syracuse, Outward Bound,* and Dodie Smith's *Dear Octopus.*

Walter Harrison saw *Hellzapoppin* and *Pins and Needles.*

S. Brown took a look at *Hellzapoppin, American Landscape,* the Jimmy Durante show, and Katharine Hepburn in *The Philadelphia Story.*

There, unless my band of skilled sherlocks are less skillful than usual, is the theatregoing record of the men who
award the late Mr. Pulitzer's one thousand simoleons to what
they announce as " the most distinguished play of the year."
Some didn't even see the play they gave the prize to. Only
one saw *The Little Foxes*, and not one saw *My Heart's in the
Highlands* or any other of the year's worthier plays.

That the Pulitzer drama prize is beginning to be a worry
even to the Pulitzer people themselves is evident from their
recent effort to defend themselves by casting mud in other
award directions and by not hesitating to prevaricate by way
of making out something of a case for themselves. Taking
over the entire contents of the *Independent Journal* of Columbia University at the time of the last Pulitzer award, they
went to the length of trying to discredit the Drama Critics'
Circle awards by attributing to Brooks Atkinson, critic for
the New York *Times* and a leading member of the Circle, a
paragraph in the *Times,* actually written by its Broadway reporter, comparing the box-office business done by last year's
Pulitzer and Critics' Circle choices. The paragraph in question allowed that while the Pulitzer prize had increased re-
ceipts in the case of *Our Town*, the Critics' prize play, *Of
Mice and Men,* was due to close three weeks later. What
the Pulitzer glee-boys deliberately glossed over were the
plain facts that *Of Mice and Men* opened on November 23,
1937, and was already naturally approaching the end of its
long and highly prosperous run, that *Our Town* didn't open
until February 4, 1938, that when the final statistics were in
Of Mice and Men showed a record of two hundred and seven
performances against only one hundred and fifty-nine for
Our Town, that *Our Town*, further, was forced to cut salaries
in order to continue, and that the Critics' award was announced on April 18 and the Pulitzer award not until May 2.

Even droller was the Pulitzeristas' publication of a large
photograph taken in front of the Morosco theatre and showing, during the closing week of *Of Mice and Men,* " play-

goers during that same week flocking to *Our Town.*" A careful count reveals just fourteen people in front of the theatre. Two of the fourteen are moving up Forty-fifth street away from the theatre, two are clearly just passersby, one is scratching her nose in doubt about going to the show, and one is quickly to be identified as a certain gentleman who always sees plays on passes. That leaves a huge crowd of exactly eight people flocking to the Pulitzer exhibit.

It is true that I may be prejudiced — and God wot, why not? — but when one reflects on the machinery and dispensation of the Pulitzer prize it is surely pretty hard not to convince oneself that it is a pure, aimless monkeyshine in comparison with the Critics' Circle's prize. Whatever may be argued against the latter, it is at least awarded by a body of men whose profession and life's work is theatrical and dramatic criticism; it is determined upon without compromise of any kind; its one, sole and only consideration is dramatic merit; it hasn't the slightest traffic with box-office success or failure; and it represents a corpus of professional opinion that is uncorrupted, forthright, and contemptuous of mob approval. Though I personally have not always agreed with the awards — on two occasions, indeed, I have been a stubborn dissenter — I have recognized, nevertheless, that they have been not without their merit and have come from the honest conviction of the majority. To allow merit to even one Pulitzer award out of every three — and that is a generous ratio — would be a difficult feat on the part of anyone possessed of even faintly sound critical standards.

That the best of our American playwrights themselves duly recognize all this has been made evident. Take, for instance, Robert Sherwood. When several years ago he was given the Pulitzer prize for his *Idiot's Delight,* which the Critics' Circle had spurned, he stated very politely that he was pleased but that it would be a lot better if the Pulitzer award were determined not by the bizarre Pulitzer committees but by the Critics' Circle. In his speech of acceptance of an award by the Critics' Circle, Maxwell Anderson in the same year wittily, if delicately, relegated the Pulitzer prize, which had in a previous year been awarded to him, to the limbo of the excessively dubious. And what Eugene O'Neill, who has received the Pulitzer prize on three different occasions, thinks of it I prefer to leave to the imagination of those who recall his message to the Critics' Circle upon its foundation.

The other annual awards may be dismissed in a minimum of space. The medal given by the Drama League of New York for the most distinguished acting performance of the season, like the medals and what not given by other such groups of stage-struck elderly ladies, represents little more than the crushes the old girls get on this or that actor or actress (usually actor). The certificate of merit and Virginia ham awarded by a " lay committee " (composed of men and women apparently picked up on street-corners) on behalf of Robert Porterfield's Barter Theatre of Abingdon, Virginia, amounts wholly and entirely to the critical and æsthetic value of one Virginia ham. The plaque bestowed by the Stage Society, whatever that is, is simply an occasion for the lady members effusively to eat a gala two-dollar-and-fifty-cent lunch in the company of various theatrical celebrities.

But be sparing of any too cynical laugh that may be brewing within you. Hold it in reserve for the prize among all prize awards since Caesar first passed out the original laurel. Hold it in reserve for the regents of the University of New Brunswick, of Frederickton, N. B. It is they who recently conferred their prime award, the degree of Ph.D. — Doctor of Philosophy, no less — upon that combined Socrates, Hegel, Kant and Descartes of the twentieth century, Mr. Louis B. Mayer.

QUESTION OF COMPETITION. The indignation of our theatrical managers over the invasion of their sacred precinct by the late Federal Theatre Project was not without its humorous aspects. With eyes abulge with alarm, they howled that the low admission prices charged by the Federal showmen would provide dangerous, even ruinous, competition. And with ears atwitch with fright, they cried that their only salvation was the segregation of the relief playhouses far from the theatre zone.

It is true that superficially it did not seem fair to have the government-subsidized shows trying to horn in on independently operated theatrical territory. And it is true that superficially it would seem that a fifty-five-cent or eighty-three-cent box-office charge might play havoc with a three-dollar-and-thirty-cent charge. But what are the hard facts? The hard facts, four in number, are the following. First, the Federal Theatre folk couldn't have horned into the managerial zone if several of the managers who did the loudest complaining had not themselves hypocritically rented their theatres to them. Secondly, the low box-office charge could not provide any more seriously objectionable competition than these same managers' frequent cut-rating of their own admission fees, often resulting in a slicing of two-thirds off the price marked on the tickets. Thirdly, the many failures of the Federal folk proved that people will no more buy a bad Federal show even for the small sum of fifty-five cents than they will buy a bad professional show even for the thirty-cent tax on free passes. And fourthly, if the managers had

any acumen they would so finally arrange their business that
they could compete with some such good Federal show as
Power or . . . *one-third of a nation* with admission fees
at least two-thirds less than they now unsuccessfully try to
get for some such professional garlic as *Close Quarters* or
Ringside Seat.

There is no such thing in the theatre as arbitrary competition. The Federal people could have taken over half the
houses in the theatre zone and, if they didn't put the kind of
plays in them that audiences wanted, would have had to
close up shop whether they charged fifty-five cents or merely
a dime. They moved into the St. James Theatre in the very
heart of the zone, produced something called *Trojan Inci-
dent* at four bits the ticket, and attracted so few customers
that they had to shut down after a few days. All the plays,
good or bad, for which they charged only fifty-five cents
would not in the least have diminished audiences who were
called upon to pay three dollars and more for the worth-while
professional plays, for the simple reason that the fifty-five-
cent theatregoer cannot afford the higher price however
eager he may be to see the worth-while professional plays.
Moreover, the managers might actually help the theatre and
its business a deal more if they would cease yelping about
such things as the late threatened Federal Theatre invasion
and themselves put a stop to the already existing shoestring
invasion. When they freely rent out their theatres dozens of
times every season to fifty-five-cent tripe box-officed at three
dollars and thirty cents and don't get even fifty-five cents for
it, they do the theatre infinitely more damage and bring it
into infinitely greater disrepute than if they were to rent them
out to Federal or any other kind of folk for three-dollar-and-
thirty-cent exhibits like certain of the *Living Newspapers* tick-
eted at the bargain price of fifty-five cents.

There is another point. Does an abandoned or empty
playhouse help the theatre? Isn't it much better to put even
a fifty-five-cent show into some such orphaned house as the

Forty-Ninth Street, the Bijou, the Adelphi, the Belmont, or any of the half dozen others than to board it up or give it over to twenty-five-cent films? And there is another point still. If the Federal Theatre Project could put on something like *Murder in the Cathedral* better for fifty-five cents than a professional manager subsequently proved he could for three dollars and thirty cents, then — much as it pains me to say it — to the waste-basket with the professional managers.

QUESTIONNAIRE CRITICAL. In his review of *All that Glitters,* our beloved critical colleague, Brooks Atkinson, wrote: " Having been victimized by his last two excursions into dramaturgy, George Abbott has now returned to comedy."

Since when is comedy also not dramaturgy?

In his review of *A Doll's House,* in an attempt politely to get out of calling Miss Ruth Gordon names, our beloved critical colleague, Burns Mantle wrote: " There will always be as many Noras as there will be Candidas and none of them, I could wager convincingly, knowing I could never be proved wrong, would be accepted by either Ibsen or Shaw as approaching his creation."

You lose your wager and you are easily proved wrong. Don't you know that Ibsen and Shaw are on record as having wholeheartedly accepted certain actresses in the rôles in point?

In his review of Lennox Robinson's *The Far-off Hills,* our beloved critical colleague, John Mason Brown, wrote: " As everything Robinson does is done only as entertainment for entertainment's sake, it would no doubt be ungrateful to complain," etc.

Done only as entertainment for entertainment's sake? Come, come! What of his *The Lost Leader*? What of his *Patriots*? What of his *Portrait*? What of his *The Big House*?

In his review of Teresa Deevy's *Katie Roche,* our beloved critical colleague, Richard Watts, Jr., wrote: " It is an unsuccessful attempt to adapt the Chekhovian method of indirection to a subtle Irish character study and I found it utterly lacking in significance."

But, whatever the method of treatment, how can an Irish or any other character study, if it be subtle, be utterly lacking in significance?

In his review of Robert Vansittart's *Dead Heat*, our beloved English critical colleague, W. A. Darlington, wrote: " The first requisite for drama is that there must be no dead heats; in the race between love, ambition, wealth and the rest, one must win or there will be no climax."

What of such meritorious and widely accepted plays as Galsworthy's *Strife*?

In his review of *Antony and Cleopatra*, our beloved critical colleague, Brooks Atkinson, qualified his general denunciation of the production by writing: " As Octavius Caesar, however, John Emery has the stature of a statesman and warrior."

What kind of criticism is that? So, for that matter, had Corse Payton.

In his tribute to his own production of *Susan and God*, our beloved theatrical manager, John Golden, wrote: " There's no woman playwright to compare with Miss Crothers. Rachel doesn't go into a room with Moss Hart or George Abbott and come out with a play. No, she goes into a room by herself and comes out with a play a year later."

In this case, wasn't it mighty lucky for her though that she met Gertrude Lawrence on the way out?

QUIXOTISM. The critics may protest all they care to, but the fact remains that if a young actress wants to make a big hit with them let her be certain to find herself a rôle that veers heavily toward the sentimental and moral. She will then stand a dozen times better chance for good notices than if she is cast in a rôle of harsher contours. The critics are much more sentimental and moral fellows than they like to admit. Thus, season before last, the most laudatory reviews were reserved for Martha Scott, as the sentimental young bride of *Our Town;* Julie Haydon, as the sentimental true believer of *Shadow and Substance;* Jessica Tandy, as the sentimental sister of *Time and the Conways;* Jane Wyatt, as the sentimental princess of *Save Me the Waltz;* Vera Zorina, as the delicate cherub in *I Married an Angel;* Uta Hagen, despite the lapse in morals, as the sure-fire sentimental Nina in *The Sea Gull;* Jacqueline Porel, as the sentimental ugly duckling in *French without Tears;* and Nancy Kelly, as the sentimental deserted child in *Susan and God.* The only exception was Frances Farmer in *Golden Boy* and even there, despite its overtone of brazenness, the rôle was preponderantly on the sentimental if not moral side. Thus, too, last season the most flattering notices were reserved for Helen Trenholme, as the sentimental nurse of *Come Across;* Lois Hall, as the sentimental little mother of *Dame Nature;* Amelia Romano, as the sentimental little orphan of *Big Blow;* Mary Rolfe, as the sentimental, beset virgin of *Dance Night;* Adele Longmire as the sentimental Ann Rutledge of *Abe Lincoln in Illinois;* Eleanor Lynn as the sentimental dreamer of *Rocket to the Moon;* Fredi Washington, as the sentimental virgin pursued by the dastardly villain in *Mamba's Daughters;* Jessica Tandy, as the sentimental defender of old ideals in *The White Steed;* and Gene Tierney, as the sentimental young love interest of *Mrs. O'Brien Entertains.* It has always been next to impossible for a young actress to fail with the critics as Kathie in *Old Heidelberg,* as Sonia in *Uncle Vanya,* as Deirdre in *Deirdre of the Sorrows,* as the heroine of *Griselda,* as Flavia in *The Prisoner of Zenda,* or as the heroine of any fairy tale. Though it is different in the case of older actresses, the young actress who plays bitches, even though she be something of an acting genius, generally has a much harder job convincing the soft-hearted Bethunes.

QUODLIBET. The chief diversion of the audience and critics directly after the opening of Philip Barry's *Here Come the*

Clowns was trying to figure out what the play was about, and in the diversion I have little doubt that Mr. Barry himself was somewhere secretly participating. As in the instance of his *Hotel Universe,* the author here again sought to explore the regions of metaphysics, symbolical philosophy and transcendental ethics and here again got lost in the dark. A grotesquerie involving vaudeville folk bent on deciphering the problem of Good and Evil, the play amounted in sum to an unintentional vaudeville of Pirandello, Giacosa, Evreinoff, and the Chesterton of *Magic,* all faultily digested. It was as confused as the hundred bits of colored glass in a toy kaleidoscope but, paradoxically enough, like such a kaleidoscope its shifting movement occasionally provided a gleaming and engaging, if still disordered, pattern. In other words, though much of the play seemed meaningless, or at least troublesomely evasive, it now and again despite itself induced in one's imaginative fancy oddly piquant little half tones and overtones.

The difficulty with Barry is that he unconsciously mistakes his own philosophical vagueness for vagueness in the philosophies themselves. He gives the impression of a man who has heard a good tune somewhere, tries hard to remember it, can recall only the first few notes, and thereupon persuades himself that the rest of it must be as nebulous to everyone else as it is to him. It is thus that a play like this *Here Come the Clowns* or one like *Hotel Universe* confounds its audience not because its concepts are in themselves necessarily obscure but rather because Barry tortures them into obscurity with his own mental booziness.

R

RETURN OF INTEREST.   What is back of all this sudden return of interest and excitement in the theatre? What causes so many of the critics, those supposedly frost-bitten fish, to write of it as if their typewriter ribbons were soaked in marijuana? Their enthusiasm has become so exotic that, if they don't watch out, it won't be long before Hollywood's " colossals ", " magnificents ", " super-colossals ", and " epics " will pale in comparison. I quote some of their reactions and tributes to various recent exhibits:

" A dramatic tornado."

" Gorgeous entertainment."

" A triumph! "

" A modern masterpiece! "

" One of the finest achievements of the drama."

" Never such an evening of riotous fun."

" Superb! A master performance! "

" Nothing so original and jovial has turned up for a long time."

" Truly joyous in every single particular."

" One of the finest, most pungent productions to enrich the stage in years."

" A work of tremendous beauty. Nothing short of perfection! "

" Relentless in its power."

" Epically beautiful."

" Every reason to beat the drum royally."

" All hats must be tossed into the air. Great stuff! "

" An explosive success."

" Utterly ingratiating."

" Immense! Fascinating! "

" Enormous wit and brilliance."

" Wonderfully captivating and irresistible."

What, as I say, is back of all this? I suggest the following eight reasons:

1. Those audiences who had deserted the theatre for the movies have found that they can no longer get any satisfaction from the movies' endless reduplication of themselves. They have also come gradually to realize that the much advertised " romance " and " glamour " of the movies is confined very largely to the outsides of the picture palaces, what with their gaudy fronts, electrical displays, imposing doormen, gilded lobbies and the like, and that once you get inside and the show begins it is like visiting Buckingham Palace, sitting at table before a wealth of gold plate, and being served a cheese sandwich.

2. In the new deep emotional surge and sweep of the world, the puny little emotions purveyed by the films are no longer sufficient and only the profounder spiritual emotions of drama can meet the cravings of a psychically beset and become serious public.

3. Even the lower forms of mentality progress upward, however slightly, with time and experience. After years of film-going, even the movie mentality seeks something finer, better, and more inspiring.

4. The critics have driven trash quickly into the discard and have thus made theatregoing safer and more profitable for the public. Their occasional noted over-enthusiasm for the relatively better plays, while critically deplorable, has nevertheless been a good thing in the encouragement of theatre attendance on the part of a public not yet altogether ready for the higher æsthetic criticism.

5. The countless amateur theatrical groups spread throughout the country, the many new college courses in drama, and other such things have stimulated an increased interest in the professional theatre.

6. The managers are no longer regularly bamboozling the road with poor plays, poor casts and poor productions and, by sending out good plays with good actors, are gradually rebuilding the road's confidence in the theatre, just as Hollywood's Grade-B and Grade-C films are slowly beginning to destroy the road's confidence in pictures.

7. Idiotic censorship has disgusted the public with many otherwise possibly entertaining films, whereas the theatre is relatively free from any such censorship.

8. And the quality of drama has improved greatly in the last half dozen years.

REQUIRED PLAYGOING. Writes Critic James Agate in the London Sunday *Times:* "When Mr. Odets' *Golden Boy* was produced here, a well-known English novelist and playwright wrote to me protesting that this was a hokum play without integrity: 'Practically every scene is jazzed up, given more punch and excitement and noise than it should have, without reference to reality at all'."

If the unidentified well-known English novelist and playwright correspondent of Mr. Agate's is correct in assuming that his criticism of the Odets play registers it as a hokum play without integrity, does not his criticism similarly and automatically stamp as hokum plays without integrity a number of the better works of Strindberg, Wedekind, Kaiser, Andreyev, and Galdós?

REVIVALS. Whenever a producer doesn't know what else to do but feels it arbitrarily incumbent upon him to do something, he either puts on a revival or casts the nearest thing to hand with a company of Negroes. Occasionally, if his mind at the moment is even less inventive than usual, he does both simultaneously. This is his idea of a great novelty, habitually and unfortunately shared by hardly anyone else, particularly the Negroes, who are well known to be a shrewd race and amusedly tolerant of Aryan theatrical managers, if any.

The motivations of a producer in such cases are several, both internal and external. If it is a revival he puts on, he does so either because he has indignantly persuaded himself that it is impossible to find a good new play (meaning simply that he doesn't know a good new play even when it is stuck right under his nose), or because a number of actors whom he likes and who are sadly out of jobs have banded together for an assault upon his tender sensibilities. In either instance, in addition, he knows he can often get the revived play for less than its former scale of royalties — and maybe the scenery out of the storehouse. If, on the other hand, it is the Negro concept that fetches his fancy, he slyly and further appreciates that the whole colored weekly salary list won't run much higher than a single white actor's laundry bill and that the critics will often with sweet magnanimity overlook deficiencies in second-rate colored players which they wouldn't for a minute condone in even first-rate white ones.

Another thing that persuades a producer to the revival idea is his strange conviction that because a play has once been a big success it will in all probability be a big success again, a conviction statistically disproved in the revival of eight modern plays out of ten and akin to a belief that someone is overlooking a grand bet in not putting Kreuger & Toll stock back on the market. And when it comes to the Negro proposition, it is his equally whimsical prepossession that what would in all likelihood be a bore if acted by whites must inevitably become a sensation if done in black-face, an idea in turn akin to a belief that one could easily make a million dollars by casting Uncle Tom in white-face and Little Eva as a pickaninny, with the Harvard Glee Club in evening dress as the plantation singers.

RIDDLE-SNIFFERS. The recent revival of Shaw's *Heartbreak House,* originally shown here nineteen years ago, again provided a gala holiday to those persons who delight in working themselves to death ferreting profound meanings out of the most simple and innocent works of art and who, however much they may actually enjoy a thing, are unwilling to surrender themselves fully to that enjoyment unless they are able to justify it with some attributed cryptic purpose on the part of the author. There is, true enough, some meaning to the Shaw exhibit but it is as clear as the blue sky and calls for no undue head-scratching. It is, simply, the muddled attempt of muddled and war-beset humanity to guess its way out of chaos. But that is not, apparently, enough for some geese. The play is by Shaw and hence must surely mean something infinitely deeper and more complex, just as any play by Ibsen, being by Ibsen, must mean twice as much as Ibsen clearly and succinctly says it does or as even Richard Strauss' *Till Eulenspiegel's Merry Pranks*, being by the anarch Strauss, must have immeasurably more esoteric purport than Till Eulenspiegel's merry pranks.

RURITANIA, ZENDA AND POINTS WEST. Let anyone put on a play laid in an imaginary kingdom with the men in uniform and the women in silks and satins and the reviewers are pretty sure to say that it would have been a lot better with music. They are usually right. First, because the average exhibit of the species enjoys a lack of quality that music would help to conceal and, secondly, because the mythical kingdom play, for all the fact that it once in a very great while is fairly satisfactory without music, is nevertheless so inextricably bound up in theatrical prejudice with music that, when music is missing, the feeling is as violated as it would be if Gorki were scored or if Strindberg were augmented with Follies girls.

In *Save Me the Waltz*, Katharine Dayton attempted to modernize Graustark by bringing in a dictator who falls in love with the Princess Flavia. She attempted all this with a straight face which now and again tried desperately to save itself by talking a little satire out of the corner of its mouth. The result was akin to listening to a recitation of the words of a blues song by a singer who has lost her voice. The very title of the play belied its scorelessness. With scenery that, in one character's observation, "looks like the Waldorf", with a wealth of uniforms and costumes that made Lehar appear in comparison like Erskine Caldwell, and with a purple moon glowing over the green and gilded palace terrace, the curtains went up and down to the tune of admiring Ahs and Ohs from the audience but that, unfortunately, was hardly enough tune to relieve Miss Dayton's libretto. For a libretto it was and remains, whatever she may fancy to the contrary. Her love scenes were sheer saxophonic sentiment; her comedy relief was straight out of Cole Porter's *Jubilee;* and her whole plot scheme was the Castoria that the children of musical comedy have cried for from the days of the old Casino Theatre. There was a rumor that George S. Kaufman did some work on the script. I doubt it. However, that line of the portrait painter's to the effect that he has painted all the dictators from Stalin to Sam Goldwyn makes me a bit suspicious.

Without music, in short, the play sounded like a tuba in the hands of a man dying of galloping consumption. Even with music, true enough, it would not have been much good, but without it it was approximately as satisfactory as an orchestra that, after a brief and piquant tuning up, lays aside its instruments and sits itself down to a quiet game of pinochle.

S

SAROYAN. For the second time in two years a playwriting
novice came out of the California that isn't Hollywood and
showed up most of his theoretical professional masters. First
it was John Steinbeck with *Of Mice and Men.* Then it was
William Saroyan with *My Heart's in the Highlands,* as bonny,
imaginative, and utterly fascinating a sentimental lark as had
come the way of the local stage in a long spell. Lit with the
gleam of a smiling fancy and stirred with a humorous compassion, this loose and gently jovial mixture of almost everything from fantasy to nuts simultaneously squeezes the laughter and tears out of one with some of the seemingly most
carefree playwriting it has been my surprised pleasure to
have experienced. The fable of a tenth-rate poet whose pro-
tective little boy worships him as a genius and of the twain's
machinations against an unappreciative world, embellished
as it is with half a dozen other characters rich in a joint tenderness and jocosity, was one of its season's few treasures.
The majority of the reviewers, while praising the play, however complained bitterly that they couldn't discern any clear
meaning in it. Which struck some of the rest of us like complaining bitterly over the absence of any clear meaning in
Brahms' solo scherzo in E flat minor, the Black Forest in the
early morning sunlight, a good hamburger with onions, or
human life itself.

As a second testimonial to his talents, Saroyan has now
followed up this play with one called *The Time of Your Life,*
which is every bit as good as the first. Its theme is an invocation of the smiling beauty that life holds and that bravery
and charity and humor should resistlessly evoke from it. The

action passes on the afternoon and night of a day in October
in Nick's Pacific Street Saloon, Restaurant and Entertainment
Palace at the foot of Embarcadero in San Francisco, and in a
room in a small hotel around the corner. The leading characters are Joe, "a young loafer with money and a good
heart"; Tom, "his disciple, errand-boy, stooge, and friend";
and Kitty, a girl of the pavements. Surrounding them is an
assortment that hasn't often been matched for bizarre variety
and that includes an Arabian philosopher and harmonica-
player; an old Indian fighter, Kit Carson by booze-parlor
name; a literary-minded longshoreman; a hoofer who wants
to make people laugh but can't; a small colored boy who
"plays a mean and melancholy boogie-woogie piano"; a
marble-game maniac; a cigar-smoking society woman; and
"a waterfront cop who hates his job but doesn't know what
else to do instead."

To try to get the plot exactly upon paper is as difficult
as it would be in the case of, say, Strindberg's *Dream Play*
and *Spook Sonata* or Gorki's *Night Refuge*. As in the instance of the last named, the play consists rather in many
variegated chips and stones that gradually settle themselves
into the mosaic of a permanent mood. There are a dozen
plots, yet on the whole no plot. What we get is a kind of
dramatic music, vagrant and often formless but with a melody that lingers when the play is done. And throughout the
oddly deft orchestration of loud laughter and gentle pity, a
vaudeville of humanity that goes deep under mankind's
grease-paint. But, above all, and beyond such critical analy-
sis, what we get is a fundamentally rich and juicy theatrical
show.

It is wild and crazy stuff and at the same time as sane
as mankind foolishly thinks itself. The well-to-do loafer dis-
tracts himself with toys designed, he says, "to drive the boredom out of children." The old Indian fighter, a liar summa
cum, brags ceaselessly of his exploits, including the time he
herded cattle in 1918 in Toledo, Ohio, on a bicycle in com-

pany with the only Jewish cowboy in existence (on another bicycle) and was disconcerted to discover that bicycles scared the beasts. A sentimental young beer-weeper falls passionately in love with a Miss Elsie Mandelspiegel who rushes bed-pans in a hospital. The loafer gets the prostitute to stop crying by giving her the toys he has been playing with — " Toys stopped me from crying once. I was two-and-a-half years old. (*To Tom*) That's the reason I had you buy them. I wanted to see if I could find out why they stopped me from crying. I remember they seemed awfully stupid at the time." The bartender's peace of mind is utterly ruined because someone has called him a dentist; scratch his head as he will, he can't figure out why. Tom, the hulking dumbhead, dreams wistfully of the day when the loafer, his benefactor, will change the scheme of the present world and run an errand for *him*. And through it all from beginning to end moves the harmonica-playing Arabian savant profoundly wrinkling his brow, magnanimously pausing to let the effect of his even profounder philosophy slowly filter into the obtuse brains of his listeners, and always singly, simply, solely, and idiotically remarking: " No foundation. All the way down the line." A mad play, a screwy play — but/and a play that brings a new and strange life to the American stage.

SCRIPTS.   It is one of the stoutest beliefs of most theatrical producers that one can tell very little about a play from a mere reading of the script, that one can never tell just how it will come out in actual production, and that only in such production can there be any true test of its real merits. This, among other reasons, is why so many producers land seriatim in the storehouse, poorhouse, and bughouse. Any fairly intelligent person who knows anything at all about the theatre and drama can tell very well what a play is like from a reading of the script and can also foretell pretty well what it will be like in production. One can't, of course, always tell whether it will be a financial success, but the average of prognostication in that direction, even so, isn't so bad. The opposite view maintained by the producers proceeds almost entirely from their own shortcomings. If and when they get hold of a good play and, after reading it in script, miraculously conclude that it is a good play, what do they frequently do? They miscast it; they fail to engage a sufficiently knowledgeable director to stage it; they hamstring it with the wrong kind of scenery and costumes; they book it into a theatre wholly unsuited to it; they open it, maybe, during a blizzard, a business panic, or an influenza epidemic; and then they derisively shout: "See! We told you! You never can tell."

The contention of producers that there is something very mysterious about scripts is, as I say, the sheerest nonsense and on a par with various other of their beliefs, perhaps chief of which is the conviction that if the critics were more lenient with bad plays the public, presumably unable to tell bad plays when it saw them, would be induced to flock to the box-offices in enormous numbers and make whopping successes of all of them. Any producer who can't recognize the merit or demerit of a play from a reading of it in manuscript has no business in the theatre and should promptly insert himself into short pants again and go back to school.

What is sometimes much more difficult than appraising the quality of a play before it has been produced is — even in the instance of the professional critic — appraising the quality after it has been produced. A case in point is Stanley Young's biographical study of George Noël Gordon Byron, *Bright Rebel*. As staged, directed, and acted at the Lyceum it impressed one as being a starchy, feeble, talky and dull job, full of sound and fury and signifying only that Mr. Young's hero's real name must have been William Jennings Byron. So much for theatrical criticism of it. But dramatic criticism, penetrating with some difficulty into and behind the afflictive incompetence of the production, could not be too sure that Mr. Young's play wasn't rather better than it seemed to be.

One could discern in it, through the damp fog, at least slight qualities that the presentation obscured. That it was far from a satisfactory script, even a theatrical producer could easily have told. That it would inevitably prove a failure, almost anyone should have been able to foretell. But, just the same, unless I am more than usually mistaken, it wasn't the complete botch that the production made it out to be. Production or no production, it doesn't take a critical sleuth to appreciate that any play which at this late day offers such rococo lines as a clandestine and flustered hussy's " Where shall I go? " at the sound of a third party's approach and her Lothario host's " Quickly, in there! ", can't be a play worth very much. And production or no production, it also doesn't take a critical sleuth to appreciate that even if the play were a good one it would stand blessed little chance of proving itself with an actor who throughout the evening indicated Byron's resolute determination by impetuously crossing his arms over his bosom, with the ladies and gentlemen of Melbourne House played by mimes evidently under the impression that it was the old Hoffman House, and with the kind of stage direction that permitted actors invariably to indicate their sentimental stirrings by passionate blinkings of their eyelids.

SELLING THE THEATRE. After many years of treating the public as if it were doing the latter an unheard of favor to permit it to spend its money on it, the American theatre has at last been forced to the realization that, if it is to continue and prosper, it must get off its high horse and metaphorically buy the public a few drinks. Its former attitude, it now has come fully to appreciate, brought it almost to the edge of ruin. Second- and third-rate touring companies sold under the original label had killed the theatre on the road. Theatre auditoriums that looked like a ten-cent stick of lip rouge smeared on a garbage dump alienated the old-time audiences. Box-office attendants who treated potential customers as if they were the pox discouraged the theatregoer from any further commerce with them. Ticket brokers and scalpers who charged outrageous prices not only discouraged him even more greatly but profoundly irritated and disgusted him. In fact, things had come to the point where about the only person who could go to the theatre with complete ease and comfort was the one who got in on a pass, and even he was discommoded by having to stand in line at the box-office to pay the tax assessed by the management and by having to wait at the entrance until the ticket-taker made certain that the pass wasn't a forgery.

As an instrument at least partly to correct these and other abuses, the theatre a few years ago inaugurated an organization known as the American Theatre Council, composed of various managers, producers, actors, playwrights and others, and with James F. Reilly, long identified in a business capacity with the theatre, as chief executive lieutenant. The aim of the Council is to serve as a public relations medium, to obtain from all and sundry suggestions as to how best to sell back the theatre to that portion of the public that latterly has had insufficient traffic with it, and to weed out the most practical of these suggestions and endeavor to put them into force. At its first congress two years ago, the Council contented itself with little more than launching exercises. There were many pretty speeches and everybody was happy, but the net benefit accomplished could have been written on the back of a postage stamp. At its second congress, held last year, it rolled up its sleeves and at least struck an attitude of getting down to some tacks. Let us, however, survey the tacks.

Mr. William A. Brady, the venerable manager and producer who is noted for an annual bellicose pronouncement that the theatre is dead and who annually for the last twenty-two years has each year assigned a totally different contributing instrument as the mortician, at last year's session of the Council declared, with a darksome look in his eye and with his voice trembling with indignation, that the disaster lay in the refusal of playwrights to write good plays. This brought something of a sardonic laugh from the assembly, as the assembly seemed to be aware that even if and when the playwrights wrote good plays Mr. Brady did not himself seem to be particularly interested in them, preferring instead for the most part to deal in the lesser quality of drama, often of a purely box-office hokum species. It was also pointed out to the orator when he roared that not one good play had been produced in New York during that season, that that season saw the production of *Of Mice and Men, Amphitryon 38, Golden Boy, I'd Rather Be Right, Father Malachy's Miracle, The Cradle Will Rock,* . . . *one-third of a nation, Shadow and Substance, On Borrowed Time, Our Town, Murder in the Cathedral, Prologue to Glory* and certain other plays, and that even the critics, whom Mr. Brady considers so much poison to the welfare of the theatre, thought most of them not only good but here and there pretty fine.

Mr. Lawrence Langner, of the board of directors of the Theatre Guild, offered as his ideational contribution to the cure of some of the theatre's ills a central promotion bureau, to be supported by an assessment of twenty thousand dollars annually, which would act as an intermediary between the New York producers with good plays and the out-of-New York theatregoers who might be interested in seeing them. Mr. Langner's suggestion was courteously received, despite Mr. Brady's wroth interruption that someone ought to put up not a paltry twenty thousand dollars for the purpose but at least a million, along with a somewhat general feeling that a man who didn't seem to know how to make a go of a single, small theatre organization like the Theatre Guild was hardly the one to have any sound idea how to make a go of all the theatres in the nation.

It was also contended by Mr. Langner that the theatre should build up organized audiences in cities throughout the country, following the plan inaugurated by the Guild some years ago and later by the Shuberts in the case of the American Theatre Society. This appealed to the congress as having some sense, at least as an idea, though there was considerable speculation on the part of critics not present as to how, once the audiences had been organized, you could keep them organized after dosing them up with road tryouts of plays so bad that they subsequently would not last a week in New York and with tryouts of even the better plays that were still in an unprepared and unfinished state.

Mr. Burns Mantle, drama critic for the New York *Daily News,* broached still another plan originated, he said, by the late Mr. Ralph Holmes, drama critic for the Detroit *Times.* This plan consisted in the wish that the theatre managers might put aside two percent of the gross of all legitimate productions, the money to be placed in a general fund under the control of the Council and employed to make up for managerial losses on attractions. Mr. Mantle's amendment to his colleague Holmes' plan was that the money, instead of being applied to managerial losses, should be used in a campaign to revive the road. The moment the producers present heard the suggestion that they should be nicked two percent of their intake to help out other producers or anybody or anything else, they sneaked quietly in a body out to the washroom.

When, an hour later, the frightened producers returned from their hiding place and felt assured that their two percent was safe in their own pockets, it was proposed by various delegates that the ten percent government tax on theatre tickets was so obviously not only a nuisance but a detriment to the box-office that every effort should be made to seek its repeal. No one objected to this idea and it was decided to get the seek under way.

It was then Mr. Orson Welles' turn. Mr. Welles, as you may know, is the twenty-four-year-old young man who, up to two years ago, was working at minor acting jobs (including a Federal Theatre relief one at forty dollars a week) and who since then and at the moment was successfully operating the Mercury Theatre, not only with considerable kudos to himself but with a self-raise to two hundred smackers a week.

Young Mr. Welles was all gloom. The theatre was too dead, really, to do anything about it, really, he said. There was no good holding these Council meetings; everybody might just as well admit the worst and go home. It is to the congress' credit that it gave young Mr. Welles what is known to native belles lettres as the raspberry, whereupon Mr. Welles, registering an expression of ineffable world-weariness, repaired to " 21 " and ordered himself up a platter of caviar (out of the profits of his *Julius Caesar*), a thick Porterhouse steak with onions (out of the profits of his *The Shoemakers' Holiday*), and a bottle of Mumm's (out of the profits of his *The Cradle Will Rock*), the while continuing to moan to Karl, the waiter, that the theatre was a corpse.

Other physicians entertained the congress on a variety of therapeutical topics. These ranged from the price of theatre tickets to special dramatic festivals and from the sending out into the road cities of accomplished ballyhooers to guarantees against losses to producers who sent their attractions out of New York. Mr. John Golden, the producer, further suggested that the dramatists and actors help the managers to perfect a sound disciplinary organization; Miss Helen Hayes contended that it would be a help to theatrical economics if the Actors' Equity Association allowed actors to be sent on the road in cars other than expensive Pullmans and that the railroads should be beseeched to reduce their present rates for traveling companies; and Mr. John Krimsky, who was in charge of theatrical entertainment for the approaching New York World's Fair, argued that it would be dandy if a national poll were conducted to determine the plays that visitors to the Fair would like to see revived for a big Fair festival.

This, then, was the sum and substance of the accomplishments of the American Theatre Council in second congress assembled. That some of the proposals were not without their share of sense is to be admitted. But that, if the public is to be brought back wholesale into the theatre as the

Council hopes, a considerably more practical and considerably less verbose putsch will have to be put in motion is as plain as mud.

The theatre today, whatever the grousers may blubber to the contrary, is healthier than it has been in years. The maligned road rushes to buy all the really good plays that are vouchsafed to it. And there is a rebirth of general interest in the theatre that in its volume surprises even the optimists. The public relations problem is, therefore, not so much to get people into the theatre as to keep them there. They must be made not occasional customers but regular ones. And they cannot be made regular ones merely by making speeches at them.

The first thing that should be done — if it possibly can be done — is to establish for once and all the sale of tickets at the printed box-office price. Ticket brokers of all and any kind should be promptly got rid of. The allowed ticket broker charge of seventy-five cents over the box-office price is a rank swindle and the managers who, through the League of New York Theatres, condone and endorse it, are helping just that much to discourage playgoing. It is their argument that the brokers serve a good purpose in acting as central agencies with which the public may handily do business. This is nonsense. It is just as easy for a prospective theatre-goer to call up a box-office or to go to a box-office as it is for him to call up or to go to a broker's agency. But, say the managers, what if the box-office is out of seats for the attraction the customer wishes to see? He then, they argue, has to call up or visit several other box-offices in search for seats to a substitute show, whereas the broker, who handles all the shows, may save him the effort or telephone expense. This is also nonsense. The broker is often out of seats for the attraction the customer elects to see and the customer has to travel around to several other agencies before he can get them. Furthermore, three telephone calls cost only fifteen cents and that is a whole heap better than paying out an added one dollar and thirty-five cents on two tickets as broker's graft.

That there doubtless will always be ticket speculators, apart from the so-called legitimate agencies, who will swindle the public, we must regretfully admit. Nor does there seem to be a ready cure for them. But the least the managers can do is to withhold their tickets and approval from the lesser but just as objectionable speculators who constitute the brokerage agencies in question.

One thing is pretty certain, however, and that is that whatever the theatre managers finally decide to do about the present ticket mess will still be not even half-way satisfactory to their customers. Already for more years than one can remember they have waltzed around the matter with so much aimless, if high-sounding, gabble that the public's good will has been tried to the point where it can't be tried much farther. It is now up to the managers to make a firm and decent decision for once and all, or else frankly inform the public that they have no intention of making one and that they continue to relish the long-established custom of irritating and cheating the people who pay to get into their shows.

Always unwelcomely ready to come to the aid of damphools in distress, I have the impertinent honor to pass out to these managers a few further suggestions touching upon the subject. First, after quickly kicking out all the present ticket brokers, let them just as quickly establish the central co-operative ticket agency which they have been mulling in their minds and thus put an end to the seventy-five cent graft which the present brokers charge for each ticket they vend. The twenty-five cent charge outlined for such a co-operative agency is fair enough in view of public convenience and the covering of operating expenses.

Secondly, the present custom of holding ordered tickets at the box-office until only eight o'clock should be corrected. Since most curtains do not go up until around a quarter to nine, it means that the customer must either lose his tickets or waste three-quarters of an hour hanging around until the show starts. Either let the managers hold the tickets longer or solicit the aid of the telegraph messenger services in delivering them ahead of time for a nominal twenty-five cent charge.

Thirdly, sell orchestra and balcony tickets at different windows. If the construction of the lobby makes that impossible, erect a small à la movie theatre booth somewhere around the premises for the latter purpose. I have often seen potential three-dollar-and-eighty-five-cent orchestra seat buyers waiting near a window for many minutes and chafing at the bit lest the curtain rise while some seventy-five-cent or dollar balcony customer, usually female, debated seat locations and what not with the box-office attendant.

Fourthly, number the rows honestly. In one theatre, tickets marked Row C are presently in the sixth row; in another, those marked A are in the fourth row; in still another, those marked E are in the eighth; and in another still, those marked H are in the very last row before the balcony rise beyond the passageway. There are numerous such instances. Sometimes, in certain theatres, the row is really that indicated by the letter on the ticket but in these houses Row G, say, is actually where Row L would be in a normally constructed auditorium. Furthermore, place charts on the box-office window ledge — and don't cheat by reducing the chart to such size that even Row X looks as if it were only half a dozen feet from the stage.

Fifthly, employ a squad of dicks from a reputable detective agency to hang around the central ticket agency, when and if it is established, and to watch the employees and see to it that they don't work in cahoots with diggers. These diggers, or men who nab tickets at the established agency fee for resale at fancy figures, are presently robbing the public in the grand Ponzi manner and under a central ticket agency with only a twenty-five-cent fee they would live on the fat of the land. (It might also be a good idea to employ another squad of detectives to watch the first squad of detectives.)

Sixthly, make every member of the managers' league put up a bond of $10,000 that he'll stick by the rules and won't load the dice. (Maybe a bond of $20,000 would be safer in the case of some managers.)

Then sit back and watch business jump!

As to the box-offices themselves, many of them are still as rude and unaccommodating as they have always been. In order to determine what justice there is in the public's accusations of uncivil treatment on the part of box-office attendants, I personally, though under another name, recently telephoned to twenty New York box-offices to inquire about seats, and out of the twenty experienced courtesy in only six instances. I had lieutenants make the same experiment in four other cities, Washington, Boston, Philadelphia and Chicago, and the relative average was no better.

The managers' habit of garbling the critics' comments in the newspaper advertisements is another item in the theatre-goers' curse list. Let a critic write of a play that it is an excellent soporific; let another say that it is highly recommended to morons; and let still another observe that the acting is first-rate ham — and in all likelihood a lot of theatre-goers will subsequently be deluded by advertisements proclaiming the play " excellent ", " highly recommended ", and with " acting that is first-rate ". To each of these tributes, the critics' names will be attached. The Critics' Circle might be of service to the theatre if it undertook to stop such misquotations.

Curtains should be advertised to rise at the time they actually do rise. If a theatregoer is in his seat at eight-thirty, having been told that the play will begin at that time, and if the curtain does not go up until five minutes to nine, he not only is properly irritated but feels that he has been sold a short-weight play. And he is justified. Last season in New York alone there were shown twenty-one plays that, excluding the long intermissions, consumed not more than an hour and ten minutes of actual running time.

These are just a few tonic hints. They will suggest a variety of others, among them cleaner and brighter playhouses, better trained ushers, banishment of movie scouts, more attractive photography for publicity purposes (the theatre might take a cue here from Hollywood), less idiotic interviews given out by actors, and the like. The theatre is all right. The trouble with it is the people who run it.

SENTIMENTALITY IN SONG. The business of capitalizing the sentimentality of the American heart proceeds apace and the bookkeeping figures inform us that the financial returns have never been better. There is renewed joy in Tin Pan Alley. Song writers and song publishers now again are able to dress as if every day were Easter Sunday, and their wives and best girls are once more to be beheld in the mink coats to which in the past they were accustomed.

Many things have conspired to bring about bonanza times. The radio, that greatest of natural-born song pluggers, is No. 1. The large favor that has greeted the musical movies is No. 2. The enormously increased number of hotel, restaurant, cabaret, and night-club bands and orchestras is No. 3. The lowered price of phonographs and records is No. 4. And the congenital appetite of our otherwise relatively realistic and cynical fellow countrymen for lyrical prevarications about love, the moon, tropical palms, and other such emotional juleps is No. 5, 6, 7, 8 and 250.

The nation, it appears, after a relatively brief and unhappy holiday spent with comical songs, has now again returned to first principles and is swimming dreamily in sentimental musical and lyrical ooze. As I write, the best selling songs are announced to be *Moon Love, Moonlight Serenade, Over the Rainbow, Wishing, Stairway to the Stars, I Poured My Heart into a Song, Cinderella Stay in My Arms, In the Middle of a Dream, Yours for a Song, All I Remember Is You, My Heart Has Wings, Let's Make Memories Tonight, You Taught Me to Love Again, This Heart of Mine, You Are My*

Dream, To You, My Love for You, Especially for You, and
I'll Remember. Just a year ago at this time the best sellers
were *My Cabin of Dreams, Sailboat in the Moonlight, Sweet
Leilani, Stardust on the Moon, You and Me that Used to Be,
So Many Memories, Whispers in the Dark, Moon Got in My
Eyes,* and *Moon at Sea.* And the favorites on the radio similarly had and have to do with the aforementioned moon,
dreams, Hawaii, confidences in the dusk, nocturnal sailboats,
memories, and old loves. Way down at the bottom of the
lists appear the songs that fail to monkey with the cardiac
E-string. There we find the melodic orphans which tell saucily about going and flying a kite, merry-go-rounds that break
down, please to stop because you're breaking his heart, how
someone is feeling like a million dollars, how all God's chillun
got rhythm, and how it happened that she married a cop.

The proletariat may cotton to humorous songs once in a
while, but in the general run what it passionately craves are
ditties like *Can I Forget You, You're My Desire, Remember
Me, Harbor Lights, The First Time I Saw You, Where or
When, Afraid to Dream, I Know Now, Am I in Love, Yours
and Mine, In a Little Carolina Town* and similar pleasurable
heart-jerkers, all habitually worshipped by devotees of the
art of the mike. Five years ago you could have got odds of
ten to one that blues singers wouldn't last in the popular
esteem beyond January 1, 1937. Today, with the blues singers going bigger than ever, you would have to give odds of
one to ten that they won't still be going strong by January 1,
1945.

You can swindle the American public in a lot of directions. You can persuade it that there are millions of dollars
to be got out of defunct gold-mines, that there are no less than
one or two hundred patent medicines that will cure a bad
cold overnight, that the late George Gershwin's *Rhapsody
in Blue* is a great musical masterpiece, that a man who can
play the violin standing on his head is a more remarkable
artist than one who plays it standing on his feet, and many

other such things. But try to make it believe that the moon doesn't promptly convert the most pachydermatous celibate into a wistful Romeo, that the beach at Waikiki isn't chock-a-block with dusky Ann Penningtons all yearning to be made passionate love to under the gently swaying palm trees, that twilight on the range isn't exactly like twilight in the Vienna Prater and that blue flies and snakes aren't present in abundance, and that love doesn't sometimes land one in the divorce court and even in jail, and it will — if it doesn't forthwith metaphorically poke you one in the nose — at least contemptuously wave you aside as a something worse than a mere screwball.

There have been many attempts on the part of song writers and song publishers to make mock of such sacred matters, but the attempts have pretty generally failed, and dismally. Now and again, at rare intervals, a humorous or sardonic approach to the moon, June, love and the hills of old Virginia may capture the attention of the more sophisticated minority for a moment. But it isn't long before even that sophisticated minority (which isn't big enough to populate even some such village as Matunuck, Rhode Island) is found once again lustily crying into its beer over the news that it is apple blossom time in Normandy, that when all is said and done one's mother is one's best friend, that when things aren't going right with one's present love one likes to think back to the girl one had in other days, and that the stars in the Caribbean are somewhat brighter and more romantic than those over the Hercules Glue Works in Newark, New Jersey.

What popular songs of the last twenty-five years have most greatly retained their original popularity? In the list, I daresay, you will have difficulty — apart from certain war and doughboy ditties which do not figure in the present argument — in finding more than two or at most three of a humorous slant. The unimpeachable majority will be discovered to be the pleasantly lugubrious and agreeably wistful songs, like *Shine On, Harvest Moon, Melancholy Baby, Rose Marie,*

A Kiss in the Dark, A Pretty Girl Is Like a Melody, Make Believe, Come with Me, I'll Waltz with Thee into Paradise, My Heart Is Yours Alone, Kiss Me Again, I Wonder Who's Kissing Her Now, etc.

It will be answered to all of this that, in this general respect, Americans are no different from the peoples of other nations, and that one and all always prefer songs that touch the heart-strings to those that play with the funny-bone. But the answer will be defective. The English, for example, relish comical songs much more than the sentimental variety. And so do the Italians and, to a considerable degree, the French. The Germans and Austrians alone resemble the Americans. Give them something lyrical about dusk falling over a lake, or about some mädel in a flower shop, or about the loveliness of the edelweiss, and the waiters in the beer gardens and coffee houses will join them in comprehensive sighs and gulps.

If anything was needed to make the heart palpitation of the American public more exuberant than it had hitherto been, the emergence of the saxophone to a place of honor looked out for that. With the advent of the saxophone as the pièce de résistance of bands and orchestras, the wistfulissimos became drunker than ever on meditations on the lunar light, the lure of the South Seas, the girl back home in the calico dress, and the power of love to cure everything from financial panics to athlete's foot. The moanings and groanings of that lachrymose instrument came as manna to, if not exactly starved, at least immensely hungry hearts, and the song writers were able in a short time to buy even handsomer wardrobes for themselves, including goldheaded canes and spats, and even more sumptuous mink coats for their wives.

What overjoys the song writers and song publishers at the moment is the claim of astronomers that there isn't just one moon, but three or four. If what the astronomers say is true and they can prove it, the song writers' and song publishers' wealth will reach well-nigh fabulous figures.

SHAKESPEAREAN PRODUCTIONS. The more I see of contemporary Shakespearean productions the more I wonder if we all weren't considerably better off with those of yesterday. I appreciate that many of the latter were far from perfect and that many of them deserved the opprobrious designation of ham which the critics visited upon them, but it seems to me in retrospect that they were at least simple and forthright and by their own lights honest, and not, like the majority of present-day productions, designed largely to show off the theories and scholarship of their producers, both often disingenuous and not a little idiotic.

The productions which we have had in the last few years have, of course, been greatly superior to the older ones in settings, costumes, lighting, and other such dramatic externals but, with the notable exceptions of Margaret Webster's for Maurice Evans' *King Richard II, Hamlet* and *Henry IV,* there has been not one of them that has not in whole or at least in part been corrupted by directorial sophism of one kind or another. I am not thinking so much of such exhibits as the Surry Players' *As You Like It,* directed by Samuel Rosen, as of the presentations of the Bard's more serious works. Mr. Rosen is a minor director and so may either be politely waved aside or impolitely laughed at for directing his characters to suggest their lively youthfulness by a ceaseless gamboling, hopping, skipping, and running about, all of which suggested lively youthfulness infinitely less than a transparently concealed, nervous, and very peremptory need to get to the lavatory as quickly as possible. I am, as I say, thinking of our more representative and eminent directors and of the strange things they do to the graver Shakespeare by way of proving to a stupid public and to the less percipient of the critics that they are uncommonly original, vastly fecund, and enormously brainy fellows.

No writer on the theatre has a kindlier respect for Mr. Guthrie McClintic, for instance, when it comes to the staging and direction of modern plays, than I have. But I believe that I may fairly select him as a typical example of the species of producer I have in mind when the classical drama is at issue. With a modern script in hand, he works simply and — apart maybe from sometimes too fancy lighting — unaffectedly to afford it its every legitimate ounce of stage life. But give him Shakespeare and promptly he seems to wish to convert himself from that simple, sound, and unposturing director into a cross between a Forty-fifth Street Freud and a Broadway Dover Wilson. We thus get a *Hamlet* in which the feigned insanity of Hamlet, that cerebral Lincoln J. Carter, is directed as histrionically even more normal than his moods of rationality and in which the undissembling insanity of Ophelia, that overnight abreactive and cathartic lily, is on the other hand directed into a melodramatically fabricated lunacy. We further get a Hamlet who is deprived of his chief line of sexual challenge to Ophelia and an Ophelia whose subsequent sexual obsession is accordingly uncued and largely meaningless. And we also get a Juliet whose nurse, deleted of her bawdy lines, is indistinguishable from a Southern mammy, a Romeo of Hamlet meditation rather than Montague mooning, and a Juliet herself who, though notoriously the more shrewd and adult of the lovers in their earlier scenes of romantic address, comports herself like a débutante grasshopper.

I have wondered at such puzzling lapses in a director otherwise so competent. Why is it that Shakespeare so often turns that scurvy trick? The answer may conceivably be found, at least in respect to one director, in an interview given to a representative of the press by Mr. McClintic himself.

In the verse drama, states Mr. McClintic, " there must not be a single detail that obscures or detracts from the central idea. For that reason, nobody eats cornflakes and cream in a play in blank verse. Take *Romeo and Juliet*. The guests who are invited to Capulet's house are bidden to a feast. And what do they do when they get there? They dance, they make love, they carry on their intrigues, but nobody eats.

Now, if you wanted to spend a lot of money, you could hire a few dozen extras and have them gobbling in the background. But there's not a line spoken by the principals to justify the expense."

"Mr. McClintic," cordially concludes Michel Mok, his interviewer, "qualifies as an expert in these matters."

Mr. McClintic, it seems to me, qualifies rather as a schafskopf. Inasmuch as he unquestionably used cornflakes and cream to represent any kind of edible in connection with blank-verse plays, doesn't he know that the verse drama of Shakespeare is full of food, to say nothing, surely, of drink, and that it ranges from everything from a single plate of mutton to a great banquet? Sometimes, true enough, the eating is begun and at once abandoned, sometimes a mere nibbling gets under way and is interrupted, sometimes the injunction is "Feed, and regard him not!", sometimes it is "Come, queen o' the feast . . . here take your place," sometimes the lament is that "all viands that I eat do seem unsavory," sometimes the food is merely sweet honey, sometimes prospectively it is Julia who can hardly wait dinnertime "that you might kill your stomach on your meat", sometimes the command is "Forbear, and eat no more!", sometimes — but enough.

We turn to Mr. McClintic's conception of the Capulets' feast in *Romeo and Juliet*. Doesn't he know that the reason nobody eats is that the eating is all over when the scene begins? Says Benvolio in the antecedent scene: "Supper is done, and we shall come too late." The scene itself opens with the servants clearing away. "Save me a piece of marchpane," bids the first servant of the second. "Turn the tables up!" orders Capulet. "But nobody eats," pontificates Mr. McClintic. Of course nobody eats. Who wants supper immediately following supper? Only a little while ago, incidentally, Mr. McClintic produced Maxwell Anderson's blank-verse play, *High Tor*. Has he forgotten so soon the lunch box and then the sandwich-eating in it? I have not used McClintic as a chopping-block. He is merely one of a number of directorial illustrations. The trouble with most of them, it seems, is that, judging from their recent Shakespearean productions, they haven't read Shakespeare.

The production of *As You Like It* by the Surry Players — a Maine summer theatre troupe — indicated that they didn't know summer was over. They did everything with the Shakespearean comedy but go canoeing in it. Evidently mistaking the play for a sports field, they indulged in so much hopping and skipping about, so much scampering hither and thither, and so much jumping up and down and running around that at the end of the first half the spectators feared that they would be worn out and that their director would have to substitute a second team. No such anticking and frolicking has been seen on a New York stage since the last appearance of Goldman's trick dogs.

You have probably guessed the reason. Mr. Rosen, like a number of other Shakespearean producers, seems to believe that the best way to depict youth on the stage is to persuade the actors and particularly the actresses to comport themselves as if a crew of invisible stagehands were constantly giving them turpentine hypodermics. Just why the average producer confounds youth with a kind of coy chorea complicated with adagio dancing is pretty hard to make out. Yet give such a producer any play in which the characters are supposed to be young folk and his idea of suggesting their vitality and freshness is to make them all act like idiots full of copious doses of strychnine and suffering, to boot, from the delusion that they are participants in an uninterrupted Mardi Gras carnival. By the time ten o'clock came around, I was so fatigued from looking at Mr. Rosen's Olympic games masquerading as a Shakespearean comedy that I dragged myself out of the theatre and sought relief watching the squirrels tranquilly disporting themselves in Central Park.

In short, save in the case of the Webster-Evans productions, the hearing that the Bard has got has, to put it very gently, been somewhat impaired. The Gielgud *Hamlet* had the unfortunate and rather dismaying aspect of a " drag ", the Howard *Hamlet* suggested a Prince of Denmark who had so exhausted himself necking the college widows at Wittenberg that he didn't have enough energy left even to hold Ophelia's hand; the Huston *Othello* permitted its Iago to comport himself so like a combination of Paul Haakon and the Rath brothers that one momentarily expected Othello to get down on one knee, shout " Allez-oop! ", and balance him on his head; the Bankhead *Antony and Cleopatra* was in every way disaster twice multiplied, as were the Merivale *Othello* and *Macbeth;* the Orson Welles *Julius Caesar* was a fabricated theatrical skeleton with hardly a covering ounce of Shakespeare's flesh; the Robert Henderson *The Merry Wives of Windsor* was so bad that it was ridiculed into the storehouse after just four performances; and the Lunts *The Taming of the Shrew* was better than most and here and there an amusing show but often so over-burlesqued that one momentarily expected Lynn Fontanne to go into a strip-tease.

SHOWMANSHIP. With the possible exception of toe dancers, nothing interests me less than champion swimmers and divers. The awe that envelops the majority of human livestock when one of their species poses himself atop a lofty scaffold, draws in his belly, raises his hands over his head, and then projects himself tail rearmost into a body of water, splashing the pants of all the aforesaid livestock within a radius of 600 feet, has somehow always neglected to infect me. Nor has the spectacle of the human female essaying to beat the herring at its own game stimulated me perceptibly more. Water has generally seemed to me to be even less satisfactory as an opera house than as a drink. But now comes Mr. Billy Rose with the magic of his sound theatrical showmanship and converts this erstwhile old infidel. His Aquacade, installed at the New York World's Fair, was not only the best show at the Exposition, but one to the taste of even such churls as myself who, until he appeared upon the scene to debate matters, were perfectly willing — indeed hysterical — to exchange all the two-legged professional piscatorialists this side of Helsingfors for a half-portion of filet de sole Marguery.

Conjuring up lights and colors, music and a convenient moon, gay silks and whirling stage sets to embellish his pool and its denizens, the petit Barnum evolved an extravaganza that pleased even a customer suffering from hydrophobia. To the tune of a soft song, the lovely Eleanor Holm — the only woman swimming virtuoso I have ever observed who doesn't suggest a brobdingnagian pork chop that has been left out in the rain — gracefully and beautifully waterwaltzed the former prejudice out of the most stubborn dissenter. Under Billy's necromancy, even Johnny Weissmuller, the Sam Goldwyn of the papier mâché jungles, dunked himself with an unwonted humor calculated to win favor from those who hitherto had viewed his wet gymnastics with stoic calm. Then, too, there was a supply of forthright clowns who sat aloft in chairs and dove chairs and all into the deep by way of dismaying any possible further doubts, to say nothing of score upon score of cuties in and out of clothes who danced and kicked themselves into a state of exhaustion on behalf of the more recalcitrant landlubbers. It was a real show, a good show, with the fair Holm, aswim with a blue ribbon in her pretty uncapped hair, alone worth triple the forty-cent admission fee. And it was still another tribute to the best showman America has seen since Ziegfeld joined the angels.

The words " showman " and " showmanship ", however, sometimes induce in the professional critics a certain amount of regrettable confusion. I have in mind in this connection, particularly, the musical show, *Mexicana,* produced here under the ciceronage of the Mexican government. A considerable number of the reviewing gentlemen discouraged future trade by lamenting that the exhibit, while intrinsically commendable, lacked the necessary showmanship to put it over. This struck some of the rest of us as nonsense, since it was the very absence of the specific kind of showmanship the gentlemen yearned for that made the show the immensely delightful thing it was.

In the dictionary of Broadway criticism, showmanship in the case of musical shows seems arbitrarily to mean speed (whether it be appropriate to the immediate materials or not), a sharply regulated variety (though an even flow of already thoroughly interesting elements might be acceptable), and a serial alternation of moods (however relatively deficient some of them may be). Any such Broadway hocus-pocus would no more have fitted the scheme of this *Mexicana* than it would fit *Pierrot the Prodigal*, a tranquil and lovely Springtime night, or a rare brandy smelling contest. The show was a sufficiently valuable and charming affair as it stood, and anyone who couldn't discern its natural and un-mechanical element of speed in its dance movement, its variety in its music and smashing color, and its alternation of moods in its terpsichorean interpretation of tragedy, glee, pity and passion should have gone out and buried his head in the Broadway sands. One otherwise estimable critic actually went so far as to demand a quota of verbal jokes in the show, which — aside from a speculation as to how he would have understood them in Spanish — seemed like asking for a quota of nifties in the Japanese No drama or the Russian Ballet.

SIMPLICITY. An exhibit called *The Happiest · Days*, by Charlotte Armstrong, followed almost literally the not so long ago news story of the two Long Island youngster lovers who, finding the world incompatible with their dreams, sought to end their lives in a suicide pact. It came to the sort of play that is usually commented upon by the reviewers as if it were a combination of filet de boeuf and cathartic. It was, they allowed, at once " tender " and " gently moving ". This one occasionally was, but it was also so ostentatiously underwritten in the apparent belief that underwriting is identical with simplicity that after the first half-hour it defeated its ends. Drama calls for body under its most simple dress.

SKINNER. Miss Cornelia Otis Skinner, who for some years has been known to the platforms of the thitherward Town Halls and Knights of Pythias tabernacles as a monologist of considerable charm and skill, lately presented herself to the metropolitan theatre stage as an entire acting company in her own dramatization of Margaret Ayer Barnes' novel, *Edna His Wife*. Though still charming and skillful, Miss Skinner committed a big mistake. Not only would any dramatization of the Barnes novel, itself schmalz, be a profound sedative even were it to be played by an all-star company gathered together from the Comédie Française and the Moscow Art and Abbey theatres, with Helen Hayes, to boot, playing the maid and Maurice Evans the waiter, but it becomes an infinitely profounder one with merely a monologist, however charming and skillful, performing it solo. A woman talking steadily for two hours is hardly my idea of entertainment, whether in the theatre or in private.

Miss Skinner is often expert in makeup and in flicking the edges of character, but her dramatic talent halts there. She is not an actress; she is rather simply the impersonator of and commentator on an actress. Nor is she a dramatist, as we may clearly detect when she bequeaths the climactic scene of her play and the big melodramatic curtain of the first of her two acts to a wholly secondary character. The net impression of the evening's garrulity was of Ben Hecht in women's clothes playing all the rôles in *To Quito and Back*. And the net critical impression of the entire enterprise took the form of speculating how far these recent theatrical stunts will go. In the last two seasons, as hereinbefore chronicled, we have, in *Julius Caesar*, seen the abandonment of scenery and costumes; in the dramatic opera, *The Cradle Will Rock*, the abandonment of the orchestra; in *Blow Ye Winds*, the abandonment of action; in *The Ghost of Yankee Doodle,* the abandonment of plot; and now in *Edna His Wife,* the abandonment of actors. It accordingly probably won't be long before they will, as a logical sequence, be putting on plays and telephoning the *audience* to stay at home.

SOCIAL SIGNIFICANCE. Those persons who believe that something is all wrong with Ed Wynn because he hasn't any Social Significance are enthusiastic to the bursting point over the virtues of the above-mentioned Marc Blitzstein's labor opera, *The Cradle Will Rock.* That its music is negligible, its libretto for the most part commonplace, and its presentation admittedly amateurish doesn't seem to matter to them. What matters, they say, is its Social Significance. In other words, because it is about a steel strike, because steel strikes have been much in the air recently, and because steel strikes and labor union troubles are matters of current public interest, Mr. Blitzstein's exhibit, whatever faults may soundly be found with it, is more signally important as dramatic and musical art and more justly to be commended than something, say, like *Der Rosenkavalier,* which deals merely with gentle dalliance, hasn't a steel strike in it from beginning to end, and has no more Social Significance than *Romeo and Juliet, Othello,* or Rosita Royce's trained doves.

The strange thing about such persons is that they reserve Social Significance for the proletariat alone. If a play shows a lot of actors in overalls loudly demanding their rights of the boss of an iron foundry and heaving rocks through the windows when they don't get them, that is Social Significance. But if a play shows the boss of the iron foundry plausibly arguing with the men in overalls that if he grants their demands the company will not have enough money left to stave off bankruptcy and, when they won't listen to him, going out and getting good and consolingly drunk, that is everything from Escapist hooey and Ivory Tower bunk to reactionary drama and commercial claptrap.

Dramatic merit, to these poultry, is anything that discloses a mob of down-at-the-heel characters indignantly protesting that someone other than themselves is entirely responsible for their condition and clamorously threatening, in most often relevantly down-at-the-heel dialogue and down-at-the-heel music, that, *donner und blitzstein,* there'll be hell to pay unless the aforesaid someone pretty damn quick does twenty times better for them than they could possibly do today in their beloved Russia.

The persons to whom I have alluded are, paradoxically enough, themselves less often members of the overalled labor class than highly solvent Hollywood scenario writers, Broadway playwrights, *Nation* editors, novelists, dramatic critics, and other such steady customers of the more expensive night-clubs and former speakeasies. The laboring class itself seldom goes to the theatre, preferring joyfully to content itself with and revel in movies in which Garbo is rewarded to the tune of $20,000 a week for having to kiss an actor and in which Joan Crawford, the poor shop girl, becomes the inamorata of the rich capitalist. The laboring class, when left to itself, is not without some humor, and when — uninterfered with by the Charlie McCarthys of radicalism and Federal Theatre pianistic revolutionists — it has a go at the stage, it proves it. In *Pins and Needles,* produced by members of the International Ladies Garment Workers Union, we have had welcome evidence that Labor can not only laugh at itself now and then but that it doesn't always necessarily regard a piano as a musical soapbox.

SPEWACKINESS. There doesn't seem to be any valid reason why plays about authors and book publishers shouldn't turn out to be as entertaining as plays about any other rascals, but a dire fate appears to hang over them. Jogging my memory, I can't at the moment recall one — and there have been quite a number — that has managed to get far in an amusement direction. In recent seasons alone we have engaged no less than three attempts to beat the jinx in the cases of *The Golden Journey, Lady of Letters,* and *Best Sellers,* and all without success. Nor has it been merely that the plays were poor plays. Even had they been much better, the characters with their shop talk and their professional doings would have proved more or less dispiriting.

The Spewack duo, who have prosperously diverted us with *Boy Meets Girl* and the book of *Leave It to Me!,* were the latest to tackle the business and they were no more fortunate than the others who preceded them. Their *Miss Swan Expects* was dreary stuff and, theme or no theme, rather hard to reconcile with their antecedent gay shenanigans. It is possible that their manuscript wasn't of recent coinage and that they dug it up out of an old drawer and embellished it with some topical allusions by way of making a sale. I should like on their behalf to believe it, since if it was a new work it might lead us to think that without the directing and editorial skill of George Abbott on the one hand or the tunes of Cole Porter, the pantomimic humor of Victor Moore, and the anatomy of Mary Martin on the other they aren't the drolls we have persuaded ourselves to imagine they are.

Allowing for the hoodoo that lay over the nature of their basic materials, they additionally calloused their customers with slipshod and confused playwriting, feeble invention, and a considerable dose of gratuitous silliness. Even in the wildest farce it would be difficult to swallow a dead-broke ghost-writer who is willing to work two whole years without a penny's pay on a tycoon's autobiography, a publishing house that nationally suppresses a book banned in Boston without putting up a fight of any kind, a firm whose partners leave everything to the sole literary whim and judgment of a cutie, and suchlike fabulous whangdoodle. And even in the most liberal criticism it is stretching a point to condone as projectiles of comedy in this day the siren who seeks to work herself into the graces of a rich old goat by telling him he is just a boy at heart and measuring him for knitted slippers, the stenographer who is kept so busy she can't get away for her own wedding, the foolish woman who imagines herself gifted in belles lettres, the big business man who likes to play with mechanical toys, and the stuffed shirt who, when called various names, stiffly remarks upon his exits, " I did not hear that remark, sir." That brand of Spewackiness could hardly make for theatrical pleasure.

SPIRITUALITY.   The earlier noted Norman Macowan's *Glorious Morning*, which enjoyed a considerable run in London, deals, as also earlier noted, with a totalitarian state that denies its citizens a belief in God and with a young woman who beholds a vision and thereupon, at the risk of her life, undertakes to flout the atheistic authorities. It is a poor play because, among other reasons, the aforesaid young woman's spirituality is written mainly in a tedious holier-than-thou mold and because not only is her description of the vision comically indistinguishable from a celestial scene in a Cecil B. De Mille biblical movie but because, further, her indication of an inner exaltation is confined largely to maintaining a facial expression suggestive of a Hollywood hussy piously posing with lilies for one of those ubiquitous stills that appear in the film fan magazines around Easter and to comporting herself with that cold physical rigidity which is commonly associated in the theatrical mind with other-worldliness and saintship.

SUMMER THEATRES.   The latest statistics place the number of rural summer theatres at close to eighty. They occupy what were once stables, churches, town halls, garages, village libraries, schools, boathouses and almost every other conceivable species of shelter, including in several instances, oddly enough, structures originally designed as theatres. Several thousands of young and middle-aged boys and girls are employed by them as actors (to allow the word a generous elasticity), and a sizable number of youths of both sexes are to be found studying the art of Coquelin and Ristori in the academies operated in conjunction with some of them.

These bucolic mimehouses, like democracy, marriage, and lobster à la Newburg, have their virtues and their defects. As to the former, whatever their deficiencies, they at least further stimulate the steadily increasing interest in the theatre and, in addition, offer a chance for possible hidden talent to demonstrate itself. As to the latter, they often with their enforced lack of proper preparation make mock of the drama they present and so unfortunately cause the abovementioned stimulation of interest momentarily to pause and dubiously scratch its cheek.

From early June to middle September the battle between dramatic art and mosquitoes rages every night but Sunday. The mosquitoes, moreover, have a lot of allies. One of the favorite plays on the pasture circuit last summer was the murder mystery melodrama, *Night Must Fall*, and this is approximately the way you got it in the rustic drama centers:

Olivia: " Well, we woke up this morning thinking here's another day." (*A sparrow that has perched itself in the theatre's beams flies across the stage, in its flight misbehaving on the actress' hat.*) " We got up, looked at the weather and talked, and here we all are, still talking." (*She brushes a mosquito off her nose and the mosquito thereupon lights upon the actor playing the policeman and stings him on the ear.*)

Mrs. Bramson: " My dear girl " (*the Fords outside set up a prodigious honking, the actress having to pause until the racket stops*), " who are you to expect a policeman — " (*a bee stings the old girl in an embarrassing spot*).

Belsize, the cop: " If you please! " (*A stray chicken crosses the stage and gets tangled up in his legs.*) " I want to hear what she's got to say." (*Six horses in an adjacent barn start neighing.*) " Well? "

Olivia: " All that time there may be something lying in the woods." (*The horses are joined by three mooing cows.*) " Hidden under a bush, with two feet just showing." (*A but-*

terfly flits across the stage and lands on the actress' hair. She brushes it off and it flies over and lands on the cop's bald head.) " Perhaps one high heel catching the sunlight, and the other — a stockinged foot, with blood that's dried into the openwork stocking." (*It has begun to rain outside and the water drips through the theatre roof onto the stage, running down the actors' backs.*) " And there's a man walking about somewhere " (*another mosquito stings her in the neck*) " and talking, like us " (*a bolt of lightning hits a tree outside the theatre and scares the daylights out of the actors and the audience*); " and he woke up this morning, and looked at the weather — and he killed her." (*The rain is now leaking onto the audience.*)

Mrs. Bramson: " Well! " (*That bee now gets the old girl where she lives and she lets out a howl.*)

Mrs. Terence: " Ooh, Miss Grayne, you give me the creeps! " (*She slips in a pool of water and lands on her rear, the splash blinding the actor playing the cop and causing him to fall over the footlights into the lap of a village grocer.*)

But please do not think I am being hypercritical. There seem to be a lot of folk, judging from the success of the summer theatres, who prefer to get their dramatic art that way instead of assimilating it in the city without these bucolic contretemps. It's all a matter of taste. As for myself, true enough, there is something slightly discommodious about trying to enjoy a play while a frog is climbing up one's trouser-leg, but I am admittedly a rather peculiar fellow. When I go to a theatre, I want to go to a theatre and not to a former stable that still smells of manure or to an ex-garage that still smells of gasoline. And I don't want my actors to spend half their time shooing away bats, wasps and mosquitoes. Of course, I've seen shows in town which would have been greatly improved if bats, wasps and mosquitoes had been imported from the country to shoo away the actors, but that's another chapter.

If you happen to live in the neighborhood of one of the

summer playhouses, maybe going to it isn't fraught with too many inconveniences. But if you have to make a journey from the city to see a performance and have to remain in the village overnight, God be with you. I've tried it, and I know. Finding a place to sleep is as tough a job as finding a four-leaf clover in the desert and, when and if you do find it, try to sleep in it! If a squad of rookie Lunts and Barrymores aren't rehearsing something that sounds like a Comanche melodrama in the next room until four in the morning, the bed in the so-called inn has evidently been built out of a section of some old abandoned scenic railway. And if seventeen drunks don't constantly mistake your room at the so-called hotel for whatever it is drunks mistake anything for, you may be sure that just as you are getting to sleep around three o'clock the bed will collapse and send you rolling out into the hall and into the room across the way occupied by the summer theatre's old character woman, who will thereupon let out such a yell that the seventeen drunks will pile up the stairs again and insist upon singing *I've Been Working on the Railroad* until dawn.

I'll take my theatres, if you don't mind, in West Forty-fifth Street.

TEKEL, UPHARSIN.   Stefan Zweig's *Jeremiah* is a 1916 biblican mothball setting forth the dismayal of the peace-loving prophet and indulging itself in the theoretically engrossing spree of drawing a parallel with the world of today. An interminable and enervating oratorical flu, it was interpreted in the main by actors who munched their lines as if they were so many matzoths and was directed with a scrupulous regard for all the stereotypes associated with drama of the species, from the hambo in the flowing white peignoir spotlighted against a panorama of night-sky and moaning his basso-profundo woes to the choreographic mime who rushes onto the stage, leaps wildly down a flight of steps, lands on one knee, and passionately bangs a pair of cymbals. The entire enterprise, in short, was a tournament of whiskers in the matter of writing, acting, and direction no less than in that of makeup.

THOUGHTS WITHOUT THINKING.   My learned British colleague, Mr. Agate, not long ago in a review of a show called *The Laughing Cavalier* observed, " What did I think of, chin-huddled in that stall, as wave after wave of nothingness swept over me? " He then specified as follows: The lowness of the Low Countries, Holland and its dykes, Dick Phenyl, Mrs. Gilfillian, Motley's *Rise of the Dutch Republic,* Mommsen's *History of Rome,* golf, children's books like *Count Funnibos and Baron Stilkin,* Catherine of Russia, *St. Joan,* E. V. Lucas, black tulips, white tulips, red tulips, Van Tromp, icicles, *Twelfth Night,* Noah and Mrs. Noah, Hazlitt, the poor hotel accommodations in Rotterdam, bad teeth, Canning's jingles, Dr. Johnson, and cheese. There is no reason to doubt my estimable colleague's veracity, as he is widely known to be a very truthful fellow. So uncompromisingly truthful, indeed, is he that he once shamelessly confessed to me that, while reviewing a play by Dodie Smith, he had actually twice during the evening thought of the play. But for all his undoubted and unquestioned candor, I allow myself to wonder if those were the only things that ran through his head during *The Laughing Cavalier* and if there were not a number of others, somewhat less august and punctilious, that he elected not to chronicle.

In the presence of a bad play, the reviewing mind is a recalcitrant animal. When what is going on on the stage has some quality, the mind is its willing and eager slave, but when what is going on is without any trace of merit the thinking apparatus moseys far into alien fields. Take, for example, such an occasion as Karel Capek's *The Mother*. Although one could spot the exhibit as worthless after its first fifteen minutes, politeness permitted the mind to dwell upon it a little longer, say for ten minutes, but after that attention was impossible. It was thus that at 9:05 p.m. sharp the Nathan brain-pan got up on its hind legs and started to go places on its own. Here, as nearly as I can honestly remember, were some of its cogitations:

1. If they don't shut that lobby door damned quick and stop that draught on the back of my neck, I am going to yell.

2. When the Theatre Guild directors got out that brochure panning the critics for panning *Madame Bovary* and sent it to their subscribers, why didn't they stop to reflect that the play couldn't have been any more to the taste of the subscribers themselves, otherwise — as with better plays in the past — the subscribers' interest would have induced a subsequent more general interest and the play wouldn't have been carted off to the storehouse in such quick order?

3. Why is it that as most actresses' talent increases and expands their rears generally follow suit?

4. Eric Linklater's little book, *The Crusader's Key,* would make the best light opera libretto since Hofmannsthal's *Der Rosenkavalier.*

5. The title *Führer,* bequeathed by the German people to Hitler, is almost identical in sound to the German designation of the men's toilet.

6. Why doesn't someone revive W. J. Turner's *The Man Who Ate the Popomack?* It is a very amusing comedy and never got a fair chance when, some years ago, it was shown down in Greenwich Village.

7. I somehow can never look at the dreamy and languorous Garbo without laughing. As a boy, we had a Swedish upstairs maid at our house who looked exactly like her.

8. There isn't a critic over forty-five who won't tell you that the most beautiful woman the American stage has known in his time was Irene Bentley, in *The Wild Rose.* Runner-up: Marie Doro, in *The Morals of Marcus* and *Clarice.*

9. Why didn't the literary critics refer to Gertrude Stein's personal tale as *The Autobiography of Alice B. Tochus?*

10. There are certain theatrical producer first-nighters who seem to regard their rivals' openings as prize-fighters regard their rivals' dropped guards.

11. I wish I had a big glass of nice, cold beer.

12. Why all this indignation here and there because Bernard Shaw has rewritten parts of *Cymbeline?* Even actors — Burbage, for one example — rewrote Shakespeare's plays in his own day, and Shakespeare both approved of it and liked it.

13. Artists welcome criticism; actors resent it.

14. Exercise is ridiculous. I never exercise. I get enough exercise every day brushing off the cigarette ashes that start burning my trousers, pulling my tie tighter at my collar, brushing my hair, moving my face and neck into various shaving positions, opening and closing taxicab doors, sharpening lead pencils, dressing and undressing, wriggling

around under the shower-bath, looking under the bed for burglars, and running several hundred miles at breakneck speed and jumping over high cliffs to get away from the murderer who shows up on my heels every night a few minutes after I have got to sleep.

15. Why are children's school books always bound in forbidding blacks and dark browns? Why not make them more inviting to the youngsters with bright oranges, purples, sky-blues, crimsons, and other such gay colors?

16. Dramatic criticism has become largely a succession of trumpet or bird-whistle solos.

17. Some critics shrewdly practice the technique of reticent calm. So, instead of detecting their dumbness immediately, it usually takes two minutes.

18. The majority of London polite comedies are silk hats minus rabbits.

19. An actor without a playwright is like a hole without a doughnut. The most adroit ad-libbing done by actors to tide over contretemps in the last thirty years hasn't been as good as even the worst lines in such recent garbage as *Please, Mrs. Garibaldi, First American Dictator, I Must Love Someone,* or even *Clean Beds,* that arch-lulu.

20. Some of Maxwell Anderson's plays always remind me of a lover's quarrel with himself.

21. If it were not for Granville-Barker and Dover Wilson, Hamlet would still be Robert B. Mantell.

22. They will probably lose at least twenty thousand dollars on this show. For the twenty thousand they could have done a revival of Hauptmann's *The Sunken Bell* and put on a simplified production of Shaw's amended *Cymbeline,* both of which would stand a better chance of avoiding any such plunge into the red and which might even make some money. And they would have had enough money left over to buy a couple of cases of good champagne. Numskulls!

23. I should like to see a production of *Romeo and Juliet*

with either Celia Johnson or Loretta Young as Juliet and Pierre Fresnay or Maurice Chevalier as Romeo. I am tired of looking at antique piefaces of whom presumably "the envious moon is already sick and pale with grief, that thou her maid art far more fair than she" and at hunks of ham brochette described as "the god of my idolatry," compared with a bird, and complimented that "upon his brow shame is ashamed to sit, for 'tis a throne where honor may be crown'd sole monarch of the universal earth." Now, I ask you!

24. I always have to laugh at direction of the bogus suspensive species that causes any two characters who find themselves alone on the stage to pause for a moment and then cautiously steal across the room and close the doors before proceeding with their perfectly innocuous conversations.

25. I also gag at the kind of stage direction which, in the case of plays containing youngsters, causes one of the adult characters to bestow a pat upon the latters' backsides every time they make an exit.

26. Another thing I don't like is the foolish program dodge, in the instance of plays containing dogs, parrots, donkeys or other animals and birds, listing them in the cast under such names as Reginald, Hugo, Gustav, or Ham Fish and in the opposite column identifying them by the pronoun, Himself.

27. Oh, for that glass of nice, cold beer!

28. I wish to object to the tendency of a number of our actors and actresses to horn in on public affairs and other matters dissociated from the theatre. They usually make fools of themselves when they do and pitiably betray the infantile cast of their minds. Some of them aren't any too good at their own jobs of acting and might better devote the time they are wasting on alien concerns to improving themselves in their craft.

29. If anybody thinks I am going to write a detailed and extended criticism of such godawful tripe as this *The Mother*

and maybe go on and tell about all the actors in it, he is crazy.

TIPS TO PRODUCERS AND PLAYWRIGHTS.   One of the most commonly heard complaints against the critics on the part of playwrights and producers is that it is next to impossible to judge from their writings what exactly, if anything, they really like. There is no making head or tail of their fundamental tastes, argue the puzzled ones; sometimes they seem to like one kind of play and the very next day another and quite different kind. How, the playwrights and producers demand to know, can anyone therefore figure out how to please them?

I herewith come to the puzzled gentlemen's aid. From close association with the New York dramatic critics over a period of years I have become savvy to their personal tastes, prejudices and predilections, many of them somewhat fantastic, and offer them as alleviating hints to our worried theatrical impresarios.

If the latter wish to please Brooks Atkinson, critic for the *Times*, for example, let them become acquainted with the secret that a play that sentimentalizes New England or one in which the Hudson River figures is pretty certain to get something more than a good break from him. A New Englander by birth and a Harvard man, Prof. Atkinson apparently finds himself moved willy-nilly by plays that cry softly into their Schlitz over almost anything at all concerned with New England. Just why the Hudson River should exercise the effect upon him that it does, I do not know; but the fact remains the fact. As a member of the Critics' Circle, his vote for the season's best play two years ago was *High Tor*, which had a lot in it about the Hudson. And his vote a year ago was for *Our Town*, which poured sweet syrup copiously over a New Hampshire small town.

John Mason Brown, of the *Post*, also a Harvard boy, shares the sentimental reactions of Prof. Atkinson and, in the seasons specified, voted for the same plays as the latter. But while New England given a marshmallow icing is likely to exercise its pleasurable critical influence on him, you can't be too sure always about the Hudson River. What is surer is any play that sentimentalizes old age, particularly if it be acted by some venerable male or female favorite of the theatrical yesterday. Although the youngest of the New York reviewers, Brown has a profound admiration for all actors, and especially actresses, over sixty-nine years of age. Young actors, and especially young and pretty actresses, he more often has small use for.

Burns Mantle, of the *Daily News,* the oldest of the present critics, is also a hound for sentimental stuff and will go big for almost anything that possesses a measure of nostalgic appeal. The one thing that he can't abide is the naughty drama. He believes that the drama should be moral in tone and woe betide any play, whatever its share of quality, that goes in for what we may sufficiently designate as sexification. Give Burns clean plays, you boys, or take the consequences!

Richard Lockridge, critic for the *Sun,* is rather partial to the Left drama and is more likely to be pleased by a theme sympathetic to the proletariat than by one cast in an opposite direction. Less sentimental than any of the three above-mentioned reviewers, he is a tougher customer when producers try to feed him dramatic molasses.

John Anderson, of the *Journal-American,* is entirely unlike Gilbert Gabriel, former hazlitt to the *American.* Dr. Gabriel was the most sentimental play reviewer seen in New York since the days of Clayton Hamilton, who will be remembered for years for a style of reviewing which was wont to describe any tender play as being " like the music of a million Easter-lilies leaping from the grave and laughing with a silver singing ". Prof. Anderson, on the contrary, is given to a considerable amount of cynicism. Show him a play which applies a heavy smear of lard to New England, or which argues that everything was wonderful thirty or forty years ago, or which stoutly denies that there is an occasional stale cantaloupe or old egg-crate to be seen floating on the Hudson, or which proves agreeably to MM. Atkinson and Brown that it is jollier to be dead and at peace than alive and having a good time — show Dr. Anderson any such play and he will let out a snort. But what gets him nine times out of ten is a play that, as the phrase has it, " says something ". That is, a play which in his opinion is a commentary on present-day world affairs. Thus, give him an exhibit in which a man and woman contentedly eating their *dinde à la Perigueux* at the Ritz in Paris are suddenly bombed by a Jap warplane, or one in which it is dismayingly proved that a pacifist conscripted into the trenches is likely to suffer from cooties, or one in which living in a tenement is argued to be not so comfortable as living at the Savoy-Plaza, and it is better than a gambler's chance that he will be more or less favorably disposed toward it.

Richard Watts, Jr., of the *Herald-Tribune,* like Prof. Lockridge, is partial to the Left drama. In fact, he is, in his own pet mathematical phraseology, six times more partial to it than Prof. Lockridge. What, down at the bottom of his heart, he prefers is the play in which Capital gets kicked in the face by Labor, or in which the young Communist hero triumphantly puts to dialectic rout the effete Schuyler Van Rensselaer Schermerhorn, Jr., or in which Fascism is shown to be more malignant than smallpox, leprosy and cancer rolled into one. Dr. Watts is also a sucker for Irish plays. Unless they are intolerably bad, he can't resist exhibits laid on the Ould Sod and in which the dialogue runs something after the following fashion:

" Murtagh he is gone now, and his share of spells with him, and isn't it a foine thing for one to be listening to the storm outside and one himself being quiet and aisy beside the foire, and it's Pat that did it. With poor Maura dead these many years, and Ignatius a-helping him whilst the quicken trees in the valley were losing their leaves in the wind, and often 'twould be a little song he would sing to

O'Reilly and me, or is it into the Galway country he would go — he, only a gossoon of eighteen or maybe twenty — and the priest counseled him to go and not to bring sorrow on his ould mother's house, and the little ladeen he marched the road betwixt the lakes, through Cornomona and Cloubur and Cong, and Oi have been going over it and over it in moi mind all the long hours of the noight."

Let Dr. Watts get an earful of anything like that and it's at least ten metaphorical stars.

Sidney Whipple, the latest recruit to the reviewing circle, who covers plays for the *World-Telegram,* is the hardest of all the boys to figure out, because he seems to like all sorts of plays equally and at the same time. The sentimental drama, however, is the one that probably fetches him the most readily. Like a number of the other reviewers, give him a young heroine in a white dress, or a little boy hugging a grandfather's coat-tails and wistfully lisping, " Say, Gramps, what's a orphan? ", or a gruff detective melting at the final curtain and letting the heroine escape with the words, " Run along, sister, and good luck; no, them's not tears; I got a cinder in my eye " — give Prof. Whipple a load of any of that and he's yours.

Now don't let me hear any more in the future from playwrights and producers as to my not being a constructive critic.

Top Achievement. Which, to date, is the best play of each of our leading American playwrights? To my mind, these:

Eugene O'Neill: *Strange Interlude* (although I can never without difficulty dismiss the short play, *The Moon of the Caribbees*).

S. N. Behrman: *Rain from Heaven.*

Maxwell Anderson: *What Price Glory?* (in collaboration with Laurence Stallings).

Lillian Hellman: *The Little Foxes.*

Clifford Odets: *Awake and Sing.*

Robert Sherwood: *Abe Lincoln in Illinois.*

Elmer Rice: *Street Scene.*

George Kelly: *Craig's Wife.*

Sidney Howard: *Dodsworth* (with Sinclair Lewis).

George S. Kaufman: *The Royal Family* (with Edna Ferber). Musical: *Of Thee I Sing* (with Morrie Ryskind).

Moss Hart: *Once in a Lifetime* (with George S. Kaufman).

John Steinbeck: *Of Mice and Men* (his first and only effort, yet a play superior to many other more active playwrights' best).

William Saroyan: *The Time of Your Life,* with *My Heart's in the Highlands* a very close runner-up.

Thornton Wilder: *Our Town.*

Marc Connelly: *The Green Pastures* (based on Roark Bradford's *Ol' Man Adam an' His Chillun*).

Paul Green: *Johnny Johnson.*

Philip Barry: *The Animal Kingdom.*

Sidney Kingsley: *Dead End.*

George M. Cohan: *Seven Keys to Baldpate* (based on a story by Earl Derr Biggers). Independent effort: *Pigeons and People.*

George Abbott: *Broadway* (with Philip Dunning).

B. & S. Spewack: *Boy Meets Girl.*

Zoë Akins: *A Texas Nightingale.*

Edwin Justus Mayer: *Children of Darkness.*

John Wexley: *The Last Mile* (based on the document of a prisoner in a Texas hoosegow).

Paul Osborn: *On Borrowed Time.*

Robert Ardrey: *Star-Spangled.*

Irwin Shaw: *The Gentle People.*

Owen Davis: *Ethan Frome* (dramatized from the Edith Wharton novel).

Mark Reed: *Yes, My Darling Daughter.*

A. E. Thomas: *No More Ladies.*

John Howard Lawson: *Processional.*

Arthur Arent: ". . . *one-third of a nation.*"
Lynn Riggs: *Russet Mantle.*
The Heywards: *Porgy.*
Hecht and MacArthur: *The Front Page.*
Frank Craven: *The First Year.*
Arthur Richman: *Ambush.*
Lula Vollmer: *Sun-up.*
Vincent Lawrence: *A Distant Drum.*
Harry Wagstaff Gribble: *March Hares.* (Close runner-up: *Revolt*).
Frederick Ballard: *Young America.*
Albert Bein: *Little Ol' Boy.*

As to Rachel Crothers, I leave the choice to you; none of her plays seems to me worthy of even a relative " best ". As to Susan Glaspell, perhaps *Alison's House* should be the choice. Robert Turney's best is *Daughters of Atreus,* but nothing else of his that I have read in script (*Daughters of Atreus* is his only produced play) seems to me to be of any consequence.

TWO-CHARACTER PLAYS. A transient little tse-tse bite adapted from the German by Gilbert Lennox and dubbed *Close Quarters* would not merit more than a sentence or two were it not that it provided us with another opportunity of smiling at that greatest of dramatic and critical frauds: the so-called full-length two-character play. We had already seen four examples in the local theatre and, like this latest specimen, all were of a charlatan piece. There have been some sound one-act two-character plays, but if in the modern theatre there has ever been a sound full-length one I wot it not.

The three-act two-character play is a double misnomer. Though the program may claim it has three acts and but two characters, the program both exaggerates and underrates. Such a play, checking off its deliberately protracted intermissions, usually runs — at most — the approximate time of two acts of the average three-act play and occasionally, as in the case of *Close Quarters,* by actual count something like fifty-five minutes. As for the two characters, it would be more precise to say two actors, since there hasn't been one such exhibit that hasn't employed, albeit off-stage, at least three or four, and sometimes as many as seven or eight, additional characters.

The circumstance that a character isn't seen in person doesn't, surely, make him less a character in a drama. Some of the most important characters in various modern plays do not appear on the stage, yet nevertheless are more influential on the action than many of those who do. From *Ben Hur* to *Family Portrait,* Christ, though He never emerges from the wings, dominates the stage. The most dramatic character that has been devised by Susan Glaspell is never brought before the audience, nor is the most positive one fashioned by Jean-Jacques Bernard. Napoleon, the protagonist of *The Duchess of Elba,* spends the whole evening off-stage, as, to stretch a point, do Odets' Lefty and, not to stretch a point, several of Pirandello's most vital characters.

U

UGLINESS VERSUS BEAUTY. Although I sadly appreciate that, in view of what I have indited hereinbefore, I shall be accused not only of ambiguity but of lamentable contradiction, I nevertheless sometimes believe that we hear altogether too much guff about beauty. As the esteemed W. Somerset Maugham says: " I do not know if others are like myself, but I am conscious that I cannot contemplate beauty long. For me, no poet made a falser statement than Keats when he wrote the first line of *Endymion*. When the thing of beauty has given me the magic of its sensation my mind quickly wanders. People add other qualities to beauty — sublimity, human interest, tenderness, love — because beauty does not long content them. No one has ever been able to explain why the Doric temple of Paestum is more beautiful than a glass of cold beer except by bringing in considerations that have nothing to do with beauty. Beauty is that which satisfies the æsthetic instinct. But who wants to be satisfied? It is only to the dullard that enough is as good as a feast. Let us face it: beauty is a bit of a bore."

The tributes that are paid to beauty might often be paid with a lot more sound reason to ugliness. I am not being speciously paradoxical. What the great majority of people regard as ugly is really, if only they pondered the matter a little, beautiful. It has, for example, always been my contention that the names of many diseases are at least twice as lovely as the names commonly given to girls and that the two might happily, for the sake of beauty, be exchanged. Pneumonia, Erysipelas, Diphtheria and Influenza assuredly have a musical sound that Bessie, Mabel, Lena and Fanny sadly lack. It would therefore add to the æsthetic welfare of the ear if the diseases in question were called by the girls' names and the girls by the diseases'. Just as Lena sounds much more like something wrong with one than Pneumonia and as Fanny sounds much more physically distressing than Erysipelas, so Malaria, Sciatica, Amnesia, Cirrhosis and Hernia have all the winning sex appeal as girls' names that Minnie, Effie, Lottie, Agnes, Bertha, Ida, Sadie, Maggie, Jessie, Amy, Ruby, Eliza, Maude, Daisy, Billie, Emma and countless other such baptismal earaches haven't. If I had a daughter, I'd fight to christen her Neuralgia or Laryngitis rather than burden the poor child through life and love with some such grating handle as Maria, Mimi, Sophie, Mozelle, Hetty or Myrtle.

It is simply the association of ideas that often blinds people to true beauty. The toadstool is infinitely more beautiful than the mushroom and poison ivy is very much more lovely than the harmless variety, but few in their prejudice realize it. Coal tar products, ugly as they are, are the bases of some of the most fragrant perfumes and some of the most delectable food and candy flavorings. The epicure isn't fooled by the superficial ugliness of liver, kidneys, pigs' knuckles, lobsters, crabs and what are euphemistically called mountain oysters; he knows the beauties that reside in them. It was Robert Loüis Stevenson who defended the popularly contemptible onion with the statement that " it ranks with the truffle and the nectarine in the chief place of honor of earth's fruit ". And only an idiot would condemn the beauties of many cheeses because of their odors. Furthermore, some of the finest and most beautiful of the world's dramas, from *Oedipus* to *Night Refuge* and including the plays of Strindberg, Ibsen, Hauptmann and various others, are built upon the ugliest of themes and the ugliest of characters.

Fate and Divine Providence, wiser than we humans and critics, seem to be against mere beauty. The most beautiful flowers die soonest and the least beautiful actresses last longest. The Lily Langtrys and the Maxine Elliotts, the Cora

Urquhart Potters and the Lantelmes, all hailed, and legitimately, as great beauties, enjoy their relatively brief day in theatrical court and quickly fade from view. But the Bernhardts and Sorels, the Rachels and the Ristoris and the Marie Tempests, none of them celebrated for beauty, live on. All of which inspires another thought.

The aforesaid thought is that beautiful people do not seem to be particularly lucky in this world. Have you ever noticed the number of tall, handsome men who are driven to eke out a living at such jobs as cab-starters, headwaiters, movie extras, floor-walkers, elevator-starters, hotel clerks, hotel receptionists, and the like? Four cab-starters out of every five — to single out just one of the jobs — are uncommonly good-looking fellows; that they look like dazzling major-generals is, indeed, a popular joke; yet the world seems to have left them out in the cold when it dispensed good fortune. Secondly, have you ever pondered who are the most successful and popular stage actors: the handsome boys or those whom nature has less lavishly smiled upon? Look over, first, the American scene; secondly, the English. Burgess Meredith, Alfred Lunt and Orson Welles are grantedly the outstanding and most sought after of the relatively younger American actors and surely none of them by the widest stretch of the imagination could be called an excessively pretty fellow. Among the older actors, we have George M. Cohan as the most successful light comedian and Walter Huston as perhaps the most favored dramatic actor, and neither in turn certainly is any trump when it comes to beauty. And in England the front-rank favorites are Cedric Hardwicke, Maurice Evans, Emlyn Williams, John Gielgud, Charles Laughton, Leslie Banks and Noël Coward, none of whom, assuredly, keeps his handsome colleagues awake at night worrying over competition in the line of looks.

It is the same, it seems, when it comes to the ladies. The three favorite actresses of the American theatre at the present time are Helen Hayes, Katharine Cornell and Lynn Fon-

tanne, none of whom, as they themselves would unquestionably be the first to agree, is anywhere nearly so blessed with
looks as Tallulah Bankhead, Helen Gahagan, Violet Heming,
Mary Ellis, Ina Claire, Francine Larrimore, and God knows
how many others infinitely less popular. Even in the movies
the Fred Astaires, Spencer Tracys, William Powells, James
Cagneys, Fred McMurrays and other such non-matinée-idol
types give the Gary Coopers, Robert Taylors and Tyrone
Powers a hot run for their money. And screen girls with far
less looks than some of the stars are beginning to edge the
latter into the discard and are claiming the attention of
audiences.

Beauty, they used to say, isn't everything. It may not be
too far wrong to say today that extra-theatrically it is, by itself, scarcely anything. It is valuable chiefly to dumb chorus
girls, dress models, débutantes who haven't any money,
movie ushers, and gigolos. Are not the very words for ugly
things considerably more beautiful than the words for beautiful things? Isn't " swill ", for example, possessed of a richer
and more charming ear-music than, say, " comeliness "?
Compare the beauty of such words as " gangrene ", " manure ", " abomination ", " mildew ", " dandruff ", " carrion ",
" garbage ", " sewer ", " cancer ", " tarnish ", " cesspool ",
" mosquito ", " gorilla " and " baboon " with the ugly sound
of such words as " eloquence ", " grace ", " pulchritude ",
" gorgeousness ", " refinement ", " æsthetic ", " peacock ",
" brilliancy ", " jewel ", " handsome ", " radiance ", " sym-
metrical " and " personable ". Which, as a name, has the
lovelier ring: Hebe or Appendicitis, Venus or Leprosy? The
word " beauty " itself, when one comes to think of it, is nowhere nearly so mellifluous as the word " hideous ".

UNSYMPATHETIC RÔLES. While it remains perfectly true that
sentimentally sympathetic rôles pretty generally contrive to
persuade the critics to admire the younger actresses, a fast-
disappearing myth of the theatre is the one to the effect that

actors and actresses in general are heavily handicapped by unsympathetic rôles. In the present-day theatre an unsympathetic rôle often proves to be the belated making of some relatively older player who, previously cast in sympathetic rôles, has had a hard time of it with the critics and public. Tallulah Bankhead, playing the rôle of a flinty and repulsively mercenary female in *The Little Foxes,* has at last scored her long waited for success with both the critics and the public. Muriel Kirkland, playing the Emancipator's bitter, nagging wife in *Abe Lincoln in Illinois,* has been greeted with bouquets which were sadly lacking in her several antecedent performances of rôles more sentimentally appealing. George Coulouris, after long and patient hope for favor, only last season got the pretty attention formerly denied him, when he appeared in the unpleasant rôle of the moral bigot in *The White Steed.* Helen Claire, after years of neglect, was accepted with open critical and popular arms upon getting and playing the gabby bundle-of-nuisance rôle of Cindy Lou in *Kiss the Boys Goodbye.* As the moral hypocrite in *The Good,* Frances Starr — despite the deservedly quick failure of the play itself — was accorded warming toots by the critical fraternity. Jeannette Chinley, after beating at the theatrical door of favor in vain, showed herself as a murderous hussy in something called *The Devil Takes a Bride* and got a round of sweet notices. Florence Reed as the supercilious snob in the revival of *Outward Bound* got more critical and popular applause than had been handed out to her in seasons of more sympathetic parts. A young Negro actor named Bryant, playing the cheap seducer in *Mamba's Daughters,* was accorded the rapt admiration of his audiences. Helen Westley, as the foul old grandmother in *The Primrose Path,* made the hit of her career. Franchot Tone came back to the theatre from his heroic Hollywood movie rôles, much to the fear and misgiving of the critics and the more intelligent portion of the theatrical public, disclosed himself in the rôle of an offensive bounder and racketeer in *The Gentle People,* and was show-ered with candy by the critics, the more intelligent portion of the public and also the less intelligent portion of the public, the latter consisting of those folk who had venerated him in his heroic Hollywood rôles. Playing two unsympathetic rôles in *Rocket to the Moon* and the revival of *Awake and Sing*, Luther Adler worked himself even deeper into the critical and audience affections than he had before. An actor named Leonard Elliott, whom no one had hitherto paid any attention to, made his first hit when he came onto the stage in *Family Portrait* as, of all things, Judas Iscariot.

All these instances, along with a number of others, have occurred in the last season alone. And the argument may be considerably reinforced by a glance at the several preceding seasons. Is it possible that the day when popularity and affection were solely synonymous with nobility of character is rapidly disappearing? Is it possible that the next time a Pollyanna and a Lightnin' Bill Jones dare to show their faces on the stage the new tough public will sardonically heave pennies at them?

VAUDEVILLE. It is the well-known whimsicality of the show business in every one of its various phases that someone is always saying it is either dying or already dead. Someone, alias Legion, said it years ago about the theatre but the theatre somehow didn't pay the necessary polite attention to it and impertinently continued on its way alive and kicking. Someone, *né* Beanbrains, said it years ago about the circus but the circus blandly continued to draw the crowds and get bigger and bigger. Someone, surname Picklewit, said it several years ago about burlesque but burlesque houses are still prosperously disseminating their perfumes in cities throughout the land. And Someone, baptized Noodlenoddle, is still saying it about vaudeville.

In the United States, it seems, anything is considered dead that isn't pretty colossal. If a town once had three theatres and now has only one, which is all it ever needed in the first place, it is dead theatrically. If the moral clean-up of burlesque cut short the careers of a couple of houses down around Fourteenth Street, burlesque is dead, even if a couple of houses in Forty-Second Street, to say nothing of one on Broadway at Forty-Sixth, sprang up to take their places, it being the logic of Someone, middle name Goosehead, that there ought to be five houses in all if burlesque weren't a corpse. And if the Palace Theatre is now a movie house, vaudeville is dead, even though there is enough vaudeville around town, all of it going strong, to choke a horse.

Vaudeville, far from being moribund, as Someone, birth certificate nomination Locococo, is currently proclaiming, is showing greater life than it has in the last decade. It is, in point of fact, so omnipresent that you can't get away from it. You go into Roxy's, Loew's State, the Audubon, the Windsor and other movie chambers to see a picture and vaudeville is heaved at you in large doses. You inquire what is the biggest musical show hit in town and you are told it is *Hellzapoppin,* which from first to last consists of vaudeville acts ranging from a trick bicyclist to a magician and from Barto and Mann to Hal Sherman and Olsen and Johnson themselves. You last season went to some other theatre in search of something in the line of drama and found a vaudeville show headed by the old Palace favorite Frank Fay and made up of a lot of other old Palace favorites like Elsie Janis, Smith and Dale, and the Hannefords. After the vaudeville shows you go to a night-club and three times out of five you get vaudeville with your scrambled eggs and highball. You go to the International Casino, to Billy Rose's Diamond Horseshoe and to the Waldorf's Sert Room and you get vaudeville again. You change your luck and go up to Harlem and you run bang up against more vaudeville at the Apollo and one or two smaller theatres. You change it again and seek refuge down in Greenwich Village and you get vaudeville with your dinner at the Village Barn and more vaudeville with your supper at Jimmy Kelly's. You seek surcease over in Brooklyn or in Jamaica and you discover that this and that cinema parlor like the Flatbush and the Carleton are also not without their stage vaudeville shows. If vaudeville is dead, it is certainly the liveliest zombie that has walked the night in a long time.

Many of our present-day musical shows and revues are little more than vaudeville shows under another name. For vaudeville even in what are referred to as the good old days wasn't always vaudeville in the popular interpretation of the term. Hammerstein's famous Victoria Roof, for example, offered fewer soft-shoe hoofers, Indian club jugglers, and trained doves than lay females recently acquitted of murder, front-page divorcées, and other such extrinsic attractions. Its chief attraction for several years, indeed, was an ordinary barnyard cow who did nothing but moo around in a cubicle painted to suggest a pasture. The celebrated Palace, in turn, built much of its reputation on such dramatic stage stars as Sarah Bernhardt, Amelia Bingham, Ethel Barrymore, Mrs. Fiske, Arnold Daly, and the like and on such plays as *The Twelve Pound Look, The Light from St. Agnes,* etc. Half the bill at the old Fifth Avenue on one occasion consisted of a somewhat abbreviated straight dramatic play, and at a Special Gala Week at one of the downtown Keith and Proctor houses I recall seeing half an hour of straight ballet, a Sidney Grundy one-act play with a couple of legitimate stage stars which took up twenty-five minutes, and a fifteen-minute lecture on the manly art by Jim Corbett. There is as much dyed-in-the-wool vaudeville, in the accepted sense of the word, on tap around New York today as there was in vaudeville's heyday.

Which, however, is certainly nothing to go home and brag about.

Having heard from various scholars of my acquaintance of the uncommonly stimulating intellectual appeal of the Hollywood movie actress, Miss Hedy Lamarr, and like them admiring cerebral puissance above everything else in the girls, I recently galloped to Loew's State Theatre to develop my mind. Miss Lamarr's picture, *Algiers,* had, it unfortunately appeared, just finished as I entered and it was thus that, driven to wait an hour and a half until it went on again, I beheld the first complete out-and-out vaudeville show I personally had experienced in at least a dozen years. I now duly appreciate why so many people argue that vaudeville is dead.

I dislike to employ the fatigued phrase, believe it or not, but believe it or not the opening act on the bill was the same opening act of grandpa's day: the man who juggled barrels on his feet. Van Cello was this particular professor's name and there, by God, he lay rapidly twirling the spangled, glittering kegs with his toes just as hundreds of Van Cellos before him had done for half a century. This novel wow was followed by The Three Chocolateers. The Three Chocolateers were a trio of Harlem bojangles who vouchsafed perspirational tap solos and who concluded their act with the stereotyped frenzied ensemble shuffling, leading them to take their bows puffing and wheezing like so many asthma clinics. Next, after the electrician turned on a purple light, came Mr. Del Casino. Mr. Casino was a spruce young man in very gray store-clothes and with plastered black hair who, in a voice bursting with tears, breathed several ballads telling seriatim how his love for his girl was as deep as the ocean and as high as the sky, how there was no girl in his life and how lonely he was until his present love came along, and how it was a case of just you, only you, you alone, with his new girl. Responding to the applause at the finish of his act, Mr. Casino, humility personified, said: "If you love my singing as much as I love singing, you will sympthize at my pain at my not being able to go on singing more songs for you."

Now, the big coup of the bill, Roscoe Ates, the stuttering film comedian. Mr. Ates' act started out with a ten-minute stutter monologue in which he unsuccessfully tried to articulate various three- or four-syllable words and compromised by abruptly substituting one-syllable synonyms for them. Thus: "He's a hyp-hyp-hyp-hypoc-hypoc-hypocr-hypocr — oh, hell, louse." This was followed by the announcement that he would play a saxophone solo. "Have you a saxophone?" he inquired of a player in the orchestra. "Sure," was the response, whereupon a trombone was handed to Mr. Ates who tooted several sour notes on the instrument, which then fell apart. Mr. Ates now entered into an exchange of facetiæ with the orchestra leader, his partner, a violently red-haired babe in a tight short skirt, having meanwhile coyly taken her place at his side. "We can make up any tune she wants to sing," said the orchestra leader in reply to a query by Mr. Ates. "You boys are out to make anything," humorously rejoined Mr. Ates, with a significant nod toward his partner.

Mr. Ates' partner now stepped to the microphone and, with Mr. Ates registering mock surprise and shock, sang a ditty describing how crazy she was about men. She didn't care what or who the men were, just so long as she could have 'em. Soldiers and sailors, plumbers and tailors, Frenchmen and Russians, Dagoes and Prussians — it was all one to her.

George Hall's swing band, with Miss Dolly Dawn as vocalist, was the hot concluding item. Mr. Hall, an ample bird in a white jacket supplemented by pants of a lovely dove shade, lifted his baton and the boys proceeded to go nuts, the electrician successively throwing the spotlight on each of those cutting up solo capers with the instruments. This done, Miss Dawn, a plump miss, stepped forth and sang a parody on *Rolling Down the Mountain*, being assisted by several of the boys in the band who put on funny hats and joined her at the mike. Then Mr. Hall lifted his baton again, the lights were sentimentally lowered, and the band played *Melancholy Baby*.

" This," reported the *Herald Tribune,* " is the kind of show to warm the heart of the ardent followers of vaudeville."

VICTIMS. *Angel Island,* by Bernie Angus, was a murder shin-dig so excessively stale that George Abbott must have bought and produced it in his sleep. But even had it been twenty times better than it was, I doubt if it could have retained much audience interest after its long first act in which the victim of the murderer was a female. Why it should be so, I don't know, but audiences as a usual thing are not much interested in plays of this species in which the victim is a woman. Quickly thinking back over a period of thirty years, I have difficulty in recalling the name of any really successful murder mystery play in which the corpse was not male. Four exhibits in the last few theatrical seasons alone, *Night Must Fall, Black Limelight, Love from a Stranger* and *Escape this Night* dared the prejudice against female victims and quickly failed. In *Angel Island,* true enough, a male corpse was also provided at the end of the second act, but that was too late to help matters.

Another point that impressed itself upon me during the performance was the danger of including a long staircase in the productions of these pseudo-thrillers and causing the numerous women in the cast frequently and palpitatingly to run up and down it. Running down it may be all right, but if there is anything in this world that can destroy the hoped-for serious attitude of an audience at some such suspense-spiel it is the periodic spectacle of a large and variedly expansive assortment of female rears jiggling and wobbling up it. *A Nude Descending a Staircase* made the public snicker, but if the artist had painted her going up there would have been a horse-laugh that would have been heard around the globe.

VICTORIAN CHARM. The very lively and active Miss Ina Claire spent most of the evening in *Barchester Towers* lying on a chaise-longue and reclining in a wheel-chair. This was a great mistake. In view of the acute lassitude and feebleness of the play and the simmering spirit and dash of Miss Claire, it would have been a much better critical and much more prosperous dramatic idea to have her and the play change places. Freely fashioned from the Trollope novel by Thomas Job and retailing the manner in which a worldly hussy from Italy inserts herself into the problems of an English cathedral town in the 1850's, the exhibit banked chiefly for its appeal on what is known as Victorian charm, that fallible resort of actresses and their managers who haven't been able to find a modern play to their liking and who pleasure themselves imagining that the box-office will respond with an ecstatic wistfulness to any plot so presently vapid that it wouldn't draw even a couple of customers to Leblang's if only they people it with actors in side-whiskers and actresses in expansive, billowy skirts, have them periodically bow at the waist, cause them elaborately to conduct their conversations after the

manner of Grover Whalen, illuminate the scene with Woolworth candles, and thus induce in the audience an overpowering nostalgia for the ineffable gentility of another day.

There is something peculiarly droll about this theatrical
business of Victorian charm. Inasmuch as three-fourths of
the dramatized novels and plays that reflect the period of the
late lamented Queen are full of characters possessed of a rich
share of bigotry, pettiness, sarcasm, equivocation, acidulous-
ness, insipidity, smugness, acrimony, wounding sharpness of
tongue, and illiberality, to say nothing of moral hypocrisy,
just where the charm comes in, aside from the costumes and
settings, is rather hard to make out. The theory, furthermore,
that characters so priggish and emotionally juvenile that they
would bore an audience to death were they incorporated into
a play of current times become instantaneously irresistible
and lovable if the scene is set back seventy or eighty years is
not less easy to comprehend. There is fifty times more gentle
emotion, more lovableness of character, more wistful heart-
ache, and more nostalgic sadness for the vanished fineness of
human character and conduct in such a play as *Of Mice and
Men* than you will find in nine-tenths of the Victorian dishes
that the contemporary stage merchants.

Vox Et Praeterea Nihil. A singularity of recent seasons
has been the effort of many of our playwrights to give body
to plays not noticeably possessing any by arbitrarily tacking
on, just before the last curtain, a big speech of cosmic significance. Most of these last-minute afterthought fireworks
give one the impression that the plays into which they have
been incorporated were fished out of trunks and through the
tacked-on harangues hopefully, if bogusly, posed as up-to-
the-minute and very trenchant and pregnant stuff. Shaw is
probably the papa of the chicane. Finding in *Too True to
Be Good* that he had written a play that didn't amount to
much and that was, even in his own judgment, pretty feeble,
he cleverly pinned onto the end of it, like a bright carnation

on a shabby, rented tail coat, a brilliantly colored, if somewhat irrelevant, philosophical oration on the present travail of humanity in the hope of deceiving his audience that what had gone before was rather meaty business and sending it out of the theatre persuaded that the eloquent finishing speech indicated a quality it must have carelessly overlooked in the antecedent parts of the play.

Our playwrights who go in for the same trick are, however, unfortunately not Shaws and as a consequence their last-minute philosophical antics only convince their audiences that the plays that have preceded the antics are even worse than they seemed. The force of the theme of a play must be inculcated in an audience slowly and gradually; it cannot be kept hiding behind a screen for a couple of hours and then suddenly be thrown into the audience's face like a custard pie. A number of the exhibits that have endeavored to lend a superficial importance to themselves by abruptly and startlingly laying down their tea-cups at ten minutes to eleven and talking big out of the corners of their mouths have accordingly not only irritated their patient auditors to the point of a nervous and embarrassing laughter but have defeated what simple purposes the plays themselves, before their authors became cosmically self-conscious, originally had. If the nonsense keeps up, we may soon expect farces like *Getting Gertie's Garter* to pause suddenly toward the conclusion of their last acts and confide to us that unless we all become Single Taxers immediately we are lost, and revivals of *Charley's Aunt* in which the uncle from Brazil will step to the footlights at eleven o'clock and make a fifteen-minute speech arguing that if Brazil ever again enters into any trade barter deals with Germany the whole western hemisphere is in danger of going Fascist.

VUE ANGLAISE. The English view of us continues to be something more than mildly bizarre. Writing in the London *Times* not long ago, Mr. James Agate delivered himself so:

" The popularity of Dreiser's *Jennie Gerhardt* in America can only be due to . . . the extraordinary preoccupation of the Americans with sex. As the Americans do not allow themselves to indulge in any form of vice except moral uplift, it follows that they never think about anything except virginal overthrow. Jennie's story is so popular in America for the same reason that every other American is a hotel detective. It is not moral to write epics about naughty girls who could not possibly go right; on the other hand, it is extremely moral to explain at enormous length how the fates conspire to make a good girl go wrong."

Let me provide James with a few pharmaceutical statistics on American popularity. In the way of books, the most popular tome in the last forty years — it sold over eight million copies — was Charles Munroe Sheldon's pietistic confection, *In His Steps.* The twenty-three other best-sellers in that period, all of which totaled more than a million sales (in some instances, very considerably more than that) were the following: Lew Wallace's *Ben Hur,* Gene Stratton Porter's *Freckles,* Gene Stratton Porter's *A Girl of the Limberlost,* Gene Stratton Porter's *The Harvester,* Gene Stratton Porter's *Laddie,* Mark Twain's *The Adventures of Tom Sawyer,* Harold Bell Wright's *The Winning of Barbara Worth,* Edward Westcott's *David Harum,* John Fox, Jr.'s *The Little Shepherd of Kingdom Come,* Jack London's *The Call of the Wild,* Owen Wister's *The Virginian,* John Fox, Jr.'s *The Trail of the Lonesome Pine,* H. G. Wells' *Outline of History,* Margaret Sidney's *Five Little Peppers and How They Grew,* Anna Sewell's *Black Beauty,* Mark Twain's *The Adventures of Huckleberry Finn,* Robert Louis Stevenson's *Treasure Island,* Du Maurier's *Trilby,* Eleanor Porter's *Pollyanna,* Jesse Lyman Hurlbut's *The Beautiful Story of the Bible,* Hervey Allen's *Anthony Adverse,* Margaret Mitchell's *Gone with the Wind,* and E. M. Hull's *The Sheik.*

Of all these unparalleledly popular books one and only one, *The Sheik* (which, incidentally, was of British origin and also a smash hit in celibate England), has been concerned with sex in the sense that Agate speaks of it. All the others, save for certain minor portions of the Allen novel, were more or less food for Sunday Schools, volitional spinsters, and the pure in heart generally.

What, further, are the American best-sellers at the moment of writing? These: Marjorie Rawlings' *The Yearling,* Cronin's *The Citadel,* Kenneth Roberts' *Northwest Passage,* Phyllis Bottome's *The Mortal Storm,* Hervey Allen's *Action at Aquila,* Lin Yutang's *The Importance of Living,* Albert Einstein's *The Evolution of Physics,* Eve Curie's *Madame Curie,* Dale Carnegie's *How to Win Friends and Influence People,* and Elizabeth Hawes' *Fashion Is Spinach.* In that whole lot there is just about as much sex as you'll find in Jane Austen or the nearest Swiss Hand Laundry.

Turn to the drama. What have been America's most popular plays in the last forty years? These: *Abie's Irish Rose, Uncle Tom's Cabin, Lightnin', The Bat, Three Men on a Horse, The First Year, The Old Homestead, Way Down East, Seventh Heaven, Peg o' My Heart, East Is West, A Trip to Chinatown, The Drunkard, The Green Pastures, Adonis, Victoria Regina, Charley's Aunt, Rip Van Winkle, The Count of Monte Cristo, Ben Hur, Tobacco Road,* and *Rain.* Passing over the fact that at least four were written by Englishmen, only two of them, *Tobacco Road* and *Rain* (the latter of British origin) fall into the strict sex category and then, even so, hardly within the bounds of the Agate animadversion.

Home, James!

VULGARITY.   There is a type of critic habitually given to a punctilious complaint that this or that is " vulgar ". He is of the species that would have Zola delicately hold up two fingers instead of saying his direct and natural say, that would have had Farragut darn the torpedoes, and that would argue the bedfellowship of Abraham Lincoln and Chick Sale.

WARNINGS. The critical demolition and box-office disaster which simultaneously overtook the not long ago revivals of *The Merry Wives of Windsor* and *The Wild Duck* should have been a warning to producers. Nevertheless, they obviously weren't, and for two reasons. First, the average producer generally has the same contempt for warnings that any other child has and, secondly, experience has taught him that his attitude is often right. This, of course, is most unhappily disconcerting to such critics as loftily believe that producers should love, honor, and obey their dicta without question. But it is true. Thus, when the critics with the completest theoretical good sense and propriety point out that immediate failure must be the lot of any classical revival produced and acted as badly as this *Merry Wives* or this *Wild Duck* and when they further point out as proof the earlier seasonal failure of the revivals of *As You Like It* and *Antony and Cleopatra*, the producers simply laugh at them. And, again, justifiably. For the subsequent revivals of *A Doll's House* and *The Sea Gull*, neither of which got anything much in the way of sound production and acting, not only were endorsed by a number of the critics themselves but enjoyed pretty good runs to boot. What is more, the producers know that the same thing has happened several other times in the last few years.

Nothing could have been worse than the first two revivals mentioned. The producer of the Shakespeare exhibit evidently confused it with Planquette's *Paul Jones* and the Bard's characters with Planquette's sailors and lassies of St. Malo. We were thus treated to the spectacle of every entrance accompanied by a merry village maidens' species of

Castle Square Opera company laughter and every exit accompanied by a Hawkshaw ha-ha. The producer of the Ibsen drama, in turn, apparently imagined, among sixty or seventy other delusions, that the best way to direct actors in the playing of aged characters was to persuade them to walk as if they had sore feet and that the best way to conceal amateur acting in general was to keep the actors standing in one position, lest they betray their inability to move properly on a stage, and to have them inaudibly whisper their lines, lest they betray their inability to speak them.

Although he has nothing to do with the classics, George Abbott is another producer who has no slightest use for critical warnings. The critics warned him a few years ago that there had been a surfeit of Hollywood buffooneries and that failure would follow the production of any more of them. So he put on *Boy Meets Girl,* delighted the critics in spite of themselves, and made a fortune. Then they told him, a year later, that after the quick failure of such boys' school plays as *So Proudly We Hail* and *Bright Honor* the public didn't want any more boys' school plays. So he put on *Brother Rat,* again delighted the critics in spite of themselves, and made another fortune. In the meantime, of course, he became a little cocky and put on other things in the face of warnings and lost a fortune. But no matter. The scoreboard still supported at least a measure of his snootiness. More recently, he produced still another school play, *What a Life.* Although a machine-made and feeble Broadway paraphrase of Tarkington, it got excellent notices from the critics and enjoyed a long and prosperous run. So the whole business becomes more and more bewildering. No wonder producers chuckle at the critics' judgments. No wonder I chuckle at the critics' judgments. No wonder the critics chuckle at my judgments. No wonder we're all crazy.

WEAKNESS. It is the weakness of so much of present-day drama that its emotions are fundamentally little more than moving-picture emotions in dinner jackets. Its passions are the puny tremors of puny hearts and spirits to which puny playwrights seek to give size by funneling them through a ceremonious polysyllabic dramaturgy. It lives like a worm; it thinks like a Hollywood movie director; it loves either like a eunuch or a rabbit; it feels like a gigolo; and it dies like a ham Cyrano. In it one finds none of the bewildered nobility and splendor of the higher reaches of the human heart, none of the pain and doubt and ecstasy of the human mind, none of the tortured but sometimes ringing music of human search and despair and triumph. Into the theatre of such a drama even a second-rate Irish play comes with the reassurance of a doctor's pat on the back, with the warmth of a glass of port against the chill, and with all the welcome melody of a familiar " Hello " in a strange and lonely land.

" WELL — SON "; " NOW — DAUGHTER ". At least half the talking pictures I have seen seem to proceed either toward or from the line, " But — father! "

WHY THE GUILD FOUNDERED. In a public address, Theresa Helburn, duenna of the Theatre Guild, last season confessed that " the only way we can get a sound idea of any script that interests us is to bring together a group of actors and actresses and have it read to us by parts." There you have it. The Guild board, instead of coolly and intelligently determining for itself the values implicit in a play, just sat around in a circle and let itself be suckered by the false and superficial values cleverly read into the script by actors and actresses desperately looking for a job.

WILDER. Granting that there is a certain theatrical novelty in applying the age-old Chinese stage devices to a play about a small American town and that now and again the author manages to evoke the usual sentimental emotional response to a wistful recollection of the past, what else does Thornton Wilder's *Our Town* offer on its behalf? It is obviously unfair to point out against it that in every last technical detail it is exactly like a staging of a rehearsal of one of D. W. Griffith's old silent motion pictures. Anyone who knows anything of such rococo matters will immediately recognize the play's complete identity with Griffith's method: his description to the players, all gathered in a bare room, of the scenes and settings, the acting with imaginary props, the skeletonized plot, the pantomime accompanied by spoken lines (it was a paradox that the silent-screen players always spoke the appropriately accompanying dialogue at reheasals), the employment of chairs and ladders to represent everything from a war trench to a palace staircase, and so on. But it is less unfair to point out that Mr. Wilder cheats in the use he makes of such skeletonized drama. While insisting that he abandons all scenery and props, he still compromises with his plan by employing them. He shows us no houses, but he brings out two flower-covered latticed doorways to trick the imagination into an acceptance of their presence. He shows us no drugstore, but he brings out a long panel to realize his soda-water counter. He uses almost as many lighting tricks as the late Belasco to assist his audience's imagination in the matter of his described sunsets, dawns, and sunrises. He asks us to fit into his imaginative scheme by conjuring up the picture of a garden or pasture or chicken patch and then pulls a vaudeville act by having someone in the wings moo like a cow or crow like a rooster. He concretely shows us no marriage altar, but he puts his actress into a white bridal costume and has the electrician throw a stereoptican slide of a stained-glass window above the spot where he has asked us to visualize it. He says, in metaphorical effect, "this is no theatre you are in" and yet he has steps leading up to his stage, and an actor in an orchestra seat shouting out a question to another actor on the stage, and two other players on their way to the above-mentioned marriage altar brushing against the audience on their march up the aisles. In other words, he seeks to take us out of a theatre while still insisting upon a theatre. And in other words still, he asks the child that is in all of us to visualize in our fancies the nursery of life and then distractingly assists us by making a noise like a choo-choo, blowing on a bird whistle, and giving an imitation of us sucking an ice-cream soda through a straw.

The merit of any play, apart from its theme, is plainly predicated on its characters, its dialogue, and its philosophy. In *Our Town* there is no single achievement of character drawing, no single memorable line of dialogue, and the philosophy of death which its last act expounds amounts in sum to the remarkable cerebration that while life is turbulent death is serene and that the dead wouldn't care to come back if they could, because they would be unhappy living in a world whose future they would know and could foresee. (How they would know it and could foresee it, Mr. Wilder carefully refrains from confiding to us.) The exhibit, in short, remains fundamentally a stunt. A much more literate stunt than most, to be sure, and one here and there profiting from the spontaneous emotional combustion resident in its sentimental chemicals, but a stunt nonetheless.

Although it is to be admitted that the play's panoramic sketching of birth, life, love and death in a small native community here and there by virtue of its narrative quiet and simplicity achieves the audience effect that often lies in adroitly calculated understatement and although, of course, there is always an audience emotional value in such time-honored stage cardiac seducers as the gentle and understanding love of an elderly married couple, the tender laying of a posy on a beloved's grave, the young bride in white at the wedding altar, and the like, I fear that I cannot discern in the exhibit its alleged large æsthetic virtues. While it has its few moments and while it now and again succeeds in evoking in its audiences a strange, homely emotional co-operation, it seems to me to be essentially little more than a sparse Sino-American paraphrase of Andreyev's familiar *The Life of Man* which also, you will recall, has its narrator to interpret the action, which also has been acted on a bare stage, and which aims at accomplishing its effect through the same innocence of detail.

As for Mr. Wilder's *The Merchant of Yonkers*, it is apparently predicated on the theory that outmoded situations and jests, which in 1939 costumes and stage décor would promptly put an audience to sleep, immediately become acceptably hilarious if offered in those of 1880. Derived from a farce written by Johann Nestroy about a hundred years ago and one that in the meantime had already been paraphrased at least a hundred times, this latest edition presents the usual depressing spectacle which results from the sentimental theatrical presumption that all you need do to convert a tiresome old joke into a rip-roaring one is frankly and a bit wistfully to admit it is a tiresome old joke.

I, for one, notoriously an inhospitable mule, stubbornly fail to find myself reacting properly to these hypothetical bustle-busters. I am no longer an incontrollable roarer at characters who hide in wardrobes and under tables, at Mrs. Levi speaking with an Irish brogue, at the old female servant who periodically wanders distractedly out of the confused scene muttering " The Lord have mercy on us! ", at the suitors who have only one dollar and forty-five cents between them to buy their lady-love dinner, at the humble clerk mistaken for a man of wealth and position, at the joke about the life line being so long it runs clear off an old boy's hand, at such humorous philosophies as money being like manure because the more you spread it around the more good it does, and at other such moxies of long bygone days. That is, I am no longer an incontrollable roarer at them unless the management fuels me coincidentally and constantly with ethyl alcohol, if then. Unfortunately, the management on this occasion was remiss.

WOMEN AND ACTRESSES. The average female playgoer critically disesteems an actress in proportion to her sex appeal.

WOMEN PLAYWRIGHTS. John Golden, the theatrical producer, in a recent interview projected the following statement: "In the English-speaking world there is no woman dramatist to compare with Rachel Crothers. She has put great writing into *Susan and God* and she possesses a writing competence given to few dramatists. There is certainly no woman playwright in her class!" Although Mr. Golden happened by a coincidence to be the producer of Miss Crothers' *Susan and God* and hence by a coincidence may be somewhat prejudiced in her favor, there is yet something in his pronouncement that brews a pony of meditation.

The meditation runs this way. While Mr. Golden's extravagant tribute to Miss Crothers may not only grieve the critically judicious but even incline them to a whimsical snicker or two, it implies, notwithstanding, an obliquely valuable and devastating criticism of women as a whole when it comes to the matter of playwriting. If Miss Crothers, a successful second-rater at best, is all or even half — or possibly even one-third — what Mr. Golden claims for her, why, may we ask, is it that the ladies are nevertheless almost uniformly so abjectly inferior to men in the field of dramatic composition? I do not wish to seem unchivalrous, but the fact remains that there isn't a woman playwright living today who seems to be able to confect a play that comes within hailing distance of the drama written by the more competent of her boy-friends. Aside from Lillian Hellman, who has indicated a possible future competitive challenge in the instances of *The Children's Hour* and *The Little Foxes,* and maybe the deaf Irish Teresa Deevy, who in *Katie Roche* hints vaguely at genuine capability, the rank and file of the playwriting girls, in whatever nation you find them, are a sadly negligible lot.

With Lady Gregory gone to her Maker — and what talent Lady Gregory proved was confined mainly to one-act plays — the women dramatists she has left behind are very small shakes. The situation in England is clearly reflected in the herein earlier quoted article lately published by Charles Morgan, critic for the London *Times*. Says Mr. Morgan: "Miss Dodie Smith, author of *Autumn Crocus, Service, Touch Wood, Call It a Day, Bonnet over the Windmill* and *Dear Octopus* is the most consistently successful woman playwright in England. She is a devoted craftswoman who works within her limitations while continually striving to enlarge them; she has good-humor as well as humor and is entertaining without being malicious. The problem is whether her limitations can be extended and, if so, how far? Has she anything to say or must her plays always be, in effect, popular magazine stories adroitly told?" If such a playwright as Dodie Smith is the outstanding example of successful English women dramatists and if Dodie Smith is at the same time merely a writer of pulp magazine stuff, what are we to think?

Clemence Dane, a fellow countrywoman of Miss Smith's, has tried to aim at something higher and has consistently failed. The best she has been able to negotiate has been deplorably second-rate. Ditto Margaret Kennedy. To the North, in Scotland, a woman who signs herself Gordon Daviot several years ago managed to write an historical paraphrase, *Richard of Bordeaux*, that had its points, but thereafter proved conclusively that her one good performance was something of a fluke. France has no woman playwright worth mentioning. In Germany today the ladies who once tried without success to write for the theatre are with considerably more success confining themselves to cooking and having babies. The same in Italy and Spain, where women have generally had the sense to leave the business of playwriting to their husbands and lovers. If there is a reputable woman playwright in Russia, we haven't heard of her. And so it goes.

Take America, where the girls in large numbers are trying to compete with the men. There is the Miss Crothers referred to. What has she accomplished? A number of prosperous box-office trivialities not one of which has come within a hundred miles of approaching the quality of the plays of such men as — let us omit O'Neill, Steinbeck and the like as being too obviously of the higher class — Kaufman, Hart, Saroyan, Green, Lawrence, Rice, Tarkington, Connelly, Kelly, et al. Zoë Akins in her early days began to suggest a pretty talent but never developed and realized it. Helen Jerome has thus far revealed herself only as a handy dramatizer of others' works; we shall have to suspend judgment of her until she proves what, if anything, she can do with original work. Clare Kummer has written a few minor comedies, pleasantly diverting but no more. Zona Gale dramatized one of her own novels and otherwise proved little or nothing. Susan Glaspell has a better mind than most, but has never been able to contrive a fully satisfactory play. Sophie Treadwell wrote *Machinal,* which was two-thirds strainful pretence to one-third honest drama, and with her other efforts went critically down the chute. The same with Lula Vollmer after her moderately good but still defective *Sun-up.* Maurine Watkins, as a young girl, fashioned an amusing little lampoon called *Chicago* and thereafter a half-dozen plays that got nowhere. Rose Franken contrived a fair piece of family reporting in *Another Language* and collapsed. Clare Boothe, like Rachel Crothers, is thus far simply a box-office masseuse; what she may do in the future one can't predict. And Anne Nichols has written *Abie's Irish Rose!*

The question poses itself. What is the trouble with the girls? Why can't they, apparently, cope with men in the writing of plays? And the answer poses itself in turn.

In almost all the dramatic efforts of the women writers we find that, when they tackle male characters, they go com-

pletely to pot. Their female characters often have some life
and reality, but their men are dummies. Clare Boothe's successful play, *The Women,* unquestionably owed its success
to the fact that she was sagacious enough not to try to interpret male characters and to confine her stage wholly and exclusively to women. In all the plays written by women in
the last dozen years I can't think of a single male character
— unless it be that of Stanislaus Gregg, the middle-aged
wooer of Katie in the Teresa Deevy play to which I have before alluded — that hasn't made any closely observant and
intelligently critical man in the audience emit a doubtful
grunt.

Women playwrights may know their own sex, although
even here there never has lived a female playwright who
knew women as deeply, fully and articulately as male playwrights have amply proved they knew them, but they seem
to know next to nothing of men. They see men either as
romantic heroes or as childlike and blundering oafs, either
as intellectual and emotional giants or as goats and blockheads. They seldom, if ever, see a male as occupying the
no-man's-land which stretches forlornly between, that no-
man's-land in which the great majority of the theoretically
stronger sex find themselves. The result is a series of male
characters who suggest nothing quite so much as movie heroes with jobs or shoe-salesmen who were fired years ago and
have in the meantime just hung pathetically around the
house.

We approach a second reason. It seems to be impossible for a woman playwright to stand aloof and apart from her
central woman character and not identify herself, in however
slight a degree, with her. The playwright may not be aware
of it, indeed seldom is, but just the same before the evening
is over you will observe that something of her own self and
her own prejudices has sneaked automatically and question-
ably into the character and in part invalidated it. Objectiv-
ity fails, and what we most often get is a woman character

who starts out independently and who around ten-fifteen begins to have a difficult time keeping her individuality and integrity and not acting more or less like the woman who wrote her.

To sum up, women can write pleasant, negligible little comedies, pleasant little fantasies and sometimes entertaining little excursions into parlor cynicism but, with rare exception, when they seek to come to grips with the sterner and more profound stuffs of drama they go badly to pieces. They can write; they can think; and they can feel. But their writing at its best too often is imitatively patterned after men's and hence, as in the Akins-Pinero, Dodie Smith-Barrie and Glaspell-Bernard patterns, does not ring forthrightly true; their thinking too often stumbles at the three-quarter post; and their feeling too often — surprising as it may seem — is sentimentally, arbitrarily and ridiculously prejudiced in favor of the male sex.

WORKERS' STAGE. What we get in some such Workers' Stage revue as *Sing for Your Supper* is simply one cheaply imitative of the Broadway species at its worst and distinguishable from the latter only in the substitution in its lyrics of Mrs. Shapiro for Elsa Maxwell. It is apparently the theory of the various relief and workers' stages that any such substitution promptly and effectively converts the restricted Noël Coward or Cole Porter type of entertainment into one of wholesale democratic appeal. Added to this theory is the further one that if you put in a number kidding the drama of social significance you will endear even the dullest proletarian offering to its more affluent and snooty customers. And added to this second theory is a third to the effect that if you suddenly bring the genial self-spoofing to a halt with a number that views the problems of the unemployed gravely you will have magnificently justified the whole purpose back of the enterprise.

These shows are beginning to follow a pattern twice as

monotonous as the condemned Broadway pattern. They imagine that you can make alive with novelty and import a stale fifteen-minute Viennese waltz number simply by bringing on half a dozen actors dressed as Nazis finally to interrupt it. They believe you can take a skit that wouldn't be tolerated in the poorest Winter Garden show and transform it into something pretty topically hot simply by injecting into it an allusion to Mayor Hague. And they are convinced that if you wind up the proceedings with a dozen actors dressed in overalls, programmed as WPA workers, and singing something about leaning on a shovel you will have proudly achieved a show that emphasizes the pathetic triviality of shows which conclude with fifty beautiful girls in beautiful costumes singing about the satisfaction of having a decent bank account.

X. Not long ago Hollywood, in scholastic conclave assembled, picked out one of its young movie women, a Mlle. Ann Sheridan, and formally announced to the American public that she had more sex appeal than any other houri in the whole community. Thus was added still another imbecility to the already rich roster of the California Corinth. That the young lady in question may enjoy a share of sex appeal is quite possible, although, judging from the many photographs of her which I have seen in the public prints, I feel that I personally might be able to resist her devastating puissance with considerable ease and equanimity. But that is not the point. The point is that it is no more possible arbitrarily and specifically to nominate sex appeal for the generality of men than it is possible accurately to predict their unanimous reaction to broccoli and the political philosophy of Walter Lippmann, or even to cures for colds, sleeveless pajamas, and Western sandwiches. What is sex appeal to one man is often a dose of salts to another. If proof were needed, the commonly heard query, "What does he see in her?", would supply it. And if, further, feminine sex appeal were the positive and firmly fixed attribute that Hollywood apparently thinks it is, there would be hardly a man in America today who wouldn't be going around with a black eye.

Hollywood, however, must at least be credited with the courage of its convictions, however idiotic. It stoutly believes, for example, that you can take some ex-Childs waitress with little more personality than a ginless Martini and little more natural appetizing quality than a Chinese steak and quickly convert her into a glamourous creature, whom strong men will swoon over, by the simple process of shaving off her eyebrows, supplying her with a set of false teeth, changing her name to something that sounds like a cross between a ten-cent perfume and a London hotel, and broadcasting pictures of her in a bathing suit. And it also resolutely imagines that if several hundred youngsters, most of them under the age of twelve and residing in some tanktown in Arkansas that hasn't even one movie theatre, suddenly and mysteriously write in to request her autographed photograph, the baby in question is on the sure road to stardom.

It accordingly isn't strange that any such great cultural center should persuade itself that you can define sex appeal as absolutely and irrevocably as you can define tuberculosis, a broken leg, or Paul Joseph Göbbels. There is only one thing in connection with Hollywood's rapt conviction that disturbs me. When I was last out there, I noticed that all the men somehow didn't seem to give a nickel for the girls they had designated as champion sex appealers and went around instead with a lot of telephone girls, stenographers and movie-lot extras whom nobody had ever seen or heard of, and often even with their wives.

Long before the Mlle. Sheridan was heralded the empress of sex appeal, the throne out Hollywood way had been occupied for a span of years by the late Jean Harlow. Miss Harlow, when it came to sex appeal, was in Hollywood's publicized estimation the final and lushest bloom. Yet I have the word of many men who knew her that so far as sex appeal went she wasn't of any more voltage than the average girl they knew, that so far as she herself went it was a great big laugh to her, and that her real appeal — a strong one — lay in her intelligently entertaining conversation, likable company, and ability to sit at a table with a man for hours at a time and give the impression of hugely enjoying herself. If your answer, perchance, is that all that is part of sex appeal,

I fear I shall politely have to content myself in urging you to buy a dictionary or to consult your osteopath.

Sex appeal — and here surely your professor discloses no startling news — is as undefinable as the taste of celery. You can no more tell me or any other man that this or that woman has sex appeal and hope invariably to convince than I can tell you or any other man, even when under the influence of alcoholic liquor. Asked to define sex appeal, the current Hollywood bombshell saucily tossed a theoretically tempting hip and sagely observed: " Sex appeal is mixed up with charm and personality, the main ingredients of which are a healthy, natural curiosity and an active sense of humor." Curiosity and an active sense of humor, the young lady should be sadly informed, have driven more originally impressed and palpitating men away from potential sirens than you can shake a stick at.

" Next important thing," continued the irresistible pigeon, " is to avoid being too shy. Then nobody has any fun." It is quite possible that maybe nobody has any fun, but it has long been my observation that the shy girl, however much a party killjoy she may be, still oddly enough seems to stir the boys' fancy a heap more than the girl who climbs on the mantel and imitates Beatrice Lillie or the one who sneaks up behind you and whimsically pours a bottle of crème de cacao down your collar. Shyness, though very probably not in Hollywood, is often to sex appeal what onions are to a hamburger.

Our Hollywood load of anatomical dynamite then concluded her infallible recipe for feminine sex appeal. " 1. Don't develop a sense of inferiority. 2. Don't appear grateful to a man. 3. Never laugh at a man when he is serious — about anything. 4. Don't forget that all men like to be thought pretty dangerous."

As for Item No. 1, I fear that our California authority is slightly off the track. A sense of superiority in a woman is one of the surest ways to drive a man into the arms of the nearest churchmouse, whether she be naturally and honestly modest and humble or merely successfully acting the part.

As for No. 2, the woman who takes a man's kindnesses for granted will in turn quickly drive him — if he is not already there — to his appreciative secretary or stenographer; in some cases, indeed, even to a girl he admired in other days, whom he for one reason or another vamoosed from, but who lingers in his memory as one who didn't always take things for granted.

As for No. 3, it must be admitted that our Hollywood luminary has something there. The woman who laughs at a man when he is serious about anything, even if he is a consummate nitwit, doesn't stand the faintest shadow of a chance with him. But the question of sex appeal doesn't necessarily enter into it. A child would hate even a mother who laughed at him under such circumstances.

As for No. 4, our Orange-grove Sexual Magnet is talking through her bonnet. It may be true that some college boys and older goats like to view themselves as Casanovas, but most men with an ounce of intelligence, experience and humor do nothing of the kind. If it happens that they find themselves interested in a girl, they of course and quite reasonably hope to stand a chance with her. But on all other occasions they are completely and coolly indifferent, and if some wench they have no interest in begins to pull any such performance as our Sexual Magnet recommends, they are pretty damned well bored to death.

This sex appeal business, in short, all comes down to what the late lamented Calvin Coolidge said. Said the late lamented Calvin Coolidge: "If I like 'em, I like 'em; if I don't, I don't."

It should in all fairness be remarked, however, that what the late lamented C. C. had in mind was apples.

Y

YEN FOR THESPIS. Now that Novelists Sinclair Lewis and Thornton Wilder, Bubble-dancer Sally Rand, Columnist Heywood Broun, Steelworker William Haade, Playwright George Kaufman, Critics Woollcott and Benchley, and the Ladies' Garment Workers Union have all duly made their appearance on the stage as actors, it seems that there are few of us left to constitute audiences any more. The yen to act has apparently got to the point where, unless it is soon checked, the producers may just as well yank out the auditorium seats.

It isn't the thousands of amateur kids cavorting on stages all over the country that I am thinking of; it is rather the countless adults whose professions are as alien to the craft of acting as brewing is to preaching. It is these upon whom the urge to mime has descended with such ferocity that it probably won't be long before the Actors' Equity Association will have to annex Central Park in order to accommodate its membership at future meetings.

Lanny Ross, the radio warbler, has turned actor in Lynn Riggs' *Green Grow the Lilacs*. Primo Carnera, the pug, made his theatrical début in Milan some months ago. Maxie Baer and Maxie Rosenbloom, his colleagues, have already acted in pictures and are on their way to the legitimate stage. Dizzy and Paul Dean, the ball players, have lately displayed themselves behind the footlights. Society girls like Lillian Emerson, Elizabeth Young, June Blossom, Whitney Bourne, Cobina Wright, Jr., Esme O'Brien and various others have gone in for dramatic greasepaint. Peter Arno, the cartoonist, lately acted in James M. Cain's play, *7 — 11*. So did Sheila

Barrett, the night club mimic. Mrs. Harrison Tweed, alias Michael Strange, has nosed the social whirl for the realm of painted canvas. Oscar Polk in turn deserted operating a Harlem elevator for the art of Coquelin, Salvini, and Corse Payton. Theresa Helburn, of the managerial board of the Theatre Guild, has gone in for acting in *Suzanna and the Elders*.

And that's only the beginning. Helen Golden not long ago left off being a telephone operator to act a rôle in *Having Wonderful Time*. George M. Cohan's valet has appeared in several exhibits with his master. Columbus Jackson, a colored gentleman, left off clerking in a Lenox avenue emporium to woo applause in *How Come, Lawd?* Patricia Morison deserted the staff of *Vogue* for the stage. Joan Wetmore has given up modeling for the sock and buskin. Jay Fasset jumped to the stage from a business desk, as Frank Parker did from the singing mike. Dr. Cecil Reynolds, well-known California brain specialist, has been playing Hamlet and other rôles on the West Coast. Martha Scott got her certificate as a school teacher and tore it up to act, landing in *Our Town*. Richard Carlson was a college instructor and overnight left his job to have a go at the performing business. And Hollywood, as everyone knows, is so full of players who were formerly cowboys, waitresses, manicurists, stenographers, real estate salesmen and what not that most of the real actors and actresses there have been crowded out of the profession.

Just what it is that makes people of all sorts want to act is a matter of opinion. Some say it is exhibitionism; some contend it is a hunger for applause (even from simpletons); others argue that it is induced by a sincere desire to follow the histrionic craft (these others are usually somewhat lit when they start any such argument); and others still assign further reasons. But whatever the reasons the fact persists that the passion to get up on an illuminated platform and antic before a congregation of customers is apparently something that human beings in the aggregate have difficulty in resisting.

While this passion has increased enormously in recent years, it is no new thing. The stage of past years has disclosed all kinds of folk who have tossed over their previous jobs and presented themselves to audiences in the guise of actors. Bob Fitzsimmons, Jim Jeffries, Jim Corbett, Jack Dempsey and various other prize-fighters have turned histrio and revealed themselves in everything from knock-'em-down melodrama to plays by Bernard Shaw. Rube Marquard, Christy Matthewson, Mike Donlin, Mickey Cochrane and other ball players have all heaved themselves onto a stage at one time or another and flirted with the bravos of ticket buyers. Louis Wolheim deserted the post of instructor in mathematics at Cornell to make a name for himself behind the footlights. And Cora Urquhart Potter abandoned the social life, as did Elsie De Wolfe.

Tod Sloan gave up jockeying to have a fling at acting. Edward S. Abeles was a lawyer in St. Louis before the bug got him. John E. Dodson also started out in the legal profession, and James O'Neill, Eugene's papa, went to the stage from clothing store clerking in Cincinnati. Maclyn Arbuckle was a lawyer and Edwin Arden was a cowboy, clerk, politician and newspaper reporter before the smell of greasepaint got the upper hand in their nostrils. Will Cressy was successively a carpenter, machinist, marine engineer, watchmaker, commercial traveler and hotel clerk and then one day got off a train at South Norwalk, Connecticut, and became an actor in something called *The White-Caps*. The admirable Sara Allgood worked in a furniture store in Dublin as preparation for an acting career with the Abbey Players. In point of fact, most of the Abbey Company's actors were in all jobs but acting when the stage beckoned to them. Weedon Grossmith was a portrait painter, Lawrence Grossmith a mechanical engineer, May Robson earned a living painting china and menu cards, and Fanny Ward was an artists' model when the call of the stage started buzzing in their ears. Neil Burgess, who later gained fame in *The County Fair,* was a Swiss Bell Ringer, Clara Bloodgood was a figure in metropolitan social life, Robert Edeson worked in a box-office, Nat Goodwin was a dry-goods clerk, and Ezra Kendall was a printer and then a reporter on the old New York *Herald* and on the Olean, N. Y., *Times,* before succumbing to the histrionic itch.

William A. Brady, unable to resist the ham business after half a century — he first became an actor fifty-six years ago the day after he stopped selling candy on a Southern Pacific railroad train — not so long ago stopped managing theatres for the moment to play a rôle in a melodrama. It made him terribly happy. Frank Shields has declared his intention of giving up tennis and becoming an actor in Marc Connelly's next play. William Tilden left the tennis courts to act several years ago, and before acting John Wexley was a waiter, a bellboy, a floorwalker and a tin roofer. Although they have not yet appeared on the stage, recent performers on the screen have included Supreme Court Justice Felix Frankfurter (*Law Film Classics*), Prof. Albert Einstein (*Peace and Democracy*), Dr. Irving Langmuir, Prof. Charles Townsend Copeland (*Charles Dickens*), and Prof. Joseph Henry Beale, who for forty-eight years has been on the Harvard Law School faculty, who has performed in *Jurisdiction for Divorce,* and who afterward confessed to the producer, E. L. Dorfman, that "my secret ambition is to be an actor." You can't, apparently, stop any of them. Otherwise, Stiano Braggiotti would still be socially braggiotting himself in Boston, Hope Williams would still be socially parkavenuing herself in New York, John Cromwell (lately the Rosencrantz in the Gielgud *Hamlet* and the Byron in *Bright Rebel*) would still be socially bernardsvilling himself in New Jersey, and a whole lot of actors of the past would, like Fred Frear, the celebrated Hadji of George Ade's *The Sultan of Sulu,* have remained bookkeepers, like Henry Jewett, bank clerks, like Charles

Ross, of the old Weber and Fields Music Hall company, handymen around racetracks, and, like David Warfield, ushers.

It looks as if relatively few actors start out in life with the intention of becoming actors. Out of a list of several thousand there seem to be only seventy-one who have gone directly into the histrionic trade. Most of the rest have got the yen after entirely different starts.

YOUTH AND THE VERSE DRAMA. The first thing one of our younger American writers does when he feels a play in rhymed dialogue coming over him is to take hold of a plot that has already served two dozen Italian dramatists who have laid it either in Rome or Sicily, to say nothing of Somerset Maugham, who has laid it in the Straits Settlement or South Africa, and then proceed to transfer it almost intact to some section of America prior to the Civil War. The second thing he does is to make it so excessively strong and masculine that Ernest Hemingway would be afraid to fight it even if it had both its hands tied behind its back. This strength and masculinity usually consist in referring to the women characters as bitches and whores, in numerous allusions to the luxuriant hair on the men's chests, in a copious tippling, in the overpowering longing of the frontiersmen for copulation with a white woman, in the inclusion in the blank verse of several goddams, bastards and sons-of-bitches, in a lofty contempt for personal bathing, and in at least two references to the softening effect that cities have upon men. The third thing the young playwright does, though he is never aware of it, is to populate his Kentucky or whatever it is with actors instead of characters. The fourth thing he does is pretty generally to include in his opus an idiot boy or some other such witling (one who has been purposely dropped on the head by the villain at a tender age and who is the illegitimate son of the aforesaid villain and Anne Hathaway), to constitute him a combination of drooling *raisonneur, deus ex machina* and bughouse *compère,* and to cause him to meander aimlessly through the action spouting ominously about the fairies sleeping in elephants' ears until, at five minutes to eleven, he enjoys a moment of comparative lucidity and kills the villain just as the latter is gloating that he has triumphed over the hero, who has ever been the moron's friend. And the first thing the director hired to stage the verse play does is to insist that the actors sedulously read the verse as if it weren't verse, thus making the whole enterprise doubly ridiculous.

Z

ZAPFENSTREICH. The present theatrical season finds me relinquishing, after two years of service in the field, my post as Generalissimo of the Drama Critics' Circle. I accordingly herewith address my farewell to my loyal and faithful troops, and beg their fond leave paternally to bequeath to them various advices, suggestions and recommendations looking to their future health and prosperity, and to the health and prosperity of the theatre no less.

Gentlemen, Officers, and Soldiers of the Theatrical Republic:

1. Do not in the future, as some of you have in the past, believe you can help the theatre by now and again charitably letting down easily some unworthy play. Your good graces in such instances, far from helping the theatre, only hurt it. Those readers who have faith in you will be fooled into paying their good money to see the play and will come away not only distrustful of you but further distrustful of the theatre itself. You are thus betraying a double trust.

2. Although patriotism is as commendable in a critic as in any other man, don't let it run away with you professionally — as it does with some of you — to the point of esteeming a play simply because of its Americanism. During and directly after the World War, the French critics made a laughing-stock of the French drama by proclaiming as a masterpiece every play that whooped it up for the Tricolor and La Belle France, and the French drama hasn't yet, these many years later, recovered. What similarly chauvinistic criticism has done for the present-day Russian, German, Austrian and Italian drama, you all know. If you laughed at the flag-

waving plays of George M. Cohan in less uneasy days, don't
— if as critics you are worth your salt — stop laughing at the
flag-waving of other playwrights simply because the national
days are more uneasy. The criticism that is not beyond and
above immediate concerns is valueless — and not only valueless, but ridiculous.

3. Those of you who are considerably younger than the
rest of us and who are relatively new to the business should
try to exercise caution in competing with the theatrical and
dramatic memories of us grandpas. Write only of what you
yourself have enjoyed by actual experience. Memory often
being what it is, you will get into enough trouble without
jumping over strange fences and frolicking in pastures that
are unknown to you. During my term of office as your
Führer, I on no less than eleven occasions read things some
of you had written which, if you will forgive me, indicated
that you didn't know whereof you were speaking quite as
unmistakably as musical allusions inevitably betray the novice in like circumstances. It is hard enough even for us older
boys who have fought in many more wars than you have.
Here, for example, I read my widely experienced London
colleague, James Agate, who is sixty, reviewing Rutherford
Mayne's new play, *Bridge Head*, referring to the author as
a new and hitherto unknown playwright and marvelling
at his " extraordinary professionalism ". One of the earliest
plays I ever reviewed — it was more than thirty years ago —
was, I recall, one by this same " new and unknown " author.
Its title was *The Drone;* it was produced at the old Daly's
Theatre; and its leading actor, if my own memory doesn't fail
me, was Whitford Kane.

4. Do not, in order to support and popularize a critical
prejudice, uppishly pontificate on æsthetics. It will often
throw you for a loop, unless, that is, you happen to be a
true Prof. Dr. Take you, Lieutenant-Colonel Atkinson of the
Times, for example. You are a valuable officer and a gallant
soldier, but what did you write by way of defending and

eulogizing your favorite play of the last season, Sherwood's *Abe Lincoln in Illinois?* You wrote: "In judging a work of art, the choice of subject is the first fact of importance. Everything else derives from that. Mr. Sherwood has chosen one of the most glorious subjects to be found in the common domain of playwriting."

What kind of æsthetic rumble-bumble is that, my dear fellow? In judging a work of art, the choice of subject is a fact of relatively minor importance. The subject of one of Rembrandt's finest works of art is an old woman cleaning her fingernails. The subject of one of Bach's is a protest against the drinking of coffee. The subject of one of Dostoevski's is an adult epileptic with a child's mind. The subject of one of Gorki's is alcoholics, thieves and whores. The subject of one of Michelangelo's is a lot of dirty soldiers bathing in the altogether. If Sherwood's play is fine stuff because in Lincoln he has chosen "one of the most glorious subjects to be found in the common domain of playwriting", then surely most of the feeble plays that have been written about one of the even more glorious subjects to be found in the common domain of playwriting — Jesus Christ, to wit — are even finer stuff.

5. While I am addressing myself to you, my dear Lieutenant-Colonel Atkinson, may I take the liberty of an older soldier than yourself and one whose hair has been grayed by longer campaigns to urge upon you, whose theatrical audience is so large and potentially valuable, a lesser prosaicism and more liberal blood-pressure in your contemplation of the arts, the drama in particular? I have here in my hand, as I stand before you, my troops, in this West Forty-fourth Street Yorktown, a copy of the Lieutenant-Colonel's criticism of the Benét-Moore folk opera, *The Devil and Daniel Webster.* In the unfavorable nature of that criticism, I myself entirely concur, but in the points wherewith the Lieutenant-Colonel seeks to solidify that unfavorable criticism I find a deficiency which is not always absent from the unfavorable

criticisms of some of the rest of you, my good men and true.

"If science has driven the supernatural out of the modern world, what is the point of clinging to it in music and letters?" demandingly asks the Lieutenant-Colonel. Now for God's sake, my boy, what in the hell kind of way is that to talk? In the first place, what has science got to do with art? In the second place, with that sort of critical logic you'd have killed off in their day — assuming that science was then where it is now — Shakespeare and Wagner and Ibsen and others of the world's eternal great. In the third place, even in this more modern day you and your criticism would doom to dissolution such dramatists as the Hauptmann of *Hannele* and *The Sunken Bell*, the Synge of *The Well of the Saints*, the Maeterlinck of *Sister Beatrice*, the D'Annunzio of *The Dream of an Autumn Sunset*, the Moody of *The Faith Healer*, the Yeats of *Countess Kathleen* (like the Benét work, a rendering of the Faust legend), and some dozen or more others such, including maybe even the Shaw of *Saint Joan*. To say nothing, on occasion, of such belletrists as the late Anatole France and G. K. Chesterton and, to mention only a few of the still living many, James Joyce, James Stephens, H. G. Wells, W. S. Maugham, Ellen Glasgow, Theodore Dreiser, and James Branch Cabell. And, since you would include music, also such modern composers as Massenet, Humperdinck and Richard Strauss. And what is still more, spitzbub, you would have deprived your own self of your own pleasure in the two plays you voted for as candidates for the Critics' Circle prize, *High Tor* and *Our Town*. So, I repeat, what in the hell kind of criticism are you dispensing?

But, not content to stop there, our Lieutenant-Colonel of the *Times* goes on thus: "What is the point of taking a stand in art that you would never dream of taking in your workaday life? The plain, useful truths are always so much more engrossing."

This philosophy, I need not point out to you, my men, would restrict the purple flight of the arts solely to the contemplation of every day's prosaic humdrum. It argues that such plain, useful truths as the efficacy of castor oil and the nutritious quality of spinach are much more spiritually engrossing than the wild, unpragmatic and mystical imagination of a cherubim-painting Botticelli, a *Damnation of Faust*–composing Berlioz or an Ariel-writing Shakespeare. It would convert artists into business men and dubious dramatic critics.

6. Do not, as some of you alas do, consider it undignified and lowering of the critical standard to let go in the case of a particularly pretty and provocative girl. You go the limit in your admiration of beautiful scenery, beautiful lights and beautiful costumes, but you are — some of you — apparently scared to death of saying as much about a beautiful young woman. What are you afraid of? It never in the least diminished the dignity of Bernard Shaw, or Max Beerbohm, or A. B. Walkley, or Henri Béraud, or James Huneker, or any other critic worth his salt. In point of fact, it raised them in the estimation of all intelligent men. And, certainly, in the estimation of their wives and all other intelligent women. Shaw, indeed, supported the merit of the critical contention by personally falling in love with two of the beauties, Ellen Terry and Beatrice Stella Tanner (Mrs. Pat Campbell); the incomparable Max married one of them, Florence Kahn; and the noble Jim Huneker, eternal flowers to his grave!, was wobbled and wobbled in turn one-third of the lovely feminine American dramatic theatre of his day, to say nothing, on the side, of the whole Metropolitan Opera House.

7. Do not exercise an arbitrary politesse in the case of foreign stars. If art knows no boundaries, the histrionic practitioners of an art should not be regarded as guests and treated to an especial critical consideration and hospitality. You insult our native mimes by any such attitude. A square deal for all and credit where credit is due, but no undue bowing at the waist in the reception of foreigners with the coinci-

dental unavoidable projection of the rear at American actors in the background.

8. Don't sneer, as you often do, at fashionable opening-night audiences. Your idea that any man in a white tie and tails is *ipso facto* a moron, and in all probability under the influence of spirituous liquors, is the mark of the hayseed. Furthermore, so many of our theatres are drab and dirty that a decorative audience, whatever its cerebral competence and measure of sobriety, helps a lot.

9. Criticize your fellow critics all you wish to — it sometimes is valuable — but do not, as I periodically observe amongst you, derogate dramatic criticism itself by way of spuriously making yourself out to be superior to your craft. None of you, and certainly not myself, is yet within hailing distance of the top reaches of the critical art. So let none deliberately make a fool of himself. That job is often accomplished without the slightest personal effort.

10. One of my valued staff, Major John Mason Brown, of the *Post*, during my term of military command permitted himself to be cozened into paying tribute to the eminence of Miss Rachel Crothers, a writer of Broadway box-office plays, at some kind of laymen's theatrical doings in the White House. At a private court-martial conducted between the two of us in Jack and Charlie's barroom, I denounced the Major for leaving off his otherwise honorable critical judgment and pride in going so far as to eulogize one for whom he himself had no high esteem simply because the White House was provided as the scene. " But sir," he interposed, " I thought it would be a fine idea at last to bring the theatre, in whatever way, into the White House." I said no more, but drank my drink in silence, and meditated upon my sword.

Ah me, I thought, can it be that a critic believes to honor our theatre and drama by indicating a proud niche for such a playwright as this Crothers? Ah me, I thought further, while trying to extricate my left leg from both my sword and the Major, does not a critic drolly realize that the White House had already been so chock-a-block with people of the theatre that occasionally there wasn't room enough left for Cordell Hull's tea cup, Louis B. Mayer's and Ginger Rogers' hats, or any slightest portion of Hendrik Willem Van Loon. The day that Eddie Cantor doesn't happen to be there, you'll surely find Kate Smith. And if Eddie Dowling isn't in Lincoln's old bed, you'll find Katharine Cornell or Helen Hayes in Abe's quondam hay.

The issue, I reflected, checking my sword with the hat-room boy, propping the Major against the bar, and ordering up another drink for him and two for myself, was not bringing the theatre to the White House but bringing the White House to the theatre. You can bring all the theatrical people in America to the White House, but if the White House doesn't go to the theatre it will not do the theatre the faintest good. And the sad fact is that, while the present First Lady does patronize the theatre, there hasn't been a First Lady or a President since Taft was inaugurated thirty years ago who has indicated by her or his attendance the least real interest in the theatre. They have now and again gone to vaudeville shows, like Woodrow Wilson; maybe one or two of them have seen one or two showy popular plays during their occupancy of the White House; but if a President of the United States or his wife (Mrs. Roosevelt as the sole honorable exception) has gone to see a first-rate American or first-rate European drama since Taft's remote day, the records do not disclose it.

And now, my fellow soldiers of the Circle, I pass my sword as your General on to another and bid you a fond executive adieu. I kiss each of you on the cheek, and thank you for your loyal service, and wish you God-speed. I return to the wars once again single-handed and alone.